*Alan Perry was born in Swansea in 1942 and is a pai
and short story writer. He has held numerous one-r
verse play "Occupied Territories" (co-written with Lloy
UK Year of Literature. The book-of-the-play, "To Liu anc
the same year.*

*A past winner of The Eric Gregory Award for poetry and The Leslie Moore Award
for painting, he has taught Art and creative writing in schools, colleges, adult education
centres and prison and read and performed his work up and down the country, as well as
in Canada and the USA.*

*A dramatized selection of extracts from this book was first staged in the Dylan
Thomas Centre in May of this year.*

*He works part-time in the Cyrenians Cymru hostel for the homeless in Paxton
Street, Swansea, and is currently illustrating an unpublished collection of comic verse for
children by Vernon Watkins.*

MUSIC YOU DON'T NORMALLY HEAR

Alan Perry

Alun Books

First published 1998 by
Alun Books (Publishers)
3 Crown Street
Port Talbot

ISBN 0 907117 78 3

Printed and bound in Great Britain by
CIT Printing Services, Haverfordwest, Pembs.

By the same author:

CHARACTERS

LIVE WIRES

BLACK MILK

FIRES ON THE COMMON

POST OF RESPONSIBILITY

WINTER BATHING

NEWS FROM INDONESIA

POEMS FROM THE SUBURBS

MESSIAH

LIFE SENTENCES

DOOMSDAY SIMILES

ROAD UP AND OTHER STORIES

55999 AND OTHER STORIES

U TURNS

THE GREAT LUMINARIES

NIGHT CLASS: A PRISON JOURNAL

TO AL AND BACK: (A Journal of the first Canadian/Welsh Writers' Exchange)

DILLWYN LOMAX SLEPT HERE

IN THE DAYS OF THE COMET

THE CIRCLE

SHARDS

OCCUPIED TERRITORIES

TO LIU AND ALL MANKIND

The houses are growing.
In their walls runs
the white blood of the just.
On the breath of millions
the moon rises,
the immense heart
rolls night towards day.

Miroslav Holub.

"...I was sleepin over in the shelter in front of the toilets by the sea front the other day. I wasn't exactly drunk but it was a freezin cold night and I was lyin down tryin to get to sleep - no blankets on bare pavin stones - and I could feel the cold getting into me. Then, all of a sudden, I started hearin this music - and it was beautiful music. Music you don't normally hear..."

Belfast Danny.

CONTENTS

Foreword   Conrad Watkins   *10*

PROLOGUE
Will   *'A Grand Opus...'*   13

DECEMBER
Paul (1)   *'It's like a language but you've got to know the words...'*   19
Darren   *'Even long lanes have their turnings...'*   26
Vince   *'The train now standing on Platform Nine...'*   30
William and Teresa   *'Jack and Jill and the nine halfpennies...'*   35
Belfast Danny   *'Music you don't normally hear...'*   43
Nigel   *'A hole in a wet Echo...'*   50
Alec(1)   *'Last Train to San Fernando...'*   57

JANUARY
Wayne and Lyn (1)   *'Ichad and Obet aped a abbit...'*   65
John   *'No tramp or drinker of wine...'*   74
Nick   *'The King and I and the marsupials...'*   78
Robert   *'As distant as drums and Novia Scotia...'*   86
Alec and Frank   *'Telephone Jock and Memory Man...'*   93
Little Ritchie   *'Catchin the Summer somewhere else...'*   99

FEBRUARY
Ceri   *'Tea in the Star Dust...'*   106
Bernie and the Bowls Team (1)   *'Until Good Friday lands on a Thursday...'*   112
Terry   *'This, that and the other...'*   119
Alec(2)   *'Huggy huggy huggy, kissy kissy kissy...'*   127
Cardiff Karl   *'Feels like we're invisible...'*   132
Rocco   *'Number One, High Street Car Park...'*   138

Tom and Sylvia (1)   *'Aunty Mary had a canary...'*   145

Wayne   *'Delta, Alpha, Romeo, Victor, Echo, Lima, Lima...'*   158

MARCH

Nicki   *'The Search for the Dragon's Egg...'*   163

Sara   *'Somethin in the back of my mind all the time...'*   167

Bernie and the Bowls Team (2)   *'He aint heavy...'*   175

Neville   *'Geographically mobile...'*   191

Kathy and Robert   *'Wanderin wanderin, nowhere but anywhere...'*   201

Bill and the Bible Class   *'I once was lost but now am found...'*   211

Steve   *'Speaking as God...'*   218

APRIL

Bob   *'Left, right and centre...'*   225

Lyndon and Douggie   *'Bad crack. Bad crack...'*   230

Ian   *'Shooting off on tangents...'*   236

Lyn   *'Don't worry, be happy...'*   245

Randall   *'Mornin night, mornin night, mornin night...'*   248

The Collective   *'Good as gold...'*   253

Bernie and the Beach Boys   *'Show me the way to go home...'*   257

MAY - OCTOBER

Evelyn   *'Like something out of Clockwork Orange...'*   264

Frank   *'The background, the foreground, the light, the shadows...'*   272

Gavin   *'The Landlord, the Butler, the Cook and the Maid...'*   279

Tom and Sylvia (2)   *'Takin off again...'*   286

Wayne and Lyn (2)   *'The Dam Busters...'*   289

Sid   *'A good time were ad by all...'*   295

Paul (2)   *'Don't look back in anger...'*   301

Baglan Benny   *'Take it as it comes...'*   304

EPILOGUE

Sylvia (3)   *'Waiting for Eric...'*   307

AFTERWORD   *320*
DEDICATION   *324*
ACKNOWLEDGMENTS   *325*

FOREWORD

The idea for this book developed over several weeks in the early winter of 1996. At the time, Alan Perry was working as an artist-in-residence, with the support of the Arts Council of Wales, at the Cyrenians' homeless hostel in the centre of Swansea, preparing material with the residents for an exhibition at the Glynn Vivian Gallery over Christmas.

The exhibition proved a success, not only in its visual impact, but as a demonstration of the level of interest in creative work among the homeless population in Swansea. The problem was, how to keep the momentum going? Given Alan's proven talents as both artist and writer, we agreed that the next step should be in a literary direction and proposed a compilation of the experiences and opinions of those who have, through misfortune, found themselves homeless and in need of the Cyrenians' services. The Arts Council of Wales received this with enthusiasm and agreed to support an extension of Alan's residency through the spring and summer of 1997.

The unifying theme of 'Music You Don't Normally Hear' is homelessness, its causes and effects, and the common thread is contact through the Cyrenians' hostel. The tales that are told herein contain, as one would expect, a lot of suffering and anguish, but also philosophy, humour, resilience and hope.

Most importantly, it has given those who are too often 'spoken for' and 'spoken about', usually by people entirely ignorant of their true circumstances, a brief opportunity to speak for themselves to a wider audience. As John Major should have said: 'We should condemn a little less and understand a little more.'

This book is dedicated to the memory of Betty Williams, who founded the Cyrenians in Wales and who devoted her life to listening to people in the depths of homelessness. She died shortly before this book was published.

Conrad Watkins, August 1998.

PROLOGUE

'A Grand Opus...'

Will

Are you thinkin of a Grand Opus or short stories? Ow will you *float* it? The average cost to float a book is two thousand pounds. Unless somebody latches onto you. Can you write TV scripts? There's much more money in that.

July 5th, 1997: an American space probe has just landed on Mars. I bump into him by chance in the early morning in St. Helen's Road: a tall, wiry Quixotic-looking man with a beard and a lumberjack's hat with ear-flaps which stick out at right-angles to reveal a pair of Walkman headphones. For years, he dossed in a ramshackle wooden hut in the grounds of the derelict St. Paul's church. He had a table in there and a chair and a small primus stove. After cooking himself a meal and eating it, he liked nothing better than to relax with a bottle of wine and a cigar. After the shed burnt down, he spent a brief spell down the Marina but eventually returned to his old haunt, sleeping out in the open now: either on the church wall or an adjacent grass verge. Two nights ago he was badly beaten up by a local teenager. The blood is still congealed on his face and clothes.

Now here's a bit of information you might not know. Are you listenin? When the first recordings of Native African music were made in Africa for transmission by the Beeb, the batteries were so heavy they had to be carried by the *Marines*. That's a *fact!* They weighed a couple of ton. Now if only somebody had thought of a small generator and a bit of wind it would have saved them a lot of trouble but they didn't think *that* way in those days. Fascinatin, isn't it? The more you know, see, the more interestin it becomes.

My favourite music is the music I'm listenin to at any given point in time. When I was young, I used to listen to Beethoven's String Quartets and think 'I'll *never* be able to appreciate these but *now* I do. And then again, I *thought* I understood the 'Hammerklavier' but I don't think *anyone* ever *will*. Now, when somebody gets up there on Top of the Pops, in theory, it doesn't matter *who's* music it is: it's the *arrangement* and the *quality* of the art they're tryin to get at, that counts. But how the harmony evolved is unbelievable when you listen to music. You know Brahms's Second Symphony? Well Von Boller thought there'd be a natural eclectic projection but he couldn't hear the *harmony*. Very *fit* man, though, Brahms. He used to go mountain climbing at the age of forty. But there was someone he loved in the past, see. And Beethoven's 'Fur Elise.' D'you know that was written for a young woman as well? But you can't *eulogize* these people. There's a guy around now - I've forgotten his name but it's Eastern European-sounding and he's written a *cadence* but he's made it too complex and there's no *need* and I want him to rewrite it in manuscript form to make it intelligible to an orchestra. It's gotto be *communicable*.

Mahler! He's *elemental:* like Barbara Hepworth and Dennis Mitchell but Gabo became too Baroque. Now, Richard Glynn Vivian! *That's* the life history you want to read. Quite remarkable! When Dore came over, he was drawing the Docks but it appears he had a strong social conscience cause he was drawing the prisons as well and Richard Glynn Vivian thought he was more than what he appeared but the actual act of refurbishment was a work of Art in itself. But we've always got that timorous feeling that they might have scraped a bit *too* much off the Sistine Chapel even though they must have been careful. Well, take Van Gogh. The originals were technically *brilliant* but when he first started, it wasn't *expensive* paint. But I actually heard a recording on the radio, verbatim, of a script written in the Twenties, commenting on Van Gogh. So I was tryin to tell this friend of mine what was more or less the truth about Van Gogh but he didn't want to *believe* it. And the ridiculous thing about him is that he was probably in a bit of a hurry one day and cut himself shaving. That's all. That's what probably *really* happened: he just cut himself shaving. But he was fuckin *tampin* and he said 'Oh, I'm *dying,* I'm *dying* - I'll paint myself **dying!'** He was a bit of a boy, like, see. But he was brilliant. He used to have to tell them **'Look!** *Look at the* **trees!** *Look at the* **sky!'** and people *do* look now. And the camera hasn't destroyed *eclecticism* in Art yet. It's still goin strong.

Sailing's been an obsessive passion all my life. I'm tryin to design a boat and it's rather like writing the 'Hammerklavier', if you follow me. It's a concept which is now coming close to fruition but you must declare your eclecticism. I might borrow some of the A.P.T. technology cause when a train hits the kerb, a natural rock on the chassis reduces the centrifugal force and makes it a more stable transit vehicle. Perhaps somebody else has built it by now. We *export* ideas but we don't always *develop* them, for various reasons.

They were goin to electrify the railways in the Thirties but there's been so much vandalism now that they *can't*. It's ridiculous, isn't it but I suppose we *will*, eventually, reach out into the Twentieth Century.

I don't want to keep a boat in a cage: I want to try it out on the sea. I might get a yacht or a nice little coal-fired steamer. I saw an article in a yachting magazine and I imagine I would sail to Chesapeake Bay in Baltimore - cause it's a natural harbour - or the Caribbean. But I don't know: it's nice *here*, now, isn't it? A bit of sunshine at last, on the old Town! A hundred and forty million pounds a year, the Tourist trade brings in and they've got to realize if they back-peddle now and destroy that, they're destroyin their own livelihood.

Now what are *you* interested in? Writin, is it? I see they're puttin that Cordell book, 'Rape of the Fair Country', on in the Grand. Read it many years ago. It had a certain imagery which I didn't appreciate at first. It seemed too - I wouldn't say 'synthetic' - but it had a certain *artificiality*. He was a Resolven boy, apparently, but whether he was born in Resolven or came to live there, I don't know. The Americans are good writers, though, aren't they? Have you read O'Hara or Steinbeck? What about 'Sweet Thursday' or 'Tobacco Road' or 'Travels with Charlie?'

I used to spend a lot of time in the Library but I had to make a fuss in there the other day about the education system because we've had eleven years of electoral dictatorship. But I don't read any more. I've got music and I'm thinkin about the boat most of the time.

I was educated in Neath Tech: Special Entry, Second Year. The first job after my apprenticeship folded was on the United Welsh buses in the late Fifties but I haven't worked for years. I'm pushin sixty now and, in theory, I've *always* been on the streets. I'm fit but I don't cycle any more cause I'm a bit too dangerous on a bike. I'm camping down there in front of Joe's, quietly. When I'm out of gas, I cook on wood. But I always clean the site up after me if possible, except if I've got to leave in a hurry - like the other night, which I can't say any more about at the moment cause it's all *subjudice*.

Did you see Twin Town? D'you know how long they filmed Lenny dancin? Forty minutes! And d'you know how long he was on? *Three seconds!* I was an Extra, too. They just had one rehearsal and two takes with me and it went smoothly. They apologized after the first take but I didn't mind. No, that wasn't *me* outside the Indian Restaurant: the street bum was played by a *genuine* street bum. But you've gotto rationalize your film budget these days because it *costs* and, of course, the video pirate doesn't *care.* But I'm glad there was a second film made in Swansea. Peter Sellars was marvellous in that other one, wasn't he? Eh, being serious now for a minute: could you work with Peter Sellars? I couldn't either: he was a *giggler.* Once he started there was no stoppin im! If I was in that lift scene with him, I could have done the fart but they would have had to tape my lips, cause he was such a terrible giggler. Yes, I could have won an Oscar for the fart!

Warm, isn't it? Well, is that worth anythin? Are you skint? Give us a fiver, then. I'm dyin for a drink.

What if the Krays had taken up Art when they were younger? The one who kicked the bucket had a heart attack and guess who he was howlin for? His *mam!* Oh, aye! Is your mother or father still alive? Mine are long gone. In the crem instead of planted so I want them co-joined in the Book of Remembrance before I emigrate - *if* I emigrate.

Anyway, not to worry! Now, you know the ceramics industry in Japan? It's probably *Korean.* And it's important with pottery work to learn to handle the media first. Sling it on, work it till it goes to slurry, *then* make your pot. You know the first screwdriver I made was out of a bit of three-eighths carbon steel. I was never good at heat treatment but I wasn't twp: I got the striker to do the work. I'm not a skilled blacksmith but I may get a small anvil some time although, more than anything, I like *thinking.* This boat design: I got it *close* now. I might share it with a friend. We've gotto *dimensionalize* it next. One of the boys has got a hi-fi computer, so we'll see what the computer makes of it. Design today: everything's shaped like a cardboard box with the corners filed off; in the old days: *acceleration* - that's all they learned. Then they stuck it in the wave box or in the wind tunnel. Now K is a constant, but things *change.* They're goin to redesign the exhausts now. D'you know Mk.1? 760 Sea Level? Mk.1 is *relative.* It's goin to go *up.* Like nought. Nought is a relative. It's not a *finite.* And you gotto know what you're doin out there cause if your electrics go, you've *ad* it.

There's pictures coming through from Mars today. I heard something about it on the News. Excellent venture, isn't it but *I* wouldn't go. Oh, no: 'Me, *Earthling!*'...

So you're thinking of a Grand Opus, are you?. Now make it a *real* Grand Opus with *real* characters in. Write about South Wales, Africa and Ascension Island. Cetewayo, the great Zulu Chieftain, was put on Ascension Island. And the finest accolade for the

South Wales Borderers was not the Victoria Crosses, it was the Zulus beating on their shields with their spears. They had their gongs on the spot then, see. They didn't have to go to Buck House. You could conceive a Grand Opus about South Wales, which is a *progression*, and you could have real characters in it like Dick Sperry or my Grandfather. He was at Mametz Woods - up to his waist in water. There's a field of Jocks there, you know? My Grandfather went there and he cried. A field of Jocks! And the Germans called them 'The Screaming Women of Hell.'

And d'you know the Anzacs? The Anzacs would talk to the British Brass Hats as if they were mud. And d'you know what the Brass Hats did? Chucked them in the front line! There's always a lot of cock-ups in the military. In the Second World War a lot of the pilots were bombin their own planes! And in China - a long time ago - British soldiers were ordered to *stand* and not take evasive action. Whether they had their full kit and rifles, we don't know but there was just one sergeant there and he ordered them to stand: 'You must *stand!*' he said and they stood there and the local populace threw shit, rocks and all sorts of crap at them and they didn't *flinch* and it's always been treated by the British as a moral victory. In China, many years ago...

DECEMBER

'It's like a language but you've got to know the words...'

Paul

I was named after Paul Mcartney. But it's funny: a lot of people say to me 'Why do you base yourself on Noel Gallagher?' And this girl Alison said to me in London the other day: 'Are you into Oasis?' I wonder why they say that. Is it my hair? Is it the way that I dress? The way that I act? A lot of them are jealous that I can dress like this and get away with it. Not a lot of people like Oasis but it's the 1990s and they are the *in* Group. In the Eighties it was Madness, in the Sixties it was the Beatles. Some people may think I'm mad but that's the best way to be. If I get a reputation for being mad, that's all right by me...

Familiarly known locally as 'Tall Paul from Porthcawl', he's two and a half hours late for our meeting but the Hostel's annual Christmas party was held last night, so I'm not surprised. A former resident but now a volunteer Worker, he's trendily dressed and his hair has recently been dyed a carrot colour. Last summer he had a small part in 'Twin Town', a big budget film which was made in Swansea.

I was born in Bridgend but I lived all my life in Porthcawl. My family was from the Rhondda Valley but my parents had to move because my father had a bad chest from the mine and the doctor advised him to go down near the sea.

We lived on a caravan site in Nottage first of all, then we moved to a council estate in Happy Valley. I had two sisters and one brother but by the time I was sixteen or seventeen they'd either married or left home.

In School, they stuck all of one bad lot into one group and that was the group I was in. Some of them were glue-sniffers and some of them were on magic mushrooms. There were fights all the time and sometimes some of my class would beat up the teachers. I was one of the *quiet* ones so you can imagine what the *rest* were like!

We got on best with the PE teachers. There was one called Mr. John who'd been teaching in Borstal. We were supposed to be doing Social Studies with him but he knew we wouldn't work so he let us play football and baseball instead. He used to give us Art sometimes just to see what was going round in our heads. Most of the people I was friends with in School, never left Porthcawl. They've been there ages but I don't go back much and when I do, there's a lot of them I don't cross because they've gone from bad to worse.

I worked for No-Go Darts in Cowbridge when I left School. That only lasted two weeks because I didn't like the way they were treating me. They put me on this machine: it was sort of barrel-shaped with a big blade and these shafts were shooting out of the barrel into these trays at the rate of about a hundred a minute. I didn't have time to breathe. One day it stopped and what I didn't know was that it needed time to cool down so I stuck my finger up it and, with that, it started again. Nearly chopped my fuckin hand off. There was blood all over the trays and the Supervisor came across and said 'You gotto go to hospital,' but it was in the middle of the day and there was no one to take me, so the Boss of No-Go Darts came down with his big suit and his flashy tie and took me to his big flashy car. Then he looked me up and down and said 'Are you *dirty*?' And I thought 'Cheeky fucker! *Of course* I am. I've been working in that shit all day and I'm black and bleeding and covered in blood and all he's concerned about is me getting in his fuckin sports car.' But anyway, I had my finger done and I was back at work the followin morning. There was no feeling of 'Are you alright?' nor nothing like that. I had a big bandage on it but the Supervisor said 'You'll have to go up there and work on the shafts again.' I was taken aback but I did it again and the bandage came away and the stitches came out of my finger and the blood just pissed out everywhere. And after that, I said 'Fuck em! I'm gettin treated like a right dick-ead ere!' So I jacked it in. Fifty-two pounds a week back in 1985: that was a lot of money in them days but I wouldn't do it now. Nine to five-thirty: fuck *that!* Then I got onto a scheme called Community Industry. I worked for this old guy, Mr Hussie his name was. He used to clean up antiques with sandblasters. He took me on as a trainee and I worked there on a trial basis sandblasting metal ornaments. One day I was doing this vase thing and I was cleaning it up so much it got wafer-thin and when I showed it to him he nearly had a heart attack: 'Fuck me,' he said, 'if I keep *you* on I'll be out of fuckin business by the end of the week!' So I had to go. But at the end of the day, the job I want to get is Prime Minister or something like that: twenty - or even thirty - grand a year, for doin fuck all.

I've had my fair share of girls. I met this girl in Port Talbot a day before my twenty-first birthday. What a fuckin nymphomaniac! I fucked her and the next day I met the mother of my daughter and I fucked *her* as well. We weren't married but we started living together. It was off and on for a bit - she used to get in these moods - but then we moved to her parents' house in Happy Valley.

Her mother said to me one day 'Take precautions There's an old saying: "If you get on in Bridgend, remember to get off at Cardiff. Don't go all the way to London."' But, of course, I went all the way to London. So all of a sudden my daughter came along and my life changed *completely*. I was twenty one years of age and jobless with two mouths to feed. Her mother kicked us out when Francesca was a couple of months old and we went to live in a Crisis Centre for three months. Then we moved to a house in Llangarw, up the Cwrw Valley. I call it 'The Bronx'. The houses are shite up there and the people are *beyond*. We stayed there for about eight months. I put in for a Crisis loan and they gave us two hundred and sixty-six quid to deck all the house out. We had no carpet nor nothing, so what I had to do was paint the stairs yellow so it looked like we had a carpet going up the stairs. The state of those houses and the people round there, just done my head in. I thought we were the perfect modern family but she did the dirty on me. She started playing team football and darts in the evenings and that's how it all started. I didn't want to go out. I'd rather have stayed in and babysat. And then she came home with love bites. She told me she was staying down her friend's house but she wasn't. She was sleeping around - so it was really doing my nut in. I was only twenty-four at the time and I thought what am I going to do now? I'm on my *own*.

I stuck it out for three months and then, when we'd finally split, I said to her one night 'I'm goin to Stormy Down tonight to start afresh.' So all of a sudden, I drank a bottle of sherry to get Dutch courage and I went. It's a Homeless Hostel run by the Social Services. It was a Saturday night, I think it was, but I wasn't allowed to stay there long because you're not allowed to have someone in the family working there and my ex-girlfriend's mother worked there as a cook.

If I seen Anthea now I wouldn't fuckin speak to her. I feel angry. The guy that she married has got *nothing* on me. He's from Wolverhampton and he's been married twice before. The way I see it, is that he picked on her because she was so young and had a three-year-old kid. I could go down any time but the last time I saw Francesca was in the winter of ninety-two. I was living here at the time and I went down on a Tuesday. Gareth in the Office gave me a lift so far and then I took a bus. I knocked the door and she opened it and said 'What are *you* doin here?' I went in and I could see Francesca was there but when I looked across the room I could see this guy sitting in *my* seat! Going bald he was: moustache, glasses. Looked a right *wanker*! I only wanted to see Francesca but the first thing she said was 'I think you should be the first person to know that we're getting married.' '*Oh*,' I thought, '*Brilliant*! **Yippee-yi-ay**!'

Then, all of a sudden, they moved to Cwmavon. Maybe they thought I'd be turning up every five minutes. I've got a good idea where they are and legally, I'm entitled to access but that'll take ages. I suppose we're both partly responsible for what happened and we could sort it out ourselves but she doesn't want to. And *I'm* the one that took Francesca for walks and all that! Some fathers would have went down before now and would have had it out but I thought 'Lay back, it's not the right time.' But the years are going on now. Will my daughter recognize me? Will she know me? I don't know where to send any cards or anything at all. I know where her nan lives and I know where her father lives. I seen him last summer in Porthcawl and he was saying things like: 'Oh, Francesca's doing this and that now,' and 'Francesca's doing *gymnastics*!' I feel I'm missing out on the best years of my daughter's life. And when things build up inside me I've got a tendency - if I went down there and didn't like what I saw - to go off my head. Beat somebody up first and ask questions afterwards.

The damage what this guy has done! If I seen him on the street, he'd recognize me. And if he had Francesca with him I wouldn't walk past my own daughter but if I did see her, I'd like to turn away because things like that can really upset you. I only went to court once during the Social reports and then I went to Stormy Down. I didn't have people from Paxton Street to back me up or to say what I'm really like. Now I feel I could go to court and win and if they said 'Why haven't you bothered before?' I could say I didn't know where they were, that they blocked my side of Francesca's life off completely and that this cunt from fuckin England - hasn't been in Wales long - comes in and takes away somebody's flesh and blood. And he's got kids by Anthea now. I'd like to *mince* him up...

I started moving around the country because I had to sort things out in myself. I've been to all the major cities in Britain. Edinburgh, Manchester, Birmingham, Chester, Leicester: stopping fourteen days in each, doin odd jobs here and there and then hitch-hiking back to Swansea to get my Benefit. *Richard Kimble: 'The Fugitive'!*

When you get to a place, you've got to know where to go. I'd go to the Council or a Day Centre - never to the Police because they might do a check-up and put a warrant out for you. I'd talk to people and you can always find out where the Hostels are from looking at people on the streets or from the Big Issue sellers.

'Sub-culture': that's the new Conservative word for 'homeless' and when it comes down to it, a homeless person is just a number in Social Security. If anything happens when you're on the streets and you get picked up by the police, you're automatically a suspect. Street people have this special language. It's called Back-Slang. They use it in major cities and if you haven't heard it, it's like a code. If the police pick two of you up and you're sat talking to the other guy, only you and him know what you're on about. I've heard it in Cardiff and Newport. Back-Slang, it's called. It's like a language but you've got to know the words.

But I can survive in my own environment. Some of the people livin here who haven't slept on the streets, annoy me. It really pisses me off when they complain that someone in off the street is havin a meal here. Those sort of people aren't in my league. I can tell them what it's like out there. I've *been* there. I've got the T shirt.

After two years on the road, I knew I didn't want to do it for the rest of my life - like some of the old guys I was seein. My legs were starting to go. A nurse gave me some cream for them. She said I needed to recharge my batteries. And she was right. All I want to do now is put my feet up and settle down.

I took a chance in coming here. That's what I always did and I was always lucky. I was only going to stay one night but the Hostel made a big difference because the staff and everybody really put themselves out for me. I did abuse that at one stage but now I'm tryin to prove to them that I've grown up. I'm still wild but in a different way.

If Swansea's going to progress by the year 2000, it's going to have to have something rapidly done to it, because it's becoming another fuckin Coventry. People will be saying 'We'll send you to fuckin Swansea!' next. It's got nothing going for itself: five, ten minutes, you can walk right through the fuckin Town.

Christmas is the only time people hear about the homeless. In the New Year, Swansea's really got to look at what the homeless need and push for it or get petitions going. They're opening a new Hostel, yeah, but for under 25's and half of them will be from Swansea: kids who've had an argument with their parents and left home. Swansea needs a permanent Day Centre and a permanent Night Shelter. As a Labour Council, it should be doing more. The only way you can survive going round the country is to go into a Hostel. A lot of people think 'Oh I could *never* do that!' but one day they might *have* to because if it can happen to me - and I was so cock-sure of myself - then it can happen to anyone and when it does and you end up on the street, it hits you *hard*.

They were going to call the film 'Pretty, Shitty City' then they changed it to 'Hot Dogs' then they changed it to 'Twin Town'. It'll be out in April and there'll be a film-of-the-film and I'll be on that as well.

My character didn't have a name. I was in a scene with the policeman's girlfriend. She'd walked across the Night Club floor and I was talking to her and he comes over and I didn't believe he was a copper and he had to show me his badge. And I had to react to that. I didn't have a line as such, it was more a reaction. And because I was wearing shades I didn't have to do much with my eyes. I was like taking the piss out of Oasis and making it part of the character. I did things not in the script - things that just come to me, out of my own head.

I got on well with everyone on the Film crew. They all know me now: Kevin Allen and his brother Keith, Paul Durden, the people in the offices and from Polygram. I got £150 for five days work in the Office and £300 for the film. As well as acting and the office work, I helped make the big papier-mache hot dog. I'd like to take it further because I was with people that were educated, with loads of cash. *They* didn't know I've been on the streets, so if anything does come of it I can say if *I* can do it, anybody can. If you don't stop dreaming, dreams can become reality. Not only my friends can watch me now but *millions* all over the world. Jack Nicholson started off in a small part, and look where *he* is today. I'll actually be in the fuckin *credits*. And the thing is: *me* coming from a small town called Porthcawl to being *this!*

It was great going over there this summer and helping out. They put on a big party for the Hostel towards the end. But the last day was the hardest. I helped this guy Ben shift all the stuff out. When we shook hands and everyone had gone, it was really sad, like. At the end of the day I just felt 'Oh fuckin hell, what am I going to do now?

If you put your mind to it you can do anything. I don't want to be doing what I'm doin now, for the next twenty or thirty fuckin years. I want to go *up* in Society - sell myself - cause I got more chance of goin into films than winnin the fuckin Lottery.

I'm twenty nine now, thirty next May. I haven't got much but that's the way I like it, because if I had *too* much it would go to my head. Some people think I'm the biggest bastard they've ever met but it's just that a lot of them are jealous of me, cause *they* didn't do it. A lot of people have fuckin stage-fright in front of a camera but I haven't. I enjoyed having the chance and I'm not going to let it go now. When my daughter comes to a certain age, I want her to say 'Fuckin hell, wasn't my dad **good!**'

Things are *happening* - and I'm not just fantasizing. I'm not greedy but I want the best now cause I think it's long overfuckindue. I want to *progress.* I don't want to be just a *person,* I want to be different: different to my friends, different to *everybody.* I want to be someone people will recognize, not just a sad fucker called 'Tall Paul from Porthcawl'. If this comes *big* next year, I'm fuckin off, man. I'm goin for the big lights. I want *everything.* I want to be up there with the *Big Boys.* I want to get out there and grab it all by the bollocks...

'Even long lanes have their turnings...'

Darren

I've got my own life now. I've learnt to come to terms with what's happened and push it all behind me. You can't change the past, you can only change the future, that's the way I look at it. When the time comes and I meet the right girl, I'll get married and have a family and make a go of it but there's no one at the moment. I'm just waiting to see this flat I've been offered. It's only one-bed-roomed but from what I've been told it's really nice, so I think I'll take it. Which will be good for me because I'm good in the kitchen and I can keep a place clean. You may see bits and pieces in my room now but it's *clean*. I take care of my rent and my debts and basically I'm independent. In the future, I hope to get a job in mechanics, catering or painting and decorating. Something *constructive*. Pass my driving test, buy myself a little motor, maybe even start my own little business. I'm not willing to settle down yet because I don't think I'm strong enough. I want to have kids but I want to be able to say to people 'Look what my children's got. I've given them things I never had.'

His room overlooks the street. It's small and has been hurriedly tidied before I enter. He's 21 and has been a resident for only two weeks. We sit either side of his bedside cabinet, on top of which, is a bible. Behind him, on the wall, are half a dozen centrefolds of naked women in a variety of soft-porn poses. It's a sunny day outside. He's immaculately groomed in clean white shirt and dark waistcoat - as though for a day's competition at the Crucible. He speaks quietly and matter-of-factly, with little outward show of emotion...

I was born in Llanrumney. It was a very rough area so after a while we moved to Rhymney, which was quieter.

When I was six my father started abusing me, not only physically and mentally but sexually as well. As a result, my mother got a divorce but then she took him back, cause he said he'd changed. Things were all right for a while and then they started up again. I've got scars on my back and head, where my father beat me: either with a bamboo

26

cane or a leather belt or sometimes a baseball bat. Because of the abuse, I ended up in a children's home. I was only there a couple of days at the most and I started having flashbacks. One day I goes up to my room, put my music on full blast and took forty Valium and a bottle of vodka. I had my bed against the radiator and I had the radiator on full because the more heat the quicker the alcohol and tablets work. One of the girls I was friendly with came up to my room and knocked on the door. When she pushed it open, she seen the empty bottle of vodka and the empty bottle of tablets and me laying against the radiator. So she ran downstairs and got one of the care assistants, who phoned an ambulance and got me into hospital. When I came out, I sat down and had a talk with the girl who found me. She understood what I was going through because she went through it herself and she said I should talk to the Staff and try and get some help and if *I* didn't want to talk to them myself, *she* would. She told me it wasn't my fault what happened with my father. I hadn't understood what was going on. So I did that and eventually the N.S.P.C.C. were brought in and the police were called and my father was arrested. During the time the police were collecting evidence I ended up in prison for robbery with violence. I was in Brizemarsh in Dorset but somehow my father found out where I was and sent me a letter telling me to drop the allegations, otherwise when he got out he was going to kill me. So I went to the Governor at the prison, showed him the letter and told him the full story. It was hard for me to talk about it then because I didn't know if anybody would believe me. The Governor handed the letter over to the police and after that I had to go to court to give evidence against my father. The case went on for six weeks and during that six weeks, they unearthed thirty nine children who also gave evidence against him on charges of indecent assault, rape and buggery. He's inside for good now and he knows not to bother me cause if I have any letters off him, I'll take them straight to the police. I don't know where he is and I don't care.

Since coming out of prison, I've moved from town to town, dossing down all over the place: shop doors, bus stations, train stations, parks. I've slept in them all: anywhere where I can get my head down. The Salvation Army helped me quite a bit but because of the abuse I suffered, I was always suspicious that people were trying to use me.

I saw a psychiatrist in Bridgend and he helped me through a helluva lot. He gave me advice on how to come to terms with what had happened. I was seventeen and still wary of people. From the age of sixteen to the age of nineteen, I had a few relationships with women. They were all a bit older than me. Some were successful relationships but others never worked. I'd be there one minute all nicey-nicey and then as soon as I got a flashback I'd be up and gone.

I can't really say when I left school because I was very rarely there. I didn't do no exams and I'd only go when there was PE, Art, Maths and English. The music teacher helped me a lot. I used to play the guitar but I've lost the old touch now. I still play the piano a bit, though: things like 'Little Donkey' and songs from 'The Sound of Music.' But whenever there's Karaoke on in a pub, I just can't help getting up and singing: Elvis songs mostly, numbers like 'Lonesome Tonight', 'Love Me Tender,' 'Now or Never,' 'Wooden Heart' - I know all the words of that. All the girls I've been with, whenever I start singing them songs, start crying. I'm good with kids, too. Like, I was with this young girl who's a single mother and she says to me one day 'Darren, I've got to go up my mother's to collect some things. Can you look after the baby for us?' So I babysat and the baby's there crying like, so I put some of Elvis's music on and as I'm feeding him I start singing. She comes back from her mother's, walks through the door and says 'Darren, I've never seen *anyone* put a baby to sleep *that* quick!" So I reckon it's a case of: either you've *got* it or you *aint*!

The artist I like the best, though he's dead now, is Leonardo da Vinci because his pictures are all about what he *feels*, what he felt, *inside.* I've got a couple of mine here that I've just done: one of a church and another one I copied out of the Daily Mirror. They had the World's Hundred Most Beautiful Women in it and she was one of them. I just copied her out. I wrote my life story, too - well, part of it - which I sent to Sue Cook in the Sun. I wrote it when I was in prison. I received a letter back from Sue while I was in there. I can't remember her exact words but it was something like 'Darren, it's good to see that you've come a long way after the abuse that you've suffered. It's good to see that you are helping other children who've been abused. Keep up the good work and thanks for your letter.' Which pleased me a lot because she also said 'PS I will use your story in a couple of leaflets which I will be putting around' - which I thought was great for children who are being abused, because now they'll be able to take note of what *I've* done and they may be able to bring themselves to take it to court.

My mother and father were *that* devious that they were able to pull the wool over the Social Services eyes. My grandmother's dead now - but she could see what was going on. She was the one person who really cared for me. You could say that she brought me up because whenever I'd run away I'd always run down to her house. I'd stay with her a couple of days, then my mother and father would come down and as soon as my father would get me in the car he'd start beating me.

I know I've got a violent streak myself but I know I can control it. I'm a Christian. I've been going to church regularly now for two and a half years. I never believed in Christ or religion until I was seventeen. I was looking for something different in my life and what started me off was I went to an Open Day in one of the first schools I was at. And my Music teacher was a Christian. She sat me down and talked to me because she'd read in the paper about what was going on with my father. She told me about Christ, about what help I could get from Christianity. So I went to church and I got in the choir and started reading the bible. My Gran couldn't understand why I was so happy but I was wearing a mask, you know. I was hurting inside while on the outside I was happy. That's the way I've always been: never showing people what I was feeling inside.

I was in the choir two years and I've done a bit of lay preaching. I've got in my Bible here a note of the places which I visit. I've got the phone numbers of Elderly People's Homes. I spoke with the Matron of the Home down by the Marina when I went down on Sunday and I've organized a carol service there with the old people.

I go to St Mary's on a Sunday. At six thirty there's a communion service with readings from the bible. When I read, I always read from John 3.3 to John 3.16, which talks about 'excepting Man be born again' and 'entering the Kingdom of Heaven.' I've got a little verse inside my bible here which I cut out of the paper back in 1973 which, if I remember correctly, is from the Sun or the Echo. It's called 'Going My Way':

> 'Even long lanes have their turnings
> And weary nights must end.
> Though you have known a cruel time
> Do not lose heart, my friend
> You have plodded on so bravely
> You have kept on hoping still
> Maybe there's sunshine just ahead
> And a joy for all the ill.'

'The train now standing
on Platform Nine...'

Vince

He opens the window to let in some air but it's still very stuffy. He hasn't had time to tidy up his room. I take off my coat and sit with my back to the window. The walls are bare and stencilled with pale silhouettes of former pictures and posters. He lights a cigarette, says he's been at a loose end and is glad of something to do.

I was born in the Shankhill Road in Belfast in 1966. England won the World Cup! My family history's very weird. My mum put me and my brother and my sister in a home. My dad was in Australia. We were going to emigrate but she got another bloke, took *his* two girls and give *us* to my grandmother. But my grandmother was too ill, and she had no choice but to go to the Social Services, or whoever it was in them days, and they had to find us somewhere, so they put us in a home. My dad come back - in '68 I think it was - and he couldn't get us out until he got married, so he got married and bought a house and his wife ended up with a husband and three kids *straightaway*. They had one son and then my mum had another son, so I've got two half sisters, two half brothers, one full brother - Roy - and a full sister.

The Shankhill Road is really rough. Every School is either Catholic or Protestant. At the end of the road's a set of traffic lights. This side of them's Protestants and the other side of them's Catholics and there's just a big wall going right around. *You* can't see *them* and *they* can't see *you*. *We* used to throw bricks over and *they* used to throw bricks over and it was just totally *crazy*, like.

My family was just working class. My dad worked in a tool company. He left there in '76, worked briefly for Rolls Royce and got made redundant. Then he worked for fifteen or sixteen years in Belfast Harbour. The Titanic was built there. That's probably why it sank!

I left school at sixteen. I was in the highest class all the way up until the fifth year and then I became a bit of a rebel. I just wanted to get out cause I had a job to go to and

I wanted to earn money. I became a Postal Cadet with the Post Office. They used to have them little motorbikes, d'you remember? But before I could get *on* one, I lost my licence, so they contracted me out to British Telecom, doing their internal mail and all that.

We used to have our pay on Fridays and I'd leave there in my uniform and we'd go to the pub and I was drinking there one day and there was a UDA bloke behind the counter and he says to me 'D'you want to join?' And my father always told me, 'Don't join *anything*. Don't even join the *YMCA*!' So I says to the UDA bloke 'I'll think about it,' and he bought me a pint and I bought him a pint and then I left and that was the last time I had a drink in that place.

Roy *did* get involved, though. His friends were all in it. He had a flat and he got a knock on the door one day and his mate Mcgeogh - he's dead now - had a bag with him. And he says 'Look, you have to keep this in your house.' And it was full of ammunition: probably two or three thousand rounds. And he had to put it in the loft and it was there for about three months and every time a knock come at the door, he was shitting himself. If the police had come and searched the house, he'd have been in jail for God-knows-how-many years and if he turned round to the boys and said 'Look, I don't want this,' *they* wouldn't have been happy either, so he got the bag one day, went to Mcgeogh's house, knocked the door and when he comes out, Roy says to him 'Look, *there* it is. *Keep* it. I don't give a *toss* - and that's the *end* of it!' They could have knee-capped him for that but we were planning to go to England, anyway.

Me and Roy came over on the boat. When we got off at Liverpool, we had ten pence between us. I was seventeen and Roy was eighteen. We hitch-hiked all the way to London and ended up in a hostel called Centre Point, right in the heart of Soho. It was only for people under twenty-five. You didn't get in there until nine at night and then you had a bed and something to eat and they used to throw you out at eight in the morning. They used to give you luncheon vouchers and then you just had to wander around London at your leisure. We stayed there for three or four weeks, then we moved into a bed and breakfast. The DHSS used to give you £232 a fortnight for yourself and the Hotel money. We moved from one hotel to another. You couldn't get a proper job because if you signed off the dole you couldn't afford to pay your rent, so we used to get jobs like washing dishes and stuff. That lasted about three years and then we got a job in a hotel in Kensington. Roy was in one hotel and I was in the one next door. We got £100 a week, free room plus we still used to get a giro for £200-odd. The owner of the Hotels was okay - he was from Bahrain - but eventually I got sacked. He sacked me four times in one week, cause I was drunk. Roy stayed, cause he had a girl in London, but I packed all my stuff and went to Victoria Station. I had about £300 in my pocket and I didn't know where I was going, but I said to myself, whatever the tannoy says is leavin straight away from the next platform, that's where I'll go. And it said 'The train now standing on Platform Nine, is leavin in five minutes for *Brighton*.' So I went up and got my ticket to Brighton - £9 or something, it was - and I lived there for six years.

It's a lot like Swansea - very hilly - but it's more of a tourists' Town. I used to live right next to the sea front in Hove. I had a nice flat there but it cost a fortune. I got a job, off the cards, working on the roads. It was good money and I was living with a girl who was working as a manageress of The Little Chef, so we were doin all right. Then I had a son with this girl and shortly after, she buggered off with him. He was two when she went. I don't know where they are now. I know where her mum and dad live and I could get in contact but she could be married now and what's the point in me turning up on the doorstep and knocking the door and saying I want to see him? You can't do things like that. It really hurts me but my father told me: 'Either do it now or *forget* it, then when he's eighteen you can go and look for him or he can look for you.'

After my girl left, I went to visit me aunt, who was living in Birmingham. I was only meant to go there one day and then go back down to Brighton. But, I don't know what happened, I just kinda stayed there. I was there five years. My uncle was a scrap man, so he used to take me out on the scrap but, eventually I got a wagon of me own. Me and my mate got drunk one night, drove down the road and crashed into six cars and a taxi. Done £20,000 worth of damage. So the judge gave me six months in jail, drink-driving. When I came out I'd just about had enough of Birmingham, so I got a bus down to Swansea, cause Roy was livin in here by then.

The first person I met down here from the Hostel was Alec - in the Duchess with Roy. He looks tough but Alec wouldn't hurt a fly. He's got the build of a boxer and the lines in the face but that's just *hard-livin* I suppose. We call him *'Pound Stretcher'* because he goes into the pub with a pound at eleven o' clock in the morning and he stays there until eleven o'clock at night and when he wakes up the next morning he's probably got £6 in his pocket because people are always giving him money. I don't know *how* he does it. But I really *like*

Alec. I shouldn't say this, but I was doing my laundry yesterday and I was tidying up, folding all my stuff up and I found a can of Strongbow there and I thought where the hell did I get that bloody can from, cause you're not allowed to bring it in here - and it turned out it was Alec. Somebody'd given him two cans and he'd tossed one into my room.

And the second person I met was Ted O' Mally. He was off his head. The first time I met him he says to Roy 'Where d'you come from?' And Roy says 'Belfast.' And he says 'What *part* of Belfast?' and Roy says 'It doesn't matter *what* part of Belfast. *That's* as far as you've got to know.' And then he started saying 'Well, I'm a Catholic, like,' and saying Hail-Marys and crossing himself and I don't know how many he'd had but then he started singing rebel songs - in the Duchess - and Roy says to him 'We don't sing rebel songs in here. *We* don't sing Protestant songs and *you* don't sing *them songs,* so just bugger off!' So he shut up then but he was just totally off his nut. He owed four or five weeks rent when he buggered off. And he was always staring at you, wasn't he? I was sitting in the telly room one day and Roy was there and he was sitting on a chair facing us. Just staring at us for about an hour. And in the end, Roy turned around and says 'Would you stop *starin*?' And he says 'I'm not starin. I'm watchin TV.' And Roy says 'Look, the fuckin TV is over **there**! Stop starin or I'll get up and *whack* you one!' So he buggered off then but he was about *an hour* starin at us. It was like something out of a *horror* film!

In Belfast, you drink where you were born and that's *it.* An area about a mile square. You go to Town, do your shopping and you go back there again. And that's as far as you go, unless you're in a car and you're goin somewhere.

I was over there two years ago when the Cease-fire was on, just for a holiday. Me and a friend of mine from Birmingham went for a week. We used to go down Town for a drink and it was always buzzing and nobody said '*You're* Catholic,' or '*You're* Protestant,' or this or that. But now the Cease-fire's gone, I don't know whether it's like that or not. I haven't been back but I don't think I'd go back down Town again. I don't think there *is* a solution unless you pull all the troops out and let the Protestants and the Catholics get on with it. Then it'd just be a bloodbath, wouldn't it?

Just because I've got this accent, people over here say 'Oh, you're *Irish* therefore you're *Catholic.*' But I say 'No. And I'm *not* Irish, anyway. I'm *British*' And they say 'What d'you mean?' And I say 'Well, I was born in Northern Ireland and Northern Ireland is part of Britain.' And if I go into the dole office and they say 'Ethnic religion?' I put down British. It totally *bamboozles* them.

'Jack and Jill and the nine halfpennies...'

William and Teresa

Teresa: I was born in County Mayo and I'm the youngest of a family of three. My parents had a small grocery shop and after my father died, we moved to Galway. I worked in the pub business there for ten to twelve years and that's how I met William.

William: I too come from the West of Ireland. I had my own business there and I got divorced and lost the lot: the business, my home, my family. And then I met Teresa. She had nothing to do with my divorce. We met afterwards...

I was at the Hostel the day they arrived, four months ago. They looked worn out. All their clothes and luggage got soaked when they were forced to hitch-hike to Cork in an open truck a few days earlier and they needed somewhere to dry them. Since then, they've become frequent and popular lunchtime visitors. Softly-spoken and with a quiet dignity, William is in his early fifties. Teresa is small, dark and pretty and in her early thirties.

William: We both come from two very well-educated, decent family backgrounds and when we met first I tried to revive my business but it didn't work. The market I was in got overcrowded and it didn't get off the ground. At the time, we were much better off than we are now. Without wishing to sound boastful, up to six months ago, we lived as good if not better, than the people in those luxury flats out there. We had our own caravan trailer and we came over here on holiday and toured around. We'd been up the coast to Holyhead but we'd never actually been through the Valleys. So I drove to Bangor, up through Merthyr and Portmadoc and it was beautiful and that's what eventually gave us the idea of coming back.

But we went back to Ireland first and settled about fifty miles away from where we actually lived. In this particular little Town, we both had part time jobs and we were signin on and we were very happy. I was working for a local man as a coach driver doing local tours and Teresa was working in a rather famous pub owned by a well-known County Mayo hurler. But it was kinda seasonal work and we knew that eventually it would peter out. And then we found out we were expecting a baby and initially it was a bit of a shock, even though we'd often talked about it. There's a stigma attached to single, pregnant women in Ireland, so when our families were informed, a bit of hostility set in. And it was uncomfortable for us, particularly because a lot of the work I was doing took me into Galway City, where both her parents and my family live.

Teresa: I'd been out of work for three months before we left because the cellar work got too heavy for me. On the way to Cork: our car broke down and we had to leave it behind. Then we had to spend three nights in a bed and breakfast because there was no sailing, so two days after we arrived in Swansea we found ourselves almost penniless. On the third day, we were walking through Town and saw two girls and three fellas sitting in a doorway with two dogs and they directed us to Paxton Street. In the Hostel, we were introduced to Sheralee, one of the workers here, and she gave us soup and coffee and got in touch with the Emergency Housing Officer who immediately came down and interviewed us and arranged for us to be moved into one of the Homeless flats. I was nearly six months pregnant at the time. We got our luggage, which was six big black bags and she drove us out there. It was teeming with rain that particular day. We didn't know what to expect but when we saw the place, it was run-down and filthy. We carried the bags up four floors, only to be told when we got up to the fourth floor, that there was no electricity, that the roof had caved in and we'd have to move all the luggage back down another floor. There was no electricity in that flat either so she decided, after losing her temper on several occasions, to put us back into a bed and breakfast for the night. We'd had bad times prior to coming over here but it was always in a place where we had friends or family whereas now we were completely alone. This woman wasn't a bit understanding or helpful and seemed to think that we were out to use and abuse the system and we were in a situation where we had no *choice* but to do as she said. So we went back to the bed and breakfast and were advised to ring the caretaker on the Monday. He told us to come back out before four o' clock and he moved us into a flat and helped us with our bags. When we went into Housing on the Wednesday, the woman didn't even realize we'd been out in the flat for two days. She assumed we were still in the bed and breakfast. She told us we'd have to stay there for eight weeks, instead of which, we've been there nearly sixteen.

William: It's three and a half miles there and three and a half miles back and it takes an hour to an hour and a half to walk it. Most of the windows are boarded up and you wake in the morning and you don't know whether it's day or night because the room's blacked-out.

Teresa: We never see daylight and we're too afraid to pull the curtains. One of our biggest expenses out there is electric light bulbs, cause we leave the lights on twenty four hours a day, for security.

William: They have a mania for breaking glass up there and you can't go out the front door because of it. If the houses are vacated *today*, the windows are all smashed *tomorrow*. Milk bottles, mineral bottles: the place is like a Diamond Field with glass. When the sun is shining you can *see* it: not just one bottle, a continuous, sheer carpet of broken glass. So we use the back door, but then you have to climb a grass bank cause there's a steel building frame bent across the path. Teresa's slipped quite a few times.

Teresa: A lot of the bells upstairs don't work, so there's always kids banging our front window to open the door to let them in.

William: There's fourteen or fifteen of them upstairs. They kick the door, throw rubbish, smash bottles - and everything lands on the bottom landing. Their parents don't seem to care. Some of them never seem to be there. There's constant noise from about eight in the morning to two or three the following morning. And these are all children ranging between the age of three and twelve. It's an absolute nightmare! The police have been up and down the stairs three or four times in the last week and people come knocking at the door at all hours asking for cigarettes or tobacco or cigarette papers. One fella came at *twenty past one* in the morning, during the New Year, looking for a *bucket.*

The other day, some kids lit a fire outside our bedroom window and the fire brigade were called. I saw the flashing lights and heard the noise and went out and saw this bloody big bonfire outside the window.

There's a man across the road, runs the corner shop - Mr Singh. And when we went there first we thought he was a right bastard, cause he was so stand-offish but after a while we realized he was a lovely, lovely man who just had so much *crap* to put up with. And from young kids - teeny-boppers - not adults or teenagers. He has a son, twenty-six, and there were kids outside there one day intimidating his dog and he chased them off and one of them shouts back to him: 'Sure, you're only an old black bastard, anyway!'

Teresa: There's nothing to do all day but look at a darkened, boarded-up window. The only pastime we have is that we take Jesse, our little Jack Russell, for walks. We've been keeping him illegally in the flat because our Case-Worker made us sign a form saying no pets, no animals - no nothing.

William: But the funny thing was, bad-minded and ill-mannered as our Case Worker was, she actually drove him around for three and a half hours that wet Sunday afternoon and didn't even know he was in the car because we keep him in that little rucksack there. We call it the Squawk. I even took it into Singleton Hospital to see Teresa when she had to go in for a week because she'd gone off eating and lost weight and needed building up.

Teresa was letting the dog out on Christmas night and the crowd upstairs were throwing empty bottles out the window. She was lucky they didn't hit her. She came into me, white as a sheet. On the other side of the building, above our sitting room window, they were throwing out dirty nappies. Some crowd made chips in another flat and poured all the oil down the sink, clogging up all the outside drains and when the kids were coming in and out, the hallway was like a bloody skating rink! And the smell! I came out there one morning and there was eggs - hard-boiled eggs - shelled and halved, left neatly on the mat outside our door and it only dawned on me after that it was to see if we'd come out and slip on them.

William: In the beginning, it took so long for our Income Support to come through - what with forms being sent back because there was a stroke of a pen or a dot over an 'i' missing - that we had to walk everywhere: in rain, hail or sleet. We were classed as a married couple and our giro was for thirty five pounds each. So we couldn't afford to take twelve pound out of that for two weekly bus tickets, even though Teresa was over seven months pregnant.

Teresa: On top of which, being concerned, we used to ring home every week and that was as much as five pounds a call. I was expecting a very small cheque from an Insurance Company after cancelling what was left to run on the car and I suppose we spent a quarter of that on trying to get through to this Company in Ireland.

William: So from then on - living in this emergency flat for the homeless with people urinating through the letterbox, kicking the doors at nights, trying to get in cause we're on the ground floor - we've suffered a terrible time. At one point I went to Bangor to a friend of mine to see if I could get some work and when I got there he was on the point of going to France with a coachload of people on a tour. There wasn't any work and I didn't have any money to get back, so I rang Teresa and she was after getting the Maternity Grant, so she got a train and came up to Bangor to bring me back. And while I'd been gone our case worker had collared Teresa and put the flat in her name and I became what's known as N.F.A: No Fixed Abode. Basically, what it meant was, I could visit Teresa in the flat but I couldn't live there. Mind you, I *was* livin there, and still am.

Teresa, being pregnant, could have been excused for being depressed but I can assure you I was getting very depressed, too - and I wasn't pregnant - and very annoyed and frustrated about it. But we were told by the staff here to come in every day and have soup and sandwiches and whatever, and it gave us great comfort and a kind of boost.

Teresa: And, whereas we were filling in forms and getting a letter back from somebody we'd never *seen* upstairs in the Social Welfare Offices, Sheralee *knew* the person to contact and she really put herself out for us.

William: So it went on and on and the case worker was mucking us about so much that I got very annoyed one day and told her in no uncertain terms what I thought of her and her outlook towards people. I told her she could stick her flat where Jack stuck the nine halfpennies. And the sun doesn't shine *there*, either!

William: We have a lovely doctor but he was missing the day Teresa was getting pains. She wasn't getting the usual kicks that you get from a baby and we got a bit concerned. We went to our practitioners and there was a locum there and he wasn't very helpful or courteous. He wouldn't get an ambulance for us, so we had to find our own way to Singleton Hospital and that upset us because we had no money. We had a single fare over but not enough for a return. But we went over anyway and she was put on the ultrascan and we were told that the baby was dead. If she'd like to stay she could but she said no, she'd like to go home. They're beautiful people out there. He said 'That's fine, that's okay. You can go home and come in tomorrow in your own time.' And there was this lovely nurse there and she said 'Have you a car?' and I said 'No,' and she says 'Where are you going to?' and I said we had to get to Blaenymaes and she said 'Oh, I'll check the buses,' and I said 'There's no need. We don't have the bus fare. We came down here in a hurry and we didn't bring any money with us,' cause I didn't want to say the position we were in financially. So she says 'I'll be back in a minute,' so she goes out and comes back and says 'That's all I've got in change,' and out of her *own* pocket, she gave us four pound, which was enough to get us home and back to Singleton the following day. Now that, to me, was what I call a little bit of Christian charity, without expecting any gains in return. So we came back the next day and they had a double room with a double bed for the two of us and they treated us the same as if we were in a Five Star Hotel. I was present for the birth and they took the baby away and dressed it up - I'm going on about this but it was a great traumatic time for us - and then they took it back. When the baby was born, Teresa rejected it. She didn't want to see it. But when they took the baby back all dressed up, she took the baby in her arms and it was so natural that you'd think it was going to move any second.

But, anyway, after we buried the baby, we offended some people that we thought were genuine. They came and took us to the funeral and were very nice and took us for coffee afterwards but what we didn't realize at the time was that they were a religious sect and that I was expected to *join* them. There was a *price* for their friendliness. So that was *another* thorn in our side because we have our own religion and we don't interfere with anyone else. And then Teresa had a bit of a bad run. She was depressed and had to go into hospital twice. And, if the truth were known, I should have been taken in with her, cause I was *worse*, but I hide it. But through all these bad times, we still came into the Cyrenians and got our soup and sandwiches and little parcels of food to keep us going. We always come in clean: I'd be shaved, clean shirt, sometimes a collar and tie. We speak well and act well and none of the Staff ever turned their back on us or looked on us as two down-and-outs. I remember coming in the day the baby was born and telling some of the people here - and their genuine shock and concern was unbelievable. So human. These people never knew us from Adam and they had befriended us so much and been so kind to us in so many ways and I've seen cases of people here who are *worse* than we are. And we haven't forgotten that and we *won't* forget it, either.

William: On Christmas Eve, we were told that there was a house available but that we couldn't move into it because there was no furniture or gas. So we were advised to leave it until the New Year, to put in for a grant and to go back down to Housing Options to see if they could provide a little bit of furniture. We got the keys of the flat on the 30th. of December and came back down to the Cyrenians, who helped us fill in the forms. When we went up to Housing Options to see if they had any furniture, we were told that there was no furniture and that we'd have to go on another waiting list. So we're still waitin.

We've got the house but we can't move into it because of problems with Benefits over a grant. I think they're going to have to give it to us, though, because Alan Morgan did a wonderful job of filling in the forms. If ever I need to get into heaven, I'm going to get *him* to write the letter for me.

Without the Cyrenians, we wouldn't have a friend in Swansea. Where we live, we go in in the evenings and we lock the door. And the only time we come out is to run across the road to the shop. I wouldn't tar *everywhere* up there with the same brush. We meet some people on the bus and we meet the odd person going in and out of the shop and there are some lovely, lovely people up there but we have never really spoken to anybody in Blaenymaes. There's nobody to talk to. We're in a boarded-up cage.

Teresa: When you stay in the Homeless flats, you won't get a job because the minute you mention them you're automatically classed as being trash or somebody who can't be trusted or somebody who's going to be drunk on the first day of work. I've worked for ten years and I'm quite capable of doing a job *well* and I'm not *stupid* but because you're homeless and you don't have money, people assume that you don't *want* to work and you're somebody that wouldn't understand plain English.

William: We never say that we're living in Blaenymaes now. We say we're living in Robin Close, where the new house is. Because one evening just before Christmas, we were going home and we went into a particular takeaway food shop on the Kingsway and there was a notice in the window said **'Kitchen Staff Wanted'** Well, we're not proud. If we get paid for a job, we'll do it. So we both went in and asked about the work and this young lady said 'Fine, I'll give you the forms.' So we filled them in and handed them over on the spot. She picked them up, looked at the name and address and said '*Penmaes Place.* Oh! Unfortunately there's a *stigma* attached to it.' Teresa had another interview for a job in another restaurant also in the Kingsway and the Manageress asked her if she'd done that sort of work before and she said she'd done bar and catering work all her life. But when she told her she lived in Penmaes, the Manageress said 'I'm sorry, the job has gone.' Now, *twice* in the one street is too much of a coincidence. And when we went to a surgery in the Kingsway, to sign on with a doctor, the receptionist took our particulars but when she got to Blaenymaes she said 'I'm sorry. We don't treat patients from Blaenymaes. It's not our area.' I don't know what became of the Hippocratic Oath. As far as I'm concerned, it's Hypo*critic*!

We're at the stage now where we're picking ourselves up. We're on the move. We're back to eating normally. We were drinking a bit heavily there for a couple of weeks after the baby died but that's finished now and we're getting some counselling for people recouping from a still-birth. There's a lady comes to see us and we talk to her and she's given us great support. And once we get ourselves a bit better organized, we're going to offer to do a bit of voluntary work. We *did* try to give a hand in the kitchen on New Year's Eve and New Year's Day and, thankfully, we didn't poison anyone!

I've applied in person to the South Wales Transport Company and been given an application form, which I'm not going to fill in until we're at our permanent address. Then I'm going to put Robin Close. An awful lot of people working for that Company, live up there, so there shouldn't be any problems.

We have talked seriously about another baby. Teresa wants another one and the circumstances will be a lot better next time because if you're living in a house, however bad a house is, soap and water will clean a lot of it. And another thing is, you can go in your front door and you can go upstairs, downstairs, out the back and into a nice garden.

Teresa: I'm thirty three years old now and I can honestly say I have learned more in the last three months about life and people than I think I've learnt for the past thirteen years...

'Music you don't normally hear...'

Belfast Danny

Victoria Park on a cold, sunny morning. The boys from the Radnor - a sea-front Guest House - told me they went there to drink at half past ten every morning but when I get to the pavilion only Danny's there, scarfed and duffle-coated sitting, staring out across the green expanse of bowling green. We talk for a moment then, at my suggestion, move out into the sun, to a bench on the other side of the green. His eyes are watering with the cold. He speaks softly and in quietly lilting tones...

I don't particularly want to talk about my childhood in Belfast. My father died when I was two, so my mother had to look after the whole family: my brother and me, two sisters and my grandparents. Me grandfather was an alcoholic, and my grandmother went senile. I was only four and she used to do crazy things like throw all our clothes out onto the street. It was an area something like Upper Killay but my mother got fed up with it. Fortunately, my father had been a Mason before he died and through his connections she managed to get us a house in a good area. And it was *really* good. We weren't rich but we had what we needed when we were children. The house had a big garden - from here to the railings over there behind the green and about twice as wide, with two big chestnut trees. And I was able to get up the chestnut trees and build tree huts and things like that - you know the way kids are. We were very near the country and there was quite a big forest - something like Clyne - nearby and we were able to play in there. I always had a bit of an education but packed it in when I got up to University level. One of my sisters is a teacher and one's a nurse. My brother's a Director of his own firm, dealing in pharmaceuticals and it's funny in the sense that I was once under threat from the law for selling drugs illegally and there's my brother making his fortune selling them *legally*.

I was married for ten years and I have children but not by the marriage. You see, we were livin in London for a long time and her excuse was she didn't want to bring children up there. She said if we wanted children, we were goin to have to move. Well, I was quite content because I had a good job and I could do more or less what I wanted. I was a Higher Executive Officer in the Civil Service - Social Security - lookin after twenty-seven thousand people. And then, all of a sudden, I found myself in the same boat as those twenty seven thousand people, and it *wasn't* very pleasant. I lost my wife and my job, through drink and having an affair with a woman at work. Until then, I used to run the entire Department but look at me now: sittin here on a park bench drinkin a flagon of cider at half past ten in the morning. And when I fell on hard times, because I'd worked in the Civil Service they thought I knew it all and that I was workin the ropes but I wasn't. I was genuinely desperate and had ended up sleepin rough in London.

I went back to Belfast eventually and did a bit of begging, then landed myself in jail for two years. I robbed a chemist: not for money but for drugs. It was the eve of my divorce. I went in and asked for some speed, just to take the paranoia off me but this guy wouldn't give it to me. So I said 'Well, fuck you, if you won't give me the *speed*, I'll take the *money*. So I banged open the till and pushed him into the back room. Then this other guy came out with a brush shaft and I told him I'd shove it up his arse if he didn't fuck off. So I pushed him in the back room as well and that was that. I was then arrested - I didn't try to hide or anything like that - and I got seven years for robbery with violence. There was no *actual* violence but that's what they charged me with anyway. I got seven years and I spent two of them in jail. And that meant being inside with a lot of U.D.A., U.D.F., and I.R.A. people: which shows just how heavy things were in Ireland at that time. I worked in the Canteen and they were good to me and I was no trouble in there at all. I was discharged a couple of days before Christmas - a week early - which I didn't really want cause I was expectin the cigarettes and the Christmas Fare that you got in prison at that time of year and I'd already fixed a date to come over to stay with this girl I knew in Hay-on-Wye, who was a doctor and had her own house. Anyway, they let me out and my mother brought me home. She gave me a Christmas dinner, then she says: 'You have to go now,' and I said 'Well, I thought I was going to stay till the end of the month' - till I was due to go to Hay - but she said 'I'm sorry, you can't stay here.' So I had to book into the Y.M.C.A. for a night and then my sister put me up. She's an alcoholic herself. Her husband used to be, but he's into collecting guns now and things like that. And I was in the house on my own one day and I got out this .303 rifle - an old World War Two thing - but it still had the magazine, so I set up this old tea-chest and made a circle on it as a target. It was full of rubbish but what I didn't realize was just how powerful a .303 is. So I'm firin at the target but the bullets are going straight through the tea-chest, out through the back gate, through this woman's back gate opposite and in through her window. I shot the hell out of her house. So that was the end of that. I got chucked out of my sister's as well.

Like I say, I'd already been in touch with this girl in Hay and I phoned her up and she said 'Yeah, come over. I says 'Look, Helen - that was her name - 'I don't have any money. So she said she'd pay the fare. Then when I went to fetch some clothes I'd left at my mother's, my mother said she'd pay my fare as well. So I had *double* the money, so to speak. I couldn't claim the dole but I had my discharge grant, so that's how I ended up here in Wales.

Hay-on-Wye lasted about a year. I'd been off the drink all the time I'd been in jail but then I started hitting it again. I was smoking proper cigarettes then, whereas normally I would smoke roll-ups. When you put a roll-up down, it goes out. But I wasn't thinkin. And this girl's a Herbalist as well as a doctor and, being in Hay-on-Wye, she used to collect her own herbs and make her own tinctures and things like that. And she had a basket full of dried herbs right beside the sink, on top of the washing machine. Well, I set a cigarette down but I was pissed and forgot about it and the ash fell into the herbs and set the bloody house on fire. So I was accused of arson and got six months in jail and that was my introduction to Swansea. This girl Helen wrote to me and she says 'I don't want to go to court. I don't want you to go to prison,' and all that, and this was read out in court, otherwise I'd have got two or three years. So, I suppose the judge wasn't such a bad old boy, really.

I thought that was the end of Hay-on-Wye but, in fact, I had to go back to Brecon when I came out because that's where I was pickin my money up from. It's about ten miles from there to Hay-on-Wye and you don't get much traffic but these people stopped - hippy guys - and they gave me a lift back to Hay and we're smokin blow the whole way back. I don't smoke blow very often but I did then because I had nothin to lose and I didn't know whether Helen would let me in or not. Summer had come around by then and up on the hill, up on the foothills of the Brecon Beacons, I'd made this - what I used to call 'The Throne'. It was a big flat stone to sit on: stones for arms and a back-rest. And, before I got sent to prison, I used to go up there to drink, because I couldn't drink in the house. So I sat there for a while and when I started to get bored, I wandered down to the house and knocked on the door. She wouldn't answer at first but eventually she did and she said 'You can stay the night but don't expect to stay here any longer'. But one thing led to another and I ended up stayin there another year. After which, things turned a bit sour again, so I came back down to Swansea and I've been here ever since - for better or for worse.

Sometimes better, sometimes bloody *awful*.

I haven't been back to Belfast for twenty years now. Well, you see, I lost too many friends there. Fourteen very close friends were shot for no reason: just because they were Catholic or Protestant. One old boy used to go into a bar at night and pick up all the empty glasses and then he'd have a free drink. But one night a guy walked up to him and says 'I'm sorry about this but I've been told to do it,' and shot him in the head. That was *one*. Another was Billy Flack - a hippie guy. He very rarely drank but one night we were in this Bar together, called The Club - and this guy walked up to him and said 'Sorry, Billy, I've been told to do this,' and killed *him*, too. But they didn't only kill him, they came back and cut his throat and battered him, so he had to be buried in a closed coffin. That was the kind of thing that was getting to me in the end.

I was born a Protestant but I don't hold with that Protestants/Catholics type of thing. It makes no difference. In fact, whenever it comes down to it, when you're livin on the street and you're on the rough, I find the Catholic fraternity are more congenial than what the Protestants are. The Protestants might give you a sandwich but the Catholics will turn round and give you a few pennies as well.

There was a girl - a very well-to-do woman - oh, going back a few years, used to always drink up by the Patti Pavilion. There used to be a bench up there on the corner. And, one day, I was coming up by the County Hall with this guy and we saw a body lying there and a load of cans. And it was this woman, sleeping there with no blankets, nothing, and she was soaking - not cause of the rain, just cause of the dew. We had money - it was our pay day - and we were goin to buy drink but we saw that she had drink so we walks over to her and says 'Oh, hello, any chance of a can?' We explained that we had money and that we were going to get a drink and bring one back. So she gave us a can each and we sat with her for a while. Her name was Louise. Her husband owned a house down in Langland - a fifty-odd thousand pounds worth house - but her husband had thrown her out. We sat talking for a while then went and got our drink but when we came back, she'd gone.

A week went by and I had money again and was walkin through Victoria Park with a half bottle of vodka, and she's sleepin up by the Patti Pavilion there, curled up on a bench. So I walked up to her and I says 'Oy! What are you doin sleepin on my bench?' It was a joke but she took me serious and she jumps up and says 'Oh, I'm awfully sorry - '

I laughed and told her to sit down: 'I was only joking. Look!' I says, 'I've got a drink. Have a drink!' So we drank the bottle of vodka and then I says 'I've got some money on me: let's walk round to Betty's, the Off Licence round the corner.' So we're walkin round there but the vodka had hit her too hard and just before we get to Betty's - Bang! Down she went. But there was an old girl watching us and she must have thought I hit her. The next thing, a police van arrived and they're pickin Louise up and I turns around - and I'm not normally verbal in that situation - but I turned around and said 'I hope you're not *fuckin* arrestin her!' He says 'No, we're not arrestin *her*, we're arrestin *you*!' and they grabbed me and threw me into the van. They took her to the hospital and they locked me up and it was a Friday of all days and they kept me in all weekend and by this time I was startin to get the shakes. When they let me out, I went to court and got a fifty pound fine, which I never did pay. But then I tried to find Louise and when I did find her, she was lying under this bush by County Hall. So I says 'Look, Louise, you don't have to stay here. Why don't you come down to the UNIFLOC building with us. It's empty and at least you'll be warm and have some blankets.' So she went down there. But summer-time was comin in and all these guys from Cardiff had arrived. And, well, I was out doin my own thing - beggin and one thing and another - so I didn't bother going back. But I happened to bump into a couple of people I knew and they says 'Why don't you come down to the Docks: we've got a few tents and a fire going.' So we walked down to the dunes and there was Louise, sprawled half in half out of this tent, and these guys who had come down from Cardiff - there was eighteen of them - had raped her. I was so annoyed, I made an excuse and left, said I had to get my giro or something. She still skippered with us for a few nights after that but I told her 'Look, Louise: don't mix with these people any more. Why don't you fuck off and do your own thing, with your own people. These people will only screw you up even more.' But after that a girl - a Christian girl - took her under her wing and took her up to a little place near Cray. She talked her round and brought her out of it and the last time I saw her was at the soup run in the Kingsway. She came up to me and said 'Hello, Danny,' and all that and she was back to normal: got her head straightened out. She wasn't sleepin rough any more. The house had been sold and she'd got her half: twenty seven thousand pounds.

The first time I went in the Radnor I'd been sleepin down by the County Hall and the weather turned bad and I was freezin to death but Bernie - a fellow countryman of mine -

invited me back there and I've been living there on and off ever since. Sometimes I'm in love with Swansea and sometimes I hate the place. But I suppose it's like any other City: you can find the rough with the smooth.

If I can get blankets tonight, I'll sleep out again. It's not that I don't like the Radnor, because some of the people there are okay, but when they get drunk they go off their trolley. You never know what's goin to happen. There was a guy murdered there not so long ago and when it happened it was one of the rare occasions when I was sleepin down by County Hall. I knew nothing about it until I went back to the Radnor in the morning and was told I couldn't come in because there was a murder enquiry going on. I didn't know if Bernie'd been killed or what and it wasn't until some time later that I understood what had happened. This guy who's serving life for the murder had been led up the garden path by his girlfriend, who's a bit of a headcase, and he murdered this guy. I don't think he actually meant to murder him but he hit him once too often and he took a blood clot to the brain. After that, I'm just very dubious about going back there, not because I feel personal danger, although the vibration is still there in the house and there's always the potential for something to happen. Most of the people get on pretty well but you never know when somebody's going to ignite so I'll only go back there if I really *have* to. All of the people that I know there have either been homeless or they've been in some sort of trouble or other and ended up going in there. They use it as a kind of Bail Hostel. There's only six people staying there but people bring friends and girlfriends back. You don't exactly know who's doing what. The landlord and landlady are only there for a couple of hours in the morning and don't really know what's goin on. It's just a Bed and Breakfast. It used to be that you could buy an evening meal but they've even stopped that.

At one time, I would have like to have got into a Hostel but it's not much different from a bed-and-breakfast. I'd have been in one fixed point then and, once you commit yourself to something like that, you're stuck with it. And it's very difficult to pick yourself out of it, especially when you're out of the cold and you're in the warm with a bed to lie in. Then the old childhood fantasies come back: you're warm, you've got a breakfast in the morning and you've got friends around you and things. But then, it doesn't last. It turns sour. So I won't stay in one.

I was sleepin over in the shelter in front of the toilets by the sea front the other day. I wasn't exactly drunk but it was a freezin cold night and I was lyin down tryin to get to sleep

- no blankets on bare pavin stones - and I could feel the cold getting into me. Then, all of a sudden, I started hearin this music - and it was beautiful music. Music you don't normally hear. It was like *elfin* music. That's the only way I can describe it. But I was travellin with the music and I was going further and further away with it and I was right into it, cause I was feelin warm then, cause it was such a nice atmosphere. Then this bloke walked up to me and shook me: 'Are you all right, mate?' he said. And he stopped it. He stopped the dream. I says 'Yeah, I'm okay thanks very much,' and he says 'Okay, son! There's a can of beer for you,' and he left me with a can of beer and off he went. Now this was about two o' clock in the mornin. Well, hard as I could try, I couldn't get back into the dream. And I *cursed* him and wished I'd told him 'Fuck you *and* your beer!' I never even drank it. First time I ever threw a can of beer away. The dream was lovely but I think if it had gone any further - and I'd gone along with the music - I wouldn't have come back. But, then again, I didn't particularly *care*. That must have been what happened to Captain Scott and all that lot, you know, when they died. They just went to sleep with the cold and didn't wake up. Cause sleep and dreams are warm, you only feel cold if you've gotto stay awake and you're shakin. It's no joy at all then, but once you get *into* the cold and you let it - the cold - just sort of drift over you, then you get warm *within* yourself. Then your dreams come. Then your dreams take over from your life-support and that's when people freeze to death...

'A hole in a wet Echo...'

Nigel

Did you know the atomic bombs they dropped on Nagasaki and Hiroshima were made with poisonous mushrooms and all the yellow gas was made with mushrooms too and if you know anything at all about mushrooms, you'd know that the most minute microscopic particle can, in itself, be left on that table there and it will *eat* the wood. It will *grow* without roots. We've got a kind of hollow in our chests and we breath it in all day and for all we know, it could try to grow in us so in a way cigarette-smoking can be helpful as well as harmful. I picked up a book called The Dictionary of Vitamins and it tells you that there's nicotinamide in every food substance in the world. It's an essential oil that we *need*. I learnt about the gas from watching a documentary film on BBC 2 but what really gave me the insight was you know when you smoke a normal Old Holborn or Golden Virginia and there's all that like brown stuff clogged up around the edge - like nicotine - well that stops any absorption of toxins and poisons and if you were to take any tick or mite or hair lice or any germ or bacteria and stick it under a microscope with a garlic and under another microscope with the nicotine: about 90% of the one with nicotine will die but only 40% of the one with garlic will die. So whether it's harmful or no, I don't know but nicotine - pure nicotinamide - can be more beneficial than the medicinal properties of garlic. I smoke between twenty and forty a day and they're very thin but when I went to hospital not long ago, they said to me: 'Don't believe for *one minute* that cigarette-smoking can in any way be good for you at all...'

I watch him put a match to the crumpled tip of the liquorice paper. The meagre little cigarette burns a third the way down before he's even taken a puff. Pale-faced and thin, with dark shadows under his eyes, he sits in the office wearing his baseball cap sideways on, like a Bowery Boy. Two weeks ago, he took an overdose in his room at the Hostel and was rushed into hospital.

I'm twenty-nine and I'm from Ely originally. I've got two older sisters and two younger brothers. I went to a normal Junior School in Cardiff but between Standard One and

Standard Three we moved to five or six different Towns throughout Wales and I think the reason was, my parents had debts. Eventually we ended up back where we started: only half a mile around the corner. It disrupted my schooling but the worst of it was I was in love with a girl in Junior School.

My parents are landscape gardeners. We all helped out but my mother did most of the donkey work. They're still together but, in my opinion, there's absolutely no love between them. It was worse when I was younger, there was violence all the time: blood everywhere, my mother's hair being pulled out and us kids being stripped and punched around as if we were rag dolls. Even though it seems impossible, my father drinks forty to fifty pints a day. There was a piece about it in the papers once. When I was nine I was sniffing lighter gas and glue. I suppose it was a sort of escapism but to me it was just fun where there was no fun - to replace all those horrors. I ran away from home a few times between eleven and thirteen. And when I was fourteen I lived in a tent in the woods. I was there for about six months, surviving by burglary. My friends used to bring food down occasionally but mainly I was stealing. I got kicked out of school and ended up in a Special School. It was two days a week from half past nine to twelve o' clock and it was beautiful. There was five people in each class and we used to go onto a farm and if ever you got stuck over a bit of work, the teacher always came over and helped you out.

Since the age of fifteen, I've been in prison numerous times and all for petty crimes: possession of hash, signing someone's cheque book and card - and burglaries. The first sentence I had: we'd walked into a hotel to get some beer and there was this key in this storage cupboard full of blankets and towels and on the key was a big ticket which said MASTER KEY so we walked into people's rooms with it and found jewellery and cash. The girls that we gave the jewellery to told their parents and the parents phoned the police.

I went to Earlstope for an eighteen month sentence and there was this big fat boy there who couldn't read or write who kept asking me to read his letters for him and write letters out and then word got round and I did it for two other lads, free of charge cause they were in trouble and come Christmas I done loads of cards for people in calligraphy cause I felt sorry for them. I was a Red Band, which meant I didn't have to go to Education but one day they put me in a class with these people who couldn't read or write and when I done the IQ test they told me I had the highest IQ that ever entered the prison establishment. It wasn't due to my schooling so perhaps I was just *born* pretty intelligent. I *do* read a lot: good books like James Clavell or James Herbert or Robert Ludlum - that's my favourite author. I've read virtually everything he's written. Anyway, I ended up hitting the fat boy. It didn't make sense that I'd done so much for him - for all of them - and then one day I saw him talking to this guy Pompeii and pointing at me as much as to say I couldn't fight or something. So I walked over, picked him up off his chair and battered him with my head. And when he went down I wouldn't stop kicking him. I lost twenty one days remission for that and got transferred to Morland but when I arrived they weren't content with that, they took me straight down the block and beat me up as well. So I had three lots of punishment for the same thing.

For three years now I've virtually committed no crimes at all. What that shows to me is that if the courts are persistent in imprisoning you, you will adapt yourself - or you will try. I took the other route. I deliberately decided to rebel. I used to tell the prison officers on the way out 'Listen! I'll be *back*!' not only because I was bitter and angry but because I used to think that their psychology in trying to change you, doesn't really work. But, in the end it got too much. Something so terrible happened in my last sentence that I don't want to go back any more. They put me in a cell with a man doing ten years for murder and he tried to *do* things to me. And *I* was an unconvicted remand prisoner and *he* was convicted and it was against the law to put me in the same cell. I complained two or three times but they refused to move me and I actually faced disciplinary action from the Governor. So now I'm trying to claim compensation but I'm having problems doing it.

I've had loads and loads of girlfriends but I'm especially attracted to *proud* women. You know: women who are *courageous* and *graceful* and won't bow the knee to anyone or *fear* the world. But as soon as they seem to show fear or let people *conquer* them, they lose their grace and there doesn't seem to be any individuality there any more.

I suppose my life style doesn't make me very attractive to the opposite sex but only once, can I say for certain, did a girlfriend finish with me because I went to prison. I'd say that the girlfriend I had when I was thirteen was the best of them all because of her prettiness but when I came out of Morland, I met this girl called Amanda Harrison. You always expect that the man teaches the woman or the man calls the shots, if you like, but she was so *experienced* and so *aware.* I was in Pentwyn and she was in Llanedeyrn, just across the lake, but that was the most incredible experience that I've ever had in my life. I learnt things that you could never imagine you're going to find out about women.

When I came out of prison, I did six or maybe eight jobs all in the space of a year. I've never actually passed *one* exam in my life but every time I apply for a job I tell them I've got 'O' level Maths and English and Economics and Cookery and things like that and I just get the job. They don't even ask me for certificates or whatever. But I'm intelligent and quick - especially with my hands - and I can do things others can't.

I started off as a kitchen porter in Steakhouse on the Avenue, then I was promoted to Assistant Chef: getting vegetables and cutting sandwiches into little triangles with no crust along the edge. Then I was a chef in Pizza Land, a door-to-door salesman for Ableglaze, a barman, an arcade attendant at Barry Island and a security guard with Centurion Security but I gave that up when the guard dog went for me. Eventually, I went to Kwiksave as a store block assistant and it was beautiful - absolutely incredible! On Thursdays and Fridays you had to do night shifts and face off every tin of beans in the store so they all said 'Heinz.' You done a full twelve hour shift and the money was good and for night shifts you got double pay plus an eight pound shift allowance. But one of the people I'd asked for a reference, wrote to them saying 'this man has been to prison. You must be *mad* if you hire him.' So they sacked me. I'd been there about two months, so they should have known I was trustworthy by then. But it was a combination of other things as well. I was going out with a coloured girl at the time and this lad who was jealous that I'd been put on the night shift called me a 'nigger-lover' in the middle of the shop, so I punched him in the face but I had a knife in my hand - the kind you cut open boxes with - and I left a little cut on him.

I rented a flat across the road from my parents after that. My father had gone to jail for three months while I was in jail. He'd told everyone it was for drinking and driving but I think it was for beating up my little sister. If he gets the chance, he's violent with anyone. My brother came up only the other day to tell me about my mother's face being cut open but I don't wish to get involved. His next door neighbour knocked the door a couple of months ago and punched him straight in the mouth. In my opinion, my father's so violent, somebody could beat him up every day for the rest of his life and it *still* wouldn't be enough for him.

I was about twenty-one when my parents sold their Council House and bought another one in Port Talbot which I then I bought off them. My girlfriend came to live there with us and I was getting money and giving it to her all the time to pay off the mortgage but one day my father came home and said 'You haven't paid *one penny* off the mortgage,' and it didn't make sense cause I'd given it all to her. So I left her and the house got repossessed and my parents went to live in Cymmer. After that, I couldn't seem able to settle, you know. I was always moving about from city to city to city. Just trying to find somewhere peaceful and quiet. Mainly in hostels.

I first came to Swansea two and a half years ago and went to live in the Cyrenians hostel in Stembridge. I also lived in the Christian Home in Canal Road. I enjoyed it there but suddenly, without explanation or reason or anything, the person in charge came to me and said 'You will be leaving soon,' and when I said 'Why?' he said 'Just get your stuff together and I'll drive you to the motorway and I'll tell you on the way.' And all he would tell me was that I wasn't *fitting in.*

The Salvation Army is easy to get into and can be long-term but it's hard to stick it out cause there's so many people coming in and out and sooner or later there'll be someone who'll find a reason *not* to like you. The world doesn't seem to accept, and governments don't seem to accept, people for what they *are.* They have to give you a label or a certificate to say you're a *psychotic* or a psychopath or this that and the other. There are people in this world that are *malicious.* They have no likes and want evil to come upon people. They desire it because of their own pangs and pains. Because no-one has ever shown them kindness or love and, as a result, they don't get to express no joy and know nothing about expressing joy. They only know retaliation for their sorrows.

Everything seems to be fine here, though. This hostel is house size but with most of them, it's like walking into a huge Asda store or something. The people seem to be okay too, in comparison to the worst hostels I've been in. But you always get someone who, if they had the chance would do you harm, if they knew they could get away with it. Like for instance, two weeks ago I came back here and went into a room to get my old suitcase and a man - who couldn't punch a hole in a wet Echo because he can hardly stand up half the time - says to me 'What d'you *want!* What are you *doin* comin in here?' as though it's a big psychological problem. And he knew *full well* that the member of staff was just trying to see if my suitcase was still in my room or if it had been thrown away. Eddie it was: the one who always looks drunk twenty-four hours a day and doesn't speak at all to anyone. He acted as if I'd just killed his children or something.

I'd definitely do landscape gardening full-time if I could. Not long ago I did my parents' neighbours' garden. I landscaped their lawn, which was just dense brambles and then they wanted this one hedge cut down to a more manageable size, so I took the croppers and cut that down and then smartened up the drive all along the side of the house.

I haven't found any proper work down here because I don't relate in crowds. I don't mix in company very well. I've had loads of jobs but I only keep them for a while. As soon as I get into an argument, I just don't bother going to work any more. It's generally older people who'll tell me to do something which is part of *their* job and I think there's no need to put up with it and I just walk out.

Financially, it's impossible to work *and* live in the Hostel because you'd be worse off than if you were on Income Support. But it wouldn't surprise me if I don't get my compensation soon. I've put in for two lots now. As well as the prison business, I disturbed burglars when I was staying up in Scotland and they kicked my face to a pulp. I'm assuming that one of them will come up then I can start up my own business and be my own boss, with no-one to tell me what to do. That's at best, but at worst I see myself in ten years time still claiming Income Support and just living in a Council flat or a Council House somewhere. I filled in all the forms here and I did have an appointment with Caer Las but I fell asleep in my bedroom and never turned up.

For the past three years I've had psychological problems. I'm on tablets called sulpiride because I couldn't seem to get any proper relaxation. Because the tablets make you slightly docile, you can relax and sleep and they give you the *impression* that you're no danger to anyone. But that's the worst problem because in reality you might hurt someone who's really your friend. You're really tense and ready to leap on anybody.

Occasionally I go into the Duchess in Town and have a drink and maybe even smoke some cannabis but my main recreation is music. I like Tchaikovsky and Beethoven but I prefer things like Andrew Lloyd Webber's Variations, Red Indian chants, The Magic Flute, and Crystal Mattresses and Synthesisers. My favourite music is sea shanties and Beethoven's oboe music. I've had some of Schubert's stuff but I couldn't really get on with him. I've just bought a cassette with some of Mozart's oboe music on but I find Beethoven far superior as far as the oboe's concerned. Mozart looks different to what I expected. I always thought he'd look very aggressive - like a wolf or something - but he's got this wig on with curly hair and he looks dignified and graceful more than anything.

I played keyboards once but I sold it a couple of days ago for bus-fare. I can't play properly or read or write music but for ten or twenty minutes, I can make it sound as though I've played piano all my life. If I settle down and get my own flat, I may take it up again but it's a bit risky to start writing music as a Mr No-one, cause people will steal the music and sell it and I don't want to spend my days, weeks, months or years, composing something only for someone to come along and stick their name on it and walk off with the prize. My younger brother, for instance, would *sell* my own trousers if he had the chance and my other brother would sell my silk hankies and ties and my best suit, too. They *all* steal off me and cheat me. Even my mother and father had my tax refund when I was in prison and they swore blind they hadn't and the Tax people said they sent it so obviously they had it and they *spent* it.

I blame everything onto my father: not only the sorrows and heartaches and all the trouble but his blatant and deliberate misconduct. He *trained* us to do wrong and he belted us if we did right. He shamed us deliberately. The fact that I picked up landscape gardening was the only really good thing about my childhood, apart from my mother's occasional kindness - and she could be *extraordinarily* kind, you know. It appeared that she was trying to protect us from my father but you can't always go by appearances. I think she was more frightened than anything else and prepared to go along with whatever he was doing.

'Last Train to San Fernando...'

Alec

Full name: Alexander Gordon Fuller. Born 1937. An orphan. In Scotland. I don't know where. I know nothing. All I know is I've got a twin sister Marjorie. My mother put us in the street there when we were two-year old. Ditched us...

He sits on a settee in my studio at half past eleven in the morning with three cans of Strongbow on the floor in front of him, one of them already opened. Familiarly known as 'Swansea Jock', everybody likes Alec. He looks like a retired bantamweight boxer but is, in fact, as gentle as a lamb. He speaks with a thick Glaswegian accent. That and the quickening effects of the Strongbow, often make him difficult to understand...

They put us in the Quarriers Home, Bridge of Wear in Renfrewshire. I was there seventeen years and I've got very bad memories of it. There were forty-three cottages with thirty kids in each, a big hospital, a church and a sanatorium. I had to get up at five every morning to make the porridge, peel the spuds and prepare the dinner. *Oliver Twist!* Oh, what a carry-on! Five in the morning till seven at night and I never got a day off or nothing. Every Sunday you got a halfpenny to put in the collection box and a bag of sweets. I ran away frae there about nine times and the police kept bringing me back. My foster mother - Miss Froome - was a very bad person. I had no comfort. No joy. No life. I was ten year old when I ran away the first time. The next time, I ran away to Glasgow. They picked me up, brought me back and belted hell out of me. I done nothin right. It wasna in the blood to do it for them. They put me the lowest of the lowest. I educated *myself. They* didn't educate *me* cause everything in my record proves it: **'X - X - X: Useless. Useless. Useless.'** The only thing I got a good mind of is football. I won a medal. Eleven teams played every Saturday morning and we were top of the East Fife League.

I went to another Hostel then, run by Quarriers and they got me a job in the fruit market in Glasgow. I stuck it there six months then finished up and left the Home altogether. I just wanted to go on my own and get my own jobs.

I started in the Fairfax Shipyard in Govan. The Personnel Man gave me a form to fill in and when I told him I couldn't read or write, he put me to work straight away. I served my time there as an apprentice painter and decorator but three months before it was up, I packed my bags and left Scotland forever. I liked the work but I didn't like what was going on there. It was run by racketeers. *I* was alright: I was servin my time - they couldn' touch me but everyone else was scared for their jobs. That's the way they work over there in Glasgow and it's still going on, to the present day. The Freemason mob were judge and jury and if you didn't like the jury, you knew what you could do! It made me sick. They seen what you *done* and what you *were* and if they didn't like it you could: *'Hit the Road, Jack!'*

Thirty years after my time, I met this Joe Brannen in Glasgow and he turns to me and says: 'Did you ever get any money for your deafness, cause they're givin out thousands of pounds?' I'd worked with the corkers and riveters and the noise had made my ears as sore as hell. So I went back to the Shipyard to try for it. I knew the Timekeeper but he says 'Fairfax's finished. There's a new name now.' So I got this lawyer in Govan and he took my case up and the first thing was, he went to the Tax office: 'Never heard of him,' they said. And I served my *time* there! I went to my Union and they didn want to know me either. Just cause I was too long away. So I got *nothing*.

I worked on Smith Docks in North Shields and Swan Hunters in Newcastle and then, after two years, I got picked up by the Redcoats. I'd had my National Service papers, telling me to go for a medical but I'd tore them up and hit the road. I got away with it, though, cause I wasn't 100% proof due to my deafness.

I hit London in 1962 and stayed in a Rownton House in the Elephant and Castle. Got a job with John Murphy on the roads there. It was pure manual labour and all I was gettin was two pound fifty a day. A lot of them were from the West of Ireland and they were *hard* men. If you couldn't keep up with the pace, it was no good being there. Seven o'clock in the morning till six o'clock at night and if there was a fault you might have to do a night shift as well. It was money-in-hand. I couldn't claim dole and I didne bother. I was payin just a guinea a week at the Rownton: one pound two and six for a seven days a week lie-down and the only time you got a breakfast was a Sunday. There were four hundred in the Hostel and the staff were excellent but it was like a beehive in there with people coming and going all the time.

I did some hop-pickin down in Kent for Courage Brewery then. We used to sleep in buses. It was seasonal work but it got me a bit of corn and kept the old stomach going, you know. Then I worked for Courage at Tower Bridge and Guinness in Acton. I got nabbed at Guinness. I was workin for a sub-contractor but he wouldn't give us any bottles, so I nicked two. Next thing, we're going through the gates and the security officers stop us. They opened up the doors and there's these two bottles of Guinness sticking out of my back pocket. I never thought, you know. 'Oh!' says this guy, 'I've got *you*, anyway!' 'Have you?' I says. 'For *what*?' And then he took the two bottles off me and says 'Right, don't bring that fella back in here tomorrow. He's *finished*!' Didn' charge me or nothin. They were all doin it but *I* was just unfortunate. That's the way it goes: up and down the merry-go-round...

After eight years in London, I went to Southport and worked in a hostel there. Then I got casual work as a Caddy boy at Royal Birkdale. It wasn't a very healthy job, the time I was runnin about on it and the hours depended on how long it took them to get to the eighteenth tee. The money was poor but if they won a Tournament, you'd be a rich man. I stuck that for a couple of months, then I left Southport for Liverpool and worked in the new Mersey Tunnel. I had plenty of money and I was enjoying every minute of it. All I was payin for my room was ten pound a week. I was just a casual man - no cards or nothing - and at the end of the day, if you wanted to go, you went. All you did was jump a bus or a rattler and go to another Town.

I worked on Southampton Dock after that but when that job finished, I started wanderin away again and sleepin rough. Things went against me. I was signing on but they wouldn't give me no money cause I had no fixed abode. I was desperate: I used to throw bricks through shop windows just to get locked up. I've got a bad record with jails all through the country but I had to survive and the only way to survive was if they took me in. The last sentence I got was a year - a solid year - for a bit of lead in Southampton. I did nine months in Winchester. Bonnie Prince Charles got married during that sentence - him and Diana. When I came out, it was a case of: another Town, another day, another dollar. I stayed a week at a Cyrenians' in Exeter and then I went to Plymouth to work on the buildings with my friend Eddie. We stayed at a place called Honnington in Buckfastleigh, run by monks. That's where they make Buckfast wine and it's a top class wine. You used to get a big meal there and a lie-down but now you only get the meal because there's a crypt down there and all the boys broke in and stole the wine and got mad drunk...

I was first in Swansea seventeen years ago. The Hostel wasn't goin then. There was a house at the back of the Tenby, owned by a Jewess - a black woman - who rented out houses and there were about twenty six of us stayin there, each man payin eight pound a week. I was travellin up and down to Carmarthen every day working for Graham Murphy on the cables. I stuck that for about four months, then I went through the country again, makin a fresh start each time but at the end of the day, it was no worth it. It was just heavy, heavy, heavy. When you hit the tarmac, you had to be a loola. You gotto be drunk most of the time when you're on the toby. Next thing there's no dykes around, Next thing you see a hedge. Next thing you're like a hedgehog there, old jacket over you, tryin to keep warm...

I came back down to Swansea through Ludlow and went straight to the Hostel when I arrived. There's all walks of life here. They come and go like flies, don't they? One minute you see them and the next you don't. I wake up in the morning and I don't know what day it is half the time and the next thing I see new faces - new customers there. You see them in the night and next day they've all disappeared again. Only George has been here longer and he's like me: he keeps himself to himself. He talks to me at odd times but I don't bother him and he doesn't bother me. If a guy wants to be alone, that's it. I don't pal up with nobody. They talk to me or they don't. I'm a loner. Ted O' Mally was the same. If he wants to go to another Town, he goes to another Town. It's in the brain, isn't it? He says to himself 'Enough's enough. I'll go somewhere else,' and he goes. One of the staff said something to him about the rent he owed and next thing he was *away* - bailed out just in time. That's what life's all about: survive. Other people in the Hostel don't know how to survive. They don't know what hard living is yet. If the Staff ask them to clean up or somethin: it's 'No, no, no.' All they want is food, food, food. Beddy, beddy bed.

I've been clean now for fifteen years but there's a warrant out for me in Leeds: Drunk and Disorderly. They put me in a dry house for twenty-one days but I broke the window and escaped. And last October they almost locked me up down here. My friend Archie had seen me into the taxi and given me a handful of change for the fare but when we got there, I didn't have enough. So I gave the driver what I had. Next minute we're at High Street Police Station. And I didn't know the carry-on with them taxis. He got out and I tried to get out too but the doors were all locked. Next thing a copper opened the door and I was tryin to get over the top of the seat to get out the other door. But he got me, read me the charges. 'Are you guilty or not?' he says. 'Well,' I says, 'I've gotto be guilty. I'm in the taxi, aren't I?' So he takes me in, puts me in the cells, locks me up. After a bit, he brings me back to the charge desk: 'Now then, Alec,' he says, 'you've got an awful bad record. How long you been in Swansea? Five years? You been doin anything wrong here?' I said 'Naw!' He says 'How're you in here?' I says 'A taxi guy - ' He says 'You tried to *fraud* him.' I says 'Oh, did I? I gave him all the money I had. I didne fraud him.' He says 'You're a runner an all.' I says 'How can I be a runner? What d'you mean?' He says 'You know, *Leeds*?' 'Oh aye, yeah - I forgot about *that*,' I says. 'but I don't think they'll bother me.' He says 'They think you're in Scotland?' 'No,' I told him. 'in Swansea.' He says 'He's getting clever. He's getting further away frae us now. The further the better !' Then he says to me 'If that was *me* in the taxi, I'd say to myself "I'm not goin to bother with this head case here." I'd take the money off you and dump you. But now I've gotta charge you.' He cautioned me but I've heard nothing about the case yet. Swansea Licensed Taxis are bringing it and I had a letter telling me I'd have to appear in court some time. I'm guilty, you know and I think it will be a big fine. Oh! Naughty! Naughty! Naughty!

I'm fifty-nine now and hopefully I'll find my sister, who I haven't seen for thirty one years. It all depends on Julie and John writing a letter for me. My sister went lookin for me a long time ago down in Govan when I was working on the shipyards. Nobody knew where she'd gone. She got depressed and was wandering around Glasgow for two days and nights. She's got a family now: my only flesh and blood in the world. The last time I was in Scotland, she got in touch with the Salvation Army and they got in touch with all the hostels in Glasgow: about thirty of them. I was working in Glasgow for a Northampton mob at the time, doin the street lightin and I came back down there to The Great Northern in Finlay Street, and the next thing there was a letter there for me in a big envelope. I opened it up and as soon as I saw 'McAllister' I knew it was my twin. I got in touch wi her that night and she met me next day. That was the last time I seen her. She's got four there in her family - three boys and a lassie - and two are married now. She says to me: 'If you go down the road again, keep in touch wi me.' But I lost her phone number and address. I know where my nephew lives: a brick-built estate in Govan. He's a Personnel Manager in the Scottish Caledonian Brewery there. I tried to get in touch but he's no answerin the phone to me. The other son's a draughtsman and the niece is in the navy. Julie and John are going to write a letter for me and make sure they're there. My sister's got a plot ready for me in the churchyard there: for me and her and her old man. She's told them all: 'My twin brother's like *me*: he's been *dragged* up in the world.' That's what she told all the family about me. She says 'He's *all right*! He went through *hell*!'

I've never seen my nephews and niece. I'm not a home boy. I run about the country too much but I always try to keep in touch with everybody. I can't help what I'm doin - that's my nature. I've got to get on with the world myself. I came to Swansea to stay for just three months, to see how I got on but here I am fifteen years later with the Cyrenians. I don't know if they'll leave me alone there. Everyone seems to be disappearin, gettin rooms. I couldn't handle a room. I couldn't pay water rates and all that. I like my drink too much. If I pay twenty-one pound a week, I'm happy, you know. The nurse came to see me the other day in the Hostel. The CPI. I was wi him about twenty minutes. 'Just came to check you out there,' he says. 'Check me for *what?*' I says. 'I'm all right.' 'No,' he says, 'I've just come to ask you a few questions about the Hostel. How d'you like it here? How d'you get on wi the staff?' 'Well,' I says, 'I get on great here but you've gotto abide by the rules. If you don't, you're out the door. They tell you that when you come in: no *drugs*, no *alcohol*. They give you your task and you do it.' I said 'That's straightforward, isn't it? Break the rules and that's *it*. You're out on your neck. When I get too much drink, I stay way up there in my rooster.' -That's my room: I call it a 'rooster' - He says 'What's a *rooster?*' I says 'Like the crow, there. The Jackdaw - ' He couldn't understand me. Didn't know what I was on about. He thought I was *out of this world*. He says 'I'm not here to put any heavyweight on you. I'm up here just to visit you. Would you like a house, there?' 'A *house?*' I said 'I never had a house in my life. I couldn't handle it. I'm always mixin with people - anywhere I go. I'm a jackdaw. I never walk *alone*.' Sounds like a Billy Connelly record, doesn't it - !

If the Hostel closed tomorrow I'd go round the country again. Nowhere in particular. The first Town that comes to me. I'll say one thing for certain, though: if they closed up there tomorrow, gave me my notice, I'd jump a bus or a rattler and I know where I'm goin to make for: maybe Birmingham, Manchester or Leeds. And if I've gotto leave Swansea and go to another country, I'll *still* make it. I *know* I can.

I cannae read or write or I'd read what I've said when you've written it out. But I can answer the questions - fiery, fiery - I'm good at that one. Can you give me a pen and paper? I'll show you my signature... I'm not kiddin you, Alan. Here's my signature: here's how *bad* I am... That's all I can write: and it's no clever.

I'm not interested in learnin to write. Nah, nah, nah. When I was in jail, they tried to put me through a school to try and get me educated again but I wouldne accept it. It's just not in me. All I wanted to be is what I am now. Accept life as it is as long as I'm getting through the country, through the world. It's a big, wild, wild world. Wild, wild Westies! I've got a Mickey Mouse brain. It's been drummed into me since I was a baby, y'know? But enough's enough. The story's all over now. And no way am I going to get it drummed into me to *do this* or *do that*, now. I just want to do what I want to do. I know I'm doing wrong there with drinkin and no eatin and all that but that's my choice. Take it or leave it. That's my way of life. Eleven o' clock in the morning till eleven o' clock at night. I don't go down the Hostel for my grub: my stomach can't handle it. They try and chase me out of the pubs: 'Go and get some food there and come back and see us.' But I say 'No. If I wanna go, I'll go. If I don't, I don't. I'm payin my dues there.' They say 'We're no worried about your dues, we want to see you doin somethin *right* for a change.'

They told me back in the Homes there: 'You'll never make it, the way you're carryin on!' But I made it up to now. They told me: 'You're leavin *good* friends behind.' Friends! I left *enemies* behind. 'You'll fall by the wayside!' they said. But I've proved them wrong. I went through tough times but I still survived and I'm happier now than I've ever been. I don't know why. Before, I was runnin around the country, jumpin buses, jumpin rattlers, workin and drinkin and no thinkin about life, you know? But now I've started *thinkin* about life.

'Dare to be a Daniel, dare to stand alone! Dare to have a purple heart and we will never stand alone!' That's one of my quotes and I've got many of them. D'you know that song: *'If you miss this one, you'll never get another one?'*... Last Train to San Fernando! That's the one I always catch. I call it The Rattler. *'If you miss this one, you'll never get another one - iddly-biddly-bom-bom - to SAN FERNANDO!'*

... Next time I'll have better stories than them for you. Brand new. All my old haunts. The real McCoy...!

JANUARY

'Ichad and Obet aped a abbit...'

Wayne and Lyn

Wayne: Our brother Paul's in hospital. He's seriously ill. It's touch and go.

Lyn: The doctors have told him if he touches another nurse, he'll ave to go.

Wayne: I just bought a new dog. It's like a greyhound only smaller.

Lyn: Whippet?

Wayne: No, I bought it.

Lyn: I was in court yesterday - for nicking shovels.

Wayne: He was looking for digs!

Lyn: My girlfriend's just gone off on holiday. To that Caribbean island where all the blacks come from. Can't remember the name of it but it begins with a J.

Wayne: Jamaica?

Lyn: No, she went of her own accord!

A freezing cold night. We're standing by the open boot of the car in St. David's Square. The Outreach minibus is out of commission. Leila is talking to a young guy called Rob, who has only recently hit Town, and I'm talking to Wayne and Lyn. They're drinking soup from plastic cups. With their stocky, well-wrapped frames, unkempt beards and recently-scarred faces, they look like time-warp Norsemen. Wayne is dark and Lyn is fair. In a much-publicised Court case, Wayne once confessed to, and was convicted of, a murder he didn't commit. Wayne examines my car, advises me to turn the car radio off in case the battery goes flat and to change my offside front tyre because it looks bald to him. A young boy appears, mysteriously, out of the darkness staggering under the weight of a car tyre which he's clutching to his chest: 'He looks tired,' Lyn quips. I fetch more soup. Wayne warns me, for the second or third time, to be careful I don't knock my head on the open boot of the car. They need a change of clothes and he needs shoes, he says. I tell him there's a pair back in the Hostel that might fit him. I also mention the book I'm writing and they promise to come to the Hostel in an hour's time for some clothes and the shoes and to give me an interview. I don't really expect them to keep their word but in less than half an hour, they are tapping on the office window.

Someone brings them a cup of tea. They settle down, side by side in arm chairs, affable and only too eager to be of assistance...

Wayne: Good afternoon!

Lyn: Good *evening*, sir! We had somewhere to go and we would have gone but we came down here, instead. A bloke told us he was going to take us up his house for a bath and some clothes so we turned him down -

Wayne: And come down here for you - cause we thought your book was more important.

Lyn: You won't find a single flea on *us*.

Wayne: They're all *married!*

Lyn: So we'll ave a little chat now and then we'll tell some jokes.

Wayne: A tapeful of talkin and a tapeful of jokes. Ow's that?

Lyn: We're brothers.

Wayne: I'm Philip Wayne Darvell. I'm thirty six years of age and I'm from Cimla.

Lyn: And I'm Lyn Eric Darvell and I'm from the same place and I'm forty-one -

Wayne: Today.

Lyn: We got eleven brothers -

Wayne: And one sister - but she died of a brain tumour - three years ago this November. She was forty-five years of age.

Lyn: We had a mixed childhood.

Wayne: Our father left in the sixties.

Lyn: He rejected us. We've been in intensive care ever since. I've been in care *and* in the hospital. I don't know if you know it: Hensol Hospital, Llantrisant? Our father worked in opencast, in the quarry.

Wayne: He used to beat our mother up.

Lyn: Ill-treat her, like, and ill-treat the family as well. But the thing is: you can have a hundred fathers but only one mother you'll ave, isn' it?

Wayne: She died. The second of February, 1980. She was a good mother. I was seven when my father left and he was eleven.

Lyn: We felt guilty when he went. Unwanted, like. Why should *we* be penalized for the sake of *them*, isn' it? If you're going to fetch kids into the world, look after them. Don't ill-treat them, isn' it?

Wayne: We went to school in Neath. E.S.N: Educationally Sub-Normal. The whole family were classed as subnormal.

Lyn: But a psychiatric hospital I was in, wasn' I? A Mental Institution. *He* had the freedom, *I* didn't. I never got on there. I kept running away. I was thirteen when I went in and I was forty when I came out. It was for young and old and disabled people: people who couldn't read or write. I was on the farm working. I can't read and write now but he's teaching me, cause he don't drink now. He goes to Alcoholic *Anomynous.*

Wayne: I been goin there three months but I don't feel it's working. I have lapses. Last night I had a bad time. I found a bottle of cider and I tipped it away.

Lyn: He threw it down the drain. Cause he said to me 'I'm goin to drink this' and I said 'No, you're not. You can pour it down there - '

Wayne: And I did. It breaks my heart to do it but I'm trying to get off it.

Lyn: I don't drink myself, see. There's more to life than drinking, isn' there? You taste your food better. Alcoholics have to *cling* to it. They get *addicted* to it.

Wayne: *'Addicted'* - Yes, that's the word!

Wayne: I didn leave school, I was kicked out.

Lyn: They done away with him.

Wayne: Not *'done away with'*. I was teacher's pet: she kept me in a cage behind the desk.

Lyn: He worked for his brother then - on the glass - didn you? That's Derek. He's a bit older.

Wayne: And more sensible

Lyn: He used to have a shop in Neath.

Wayne: W. J. Thackerel, Glazier.

Lyn: I was on the coal when I come out: carrying the bags for Eddie's the Coalman.

Wayne: We sell The Big Issue now.

Lyn: But that doesn't pay our way. We aren't on the Social because we aven't got an address. We gotto live out of the bins, aven't we?

Wayne: Whatever we can scrounge off the streets. Are we doin all right for time - ?

Lyn: We're okay. Bags of time.

Wayne: We don't mind, anyway. *Anything* for the book. But now, what we'll do, look: when that tape runs out, we'll give you another tape. How will that do?

Wayne: You used to teach Art in Swansea Prison, didn' you? Paul and me were in Swansea Prison but you taught Paul - the bald one. The drawin you done of him is still in the Prison, in the Governor's Office.

Lyn: But, knowing the Governor, he's probably put it in the bin by now.

Wayne: You were there in eighty and I was there after eighty-five. I was in prison because I was accused of doing that sex-shop murder. Nine and a half years, I done. 'Come on **down**! The price is right!'

Lyn: We go round tellin jokes to people now. We told a bloke a couple up by the Quadrant there earlier. Tell im what appened.

Wayne: Oh yeah: we told a bloke a couple of jokes up by there - and he punched us.

Lyn: He said 'We've got enough comedians already. On your bike!'

Wayne: And all I said to him was 'Ow's *your* wife and *my* kids?'

Lyn: Then I was in Court the other day and the Judge said 'You been up before me,' and I said 'Why, what time did *you* get up?'

Lyn: I've been livin rough all the time: up in London and down here. Not hostels.

Wayne: We have *been* in hostels.

Lyn: But we're not tramps, we're just dossers. We're just *unfortunate* people. Is that the word, Philip?

Wayne: Don't ask me, I'm just a subnormal.

Lyn: When I was in prison I told the Governor it was cold in the cell and he said 'Oh, don't worry about that: we'll put an extra bar on for you.'

Wayne: We just live from day to day.

Lyn: But "What d'you do when you actually become homeless?" That was what you were going to ask, wasn it?

Wayne: Well, my mother died and -

Lyn: We ad to sell the house.

Wayne: No, we didn't. It was a Council house and they evicted us. There was about two of us living in the house then: Paul and myself.

Lyn: All the other brothers are scattered. They've all got their own families and -

Wayne: There's one on crutches - Terry.

Lyn: He's down in the hostel in the Strand. He gave us a bottle of wine last night and we gave it back to him.

Wayne: There's no vacancies down there. There *were* two but they've been taken up... I lived in my mam's house for about two years after she died. This was before we were arrested.

Lyn: I reckon they were set up by the man on television. There was evidence planted and he's, well, not the type of man to do things like that, is he? *Categorically* speaking.

Wayne: Well, what *do* a murderer look like these days, anyway? And there's a lot of them about, isn't there?

Lyn: One of them tried to pinch my father's gate last night.

Wayne: Well, why didn't you tell the police?

Lyn: There was no point was there?

Wayne: Why?

Lyn: Because they might take offence!

Wayne: We'd like to get into a hostel, cause it's gettin very cold now. And I'm suicidal. Well, you can see all the marks here on my arms.

Lyn: Whenever he gets depressed - or *shitsophrenic* or something like that - he cuts himself.

Wayne: I done it last night.

Lyn: I've stopped im a couple of times, aven't I? You know: doin his throat. (Sorry I did now - no, I don't mean that!) I'm only the best boy who ever looks after you, aren't I?

Wayne: You come into the world with nothin and you go out with nothin. I've had a few close shaves. See that one there? That was the worst one. I've got scars on my arms which is unbelievable, innit? *He* don't do it cause he don't like the sight of blood. Specially his own. I do it with anything: pens, knives, you name it.

Lyn: Forks, glass -

Wayne: I'm diabetic as well and I don't get no treatment for it.

Lyn: He don't take nothing. And I got asthma and I aven't got an inhaler or nothing. Well, you can hear my chest now, can't you?

Wayne: And we can't sign on with a doctor cause we aven't got no address.

Lyn: You know, it's putting us out of gear, isn't it? We can't live on fresh air today, can we?

Wayne: It's too far to go to Morriston Casualty but Singleton Casualty is open in the nights now, so we could go there. But it's awkward, especially with his feet. He's got blisters on them and so have I. I've been to them *all* with my cuts: Morriston, Neath, Cardiff CRI, the Heath - and I seen the psychiatrist.

Lyn: And the vet.

Wayne: And the psychiatrist said to me "If I give you a golf ball, will you eat it?" I said "Yes, I'll eat it if you bloody *peel* it first!"

Lyn: We're sleepin down by the Leisure Centre. They got a big chimney down there and by the side of it there's warm air coming out of a vent.

Wayne: It wasn't enough last night, cause they turned the bloody thing off - cause of the New Year, wasn it?

Lyn: It was minus eight last night.

Wayne: Woke up this mornin and my shoes were stiff. What we usually do: the first car horn that blows, we get up. I didn't get up till *ten to four* this afternoon. Then we just wander round Town. Lookin in bins, seein what we can find to eat, you know?

Lyn: I try to play the mouth organ to earn a bit of cash but I can't bloody play it: it gets stuck to my moustache.

Wayne: They give him money just to shut him up!

Lyn: The solution to homelessness? I reckon the Government's not doing their job right. They're doin their own thing. They're takin on Paul to pay Peter, innit? There's people goin round breakin in places cause they haven't got a home and they're gettin arrested. Why don't they *give* them a home and *look after* them?

Wayne: Why don't they gather us all up -

Lyn: *Round* us up.

Wayne: Round us all up and put us

Lyn: in a big house, like, innit? There's enough empty places. Look at that one up by Toys-R-Us.

Wayne: The old U.B.M. place by the Cardiff Arms.

Lyn: That's the place we used to sleep in. Even if Labour get in next time I don't think they'll do any more for us. You might as well knock your head against a wall.

Wayne: You'd get more sense out of a

Lyn: bottle of pop! Why don't the Government get off their fat arses and *do* something. If the settee broke, they'd do something. What d'you say? Am I right or am I wrong? We *may* get them out in *May*. You never know.

Wayne: I just noticed that cutting on the noticeboard there: POLICE TO CLEAR BEGGARS FROM STREETS. Now why can't they leave us alone? We're just tryin to make a livin.

Lyn: It puts you all out of gear, doesn't it?

Wayne: It puts *me* out of gear. Must think I'm a bloody car!

Lyn: Well, I think we'll finish now with a couple of jokes. Will you start, Wayne or shall I?

Wayne: Why did the Mexican chuck his wife off the cliff?

Lyn: He wanted *Tequila!*

Wayne: Why don't British Rail train drivers have kids?

Lyn: They always pull out in time!

Wayne: This girl in the pub rolled her eyes at me. I picked them up and threw them back at her!

Lyn: We memorize most of them.

Wayne: Or make them up.

Lyn: We've managed to keep a sense of humour. Well, you've gotto, aven't you? We found an old fridge that had been chucked out the other day. He put an empty milk bottle in it. He said 'If you want a black coffee, I've put an empty bottle in there.'

Wayne: Empty bottle - get it? In case you want a black coffee.

Lyn: There's a bloke in hospital, the doctor says 'I've got some good news and bad news for you.' Bloke says 'What's the bad news?' Doctor says 'I've taken both your legs off.' Bloke says 'What's the good news?' Doctor says 'The boy in the next bed wants to buy your boots!'

Wayne: I aven't heard that one. It's good!

Lyn: Remember when *I* was in hospital? Doctor came in and said 'D'you want a bedpan?' I said 'Oh, I've gotto do my own cookin, have I?' Then I said to him 'Could you help me out?' and he said 'Aye, which way did you come in?'

Wayne: Little and Large, that's us!

Lyn: This is what we do on the street.

Wayne: To get money.

Lyn: To entertain people.

Wayne: It don't work, but it helps, like.

Lyn: Went into the Fish Shop the other day and said 'Bag of chips.' She said 'Sixty or Seventy-five?' I said 'If you're goin to count them, give me a pie!' Who're you callin Bob Monkhouse?

Wayne: I met his wife in a Travel Agent's - she was the Last Resort!

Lyn: What about that one: 'There's a Man So Mad'?

Wayne: I don't know it. Tell him it.

Lyn: *'There's a man so mad, he jumped into a flour bag.*
The flour was so rotten, he jumped into a reel of cotton.
The reel of cotton was so fine, he jumped into a glass of wine.
The glass of wine was so deep, he jumped on a sheep.
The sheep was so hairy, he jumped on the Sister Mary.
The Sister Mary had the gout: up her arse and blew him out!

Wayne: And there's one about my mother, who died:
Once I had a mother who thought the world of me
And when I was in trouble she sat me on her knee.
One night when I wa'n't sleepin, upon my feather bed
An angel came to tell me, my poor mam was dead.
I woke up in the morning to see if it was true,
My mother's gone to heaven beneath the skies of blue.
So if you have a mother, please do as you are told
Cause if you lose a mother, you lose a heart of gold.
I made that up myself.

Lyn: That's good that is, isn't it? *'London, O London's a wonderful sight! They sleep by day and they shag by night!'*

Wayne: She was 54 when she died.

Lyn: She worked in the Metalbox, makin ammunition. Hand grenades and bullets. She made bullets for her husband to fire, like.

Wayne: A boy's best friend is his mother.

Lyn: What I can't fathom out is: why do a golfer wear two pairs of trousers? Well, he might get a hole in one, innit?

Wayne: *To market, to market, with my brother Lyn!*
Somebody threw a tomato at him.

Lyn: *'Tomatoes don't hurt!' he said with a grin.*

Wayne: *This fucker did: it came in a tin!*

Lyn: Well, we aven't done too bad, ave we? Is that enough?

Wayne: We would like to thank everyone who's doin the soup runs in the night. If it wasn't for them, I think half of us wouldn't have survived.

Lyn: They could be doin their *own* thing, instead of which -.

Wayne: And I would like to thank Alan for having us down tonight - and I hope the book comes out. And whatever he makes on it, we'll have half!

Lyn: And like I say: he's very grateful for us comin down tonight like, innit? Cause *we're* doin *you* a favour, aren't we?

Wayne: I know where there's a place where we could get a bed *now* - the two of us - for £20. That's £10 each.

Lyn: But me and you was goin to go up *there* tonight, wasn we - ?

Wayne: Up where?

Lyn: Up that bloke's house, mun!

Wayne: But that's off. We've come down here to do that book for Alan cause that's more important.

Lyn: What d'you call an Irishman with two raincoats standing in a churchyard?

Wayne: Max Bygraves!

Lyn: 'Richard and Robert raped a rabbit.' Ow d'you say that without the 'r's?

Wayne: *'ichad and obet aped a abbit?'*

Lyn: No: ***'Dick and Bob fucked a bunny!'***

'No tramp or drinker of wine...'

John

He's dead on time arriving at my studio. Cap, raincoat, glasses, a Van Dyke beard and a cheery smile. As a member of staff of some five years standing and a frequent spokesman and fund-raiser for the Cyrenians, he's used to being interviewed and seems to be quite looking forward to it. He's brought with him a whole folder-full of his poems, many of which are about the homeless...

I was the middle boy of three and my father was a long-distance lorry driver. We lived in Cardiff and I was brought up in the Catholic Church, so I had a good upbringing. I was quite a religious child but, once I entered my teens, I suppose you could say I had a misspent youth. I was never in trouble with the police or anything like that - and drugs weren't known in Cardiff in the Sixties - but, nonetheless, I hung about with motorbike gangs. I had no direction in life and, if I wasn't propping up the bar at the pub, I was propping up the bar in the Catholic Club.

From early childhood, I'd had a yearning to go to Lourdes and in 1970, at the age of twenty-eight, I finally went: out of season, so I didn't have thousands of people there, and just by myself. It emptied down with rain as I remember and, to my great embarrassment, I got drunk. I hadn't eaten all day and I had a drink and it went straight to my head. But that was an experience which changed my life completely and within three years, I'd joined a monastery and found the *real* me. It was a Rosminian Order - contemplative in the main but active through necessity. Many of the monks were teachers in various institutions but the majority were in parishes. They were based in Cardiff and Swansea but I went to Wanage near Guildford. It was a comparatively strict Order with very much a thing about *obedience* and you were stuck with that. So, if your Superior happened to be in a bad mood, *you* took the brunt of it.

I was there for four years and then they sent me up to Huddersfield and that's where I decided to come out. I felt that the religious life - that particular style of life - had become anti-productive. I didn't exactly know what I was looking for but I felt I wasn't *growing* any more and I needed to make my way in life. But it had been a wonderful experience, because I really did *find* myself.

I suppose I *did* come into contact with the homeless in a way, when I was in Huddersfield. There was a group of people there in the early seventies called the Cyrenians who were going around derelict buildings at night doing soup runs. It was very much a Christian movement at the time and I started going out with them.

Their first hostel was set up in Portland Street. At the time these wonderful, big Victorian houses in Portland Street were being knocked down and when there were only two left, these Cyrenians staged a sit-in to stop the bulldozers and wouldn't move until the Council conceded and gave them those two houses. Now the Cyrenians are even more established and have a place in Spring Street in Huddersfield as well.

When I eventually left the Monastery, I decided to occupy myself more in the community so I got a job with The Catholic Rescue Society. This was a residential job looking after children - well, teenage boys, really, most of whom were well on the road to damnation. They'd had no upbringing, no discipline and they were just *trouble*. Many a time I was up till two or three in the morning searching for them and calling the police because they hadn't come home. Nice kids in themselves but no *direction* and I stuck that for six or seven months, until I realized it wasn't my true forte and I went back to college. I started learning the printing trade - reprographics and design - and from there I got a job with a Printers in Leeds. That closed down in the first of the recessions of the eighties but by this time I had become a Ba-ha'i and they needed Ba-ha'is to help with the community in York. I moved there and, before long, was offered a job with another Printers. I stuck that for six years, became Print Manager and then felt I could go it alone. I set up in my own garage and moved from there to proper premises where I was employing other people. But we weren't making the sort of money the banks thought we should be making and they lost interest and became very awkward and foreclosed on a loan of £3,000. So I lost everything and because I had everything tied up in that - the five-bed roomed house, my car and all my savings - I became absolutely destitute. I was living alone, even though I had a large house, and suddenly me and my animals were out on the street. It was a terrible shock to the system. What was I going to do? It's one thing *losing* your house but where are you going to *go?* I was of the opinion that *all* homeless people were drop-outs and alcoholics and although that's the image the media like to give, unfortunately it's not always the truth. I don't drink. I don't smoke and I'm a religious person. I've tried to live a good live but to suddenly find *that* happen, just devastates you. I'd been involved with homeless people but I never ever thought it could happen to *me*. Fortunately, a friend took me in and the Ba-ha'is of York looked after me. It took me a year to get over the trauma of it all.

I was in my mid-forties when I moved back to Swansea, with two cats and a dog and what I had left of my belongings, which I carried. Some Ba-hais put me up for a few weeks and then I got a flat and, as luck would have it, a job with the Swansea Cyrenians.

The clientele has changed considerably from when I first started with the Cyrenians. There are far more homeless women than there were and it's a growing trend. The majority of homeless used to be middle-aged and over but now you have a far greater number of young people. It's to do with Government policy and parents, too. I don't think there's the bonding in families that there was. I was brought up in a very good family. We had our problems but my parents would never have seen me on the streets. But today there's so much divorce and the kids are subjected to so much peer pressure that the parents aren't able to cope with it. Kids are more aggressive, too. I'm not sitting in judgement, but I certainly think that the family base is gone and that's the cause of a lot of youngsters being on the streets. The Government's idea was to force these kids to return home, otherwise they wouldn't get Benefit. I can understand the strategy but it was rather an aggressive way of doing it and I don't think it's actually working.

I originally started writing in the Monastery. When I was going through a bad time, I found it therapeutic. Then when I left, I did a Creative Writing Course in Night school and caught up with my English 'O' Levels. So far, I've written one and a half novels, two plays and, this year alone, some thirty-odd poems.

I had a letter this morning appointing me Press Representative for the Ba-ha'i faith in Wales and I'm also Assistant to the Council for the Protection of the Faith. And on top of that, I go around and give a lot of talks about the Faith and about homelessness. But I've been fortunate in having the support of my religious group and two communities in Swansea and, of course, in getting a job.

It was the system that let me down. But what made me different from everyone else was that I was determined not to *stay* down. I wasn't prepared to let the system beat me. Unfortunately, people who've abused all their life, don't have that backbone or determination because it's been knocked out of them. I think Society's attitude has a lot to do with it, too: you see an alcoholic on the street and you think 'Oh, it's his *own* bloody fault!' and we don't know if that's really why he's there. I think a lot of people hit the bottle *after* they become homeless. No-one *decides* to be homeless. No-one *decides* to be an alcoholic. It happens. And by that time it's often too late. We need to understand that and then perhaps we can give them back some self-dignity.

Knowing something of what it was to be homeless myself, I've been able to empathise with people in that predicament. Now, of course, I'm back on my feet. I have a job, I have my own home again but I've also come to understand that *anybody* can become homeless today, not just your drunks and your alcohol abusers and so forth.

I wrote a poem based on my own experiences. It's dedicated to the work of the Cyrenians and it's called 'The Homeless and Unemployed'. It talks about me being just an ordinary guy: *'no tramp or drinker-of-wine.'* Perhaps you'd like me to read a verse or two...?

'The King and I and the marsupials...'

Nick

He's been trying to get in touch with me since he left the Hostel. Nick was an active member of my Art class for four weeks and I chose eleven pieces of his work for inclusion in the 'Cyrenians' exhibition, held in the Glynn Vivian Art Gallery over December and January. Two days before the Show opened, I bumped into him in the street, by chance. He looked ill but promised to be there on opening night. In the event, four of his pictures sold: two portraits and two very expressionistic nudes as well as a mixed media painting we had done in collaboration. The Arts Council of Wales bought one of the nudes.

It's a few weeks after the Show ended. He's brought some new drawings to my studio for my comments. He looks a different man: fit and well and far more sure of himself. His work seems to be going from strength to strength...

I was born in Hartlepool in 1971. I've got one brother and a sister. My brother's got himself settled down with a girl now. Got a mortgage and everything - and he's only *twenty-three*! He's doing fork-lift driving or something. He seems happy, anyway, but we're only vaguely in touch. We're not really on the same wavelength, to be honest. My sister's twenty-one and I haven't seen her for some years now. I do *miss* her and I'd like to see her. As far as I know, she got in with an older man, actually had some kids by him and settled down.

My parents just *exist* really. My father's got to be forty-eight now, coming up to fifty. He was in the RAF for some years - or so he claimed - and I believe it to be true. He was away an awful lot, working in the Middle East. All sorts of weird Forces' stuff: places where there was a bit of conflict through Empire withdrawal - Israel, Sinai, Oman, Egypt - all over the shop. By all accounts, when he first went in he was in the Parachute Squadron but he transferred from that into other areas.

With him being away so much, our finances fluctuated. When times were bad, I remember the electric fire in one room and us three kids crammed in a bed in another room as cold as fuck but, at other times, when he sent some money, we were fairly well off.

I used to think that my mother had been in the RAF as well and that's where he met her and that she'd decided to give up her career for him but, as it turns out, her family history is much stranger and more extreme. Her mother died of tuberculosis when all the kids were very young and her father couldn't cope. He was a bit of a lad and because he couldn't handle it, he just left. And there were *loads* of them. There was my mother, sister Karen, sister Cynthia, sister Iris, brother Colin, brother Jim - and they all got split up and went to different homes. And some of them were badly abused at these foster places, until my Great Grandmother came steaming in to sort them out. Apparently, my mother and Iris got up to some dodgy stuff and I'm wondering if that was the score for my parents meeting or whether that was just inter-family chit-chat. Because there's always been this sort of brooding inter-family blame for almost every untoward event: for the death of *her* or the mistreatment of *these* or the split-up of *those.* And you even have Karen, at one point, accusing my mother and Iris of being *'Ladies of the Night'.* All *sorts* of weird things like that but whether these things are total fact or fiction, I don't know. It's all very mixed up.

It seemed as if they were happily married at first but, as it turned out, the marriage was a bit of a sham. I mean, we're talking serious *'mis-match'* here. It didn't show itself until much later on though and, in fact, we were led to believe my father was still working abroad, whereas they'd actually been divorced for two years.

My mother always wanted to get into acting. She had a bent for that and when they were rescued from these different foster homes, she tried to get into theatrical circles. She got me reading Shakespeare at seven or eight but she also liked classical music and poetry and was into painting and drawing. She was very encouraging of the creative bit: wanted me to paint and draw and write as well and bought me a guitar, which was the complete opposite of the old man. Whenever I painted or drew, he used to call me a poof. He came home pissed one night and smashed up the guitar because 'no son of *his*' was going to do things like that.

I suppose you'd say her sketches were 'twee' images of nature but later on she did drawings with much darker, masculine-seeming images. Unfortunately, because of her relationship with my father, I didn't get to see a lot of those. There was so much of her I didn't get to know or find an expression of. I'm not going to say there were *no* good times but the surface soundness was deceptive and after a bit we began to get the drift of things, started piecing it all together and saying 'Well, hold on. Something's *wrong* here.'

I didn't find out about the divorce until very recently, although we'd always believed that affairs had been going on. We thought she'd been having one with this huge Jamaican guy and this driving instructor and this person and that but it turns out that they'd actually had a divorce all the time.

She never really went into the abuse she'd suffered when she was fostered out but it must have been bad. Being the eldest son, I became the man of the house. She did try to talk to me about things which she must have known in her heart were too hard for me to take on board, particularly as I was only twelve and still tryin to keep the family together and deal with that as well.

There's a lot of details I've left out. My brother had gone off to a Special School at the time because she'd beaten him a lot and he'd become very disturbed. He really couldn't cope with it all and, to be honest, I don't think he ever has been able to. And then, my mother began mistreating my sister and me, in general, and it all started getting out of hand. Sometimes she'd break down screaming and I'd be trying to deal with this - from a grown woman. She was having a serious, serious breakdown, partly because my father just wasn't there but I think something was definitely *going* anyway. I remember feeling: 'This *isn't* me mother! This is a woman in *serious* trouble.'

And then suddenly, my mother did a bunk: deserted us in the way she'd once been deserted. She left a note saying 'I've left you a tenner and a bog roll. Go to the Supermarket and get some food. I'll be back.' And that was the last we saw of her. As soon as I saw it I thought 'This is a suicide note.' because I was in tune with what was going on. She'd been breaking down, beating me up - obviously, on reflection, trying to express what was wrong. I'd felt it building up for some time and I was convinced she'd gone off and done herself in.

We didn't go to school that week. We went to the High Street, to the skating rink, and did our skating, me and my sister. I cooked for her and, to be quite honest, I didn't expect to see my mother again. I really *did* think she'd committed suicide. It was up to me now to try and hold it all together and at first I was thinking I've got to take me and my sister and go with her somewhere, well away from this Town because me mum's committed suicide.

There was plenty of food in the cupboard and I was expecting to be able to survive in some way on our own but after about a week, the neighbours got involved. And eventually Social Services stepped in, which really did my head in because I knew as soon as *they* got involved, it would go from bad to worse. And it did.

My sister and I have never fitted in. We've always been seen as *different*, as weird and strange, so there was this sort of need in my mind to keep us together. It was *essential* to keep us together. To part us would have been so destructive, it would have been the last straw. But the Social Services were adamant. It seemed as if every time I suggested: 'No, don't do that - you *know* what that's going to do,' they became more determined to do it. So you had like this *kid* trying to explain to this *idiot* Social Worker: '*That* is not the rational answer. That is *not* the logical answer. If you do *that*, it's going to get worse. Can't you *see* what I'm trying to say to you!' Arguing the point to him and, of course, he's saying 'Shut up. You're only a kid. What are you talking about?' And I'm sort of thinking: 'This man is a complete *idiot!* I'm talking to a *marsupial.* Does he understand what the hell's going on? Does he have any notion of the emotional effect this is having? Obviously not.' He was so lacking in brain-power, I thought perhaps someone had picked up a chair and whacked him around the head with it. That's how strongly I felt. It was *bad* news.

And all the time, we were expecting our father to return and, eventually, he had to. He was in Egypt at the time, came over, saw us briefly and disappeared again. After that, they dropped the Children's Home idea and we went to stay with my aunty and uncle.

My mother's sister Cynthia is off her head. She had a bad experience herself with her first husband. She was *really* in love with him, had Alan, my older cousin, by him and then he just upped and went. No explanation: gone. History. Decided he didn't want the responsibility. And she was devastated. She really, *really* was in love with him. Deeply. Then she met my uncle Harry and they've been together ever since: made for each other. A perfect match, to the end of time!

At first, it was a lot better with them but there was still a lot of bitterness between the family and a lot of conflict. Aunty Iris and Aunty Karen trying to be the matriarchs and other people doing this and that and effectively not taking responsibility for *anything*, let alone their own decisions and those of others. And the repercussive effects this had were obviously quite massive. From having an uncomplicated sort of environment, they were suddenly faced with me and my sister and my brother, whenever he came over from the

Special School. My uncle Harry couldn't cope with the emotional discharge and started having a bit of a breakdown himself. And I was virtually cracking up in my own sweet way as well but not showing it because I was still trying to hold them together and be strong and everything.

About a year we stayed there, then it all got too much. Cynthia tried to be the rock and exercise the rule of law but, unfortunately, with all the best intentions, that wasn't going to work. I was coming up to fourteen and hanging around in the streets. There were terrible arguments: my uncle pinning me up against the wall and threatening blue murder. So me and my sister ended up back in the Home and from then on we were alone.

I was swapping schools a lot at this time and it was beginning to affect my education. I always did well with Art, poetry and English Language: those were very much my favourite subjects. I had various Art teachers but the one I remember the most was Mr. Chinaski - Mr. Jan Chinaski. He was a Czech bloke and *well* off his head. But really *passionate* about Art, you know? He'd kick you up the arse if you didn't paint and paint. He really wanted to get the *best* out of you. There was him and another guy - I forget his name - but I got on all right with him, too. But even Mr. Chinaski thought I was strange. One day he told us to 'paint *anything*: any subject, within reason.' So I did this sort of mad landscape entitled 'A Day in the Life of a Flea.' And what I did was I humanized the flea, deformed it and put signposts everywhere saying: 'GO HERE. GO THERE. GO **EVERYWHERE!**' and Mr Chinaski was taken aback by this and suggested that if I continued in such a vein, I wouldn't be allowed to take Art.

Then, after about a year, my father and his new wife suddenly reappeared out of nowhere and said 'Oh, *we'll* take them back.' He'd stopped working abroad and hitched up with this Jennifer, the daughter of our former next-door neighbour. And strangely enough, it was a bit like a wife-swapping job, because we found out later that our mother had run off with *her* husband. Anyway, that didn't work from the start. First of all she drove out my sister. She went back with my mother, cause my mother had reappeared at this time. The police had finally traced her: she'd been in France and then Cornwall and finally ended up living in Kilmarnock, of all places.

My father's my father and everything but I've got little respect for him quite frankly because he's weak but in other ways I can empathize - being that way inclined myself.

He's covered up the past and lied and distanced himself, not just from his failings but from the whole situation and I feel like I'm the only one - and perhaps my sister - who's analysed it, understood it and dealt with it.

Eventually, I left home as well and alternated between there and my mother's place in Kilmarnock. I got on with her new husband at first, talked to him, tried to understand what had happened but, in many respects, he was completely oblivious to the whole situation. I tried to talk to my mother about why she'd left and she tried to answer me but obviously, through a mixture of emotions: overwhelming guilt, vitriolic poison against my father and a need to defend her own position, she couldn't.

Effectively, since sixteen or seventeen, apart from occasionally flitting back and forth, I've been away from home. I had a brief stint in the military when I first went back with my mother but I don't want to talk about it. That was an attempt to please my father and try and get the fuck out of the situation. It was a very ridiculous and stupid attempt that all went horribly wrong. I went in the Welch Guards. Purbright in Surrey. It's all so *surreal* looking back on it: a load of lunatics running about in red jackets and these madmen: Guards officers, Eton boys, Drill-Sergeant Majors - huge men with twizzled moustaches and enormous chops - seriously, for real, just like the cliche of it, coming at you. Fucking ell! *So* surreal, so bizarre! It was just too much. I think they must have been slipping something in the tea actually, because looking back on that period, there's this blur of drug-induced mania. And my bastard of an old man wouldn't write me a note to get me out and they kept saying 'Oh, he's got *potential. Great* potential!' Eventually I *did* manage to buy myself out but, looking back on it, I see it as a quite extraordinary artistic experience.

For short periods after that I had all sorts of shitty jobs and a mixture of 'own' places and homelessness and sleeping round and about: parties, taking drugs, just crashing out. Experimenting with drugs rather than just taking them: a kind of philosophical experiment. All kinds of drugs, but particularly hallucinogenics, powerful amphetamines. At one point I remember working at this place - a bakery - and I was *off my face!* And it was like 'The King and I' - remember that? - where they're doing the Siamese dance. They *weren't* dancing, they were stacking bread on shelves, like, but it looked as though they were: '*We are Sia-me-ese, if you ple-ase, we are Sia-me-ese, if you don't please - '* You always manage to keep a straight face, to keep from cracking up but it's a bit hard trying to hold down a job when all sorts of things like that are going off.

I've got up to some other things as well: burglary and stuff like that. You're *bound* to! It's *bound* to happen. I can't really say *what*, exactly. All sorts of places but commercial properties mostly, never homes. It's all history that, all very much part of the experiment and development. It's got its own creativity, I suppose. I never did time and I never got caught. The closest shave was when the three of us did this place. We'd done the alarum bells, stashed the tools and were turning this corner, when we seen lights and this red van and I thought it was a Post Office van but it was a *dog van* coming towards us. And there we were, suddenly running like *fuck*. I got away but my brother leapt over this barrier and collapsed in a heap and they got him with his arse sticking out of this hedge. I got in through roofs mostly and developed this sort of 'through the roof' attitude. Everything had to be 'through the roof.' I'd even gain entry by chipping away at a brick wall and poking the bricks through. Living poetry, it was! It doesn't *excuse* it and I'm not suggesting that this is correct behaviour. Neither am I suggesting it's the ideal way to comprehend philosophy or, on the other hand, a situation of abuse or of homelessness. But I got out of that. That's *history* and I certainly wouldn't touch anything like that again.

I don't *like* the idea of having a 'steady job'. Not because I have anything against people workin or against the idea of being responsible but I have an outlook which prevents me from kow-towing or being able to deal with a job situation. People might say there's a cynical chip on my shoulder but there's not. On the contrary. Being of a creative 'bent' - that sounds dodgy, doesn't it? - I just haven't had the inclination to do many jobs.

I was married briefly. Sort of. It's difficult to describe: I met this girl and I thought *this* is the right person - a kindred spirit. She'd just dropped out of University and seemed to be creative and have the same sort of attitudes as me. I started taking her out for some bizarre reason and got deeply involved with her. She stopped me doing the crime stuff but I should have seen from the start that we just weren't in key.

She was from a well-off family and we lived in her parents house up in the Midlands. I wasn't working then but I'd got seriously into studying philosophy: Nietzsche, Kierkegaard, Hegel, modern analytical philosophers. It was a relatively stable period and I had a son by her but my continual experimenting with drugs didn't help our relationship. I was trying to take as much as I could without keeling over - hallucinogenics, a lot of ecstasy, a bit of coke - to see what happened. She took some at first but we both stopped, for the sake of the baby.

Jamie was born in Wales. I'd been applying to places to do philosophy and just generally wanted a change of environment, so we moved to a place near Lampeter. There were places in Wales *sort of* on offer but eventually I didn't get in anywhere.

Things started to go really wrong round about this time. I have to admit I got involved with a girl and, me being me, I went and told my wife and she wasn't very happy about it. It was all very wrong and I'm not trying to excuse myself in any way but really speaking, we'd always been living a lie, so eventually I just thought 'Sod it!' and left. And that's when I came to the Cyrenians.

She's got custody of the child. I don't know whether she's still living with her mother and I don't care. He's five or six now. I've got access but it's a long way to travel. I've buried her under the past. Never would you have thought that two people, who were supposed to have *loved* each other so much, could *hate* each other so much...

'As distant as drums
and Nova Scotia...'

Robert

'Long, wiry brown hair and grey-blue eyes in a pale, weary-looking face. He stammers over some of his words as though he can't get them out quick enough, often ignoring or speaking over my questions.

I'm forty-seven - a young forty-seven - and I come from just outside Sutton Coldfield. I had quite a normal childhood. I went to a Nursery school, then a Junior Infant School, and then a Grammar Technical School: Marsh Hill. The Nursery was at the bottom of Marsh Hill, the Junior Infants was halfway up and the Grammar Technical was at the top, so my school career sort of worked its way uphill.

My parents died some years ago. My mother worked in a butcher's shop and my father was a tram-driver with Birmingham Corporation. My mother was widowed before she married my father so I had three older step-sisters and a step-brother but I was the only child really. They were much older than me and all different and all non-readers: non-readers entirely. It was a normal childhood, like I say: *completely* normal. I didn't start having problems in life until well after leaving school.

I was in the A stream in school but, looking back, it was a bit pointless cause it meant that you did five years work in four, basically. So when me mates went into the Sixth Form, I stayed in the Upper Fifth but I still associated with them out of classes and I was influenced by them because one or two went on to Art College in Birmingham and London. And it was the Sixties, remember, so a lot was going on culturally with the Beatles and that kind of Revolution thing. The Beatles were my - and everybody's - favourite group but I was a particular fan of The Rolling Stones, Chuck Berry and Negro Blues. I never had the money to buy a proper instrument but I taught myself to play the harmonica and improvise and copy players like Paul Jones of Manfred Mann and American Negro players like Sonny Boy Williamson and Sonny Terry: players who are legends among musicians and Blues fans.

We formed our own group at School, cause my mate had a relation who had a pub and we practised in a spare room there on a Saturday. I played Bass for a bit: which was an acoustic guitar with the fifth and sixth strings on. My mate had a pickle fitted to his acoustic and we got a small amplifier, a snare drum and a cymbal from a catalogue. We played at School dances and things but we didn't do it seriously enough to become professional. One thing we *did* do, though, was enter a Rhythm and Blues Competition at the Ice Rink in Birmingham. There were four bands on every Monday for a few weeks and we came fourth out of four in our heat. But we got our picture in the paper and, because of that, I got a girlfriend. I was walking past the local school one day and this girl wanted my autograph, so it was quite good fun and we did a bit, even if it wasn't much.

I was never encouraged to stay on by any of the teachers and I left School after O Level. I went for an interview for a clerical job at Ansell's Brewery at Rocky Lane in Aston - which is where the HP Sauce factory is - and I must have been ahead of my time because I didn't shave that morning and the guy was old-fashioned - like they *were* in 1967 - and said 'We like our people to look *smart*,' which, if you'd ave *known* me - I mean, even me English teacher called me *'immaculate'* - you know? The way I used to dress: with a white shirt and a pointed collar and a Windsor knot with the tie. I was always very fussy when I dressed, you know, like - *particular*. I got O Level English and my arithmetic's fine - my adding-up and that - but I failed Maths twice so I didn't get that job.

Eventually, I got a job with the Post Office. I started off as a clerical assistant, took some Civil Service exams and got promoted to Clerical Officer. I thought I was there indefinitely. I saw it as a career path but, being realistic, I didn't know *then* that you can't know the future. You can grow and develop, learn what there is to learn but you don't know exactly what that is at the time, otherwise there'd be no future, would there?

I'd been living at home but by then - because I had a responsible job - I'd got a flat with friends I'd known all through School. I hadn't fallen out with my parents. Like I keep saying: I had a *normal* childhood and they were both good people - knowingly good - and they loved *me* and I loved *them* and there was only understanding at home between us and there was never any falling out, so for you to *look* for things that aren't there is a bit *small*. We were *all* all right with our parents and families and we got a flat in the normal way, through the newspaper. We were doin our jobs and had a decent social life with girl friends and so on and I was always capable and like, *ebullient*, and never the worrying kind or afraid of things like exams - either you know it or you don't - and it was all systems go.

But then the whole lot changed when I was nearly twenty when, for reasons of their own, I was *fooled* - although there was *nothing* wrong - into going into a psychiatric hospital. And it was a total injustice which, to be honest is a whole book in itself. It's not easy to say how it all came about but it's still quite meaningful to me: like it must have been to Jesus Christ, you know, when he was crucified. It's a bit of a gob-smacker to have your life ruined all at once over what seems like a minor injustice. But it changes your whole life-pattern. I know it was an injustice but I'm *biblical*. I know a lot more *now* than I did *then*. I was taught all about Art and Art Schools and Art History. I can *interpret* paintings as well as see them and I know a lot about psychology. I like Eastern philosophies: Yoga and meditation. I've read a bit of Freud and a bit of Jung, as well as my own things. And I'm a Buddhist as well, so I know that the All Saints thing was an injustice. *What* injustice? Well, I'm being as specific as I can but I can't be *absolutely* specific, can I? I can be specific about what happened, cause I've got a good memory but it might take the length of a book, if you get my point, to go through it all cause, you know, you can't be facile about something so bad and so significant. It was all based on ignorance and prejudice and the world still doesn't know about it yet, but it *will*. Because I haven't forgotten *any* of it.

I've learned a lot about psychiatric hospitals and psychiatrists. I've got lots of friends who are patients and ex-patients and I'm also well-read in the New Testament and the Book of Revelations. I'm a believer in the Judgement Day and that it's not far off. A lot of mature people *think* they're informed about it but they haven't read the significant pieces in the New Testament. One day all the bad will be wiped out by God and all the good people who are deserving - who have been kept in poverty and suffering - will be free to live freely on God's good green earth rather than in a Franz Kafka penal colony.

I can tell you how I became homeless fairly easy. Well obviously, to begin with, from the All Saints thing. Because, to keep people calm and normal, you have to have all their medication - all their Largactils, Stelazines and Depixols - which shut down the higher functions of the brain. Which is obviously evil.

I was living in Birmingham when I got married in 1985 but five years later my wife divorced me and I moved into a council flat in Wolverhampton and I was on my own for the first time properly - you know, *existentially* - in my life. I was refused a place in Warwick University round about then, even though I've actually got academic books in me - one of which comes under Philosophy - which I haven't started yet. It's still in my head. And that was the first time in my life - about the age of forty-one or forty-two - that I started getting in trouble with the police. It's just such a lot to go into but I didn't have a job and I'd started bein a writer and if I wanted to walk at night because I wanted to *think* like, the police used to stop you and ask if you were carryin anythin and, of course, you're not carryin anythin and you're not bein suspicious or doin anything dishonest like, but they look in your pockets and then they get their radios out and have to send your name in to check you out. Well, that's when I started gettin into trouble because, of course, that's extremely Fascist and I've got loads of stories about that - goin all the way back to my psychiatric injustices but, to answer your question about how I became homeless: I got arrested for something. The sentence I got was over twelve months and while I was in prison, they wrote to say I had to give up the Council flat because of a rule that says if you're in prison over twelve months, you have to relinquish the tenancy of your flat. So, of course, because you're in trouble, they make it worse - in this modern society, that won the Second World War against Fascism and evil and is nearing the end of the Twentieth Century, with all the knowledge and understanding you'd think they'd built up in the world - they make it *worse* for you. Even if there isn't an *actual* Council waiting list, you have to give up your flat or your house cause the prison sentence is *over* twelve months, so when you come out, you've got no home.

And, on top of that, the Council got all my possessions, including my furniture - although a lot of it was secondhand or what people had put outside for *anyone* to have, it was all *legal* and it was all *mine* - and I hadn't got one thing back, including small things like a watch and my writing. They were all what they call *confiscated* - a word I learnt in school, which is really a euphemism for *stealing*, if you don't get it back. But I remember. I've got a perfectly good memory because, like I say, I studied Yoga.

All this has happened since my parents died, which is where I'm biblical as well. One of the Ten Commandments is Honour Thy Father and Mother, which I've always done in my heart and mind, because there's no reason *not* to, obviously. I loved *them* and they loved *me* and, like I say, they knew the difference between right and wrong. They had a sense of proportion about things and they weren't stupid. And neither am I, you see, which is why I get into trouble, cause it's nearly Judgement Day and cause all these people I'm telling you about, do these things to you out of sheer *malice*. They certainly aren't spiritual or cultural or artistic: they're *irreligious*. They're *atheist*. And you have to be among them to find out these things first-hand rather than on hearsay. And it's fairly obvious that the police and the judges are non-artistic types and if there's good and evil in the world - as there certainly is - then they are *evil* people. And the proof is out there: in the one hundred and forty five prisons - not to mention the new Wings and the Bail Hostels, not to mention the psychiatric system and so on.

There was a few years gap between my leaving Stafford Prison and coming to Swansea. It would take two books to tell it all. But I was definitely having no more medications to kind of please everybody and I'd started getting full use of my brain back: having been a normal and intelligent person when I started my learnings.

I've been in hostels in Birmingham, Bristol, Glastonbury and London. And I've made friends with a lot of people on the same level as me, who are poor and have similar stories. Hostels are okay until you start locking horns with any of the staff because a lot of the staff in these places are quite ignorant, you know. And the moment you're resident, they automatically become in charge of you, as though it was a Bail Hostel. It's a strange thing, really, if you've got the imagination to kind of sit back and see it. Because, although you're a mature adult and you're legal and the only reason you're here is because you're homeless, the staff can easily start ordering you about as if they had a *right* to. Or as if they were your parents, like. You know, because I'm someone who's not illegal in any way. I don't even smoke cannabis for the sensible reasons that (a) it's illegal and (b) it's expensive anyway (even if I didn't *mind* it being illegal, because obviously I believe, ethically, that it *should* be legal because it's a herb plant same as tobacco and mushrooms) But what I'm saying is: I'm not criminal. I'm honest. I know my own mind and I'm a problem-solver type. Which is why I identify with Jesus a lot.

I've been writing seriously, properly, since the flat I was stayin at in Wolverhampton and, like I say: I'm a bit of a writer now, even if I *am* unrecognized. I had some good ideas then about some quite incredible experiences which I won't mention now but I remember writing a piece about vegetarianism and carnivorism: kind of rationalizing about animals, which I was quite pleased with and proud of. I get inspired when I see cultural people who are still around, referring to truth and beauty in a readable way that I can understand. Someone like Melvyn Bragg for instance: I got hold of a book of his from the library called Kingdom Come and I only read about half a chapter of it, but I know where he's at. To sum it up: I'd say he's *Sixties*, cause I truly believe that the Sixties was very biblical - like Jonie Mitchell's song Woodstock was biblical.

My poems are about different subjects. I can do short stuff, humorous stuff and serious stuff. Here's one called 'Ode to Alfred Bester'. He was a Sci-fi writer. It's quite deep and it's about me and how I kind of relate to Literature. It's two and a half sides long but I'll just read the end bit:

> *When all my beasts struck*
> *They got their hooks in*
> *And have never looked back -*
> *Like God and Jesus, Dreyfus and Cain,*
> *Robin Hood, the James Gang, Jack Hughes*
> *And that Russian whats-is-name.*
> *I'm only living and waiting to see*
> *Wailing and gnashing Death and just he.*
> *And perhaps the promise of life*
> *Will be possible to live, because now, fine friends*
> *It's really only purgatory.*
> *So when purgatory happens*
> *And recent history is known*
> *I may ask you what they asked of people*
> *On the death of Kennedy:*
> *Where were you? What were you doing from 1969 to 1983?*
> La-dee-da *dah*, la-dee-da *dee*.

Those la-dee-dahs aren't actually in it. I finished it on another sheet but I haven't got it with me right now. So it ends like that. But I've got a short one here, which is lighter. It's called Poem:

Here's a poem. It's about me.
But listen, you'll soon see
One day I'll be me
Like I am now. Although I'm not in fashion
One day, to some, I'm sure I'll be it,
And they'll be round to see me
Like flies around shit.
I'll be 'The Thing', not like that film
Like Clara Bow, I'll really be 'it'.
I'll really be now.
I'll really be happening: it'll be like a row.
I'll be in fashion: the flavour of the month. But until then,
I'm as distant as drums and Nova Scotia are now.

Yes, I really *did* write that. Well, it's in *my* handwriting so I *must* have written it.

My plans are to find somewhere more permanent but whether it will be through the Cyrenians or not I don't know. I may get a bus and go back to a drop-in I was at in Merthyr to see if there's still a possibility there. Or the third realistic alternative is getting a tent - cause the summer will be coming up in a month or two - and just going to a valley or a beach somewhere and wait until the Judgment Day and then I can come back and lead a normal life amongst my own kind.

'Telephone Jock and Memory Man...'

Alec and Frank

A quarter past twelve and the Hostel dining room is just starting to fill up. Frank is paying one of his periodic visits to the soup kitchen. In his mid-fifties, he is slim and fit-looking with close-cropped fair hair and a much-lined face. I sit between him and Alec in the third of three recently donated arm-chairs and take out my newly-acquired cassette recorder, which I'm not yet sure how to operate. Frank begins reminiscing about his time on the road and Alec soon joins in. They never met in years of travel but their roads frequently crossed. They were in the same Spikes and met the same people but at different times. It's fascinating stuff. In the middle of the conversation, I surreptitiously press Play and Record...

Frank:...I've probably met you before, Alec. I spent a lot of time in Glasgow.

Alec: I was away from Glasgow back in 1985.

Frank: Ah, but I probably bumped into you somewhere.

Alec: The last time I was up there was in The Great Northern.

Frank: Aye, I remember that. That was a helluva place. It was run by three brothers and they were all Mafia. The rooms were more like coal cupboards than rooms and there were no tops on them. You couldn't take your clothes off in there without them getting nicked. You know in most houses you only see flies in the summer? In *that* place there were flies in the *Winter* as well! It was a stinking, God-awful place. They used to get grants for this and that and all they were doin was makin money out of other people's misery

Alec: That's right. 150 Finlay Street. Some of the staff were cashing giros for people that didn't exist. They'd died or moved on -

Frank: I used to live in Partick. I used to go over to Govan to sign. Member the little ferries that used to go across? Or you could go under the tunnel but I always used to go over on the ferry. If you was in a hostel, you used to have to go to Cameron Street.

Alec: There was a guy working in Cameron Street there. A pure bastard he was: Memory Man, they called him -

Frank: Oh, *Memory Man*! I remember him. He could remember *anyone*. You could go there - he probably only seen you once before - and he knew your name and your number. He'd know your name *ten* years after!

Alec: I went there a year after he first seen me and he opens the door: 'Now then,' he says, 'I know *you*. Where you been *this* time?' A right old bastard. If he knew you were kicked out before or if he knew you were drinkin on the premises, *he* was the man who done the business: 'Right - **Out!**' and out the door you went and you got nothing. You had to come back the next day.

Frank: He'd go *fifteen* years, he'd still know you. Oh, aye: Memory Man! But what about that guy in Hanbury then?

Alec: Oh - *Telephone Jock!* He was the worst one. Every time you went in there, he was on the phone. He used to ring around to check you up. Tell him when you had the last payment and he'd check that day there and find out if you were tellin the truth. And if you were tellin a lie, he wouldn let you in. If you got your last payment in Leeds, he'd phone there and he'd come back and tell you: 'Right: you're *clear!*' He'd want to know where you'd been livin before and where you were getting your money and if you've been doin a hobble. If you were missin for three months he'd want to know how you lived for that three months, to get through the country. I never drew twice. I didne bother. Half the time I always got a bit of a hobble, like. Spud-pickin or hop-pickin down in Kent or some damn thing. Oh he was *deadly!* But that was his job. If he thought you were gettin two draws under two different names, he'd phone *America* - to check it out!

Frank: That's right. He'd phone *Alaska!*

Alec: You'd go in there and straightaway they'd get all the gear off you, search your hair for nits and put that there powder on you in case you were loused up. Then they'd give you a bath and put them long jammas on yer. I thought I were home again, you know? Or in prison.

Frank: One blanket and a bare rubber mattress -

Alec: Up at five in the mornin, bit of breakfast and you had to dig the garden for a couple of hours. They still do the same carry-on.

Frank: I'd never been to Hanbury in my life. I walked from there to Oxford and, as you know, it's a good way. And I had a big pack on my back in them days and I met this Scotch guy and we had a few pints. He goes in Reception, no problem, sees this other

Scotch guy: 'Yes, Mr Mackay,' or whatever his name was. Straight through. I goes next. This fuckin Jock comes up: 'Listen,' he says. 'You been drinkin today.' I says 'No, I haven't.' He says 'Listen: I'm *tellin* you: you've been drinkin today.' He could smell it on my breath and I didn't realize. Just two pints, like. He said 'Where did you get the money?' 'Oh,' I said, 'I begged it. Somebody bought me a drink.' He said 'When did you last have a draw?' 'Well,' I said, 'I haven't had a draw for six months' - which I hadn't. I'd been workin on the Shows, on the Fairgrounds. So I said 'I haven't had nothing for six months.' He said 'I'm *telling* you, you had money last week!' Fuckin hell - !

Alec: Oh gee! A pure bastard, this man. You oughta seen them cunts in them days!

Frank: I said 'I haven't had a draw for six months.' 'No,' he said, 'I didn't say you had a *draw* last week, I'm sayin you had *money* last week.' This is the way the cunt was. A right tough nut. So he said to me 'Listen,' he said, 'go and sit down there and when you decide you want to tell me - when you had a draw last - then I might decide to let you in.'

Alec: The cunt!

Frank: So I knew I was clear cause I hadn't drawn for six months cause I was working. So I said 'Well, you know, to be messed about like this - I may as well go back on the road.' He said 'Well, you know where it is, don't you?

Alec: Oh, a pure bastard!

Frank: Oh, he *was* a bastard! He'd make somethin out of nothin. It was nothing to him but he just had to know the ins and outs of you, didn't he, Alec? He just wanted you to know that *he* was in charge. But, if you got through him the first time you went up there, the second time he just passed you through. He'd never seen me before. I never got in and I've never been back but that Scotch guy went flyin in, cause he'd seen him before. They must have like a two-way mirror on the stairs, so they can see *you* before *you* see them.

Alec: The crack there is to get through them *first* time. Once you're *in*, you get a bath and a lie down that night and the next day the porter comes to you and says 'Right, Telephone Jock wants to interview you!' The next day does the damage. The next day he opens all them forms and he's writing on them: 'Name? Number?' Oh, you never seen a sight like it!

Frank: All over fuck all!

Alec: Think you were from out the fuckin country, you know?

Frank: But where I was unlucky was, the first day in - the first interview - *he* happened to be there. Had it of been another day, he may not have been there, Alec.

Alec: He was *always* there. That was his game. He was the Head Kidney there, was Telephone Jock. He knew what we were all up to. He missed nothing. He looked at the palms of your hand there: *'Working hands!'* I said 'I'm *not* workin.' 'How are they hard there?' You know: the wee blisters there - when you're shovellin and your skin goes hard? That's how he found you out. But he had to *prove* it first, so he'd watch your moves there and he'd have the porters lookin at you an all. See what you're doin that day there. If you're hangin about the town. Somebody takin a car or somethin, you know? Right away, you go back in the night time: 'You were in a car there. Where were you goin in that car?' Right away there, he'd think someone's giving you a casual.

Frank: Never missed a thing.

Alec: Oh no. That was his *business*. That's what he was paid for and no way was he goin to get sacked there. If he knew you were workin, he'd take fifteen pounds a week off you. I know myself. This guy was workin there but he slipped up. Telephone Jock seen him. 'Before you start performin there,' he says 'what money you got? And why you just come out of that wagon?' Next thing: fifteen pound a day for bed and breakfast. I came out of Reach there once and he says to me 'Are you still at this carry-on now? Where d'you live?' I says 'No fixed abode. I can't get money out of the Social and you people are fuckin me around here.' He says 'You know you're gettin nothin out of me. All I'm goin to give you is fuckin **stick**!' 'You keep givin me stick, pal,' I says, 'I'll stand with it. You've got the fuckin hook in me. But you can do anything you want to me: jail me, *any* fuckin thing - I'll not care!' Oh, a terrible carry-on!

Frank: The cunt was no good to Society!

Alec: I was on the gas line in Hanbury there. Doin a big job for Southern Gas and the Social would send guys out lookin for you, you know? To spy on you. But I had a pair of dark glasses on and a hat and they didn't know who I was. Next thing, they're takin photographs and a few of the guys were fired there. Next thing, they showed me a photograph of the gas line in Hanbury. There was ten men in it and there I was with the dark glasses on and the hat. I nearly collapsed. I says to myself 'Oh, I'm goin to get nicked here - nippy-nippy!' Telephone Jock says 'D'you know them people there?' I says 'No, I don't know them guys.' *'I* know them,' he says. 'Well, you're a *good* man,' I says. 'No wonder they call you Telephone Jock.' He says 'They're only in the same hostel as you, aren't they?' I says 'I don't know. I'm never here. I'm always away drinkin.' He says 'Who're you gettin your money frae, when you're drinkin all the time?' I says 'I'm away kerry-beggin. *Ham and eggin* - ' That's what they call it up there in Scotland. He *knew* I was at it but he couldn't prove it.

Frank: Friends of mine got jailed through him in Hanbury. Two years and five years, for fraud. For doublin up on the Social. There was a guy gettin *three* draws a week! He found them all out. That's what he was there for. That's why he used to phone right away: 'When d'you get a last payment?'

Alec: He'd phone the end of the *world,* to see if you got a payment there! That's how bad he was. Oh he was *deadly!*

Frank: It's all finished now, though. You can't do it any more. Once computers came out, the Telephone Jocks of this world were obsolete. All they got to do now is press two buttons and they can tell exactly where you've been and where you've drawn. They're goin to tax you for *everythin* now. Even for potato-pickin.

Alec: Telephone Jock's retired now. They sent him up to Edinburgh to finish him off. I *seen* him up there. I came out of Newcastle and went up to Edinburgh there years and years later. I got the biggest shock of my life. I thought I was back in Hanbury. Soon as I walked in and put my B1 in, I heard the voice. I nearly went through the fuckin wall! I says 'It's **Telephone Jock**! He's supposed to be in Hanbury!' I said 'What answer am I goin to give this guy now?' Next thing: Cubicle One. Interview. He knew my face straight away. Soon as he seen my name there. My date of birth. 'Keep out the door there!' he says, until my name went through the computer. 'Now then, Alec,' he says. 'You still runnin about the country doin no good to Society? What're you doin up in Edinburgh? There's no work here.' I says 'There's no work *anywhere.*' He says 'But you obviously can get work here - but we can't catch you out.' I says 'You must be *jokin!* I'm at leisure now. I *can't* work.' He says 'You're the man that's runnin about here, there and everywhere: Tom, Dick and Harry. Like the rest of the play actors.' He says 'You're always a move ahead of us.' I said 'No way,' but I had a job and he couldn't prove it. Next thing, I says 'What's goin to happen now, then?' 'Well,' he says, 'I'll tell you what I'll do with you: I'm retirin soon and I'm happy to finish wi it all, you know? My duty's done so I'm goin to give you a good hand-out.' And he give me *eighty-odd* pound on the counter there. I couldn't believe my eyes! 'Now you make sure you go down to the Glass Market in Edinburgh there,' he says, 'and book yourself a bed for the night. Greyfriars Hostel.' *Eighty pound!* And all cause he was retirin. If it wasn't for that, I'd have got *nothing*...

'Catching the summer somewhere else...'

Little Ritchie

Basically, my childhood was shit. I been an alcie since I was eleven. The only breaks I had was when I was in the Farm School and when I've been in the nick. My mother spent all her time in the pubs. She'd come home tea time and go back out again in the night. We were lucky to be fed. My old man didn't have a drink problem. He liked a sip of wine and that was about it. I remember him tryin to stop her goin out once and her sayin 'That's all right: I'll climb out the window...!'

*I last saw him at night in the Car Park in High Street a few days after the death of his friend Rob, who'd overdosed in a tent outside County Hall. Long-haired, dishevelled and distraught, Ritchie looked like some mad prophet then. He was drunk and crying and had wet himself. 'If He ad to take someone, why didn't He take **me**?' he kept bawling. Now, two weeks later and readmitted to the Hostel after a lengthy ban, he is clean-shaven and sober, although with a bad case of the shakes. We eat breakfast together and I watch him trying to put sugar in his coffee: only half of what he scoops up, actually reaching the cup. We go into the front office. He wears a little woollen hat which, perched on top of his pale, round face, makes him look gnome-like. He speaks in a hoarse, slightly breathless voice, punctuated with frequent sniffing...*

My father came to this country from Hungary just after the War and couldn't speak a word of English when he got here. He never told me anything about his experiences in Hungary and I never got round to asking. I got on all right with him but, after their divorce, he married again and, basically, he had more time for his other missus's kids than he did for us. He was working in the Mond up until the time he had to stop cause of his heart. I was seventeen when he died. This doctor in Clydach had been giving him pain killers whereas what he really needed was about eight heart operations but it was too late by then. So he was better off going, to be honest.

I went to Sunnybank School first, but I was never there. They counted up my half days over a year once and it came to ten days altogether. It wasn't because I didn't *want* to go to School, it was because in them days I was so shy, I just couldn't handle it. Sunnybank wasn't so bad because there was only two hundred people there but when I went to Pontardawe, there were over seven hundred from all parts of the valleys. I'd walk around lookin at the floor, you know. I'd catch a bus in the mornin - the free Bus - and use my dinner money to catch a bus back home. I'd just ang about in the day, then. They put me in Neath Farm School for three years cause I was uncontrollable for my mother. Which was understandable after what she was doin.

Cause she's remarried and looks respectable now, she tends to think that *nothing* ever appened. I mean, all I've ever wanted is for her to *genuinely* apologise, but she hasn't. She's using her head at last, but it's all right to do it *now*, she should have done it *then*.

I started becoming a junkie at seventeen. This girl introduced me to speed. Up till then, I'd been takin stupid things like Marzine travellin tablets, cause you hallucinate on them but if I'd have carried on with them, I'd ave cracked up.

After I'd left Neath Farm School, I started sleeping rough. My mother had buggered off and left me with a three-bed-roomed house, which I got kicked out of because the Council wanted it back. The Council gave me a flat then but I got kicked out of that, too. Too many of the boys were coming back and tripping and smoking or what-have-you. So, first off, I started sleeping rough in Clydach, cause there's millions of places to sleep and loads of woods up there. No sleeping bag. Nothing. Then, it was like: a week here and a week there, in between staying in some girl-or-other's house. That went on for fifteen years but then I got in the Hostel in Stembridge. I met Dan Piper there. He used to go out for his bottle of sherry and I'd go out for my bottle of cider and we'd sit somewhere out of the way, sort of thing, and have a drink. We used to drink a lot together but once I got kicked out of Stembridge, I'd only see him here and there. I don't really know what happened exactly in Stembridge. All I know is I put a knife to one of the staff's throat. I wasn't on anything at the time. I was just pissed. I don't get nasty like that any more when I'm pissed. And I wouldn't have used it, no, but I won't carry one now because I've been kicked out of two Hostels and I'm scared I *will* use it.

I've been in prison four times. The first time was for burglary, which I deserved to go down for. The second time was for a smash and grab on an Off-Licence window. There were more than one of us but I took the blame for it all. I could have fought it, cause it was literally impossible for me to have carried all the liquor on my own. The third time was only remand for about four and a half weeks and the fourth time was nothing to do with me. I was sleepin in a doorway and this guy walked into this woman's house and grabbed her handbag. She came out and *he* was pulling it and *she* was pulling it. But he yanked it off her and she fell back and scraped her arm and they done *me* as a look-out and I was *sleepin* in the doorway! How could I be a look-out if I was sleepin in the doorway? I was drunk and I wakes up, cause I could hear the scuffle and he only runs up the road with a black bag, doesn't he, and drops it at my feet and all these neighbours come out and shout 'Don't move!' And I said 'I'm not *movin*. I aven't *done* nothin'. I had five and a half months on remand for that. He stayed in Swansea, I went to Orfield and I tell you: I *shit* myself up there, cause - I'm not a racist - but I saw big black people: big dealers from Bristol and all that. I was glad to get back. And the thing is, the guy who done it to the old woman got off the same day as me. He should have had at least two and a half years for it.

I was quite a few years off and on in High Street Car Park but, as I say, just before I came in here, apart from when I started kipping outside Iceland's, it was eight months solid in the Car Park. It's a dangerous place. I got my head kicked in in there. I went to sleep one night with a sleepin bag and when I woke up I had a blanket over me. So I went across to this guy and him and this girl were sleepin in my sleepin bag. So all I done, I went up and I poked them and said 'Can I have my sleepin bag back?' and when they didn't answer I thought 'Oh well, leave it till the morning.' So I went back and lay down but next thing he comes over and while I'm still layin down, he kicks me in the head about eight times with his steelies on. I had to go to hospital twice over it. It *is* a dangerous car park. It's too open, like.

I can't remember when I first met Rob. He'd been down here for quite a while - maybe longer than eight months ago. I probably met him through other people - I don't know where - and then we just started hanging around together, like. Sleepin in the Car Park together or sleepin here or there together - wherever. We were both needlin: amphetamine. Like I say, I hadn't done it for sixteen years, so I was a fool to go back to it. But I stopped as sudden as that, cause I was stood in the High Street this particular mornin and I think it was Bob, with the dreadlocks, come along and said 'D'you realize Rob's dead?' So I said 'No, you're kiddin me,' and he said 'No, he's dead. He overdosed.' I cried four times that day. I don't know ow it happened exactly. He'd only just bought a tent - that day, or the day before - and pitched it on the grass down by the County Hall. Forty pound he paid for it with money he'd made from selling the Big Issue and begging. Adn't even had a chance to use it properly. He'd bought another dog the day before, too - a greyhound - and then this guy sold him the stuff. Rob wasn a big drinker, so either the ampule had been opened and something added to it or Rob done the lot in one go. He should have done half and then done the other half an hour or two later.

I went to the funeral. It was in Monmouth. The Big Issue took two vans up and it meant a lot to me that I was invited, because I said to Paul Burrows 'What if there's no room?' And he said 'They've talked to me on the phone and they are expectin you to turn up.' So I was *definitely* there. Went for a drink first, obviously - but kept myself sober. Sad. It really was, like. There had to be fifteen to twenty of us - mostly Big Issue sellers - but nobody knew which church it was at, so we had to ask directions. And when we got there, there was just the hole and the coffin in it. Nobody else there - none of his family - nobody except for this guy who said he'd be back before long to fill it in. So we all just started doin it ourselves, takin turns to chuck a couple of shovelfuls in, which sort of confirmed it for me, like sayin: 'Yeah, now I can believe he's *actually* gone,' sort of thing. We didn't even see the coffin being brought there and nobody said anything over the grave. I would ave liked to ave but, on the other hand, I suppose everybody would ave liked to ave. But nobody said anything. It was just, basically, fill in the grave and we chucked some wreaths in and buried them in with it and then put some on top as well. Then, everybody went for a drink after, in memory of him. So, like I say, going up there meant a lot to me, but I'm never goin to get over it, cause he was too young, mun. He was just a kid.

Monmouth! That's what I can't understand. Maybe that's why there wasn't any family there. He only had step-parents. I never discussed any family with Rob. It's not the type of thing we discussed. We just tried to have a laugh and get through life, you know? I don't know, I *really* don't know why he was on the streets so young. I don't think he was interested in finding a Hostel or anything like that. He was just happy to be out there and stickin a needle in his arm.

When Rob died, a guy gave me a knife and then, afterwards, he said 'Look, I want the knife back.' Cause he knew I was goin to stab the guy who give him the stuff that killed him. So he give me a watch and a lighter instead. I *would* have used the knife - I *know* I would ave. But the guy - Tex. Got green hair. D'you know him? - got beat up in Burgher King later, by Rocco. Cause Rocco shouted out in the middle of the shop 'You're a *murderer!*' And all the people in the shop were all for it - for him to kick his head in. They all just parted and let him get on with it, like, you know? He might have gone to Cardiff now, cause he's had a few kickings since and I haven't seen him around.

When I think about it, all I vision is Rob laying dead in High Street Car Park, to be honest. That's what I *see* in my head. He must have been well off it. I don't think he would have remembered much. I don't think he would have been in pain when he went, which I'm glad of. I think we were both plannin on shootin off in the Springtime - as it was coming up to Summer. Shoot off to some other Town - up in England or somewhere. Cause I lived in Bournemouth for eighteen months and worked up there for fifteen. And then we'd catch the summer somewhere else. Unfortunately, it didn't appen, did it?

I'd still be out there on the streets, if it wasn't for Rob but after that happened, I just wanted *out*. It was in the afternoon, about two weeks ago now: I'd had too much to drink and I was just goin to put my head down outside Iceland's when Paul Burrows came along and said 'Come with me,' put me in the van and brought me down here. I thought it was goin to be just for the night but they signed me in. Which I'm happy about, cause it's nice to have somewhere for a change.

I'm on Incapacity for life, so I get sixty-eight pound a week, out of which I pay twenty-five pounds rent, which isn't bad, really. I go begging in the subways if there's nobody else in them and I'd do an obble off the books if I could, but it's finding one, isn't it - without the Social knowing? I've definitely taken the right course in coming here. Best thing I've done in the last few years. When I was in Stembridge, it was different. I was around *too* many people that I knew up in Penlan. When I came here I hadn't eaten for three days and all I could do was pick. I just *couldn't* eat. Now I've started getting back into it and I feel a lot better for it. I would say I've cut down on drink a bit, too. In Dinas Fechan, if you came back drunk, they'd tell you to go and take an hour's walk to sober up whereas here, although there are certain limits, you can go out and get drunk and come back as long as you go straight to your room and don't hassle anybody. Which is fair enough because, that way, they're not expectin you to give up your needs. I drink cause it helps

103

me sleep but I try to curb it, because this time I don't want to spoil it. I'm thirty-six now and not gettin any younger. I don't want to be back out there if I can help it.

Non-resident, Paxton Street Hostel soup kitchen, Winter 1996.

Top: *Residents at work in the Hostel dining room.*
Bottom: *Betty Williams, founder of the Swansea Cyrenians, opens the Cyrenians' exhibition in the
Glynn Vivian Art Gallery, 1996.*   *(photo: Kevin Quayle)*

Top: *The author with 'work-in-progress', Glynn Vivian Art Gallery, 1997.*   (Photo: Bernard Mitchell)

Bottom: *Victoria Park Bowls Pavilion, Winter 1997.*

Top: '... X-X-X. Useless. Useless. Useless.

Bottom: '... My character didn't have a name ...'

FEBRUARY

'Tea in The Star Dust...'

Ceri

Yes, use my *real* name - you want the *truth,* mun - and ask me any question you like: I don't care. I've been on the radio *and* in the paper before now. John Griff called me into the office one day: 'Hey, Ceri, you're wanted on the phone! Radio Wales want to record you - about the homeless.' *And* there was a photo of me in the Evening Post on the last Soup Run. They had a final run cause the Crisis fund money had run out and I was *there* in the photo eatin a sandwich.

He's called in, out of the blue, to say hello to another member of staff. I've seen photos of him on the previous year's Soup Run: barefoot, unkempt and glaring at the camera. His behaviour then was manic and unpredictable but in the intervening months he's been having regular monthly injections and the physical and mental changes in him have been dramatic. As he settles into the office arm chair, he's talkative, friendly and full of good humour.

I was one of twins born on Christmas Day nineteen-forty-seven in Birmingham of Welsh parents. My mother was a housewife and my father worked as a secretary in the Lucas factory. He then worked in a furniture shop and in a variety of places all over the country. They came back to Llangennech to live with my father's mam and dad and he worked on the railway in Llanelli for sixteen years with the laying gang. He had a job in the RN there in the village but he suffered a heart attack at the age of fifty-five and died.

It was a happy childhood - oh yeah! - and I *enjoyed* school. I was in Stradey Secondary Modern. My brother and me were in the 'A' class. Mr Reed, Welsh, was our teacher and my best subjects were Welsh, woodwork and metalwork and my weakest subject was Art. Oh, no *shape* at all in Art!

I left school at sixteen and went to the Coal Board as an apprentice wagon repairer for seven years. Then I worked in Thyssen in Bynea but when I went back after the Christmas holiday, the place had burnt down. So I went to the RN in Llangennech, building a new hangar for Douglas. Then I worked for Kelly's as a sheeting ganger, as a welder's mate for Maindee Engineering and then as a grinder but I was made redundant again and I got very depressed about it. I lost good friends, a good job and good money. I was *so* depressed I went very independent and wouldn't mix with anyone. It got so bad I paid to see a Specialist in Sketty. He put me on Naphran and Ativan and I started to feel better. Then I went to see another Specialist and ended up in St. David's in Carmarthen. I was in and out of there for about six months. My Specialist was Dr. Grey, a woman. Very strict. She put us all on two hundred and fifty milligrams of Halidol a week, for depression but it didn't agree with me. Then I went on fifty grams a fortnight Modecate injections but they didn't agree with me either, so I refused to take them in the end. When I came out, I decided not to go back in. I was determined to fight my illness on my own. Hospitals are all right when you're *ill* and we're lucky we got places like that but I don't *like* them.

I haven't been to St. David's since - and that's a good eight years now. I'm off medication and injections and I'm on Invalidity Capacity money, so I'm better off money-wise now than I've been for a while - and healthier.

My brother's single. We're not identical twins: I'm about an inch and a half taller than him but he's stocky. He worked for thirteen years in Bearings in Bynea making components. But he's not a *happy* man. He was always picking and niggling at me for nothing for years and my mother would cry and get upset. He came home from the Club one Saturday night at about twelve o' clock and I was watching a Western and he switched the telly off and said 'Are you payin for the electric?' *That's* the kind of man he was: very spiteful. Even his own mates in the Rugby Club said 'What's the matter with your brother? That's all he does is *moan* mornin, noon and night.' We used to fight now and again and in the end my mother'd had enough - she couldn't take any more. Cos she's 84 now. But it was *me* that had to go. They got an order and *I* had to go. And when I left home I was not allowed back in the house again. Not even past the front gate.

I went to Llanelli to live after they kicked me out. A lodging place upstairs right next to the Hazel cafe. I was there for about a week and I thought what am *I* doing *here* in the Hazel when I've got a mother and a brother *there?* So I thought I'll go and see my mother. Went to see her on a Saturday and she made me a meal and a cup of tea and then she said 'Don't bother coming back again. Every time I see you my nerves go. You're not *allowed* anyway.' I still went back and fore in the winter but they wouldn't answer in the end. My brother came to the door once and phoned straight for the police. They came and got me and put me in a cell. I was on a loser, you know? So I went to live in Burryport in Pembrey.

There's a pub right on the corner there - oh, *what's* the name of it! - and I was there for about a fortnight. There's nothing special about Burryport is there? I know it's pretty but there's something about it I don't like. There's no *life* there and not many people about. Then I went to - where did I go then? - Swansea! My Social worker took me from Burryport straight to the Radnor and, apart from nine months with the Cyrenians, I've been there ever since.

I've been to prison three times. First time I burnt a car in Llangennech. I'd had too much to drink and I'd mixed it with medication and tablets. On a Sunday night it was. I wasn't drunk but I wasn't feeling right, you know? Oh, *what* was the name of the guy whose car it was? His daughter's name was Maureen or Doreen. It was a very old car: Fiat something. It wasn't that I didn't *like* him - I didn't know it was *his* car. They told me the following day that I'd bump-started it downhill from the house cause the battery was flat. I ended up in court for that and jail for two weeks for social enquiry reports. I had a two hundred and fifty pound fine and two years probation.

Another time I was jailed because I was homeless in Port Talbot. I was in the Bail Hostel there for nine weeks waiting for social reports but I broke all the rules of the house. I went out and I shouldn't have, so they called the police and I was arrested. I appeared in court and cause I was homeless, they sent me to gaol. And what was the third time? Let me think a bit... no, it's *gone.* Anything else you want to know? Ask me an *important* question while I'm thinking...

I was homeless for nearly two years. I slept in car parks, in doorways on beaches - everywhere. In the summer I went on the beach and in the winter in the multi-storey in High Street with Tattooed Sara and Little Ritchie. They're still there now.

I'm eating now and having meals but a year ago I didn't even have shoes. I ended up in hospital for four days: Ward R, Morriston. I was walkin on *bare* feet! Oh, I tell you what: I was standin on glass an all! They were bleedin terrible - and the *pain!* People don't *know!* I couldn't bathe my feet and I was on the verge of gangrene. Julie will tell you. She saw me one night in the Citytax office in Mansel Street and she seen them then. *Terrible* mess on them! Everybody was concerned. They rang Cefn Coed one evening without telling me. They wanted me in hospital but I refused to go. No way, I said, no way. But they persuaded me and persuaded me and in the end I *did* go.

The Radnor has got a bad reputation. People that are there, their families have rejected them. They're there cause of court injunctions to get them out of their homes. And it's the same with hostels. People that are there: their families don't want to know them.

The man who runs the Radnor's got a wife and three kids and they live in the Mumbles. He comes to make our breakfast about twelve in the afternoon - cause he's got three jobs and his wife's working - and he leaves about one. There's about eight of us in there at the moment and we all go our own way: Ray, Bernie, Danny, Gerry, Mike, Jack. I'm in room number four. There's a shower, bath, wash-up basin, bed - *everything* there. Only trouble is, Belfast Danny broke the front door the other day. He couldn't find a key so he smashed the window to reach the lock and it's been like that ever since. *Anybody* can walk in the house. It's disgusting.

I left the first time cause they're all alcoholics. It wasn't my scene, see. I like a drink but I'm not an alcoholic. They were up in the attic all night drinking and arguing. I was back on the road when that murder took place. I knew the guy who was murdered and he was a *gentleman.* Everybody liked him. From St. Thomas. I know his daughter Tina. He used to visit her every Thursday. She writes poetry about her dad now, you know. Sad, mun. Bernie's got some of his ashes and poems that Tina wrote. They were very close. I knew the murderer and his girl friend, too: Big Kenny and Mad Moira. Not many liked her. In drink she was violent and abusive and very aggressive. She told Big Kenny that a year earlier she'd been raped by five men. She mentioned five names and one of them was Peter Davey. I don't know if that was true or not. And after he heard that, unfortunately, he took Peter Davey's life.

I don't plan for the future. I'm happy and I'm on top. I've been homeless but I'm back in the Radnor hotel and I keep myself clean and I'm better in mind and body. I've been lucky but I feel sorry for people who are still homeless. I know them all. Some are good, some are bad. but it's a *hard* life. You get verbal abuse from people and they look down on you.

I'm out most of the day. I'm up early and in the Quadrant at eight every morning. From there I go to Hypervalue and then I call in the Picola Cafe next door to meet the boys. I go to the Star Dust machine gaming place for tea every day and back to the Hotel by eleven for my breakfast. I leave about one and go back for another cup of tea in the Star Dust and then go around Town to see more of my friends. I'm well-known in Swansea. People have got respect for *me* and I've got respect for *them*. I meet lots of alcoholics and junkies and most of them are *tidy* people.

I go to the Cyrenians' Soup Runs most nights, on Saturdays to the Kingsway Coffee Bar and on Sundays to the Salvation Army Soup Run. They're all *good* people! Bill's Coffee Bar is from about quarter to seven till about half past eight. Bible study first and then food. I like going there. Bill's a nice man, you know. He'll be there tomorrow outside St. Mary's with that loudspeaker thing. We all take turns at reading. I've been to morning and evening Sunday school since the age of about twelve. Oh aye - I'm very religious! *He's* looking after us all the time, God is. Of course He is, mun! He *died* for us, didn't e? I'm not *deeply* into it but you've *gotto* have faith in God, haven't you?

There's been a lot of trouble in the Coffee Bar - with alcoholics. I musn't say no names but Ritchie's one of them and Sara and Irish Rick. They've been callin for months now, drinkin and swearin and arguin and shoutin. Oh terrible! That's a place of worship, isn't it? Bill told them *no drink allowed* and they kept away in the end. They were just there to cause a disturbance, you know? Not interested in the Bible nor nothing.

After the Coffee Bar I go back to the Hotel to see Bernie and the boys or to the Brooklands or the Tredegar for a drink and I'm usually in bed before one.

Looking back, my advice to youngsters now is: don't go with the wrong company. I know times are hard - no work and that - but don't mix with the wrong crowd. That was my mistake, as a teenager. I went to The Guild every Friday night in the church hall. Games and stuff, you know? Table tennis, snooker. I was there for about two years and I wouldn't say I was a bad boy but I was easily led. Got in with the wrong crowd: 'Ceri, do this! Ceri, do *that!*' And I'd do things I shouldn't have done. We weren't violent just silly. We couldn't see the mistakes we were makin and we regretted it after. Always try and go with *tidy* people - good people who've got an interest in youth clubs and church, scouts - anything. Have interests in life and don't hang around street corners and in and out of pubs. I didn't *see* it at the time and I suppose the youngsters today don't see it at the time but looking back, I could write a book about what I've done wrong. And I've regretted bringing trouble on my mother and father. They were very concerned about me. My brother mixed with the *right* company, I mixed with the *wrong*. If you're in trouble at an early age, you get in more and more trouble until you end up in prison and people don't want to know you. In the end you're a loner.

My brother and my mother sent me a Christmas card this Christmas and a letter to say they're thinking of me, how I am and how I'm getting on. I've got another social worker now. His name is Melvyn James. I see him every Friday morning about tennish and he pops down in the day if he's goin Llanelli way to see my mother and brother and tell them I'm looking fit and well and send my mum my regards. But there's no chance we'll get together again. No chance at all.

'Until Good Friday lands on a Thursday...'

Bernie and the Bowls Team (1)

Victoria Park on a cold, sunny morning in early February. I'm ten minutes late getting to the Park and they are just coming out through the gates. Jack shakes hands with me, says they'd just about given me up. We all go back in the Park and they sit six abreast on a bench in the pavilion. Also present are Belfast Danny and a black Alsatian dog. All but the dog look severely hungover. Last night on the Soup Run, Bernie and Mav, one of the Outreach workers, gave an impromptu jam session on harmonica and tin whistle outside St David's church. Afterwards, while I was talking to Bernie, he reached in his coat pocket and put a small polythene bag - of the kind that banks keep change in - in my hand and asked me what I thought it contained. Some of the contents was leaking. It felt granular, like cannabis, but he said it was some of his friend's ashes, which he always carried around with him because they'd been so close.

Jack: I'll start it off and say my name's Jack and I'll be fifty in October. I'm from the valleys originally. Up until 1989 I worked in the mines but lost my job and went to prison. I was married at the time with three children. I done my bird and came out to find that my wife had absconded with my best mate. I went into drugs in a heavy way: methadone, speed - you name it. Now, it's the drink. We're all killin ourselves slowly but I'm not goin to stop drinkin. Not at the moment, no...

Gerry: My name's Gerry and I'm thirty-four. I come from a good family but I've gone off the short and narrow and been in custody on many occasions. I'm not proud of it. It's just the simple fact that drink's been my downfall. There's no point in condemning it because, like my mate just said, I *won't* stop drinking until I can get accommodation suitable to my way of life.

Mike: My name's Mike and I'm thirty-four. I've only been homeless for five or six months. I'm from Coventry originally and I come down here with my friend and met the lads and started drinking. I'm a registered alcoholic - we all are - and for the last six years it's been a matter of getting my life together. I been in a Hostel and I've been in detox. I've been off

112

the drink for three years and then back on it again but, at the same time, I enjoy it. I like the company.

Bernie: My name's Bernie and I'm forty-two. Mine is a long story. I came to Swansea from Belfast nine years ago. I lost my wife, you see, and she was only twenty one years old and I've been here ever since. When I first came, with my friend Marcus, we didn't know the score: where to get blankets or food or whatever. The first night in Singleton Park, it was teeming from the heavens and all we had between us was Marcus's overcoat. At four o' clock in the morning there were slugs falling off the trees and I got paranoid because they were stuck to my hair. So Marcus walked two miles to find us a better place to sleep and we ended up in a little shed in the Dog's Home. We lived there for about three or four months and that's the God's truth. I don't want this life, to be honest with you. I didn't choose it. All I want to do is go back home again and be happy, cause we sleep in the Radnor Hotel over there and you might as well sleep in that field. Cause it's cold. You've got no blankets hardly. You got *nothing.* Everythin is just upside down and we cause a lot of that upside downness cause we drink and we just don't care any more. I've got a room and the sink doesn't work: you can't have a shave, you can't have a wash, you can't do nothin. That's not a Hotel, that's just a skipper. Back home, my sister's got a beautiful flat with everything: furniture, tv - you name it - the lot. But when I go home, believe it or not, I miss these boys here - all of them - because they're good company. I have to come back here again and now I can't escape. If I was back home, I could stay off the drink - I wouldn't even think about it - but not here. One of these days I'm going to have to get myself sorted and work out what's goin to happen to me. Sometimes I feel suicidal. I can't read, you know, but I can *think*. And if you can think, that means you've got a memory and if you use your memory day by day, it keeps you alive.

Ray: My name's Ray and I'm forty-seven. I come from a good Christian family. I used to have good jobs as a fitter and turner but I've lost them time and time again. I could never survive in a Company for more than six months or a year or whatever, due to alcohol. I started shop liftin and sleepin rough and ended up in prison. They wouldn't let me out of prison unless I went in the Radnor. And this is where I am today: out on the streets, more or less livin rough. I can't get a job now cause I'm too old and I'm an alcoholic and I've got criminal convictions and I'm in one helluva mess. I don't know where to go from here - it's as simple as that. And as Mr Malloy just said, the Radnor is a real dump. You got no blankets, no mirrors to shave in, no hot water and no

Bernie: door.

Ray: No front door - well, the door's there but there's no glass in it.

Bernie: There's about six or seven of us staying there officially but we bring others in off the street. Gerry shouldn't be there and Danny shouldn't be there but we take them in to give them a bit of shelter and keep the rain off them.

Ray: They make breakfast there - sometimes but not all the time - at half past eleven but we get no other food there, so we got to rely on the soup runs and whatever.

Bernie: We pay *money* there - and for *what?* For *nothin!* But that's all we've got at the minute. There's no place else to go, cause I couldn't sleep rough any more, to be quite honest with you. It would kill me. That's one thing I *do* know.

Gerry: It's all right people coming out of the County Hall or the Guildhall, out of *beds* in the morning, and then looking at you and classing you like as if you're some waster: they ought to live how we're livin, then perhaps they'd know exactly what living out is all about. Proper facilities is what we want. I don't want to go to a hostel, to be honest with you cause, like I say, I've been in custody a lot of times: be in by eleven o' clock and do this and do that. I likes to be my own man. Do my own thing. As long as I had a key to my own door, so I could go in and do *whatever* I wanted, that would be ideal for me. Then I would start thinking of looking for work. I've tried Housing Options but they just puts you on the waiting list and that waiting list could be until Good Friday lands on a Thursday. I know they're supposed to house you straight away if you're a health risk but I don't class myself as a health risk, to be honest. The boys will tell you: I've slept out for years and years and all over this bad winter, right up until now, and I'm used to it. So this weather *now*, is coming *mellow* to me. It's like Autumn. I remember sleeping on Fairwood Common New Year's Eve night, waiting to go to Nazareth House in the morning, to get a dinner. Now *that's* what you call cold! This, now, is nothing. It's coming *summer* as far as I'm concerned.

Jack: Gerry's talking a lot of sense there. People come out of the County Hall with their three-piece suits and their brogue shoes and God-knows-what, but they haven't got a clue! I mean, where do we draw the line? The Government's got all that money tied up and we haven't got a place to sleep. Why don't they give us an hotel or *buy* us an hotel? We'll willingly pay them weekly, as we are doing now. But we don't feel safe where we are.

Danny: I sleep with one eye open.

Bernie: That's the way it works in the Hotel: one eye open and one eye shut. Sometimes I kip on the floor to give someone else the bed. We gotto put boards up against the door, just to make sure. And there's no escape, unless you jump through the front window.

Gerry: Sometimes we go to bed with an ammer at the side of us. Am I right?

Bernie: You're right, son.

Gerry: Anybody can come in. *Anybody.*

Jack: The police walk in and out as though they owned the place.

Bernie: If they only put the pane of glass back in the door. It would only cost a few shillings.

Jack: It's simply a squat.

Gerry: There's a landlord and a landlady but what it boils down to is that they're screwing us.

Jack: But we can't knock them because we'd be out -

Bernie: I open the letterbox in the morning and they've got so many rent cheques coming in there, you wouldn't believe! And I don't even know their names. They're not there. There's *nobody* there. They're claiming for Gerry: he's not supposed to be there. They're claimin for Danny: he's not supposed to be there. And a lot of other people as well. And when the police come to the house for anything at all, it's *I* got to answer the door. They run out the back and they're gone, know what I mean? I just act dumb and say I don't know *this* and I don't know *that*, cause I'm not the type to squeal - never was, never will be. But it's bloody ridiculous down there, I'm tellin you!

Jack: We need a tent or something where we can be together.

Gerry: Down the Gower or somewhere. Like a bender. But a communal bender, cause we're all in the same boat.

Jack: We'd be happy in a tent. Build a little fire, keep us warm, cook for ourselves -

Gerry: And just carry on the way we are. I know the Cyrenians could put us up in a b and b for a few nights during the cold spells but that's just temporary, isn't it? They brought the cabins down there a couple of years ago but only for the Christmas period. A night shelter should be all the year round.

Bernie: Remember what happened to Joe Tanner?

Gerry: In the Glass House.

Bernie: What used to be Ableglaze, down by Castle Gardens. He died of hypothermia.

They wouldn't let him stay in the cabin all day: he had to be out at nine o' clock and come back at four. The man was ill and they didn't realize.

Gerry: Me and Bernie was in a cabin up in Cardiff. You see some crazy people in there. About thirty of them in bunk beds and you've got a night watchman coming round every hour with a torch but you could be *murdered* in that hour, man!

Bernie: I tell you: I'd rather sleep out than sleep in Cardiff.

Gerry: It was *rough*. This guy came in drunk one night and reckoned I was in the wrong bed. And all I could see of him was just a silhouette coming towards me. Well, I gave him a good kicking and Bernie heard it and got down off his bunk and laid into him as well. But in the morning this guy was as nice as pie - apologised and everything.

Bernie: You see, it only takes a split second for something to happen, for someone to pull a knife out or whatever - just one split second is all it takes. So we all end up paranoid. I'd love digs - proper digs - cause I can't sleep rough no more. People should try and look after other people. Like sometimes, at night, we have to go out looking for the rest of the boys.

Gerry: Bernie came out for me last night. I was over by the swimming baths and he came over and took me back. If he hadn't, I'd have ended up either in this park or Singleton Park. Singleton's my bedroom, as you might say, but what with the pigeons and the cuckoos and the ducks wakin you at six in the mornin, it's like Pensycynor Bird Gardens down there! I've got a sleeping bag stashed away but I don't know whether it's *still* there. The Parks Department have got a habit of either dowsing them with water or putting them in the back of the van and driving off. Then when you come back, you aven't got no blankets. So you've got to go out of your way then to try and beg, do anything to get something to warm you up. There's a lot of Security Guards at County Hall will tell you that they've seen me sleepin there, curled up with *nothin* - just what I've got on. And they've come along at six o' clock in the mornin and told me I've got to move on because people are starting coming into work -

Bernie: I've seen that man there - Danny - full of frost. Frost! No blankets, sleepin on the beach in the wintertime. He can tell you himself. In the morning, he couldn't even stand up. That man is *strong,* to stay alive in that weather.

Jack: And the Radnor can be a very dangerous place.

Bernie: I lost my best mate in there. Peter Davey or Peter 'Pan' as I used to call him. My other mate kicked him to death. D'you know Mad Moira? I don't know her last name - she said Peter had raped her years ago, which was a lie, because Peter could hardly walk. So Big Kenny started on Peter Pan and I had to take him into my room. But then I took some sleepin tablets and while I was out Peter went back into Big Kenny's room again, didn't he? When I woke up round about midnight, I saw Peter Pan lyin on the landin with his head cut open, but he was still alive cause I could hear him snorin. So I dragged him back into my room. I didn't realize properly what was happenin because I was so full of tablets but Ray stepped over him, didn't you, son?

Ray: Yep. I thought he was sleepin. I didn realize he'd been beaten up.

Bernie: I took some more sleepin tablets and when I woke up at three in the mornin, I put my hand down and said 'Peter, son, are you all right?' And he was stone cold. Everyone loved Peter. You loved him, too, didn't you, son?

Jack: Yes, I did. He was a gentle giant. You couldn't wish for a nicer feller. He'd have a drink, yeah, like we all would but then he would just go to sleep sittin up and if we went out in the meantime, he knew where to find us later. He was a gentle giant.

Ray: All he had for breakfast was a boiled egg -

Bernie: I used to have to make him eat because the man wasn't well - and then he'd bring it all up again in the sink. But I blame myself for his death because if I hadn't of took the tablets, I could have saved his life. I always stopped Big Kenny from hitting other people in the house, didn I? He was a big bloke but I always stopped him. But *that* was the time I shoulda stopped him and I didn even know about it cause of the tablets. Then we all went to Court and the case went on for a full week. Jack was in court with me and Ray and - who else?

John: And Marcus and Mick-

Bernie: He set fire to Mick. Put petrol on him and set fire to him. And he stabbed Jack here -

Jack: Slashed me twice.

Bernie: And he done Lal. Oh, he done a few boys but he never ever touched me. They were frightened of him but I wasn't because I was the only one who could talk to him, see. He always picked on the boys when he got a few drinks in him and when he'd had cider he always used to say 'I'm a psychopath!' He stood and looked out of the window one day - Marcus will tell you - and he said 'Before tonight I'm goin to kill somebody.' And that's the God's truth. And he did. But he got twenty-five years for it and I was *glad*. D'you know why? Cause he's doin a life sentence but Peter Pan's not. Peter Pan's happy now, he's somewhere else but Big Kenny's got to live with that on his mind - for twenty-five years, if he lives that long, which I very much doubt. It could of been me instead of Peter Pan and I'd rather it *had* of been me. It's hard to explain sometimes, you know, but I *miss* him. I always carry this little packet of ashes around with me that I got from his daughter Tina. 'D'you know, Bernie?' he says to me one day, does wee Peter: 'I don't think I'm goin to last too long.' Cause he was weak: he could hardly walk. And I said to him: 'You'll live as long as *I* will.' But he didn't. Three weeks later, Big Kenny took his life away.

'This, that and the other...'

Terry

This girl I've started goin out with said to me the other day 'If we won the Lottery, where would we go?' I said 'Where d'you get this *we'* from? *I'd* be in Switzerland: *first* plane - **Gone!** 'Why Switzerland?' she said. I said 'I've been there before. It's the most beautiful place I've ever seen. It's like a postcard. There's no tax there and it's a *neutral* country.' Yes, it's definitely Switzerland for me - or Porthcawl!

A tall, thickset, happy-go-lucky bear of a man, with craggy features and pale-blue, watery eyes who appears regularly at the midday Soup Kitchens and often stays behind for ages, chatting to his good friend London Mike. We sit either side of a desk in the front office of the Hostel.

My mother and father met during the War. He was from Bristol but she was from down here. They got married and moved back to Bristol, cause that's where his business was. He was a long-distance lorry driver but not your nine-till-five sort of job. He'd go out on a Friday and come back on a Sunday, so my mother was on her own for all that time. She got so homesick, my father had to call the doctor and he advised her to go home while he was away, to be with her mother and sisters. So she came home for a weekend and just never went back. There was no nastiness and it wasn't an acrimonious split. He came down to try and sort it out but eventually they said so-long on High Street Station and that was *it.*

Of course, shortly afterwards, *I* popped out. And my mother had to start work to support me, so my gran and grandad brought me up. When my mother remarried, she and my stepfather moved to a house nearby and she had five daughters there within the space of about four years. Me and my stepfather never got on. Whether it was because I was a boy and he always *wanted* a boy or whether it was because I wasn't *his*, I don't know. We were like cat and dog. I was sixteen and had a job in the Market as a butcher's boy by this time but *he* wouldn't work and when he used to go down and get his dole money, he'd come back steaming from the pub late at night and pick an argument over the least thing.

He never hit my mother but the states he used to get in, I don't suppose he could *see* her to hit her. I was sittin there one night in what he called 'his chair' and he comes rollin in as usual and says 'You're in my chair!' and slaps me across the back of the head. And I thought 'That *does* it!' So I ran to the kitchen and came back with a carving knife. I had my mother dragging me back by the hair and my uncle pullin me back by the waist but I had my stepfather pinned up against the airing cupboard with this knife. I was goin to kill him, I *really* was, cause I'd had enough. My uncle moved out shortly after cause he'd had enough too, but I sort of persevered cause I played badminton six or seven nights a week with my friends and was more or less out of it.

There was four of us: me, Ricky Legg, Howard Rowlands and Kenny Barnes and they used to call us The Four Just Men cause when you found one, you found the other three. Every weekend we'd go to the Local for a drink and I remember one Saturday or Sunday, Ricky saying 'I'm fed up with this place. Let's go somewhere else.' So we ended up in the Rhyddings in Brynmill and I sees this girl and we start talking and I asked if I could take her home. And one thing led to another and we got married.

I'd quit the butcher's by now cause the hours were killin me. I was startin at five thirty in the mornin and not gettin home till half past seven, quarter to eight at night. All I was was a *gopher.* *'The van wants loadin!'* or *'Cycle down to Mrs Griffiths in Derwen Fawr with her meat!'* Rain or shine - oh! And my mates - the other three Just Men - were finishing at quarter past *four!* They'd come round the house at quarter to eight but I'd be so tired, I'd be in bed. So my mate said 'Why don't you get a job with me on the ashcarts?' I said 'I'm not humpin *bins* around. What d'you think I *am*? I've got my *pride!*' Then he mentioned the money. It was four pound a week *more* with the Council and four pound back in the Sixties was a lot of money. You could get a *suit* for that. 'And I'm home every day by two o' clock,' he said. So that *swung* it.

We had the weddin reception down in the Mermaid in the Mumbles and in the night we went up the Local and my stepfather was up there, drunk. So my mother said to me 'Do me a favour: get him into a taxi and get him home. Cause we're all goin back to the house after for a nightcap.' So I goes on to him and says 'Look, Dad, do us a favour: if I phone you a taxi, will you - ' But before I could finish, he grabbed me by the lapels. Well, I mean, I'm well over six foot and I'd put on a lot of weight and I thought *'Right. This* is *it!* I've been waitin a *long* time for this - ' And I raised my hand back to hit him and the next thing I know, there's a fist comes over my shoulder and he's on the floor! I turned around and there's my father-in-law. He was like John Wayne: six foot four and seventeen stone. I mean, he's seventy-odd now and I *still* wouldn't argue with him. And we got my father up and bundled him into the taxi. Then me and her flew out to Jersey Sunday mornin and coming back, I bought him a present cause I was afraid to go up the house. But anyway we walks in and, as fate would have it, my mother collared me first and said 'He thinks *you* it im!' So I thought, well I'll play along with that. I went in and I said 'You all right, dad?' And he looked up at me and said 'By Christ, son, you can't alf swing a right ook!' I didn't tell him the truth and I never will - well, *why* destroy a dream, isn't it? - and that's thirty-odd years ago, now. And since then, we've got on so well, we're *closer* than father and son.

So we had a flat in Cwm Level Road in Brynhyfryd and we'd been married about three years and I happened to be working up at Townhill so I called in my mother's. And she said 'Is there anything wrong with you and Rita?' I said 'No, we're fine. We're like a couple of kids.' 'No, I don't mean that,' she said. 'Are you able to have *children?*' I said 'Well, Christ, *aye!*' 'Oh, Dad is wonderin why you haven't had any, cause you've been married three years.' I said 'Well, Mam, I'm only *twenty-three*, you know. Let's ave a bit of *life!*' Anyway, I think the old man must ave put the curse on us, cause a year later my daughter come along. And she was my *two eyes!* I stopped goin out with the boys. I packed in my football. I packed in my beloved badminton. I even went on the sick for a week, after she was born cause I didn't want to be away from her. 'Melanie' we ended up callin her. Then, three years later the boy came along - and I was disappointed. I always wanted *two* daughters: two little girls for daddy to fuss about and this, that and the other. When I phoned the hospital, they told me he was eleven pound! So I went up and told my mother and she played *ell* with me for givin my wife a baby that size and I said 'Well, *I* can't help it. I just did what came *naturally.*' Then when I went down the hospital and told the nurse I'd come to see Mrs Pierson, she said 'Oh, you've come to see *The Bull,* have you?' They called my son 'The Bull.' And I don't know whether you've done this, but when you go in Maternity, you look in other cots to see how other kids compare and with most of them the blankets come up to their chins but on my son the blanket only come up to his chest - cause he was *huge* and his face was so fat, he only had slits for eyes. 'Oh, there's a *job* I had with him!' she said. 'What are we goin to call him?' 'Jonathon,' I said, cause 'John' is a *strong* name. 'Don't *like* Jonathon,' she said. 'Well, we can't call him Stephen,' I said, 'because your sister's just called her baby Stephen and we can't call him Richard cause they'll end up callin him Dick - ' And she was comin out with things like 'Jason' and if you hear somebody call 'Jason!' you expect to see a dog come runnin. 'Oh, listen,' I said. 'Call him Steve Austen after the Six Million Dollar Man.' So she said 'Well, what's Steve Austen's *real* name?' I said 'Lee Majors.' 'That's *it*, then!' she said. 'We'll call him Lee.' And I said 'Well, he's havin my middle name. So we called him Lee Edward.

The Council eventually offered me a job on the Civil Amenities site: handling things like washing machines and mattresses, stuff that was too big for people to put out with the rubbish. I had to talk it over with my wife first because you had to work Saturdays and Sundays. You got days off in the week but there weren't any set hours and you worked what's called Dawn till Dusk. If it got dark at half past four, you went home and if it got dark at nine o' clock, you went home. In the summer I was goin home with £700 but in the Winter it was £120, so we saved the money from the summer to compensate for the Winter.

I bought a new house in Morriston and I put *everythin* in it: central heatin, fitted kitchen, cupboards, shower. But, of course, in the Summer I was startin work at eight on a Saturday and Sunday and not finishin till eight or nine at night. And the kids had grown up and wanted to go down the beach and I had to tell them I was workin. I was only seein them for about an hour in the summer and when I got home, they were goin to bed. Then she said 'I've got a chance of a job in the evenings in the Lamb. Only three nights a week.' So I said I'd see my boss about rearranging things so I could be home in time for her to go to work and he was as good as gold about it: told me to finish at seven and he'd book me out at eight. Course, she goes to work now and we're basically passin each other in the passage. She was goin out to the bus as I was comin in and she was shouting back 'Dinner's in the dog!' or 'Salad's in the fridge!' or what-have-you. Course, after a bit she meets somebody else - and I'm out. I'd given her everythin and I walked out of the house with the record-player on one arm and a suitcase on the other. They kicked me out and the house was worth over seventy thousand pounds! But, oh, I *laughed!* She said to me 'Can you sign your half of the house over to me?' I said 'Yeah, no problem.' 'Well, there's *good* you are about it,' she said. 'I thought you'd ave fought it.' But what was the point?

You can go to any court in the land and the woman always gets the house: cause she's got the children. So she says 'Can you meet me at half past two outside the solicitors?' And, of course, who turns up with her but *Mr Wonderful* himself! I said 'I don't want *him* in there. It's got nothin to do with *him!*' So the solicitor hands out all these documents now and I'm signin them and handin them back and 'Oh,' he says, 'that's very unusual - ' *'What* is?' she says. 'Well, he's signed his half of the house over to the *children.'* Oh, she went **ape-shit!** She went **ballistic!** 'You *can't* do that!' she said. I said 'Scuse me, Mr Prosser: *can* I do that?' 'It's quite within your legal rights,' he said. 'You can pass it over to a stranger in the street as long as I've got your signature.' So I signed my half to the kids and explained to them that when they were eighteen they could turn round to her and say 'We either want to buy you out or we want the house put up for sale.' Then I went back to live with my mother. But two days was *enough!* She thought I was still sixteen: *'Your tea's ready. Where you goin all dressed up? You're not goin drinkin, are you?'* 'Mam!' I said, 'I'm thirty-*one!* Let me do my *own* thing!' So I ended up in lodgings with my friend and then I met somebody else: through my sister. I was at her house one night and there was a few girls there and I takes one of them home and moves in with her. I don't know what possessed me. We're together about a year, ends up getting married but it only lasted ten weeks. She was *worse* than my mother: *'Where you goin? What time will you be back? How much money have you got on you? Don't have too much - '* I thought 'I don't *need* this!' She was a drinker, too, which didn't help my cause one little bit. *Fatal!* I was still earnin good money and we went out four nights a week but she'd drink half a bottle of whisky while she was gettin *ready:* before we even hit the open air. So I moved out and that's when my drink problem *really* started cause I was on my own and I was pickin up £400 pound a week and I was only payin £30 for a room. By the time I'd paid maintenance and done a bit of shopping, it left me with about £250. So what d'you do in the evening other than go for a pint? And it starts off two pints a night and ends up two bottles of vodka a *day.* And, oh God, my weight halved! I went right down to about nine stone. My Civil Amenities job went down the drain. I only had to get into work, open up my cabin and *sit* there. I didn't even have to get off my backside but I was even drinkin in work: bottle of vodka a day before goin home. Course, I got caught. Somebody complained when they saw me drunk on the job - *blah! blah! blah!* - and I was *out!*

I was thirty-five or thirty-six when I met this other girl but she was already married.

I hadn't seen her or her husband for twelve years and she said 'You're lookin *terrible, Terry.* Look at you! You're about seven stone and white as a ghost! Where you livin?' So I give her my address and she said 'Well, I'll try and come down as often as I can.' And she come down that night with two or three carrier bags full of shoppin for me and cooked me a meal. She'd take my clothes home and wash them when he was on six till two or two till ten and bring them back. She was bloody marvellous! She got divorced and we started going out together. For three years everythin was fine. I got on with her daughters, and her mother - what's the word? - *tolerated* me. Her ex-husband didn't like me at all but he was all mouth and trousers: *'If I catch you two together, I'll -!'* 'You'll *what*, son!' I said. Mind you, if he'd swung I don't know what I'd have done. I might be tall but I'm no fighter.

So then the oldest daughter, Anita, had a baby and the boyfriend done a runner. And Anita started workin in Cardiff and stayin up there four days a week, which meant that Gina was preoccupied with her grandson and, after bein the mainstay in her life for so long, it felt funny to come *second.* So what did I do? I started hitting the sauce again, didn't I? I'd go out and have a shedfull and instead of goin back to the house, I'd go up my mother's. Well, of course, she met somebody else and she's livin with him now and good luck to her! She's *happy,* so there's no hard feelins and this that and the other.

Then I got kicked out of my flat, cause of an argument with the neighbour and ended up in the Hostel in Stembridge Avenue. I was there for three and a half years, and down here for two, until they got me this place over in St. Thomas.

I've only ever lived a year on my own, which means I still can't boil water! I'm gettin into it now, though, cause you *gotto.* You either learn or you starve.

When they offered me this place in St. Thomas, I asked if I could have a look at it before I decided. They said 'It's a house but you've gotto share it with *three* women.' I thought: 'That'll do *me!* Look out, *Tom Jones!'* So I goes over there now and oh, my God: they was like the *Witches of Eastwick!* I'm not bein derogative or nothin like that but one was about seventy and an alcoholic, another was six foot two and eighteen stone and built like Mervyn Davies and the other one went around all day makin the Sign of the Cross cause she was a Jesus-Freak. And you know what women are like in the mornin, once they get in the bathroom. I used to get in there about quarter past two in the afternoon! And then I couldn't *see* for steam and talcum powder. I said to my Key Worker: 'Listen, I can't handle this at all.' He said 'You've only been here ten days,' 'I know,' I said, 'but that's *it!'*

So they put me over in Port Tennant Road then, which I'm quite enjoyin. I've got a nice room, a brand-new bed, a Continental quilt one of the Key Workers has given me and I've just bought myself two pillows. I got a shower there, bath, fridge, cooker, pots and pans, wardrobe and my own T.V. I can please myself what time I get in and if I want to whip up and get a quick meal late at night, I can.

I fell out with my sisters just before Christmas because I'm forty-nine and they're still tellin me how to live my life. They don't like to see me drinkin - which is part of the reason I quit really, plus the fact I kept fallin over all the time. They're always sayin 'Come up the house for dinner,' or 'Don't go ome: come up and ave tea and sleep on the couch.' It's nice of them but I like my independence. If I want to watch Match of the Day, my sisters will say 'You don't want to go watchin bloody football: we've got a *video*.' And I'll say 'But I don't *want* a video!' So the crunch came when one of them said 'There's a flat goin over by the old Tower.' I said 'I don't want to come back to Townhill.' 'Why?' she said. 'Mam and Dad's up here. We're *all* up here.' I said 'That's just *it:* we're goin to be in and out of each other's houses all the time.' 'That's the trouble with you,' she said. 'You're *ungrateful.*' I said 'I'm not ungrateful. I just *don't want* to come back up Townhill. I don't mind comin up for a couple of hours to see you and the kids.' And then one thing led to another and, in the end, I stormed out. But I saw my stepfather in Town a few days later and he said 'Come here, *you!*' And I thought oh, here we go again, so I said 'I'm sorry about that Dad, but - ' 'I don't blame you, son!' he said. '*I'd* have done the same in your position.'

I can't work cause of this tremor I've got in my hands. If that was right, I'd be back in work as a painter and decorator but as it is I spend a lot of time in the library, cause I love readin. This is why I've gotto start wearin glasses, cause I'm readin so much my eyes have gone. I love my books but I don't like this Mills and Boon or Barbara Cartland sort of stuff. There's not a film star or a pop star I haven't read about. And, I know this is cruel, but there's not a murderer I haven't read about either: Jack the Ripper, The Boston Strangler, Charles Manson. I don't like fiction. They gotto be true to life: the real McCoy!

 I'm pushin fifty now but I don't make plans. Every time I do, I've been shot up the arse. It's like they tell you in AA: *'Day by day'.* Tomorrow I could be fallin down drunk but today I'm sober and I *know* I'll be sober tomorrow. You can never control it but I'm a hundred times better than I used to be. I only went to AA, *once*, and I won't be goin again. I went in and this woman said 'What's your name?' I said 'Terry.' She turned round to the others and said '*Listen*, everybody! This is *Terry* and he's an **alcoholic!**' I nearly died. I'd been tryin to keep it quiet for years and she goes and announces it to *everybody!*'

Thursday, I'm goin over to see my daughter who works in a pub but I'll stick to soft drinks. They tell you in AA to stay out of wet places but I think the challenge is goin into a pub to see if you can say no. It's all right sittin in the house with no beer, thinkin this is easy cause there's no temptation there. When I first quit the booze - which I did for two and a half years - I went out and bought six bottles of vodka and put a bottle in each room in the house. So wherever I went there was a full bottle of vodka there and I didn't have to go looking for it. In the end I sold them to an Off Licence. It's been two and a half weeks since I touched a drop. It used to be only two and a half days or two and a half hours. I do anythin to pass the time. I'll walk around Town all day, lookin in windows, lookin at holidays I can't afford. As long as I've got a packet of fags, milk, sugar and tea bags, I know I can come down here for a bit of soup and, as often as not, blonde Julie will say 'Stay and have a bit of tea with us.'

Never ever seen my real father. I've seen a photo of him: my aunty showed it to me. His name's Arthur. He's got black, wavy hair and a black moustache and, apparently, he's six foot eight. My mother won't talk about him. I've asked her but 'Oh, *gone!*' she says. 'All in the past.' He's still alive but he's gotto be in his seventies. My aunty gave me the number of his Club, where he plays snooker, so I phoned him and spoke to him but he denied any knowledge of me. I hit him with some details he couldn't get out of: his name, my mother's, where they met, when they married. He changed the subject. He said 'I've gotto go now, I'm bein called.' And he put the phone down. But, apparently, there's only me and him left. When he got divorced from my mother, he went back to live with his mother and sister. They both died and left him with a farm. And the haulage business he had, picked up so he bought up another one and a fleet of lorries. I keep lookin for Wills in the local paper. But knowing my luck, he'll leave it all to Bristol Zoo.

'Huggy huggy huggy,
kissy kissy kissy...'

Alec (2)

In the weeks since my first interview with him, staff at the Hostel finally contacted his sister and arranged funding for him to travel up to Scotland.

Two days after his return, there's an early-morning knock on my studio door.

...Some organization paid for me to go up. Church people. Some woman: Pat somebody-or-other. Pat *Ward* - that's it! Paul Burrows fixed that up for me. But he had to go through Conrad in the office and Conrad says *'Yes,'* so Paul went and contacted this Pat Ward somewhere down in the Mumbles and she done all the business for me.

I left here at twenty minutes to eleven Thursday morning and I got there at quarter to nine at night. My sister didn't know I was coming. No way I could get near her till Friday morning, so I booked into The Great Northern. That's about eight mile away frae my sister's place. I was in there seven year but a lot of the boys are dead there now. When I went in, they couldn't believe their eyes: *'The Good Samaritan again!'* they says. 'How does this man *survive?* Everybody's goin under but *you* keep coming back, gettin stronger and stronger.' I said 'It must be the Strongbow!'

The followin day I went out there to Cross Maluf and Ken opened the door to me. He recognized me straightaway. He says 'Come in, Alec. I been lookin for you for a long time. Your sister there's no keepin too well. She's been depressed about you.' And then she heard my voice in the back room there and she calls out *'That's my brother, Alec!'* Then she comes in and looks at me and her face lights up and she gives me a great big hug and a kiss and all of a sudden she's cryin. Next thing, Ken gave me a cup of tea and then he turns round and says to me 'You done a fast move on me, Alec. I went lookin all over Glasgow for you. I went to The Great Northern and I was told there you were missin. The police were lookin all over the place for you. Searched all the grounds. Nobody knew where you was - ' Ken told my sister they thought I must have got murdered somewhere, cause I never notify nobody when I go, you know? I just walk away out of Town and that's *it*. So I says 'Hang on, Ken. Let's sit down and sort things out. When I hit the road again I went all round the country and I lost your phone number and address and that was *it*. I couldn help it. That's the way it goes in life. But I been tryin to get in touch with you - ' Then Ken turns round and more-or-less starts blamin *me* for the carry-on so I says to him 'Ang on, Ken. No way is it *my* fault. You cannae put the blame on *me*.' He says 'Alec, I'm no puttin the blame on you. You jus went away. You never got in contact wi anyone and now, all of a sudden, you just arrive here. Out of nowhere.' I says 'Ken, I *did* get in touch with you. I got in touch with that nephew of mine, Gordon, at the Brewery.' The lady in the Hostel wrote and explained my case for me. Next thing, Ken turns round and says to me 'No message come here.' 'Well,' I says, 'it was stamped and addressed to the Personnel Manager, Scotch Caledonian Brewery.' So after that, he cooled down on me a bit, you know? He realized what had happened there: that the nephew hadn't passed the messages on. For no reason at all. I never done no damage to the guy, you know. Never seen him in my life. Then Ken says to me 'Are you still a heavy drinker?' I says 'Yes'. (For no use tellin a lie.) 'Are you still gamblin?' I says 'Aye.' (For what more can I say?) I says 'Well, that's my caper. I gotta get along there with my life, you know. You get on with *your* life and *I'll* get on with mine.' And he turned and told me: 'You never get depressed cause you're drinkin all the time.' I says 'What d'you mean by that: *I'm drinking all the time*?' I says 'I drink when I get a few bob.' 'And how d'you get your money?' I says 'I've got a good begging pitch.' 'And what you doin in Swansea?' I says 'I'm in the Hostel down there - Cyrenians. It's a good place. It's a better place there than The Great Northern.' I says 'At least you get four meals a day there and a bit of peace of mind.' He says 'How did you find that?' I says 'I'm a man that runs about the country. I know what's goin on.' He says 'Who runs it?' I says 'All I know is the address there is 'Cyrenees'. 'What organization is it?' I says 'A charity mob.' He says 'You doin anythin beside it?' 'Well,' I says, 'I got a wee turn now and again, you know?' He says 'You're lookin well, anyway.' I says 'I *always* look well.' I didn't tell him I'd been skipping and all that, you know?

I was up there three days and two nights. I didn't stay long. I just had an hour wi them. Was glad to get out of there for another drink. When I was goin away there, my twin sister was all huggy huggy huggy, kissy kissy kissy. 'Alec, keep in touch with me, *please*. I'm depressed about you. There's just you and I left in the world there.' Oh, she's right an all, you know? And Ken turns round and says to me 'Well, Alec, before you go: here's my address and phone number. And whatever you do, please keep in contact wi us all the time - once a week anyway. Just to keep my wife happy. We're on the phone, or write us a letter. Let us know - '

I said 'You're right, Ken. That's it: I'll always keep in touch with her. That's what I'm all the way up frae Swansea for...'

I met up with a lot of old friends in The Great Northern: my namesake Alec Clooney. And Archie Short. Bill Green, the Porter and Lottie Green, his sister. Still there after all those years. Oh aye, they were surprised to see me. I came out of the blue.

That's the only hostel I've stayed in in Glasgow: The Great Northern. They don't call them hostels up there, they call them *models*. I don't know where they get the name of 'model'. There's more vacancies up there than down here. There's about thirty odd vacant places in The Great Northern alone. Models. They're all over Glasgow. There's even a big Night Shelter, Kingston Halls, under Kingston Bridge, where you can get a nice lie down, then they put you in a model next day.

Two hundred stay in The Great Northern. It's a six-storey building but the top floor's all open. That's for the pigeons. They own the top floor. Free digs. They've got a big dungeon down the stairs, used to be for transport at one time, you know. There's old people cannae walk been put down the basement now cause the elevator's out of action. They've cleaned it all out and put carpets and beds and furnishing in. I've got their phone number: 150 Finlay Street. It used to be run by a bunch of villains. Pure rogues they were. They all got sacked. Six of them. They're due in Court for fraud anytime: claimin for dead men. Hibernian Homes have taken it over now. They've got proper chefs in it and you get your meals there any time you want them. It's sixteen quid for two nights bed and breakfast but I didn't bother with the breakfast. The pubs open at eight o' clock in the mornin till one o' clock in the night. Oh, nonstop! Whisky *Galore*!

I went away down the road there to a pub called the Strathshuey and I put twenty pound behind the bar there, you know? Next thing, Neil Duffy, the owner says 'I never forget a face. When'd you come back?' I says 'Thursday.' He says 'Are you stayin here for long?' 'No, I'm away on Saturday again.' He says 'Why you up here?' I says 'To see the sister.' He got me a couple of whiskies and one of the barmen turns round and says 'What made you come up so quick?' 'Well,' I says, 'That's the way of life, isn't it? You try and get

129

in touch wi somebody but if you *don't* you've gotto come up be bus. ' He says 'What's the fare there?' I says 'Forty-eight pound return. One of the staff in the Hostel got it for me.' He says 'How d'you like it down there?' I says 'Oh, it's a great place. The staff are great altogether, you know.'

I left Glasgow at quarter to nine in the morning. When I got on the bus at Cannock Street Station the busdriver turns round and says to me. 'You're in an awful state there,' Cause I'd fallen and hurt my ribs and I was all patched up with muck and everythin, you know. He says to me 'When you get in this bus here, you'll hear the tannoy goin and we'll be warnin everybody about *drink*.' Next thing, as soon as the coach left the Station, the stewardess started talkin to them over the tannoy: *'Welcome to National Express. Abide by the rules. No hot-footin' in the bus. No alcohol. No smokin. Yer luggage is safe. When we pull into a station, you can have a smoke and stretch your legs - '* The whole bus was packed out. I was away in the back seat there. The driver kept lookin at me in the mirror. I couldn't do nothin. I couldn't even get a smoke. I tried to go to the toilet but I couldn't make it: my ribs were too sore, you know. The first stop was up in Scotland there - Carlisle - then it was straight through to Birmingham. You gotto wait an hour there, so I had a couple of pints. I came back on the bus and the steward there smelt my breath. He said 'You got a drink in you again.' I said 'I've no drink *on* me. I had a couple of pints across the road. I'd an *hour* to wait.' 'Well,' he says, 'You'll hear it again, there!' So next thing, the coach pulls out of Birmingham and it comes over the tannoy again: *'Alcohol not allowed. If you're caught with it, we'll pull up and the police will come and dismiss you off the coach. And you've lost your fare. Otherwise, stick by the rules of the National Express Company and we wish all our passengers a very happy journey.'*

From Birmingham it was straight to Swansea but you gotto go to Bridgend, Port Talbot, Neath and then Swansea. Quarter to nine till half past six! Got back at night time. And as we're comin off the bus, the stewardess turns round and says *'Welcome Home again! Come back and see National Express!'* I kept goin! I couldn't get away quick enough! Went straight to The Duchess and there was Mr Burrows himself. He was *delighted.* I showed him the address and the phone number and he says 'That's *it*, Alec! That's great. You've done the business!

I haven't got plans to go up again, but I know where they are. They may come down and see me, for a holiday. He's got a car. I says 'I'm next to the seafront. There's hotels all along there. It's ten pound bed and breakfast.' She says 'You sure?' I says 'Aye.' So she may come and visit me for a couple of days. Have a look at the Hostel, see the way I'm livin.

Oh, it was good of those people to pay the fare, you know. Very *great. All Creatures Great and Small! All things wise and wonderful, the Lord God made us all!* My old ribs are still sorey-sorey but I cannot stop laughy-laughying...!

'Feels like we're invisible...'

Cardiff Karl

I went into Paxton Street the other day, with my mate. I was goin to try and get in but, as we went through the door, a bottle of vodka fell out of his hand and a bottle of cider fell out of mine and that was the end of the story! You can go in there paralytic - you can actually *fall* in there: but you can't take drink in. But there's a porto-cabin over behind Argos and the fella in there's pickin me up on Tuesday to find me a place. You get drug-users in most of these hostels so I've told him I don't want to go in one of them. I want a clean house. He knows of one shared by four people, all in the same boat as me - all coming off - so, hopefully, we'll all help each other.

We sit on the pavement outside Iceland's on a busy Saturday morning in mid-February: Karl, Sara and a man they call 'The Brigadier.' Karl hasn't been in Town long and is something of an unknown quantity, though he seems pleasant enough. A tall, unshaven, sturdily-built young man with a slight cast in one eye, the Soup Run supplied him with blankets only last night, as he lay sleeping in the High Street Car Park.

I'm thirty-four and I'm from Ely in Cardiff. My mother used to work in petrol stations and things like that but my father had a *real* good job. He was Chairman of the Union in British Steel: umbrella, briefcase and a limo to come and pick him up whenever he had to go somewhere. He used to bring people out on strike or *not* bring them out on strike.

My mum was the nicest person you could meet. My father used to give her twenty pound a week to keep that house. *Twenty pound a week*: to keep her and him and me and my two sisters and if there wasn't a meal on the table when he came home, she'd *ave* it!

He was a gambler through and through. He used to run a big Pools syndicate in work and, once in a while, it would come up and there'd be like eight hundred pounds to pay out - but he *wouldn't have* put anything on. So he'd come home and my mum used to have to go to all these different Loan blokes, to get the money for him. Me and my sister used to sit in the bedroom on a Friday and Saturday night and when my father got off at the bus station, we'd know by the way he walked, whether my mother was going to have a hiding or not. If he'd lost, he'd be empty-handed. If he'd won, he'd have a carrier bag in his hand with little toys and presents for me and my sister. But we used to dread Friday and Saturday nights: being upstairs and hearing my mother getting battered downstairs, running to the neighbours and askin them to ring the police. In the end, we used to run away from home on a Wednesday, so we wouldn't see it, and sleep anywhere: in an open car, in a squat, in an old building, and survive by stealing milk off doorsteps. Then, after a couple of days, the police would find us and my mum and dad would come and collect us and take us home and give us a hiding and three or four days later we'd be off again!

My father had to pack his job in in the end and leave Cardiff, because the syndicate won sixteen thousand pounds and my mum couldn't go getting loans for *that* amount. And that's when they split up.

I kept running away after that but they always caught me. My dad had me for this one weekend and we got caught stealing shoes in British Home Stores. He'd load the bag up and leave it on the side and, cause I was little and nobody'd suspect me, I had to pick it up and walk out. He got remanded in custody and I was sent back home to live with my mum but by the time it came to court, they persuaded me to say that *he'd* come in the shop and caught *me* shoplifting and I'd run off with the bag. *E* got found 'not guilty' and I got sent to detention centre up in Gloucester.

As soon as I was sixteen, I walked out and moved into a squat in Newport Road. There was a lot of addicts in the squat, so I started dabbling and, in the end, I ended up on a script to get off heroin. The average person on the street is on twenty to thirty mils of methadone a day but *I* was on *one hundred* mils. I tried hard to come off it. The doctor told me 'You *can't* kick methadone just like *that* or it'll damage your insides. You've got to drop it down gradually to fifty, forty, thirty and so on.' So that's why I hitchhiked down to Swansea: to get away from my associates up there, who were *all* methadone freaks.

I started skippin in the High Street Car Park almost as soon as I got here and that's where I first met this lady here - Sara - and Rocco and Nicki and Rob. I last seen Rob on Christmas Eve, when I give him a Christmas card. He normally got his methadone in diluted form but, the way I heard it, this guy Tex sold him a five-mil capsule and he popped it all in one go. Killed him stone dead. Tex was *in* the tent when he took it and when he keeled over, instead of goin an makin an anonymous phone call to say somebody'd just o.d'd, he *walked.*

Rocco saw him in Burgher King a few days later. The place was full and everybody'd heard about Robbie and Rocco shouted out in front of everybody: '*There's* the murderer!' Tex threatened to do this and do that but loads of people stood up and said 'You're a *murderer!* You murdered Robbie!' He hasn't been seen since. But he can't deal no more and he can't come into Swansea either cause, word is on the street now and anyway, he's under investigation for homicide.

Rob was my brother and so is Rocco. When I say brother, I mean blood brother. Rob looked after me and I looked after him. You've gotto have that on the street: a shoulder to lean on when you need to. We went to Rob's funeral from The Big Issue office. Everyone done a couple of shovels and afterwards - d'you know what I done? I writ down my family's name and address and phone number and give it to Nicki and Rocco because if anything happens to me, they can contact my family. Cause, with Rob, nobody knew how to get in contact with anybody. He was just a pauper's beggar. He never told anybody nothing at all about his parents. He was on his toes. He was on the run and when you're on the run on the street, you're awful discreet. You change your name, you change your life history, you change it all.

There's a Security man down here in the car park - Viv: brilliant bloke! A real nice fella. Wakes us up in the mornin, makes sure we're breathin, gives us a fag each: and not just *one* mornin - *every* mornin! And there's a cleaner down there - an old, retired man - and once he's done his cleaning, he goes hunting: for *blankets!* Now, we're not untidy people. When we leaves in the mornin, we puts all our rubbish in a carrier bag and bins it, so it's not as though we're leavin him a mess. And we don't just scatter our blankets around, we *saves* them - puts them up on the pipes or somewhere safe. And then *he* comes along and takes them away or gets the fire hose out and *hoses* them. Sometimes he even hoses while we're sleepin: he don't shout a warning, he just soaks us. Last night he'd hosed my sleepin bag and Sara had to take a blanket off herself and put it over me. That's a very *sad* man, that is, mate: a very *sad* character.

D'you want to know the solution to homelessness? I'll tell you. Look at that building over there: that empty furniture warehouse. It's been empty for nearly two years. If that was *my* place, I'd black the windows out, bed it up, open the doors and say 'Get in there!' And then find two sensible boys - somebody like Rocco and myself - to look after it.

There's not enough houses in this world to cover the people what's on the street. Go into Housing Options: unless you're a woman and you're pregnant, they don't want to know. You go down the Social: they don't want to help you.

The other day, this lady had a fifty pound fine for peein in the street. Now where else can she go and pee, mate? She's banned from the Station and all the pubs. The other day she went to Port Talbot to see Irish Rick in the YMCA in Port Talbot. She came out of the Station, walked round the corner and they arrested her, brought her all the way back to Swansea for this fifty pound fine of peein in the street, yeah? And, like, the lady don't do it *in the middle* of the street, she's *discreet.* Took her from here then and gave her seven days in Eastwood Park in Gloucester. When they released her, cause it was for fines she didn't get a discharge grant, she just got a travel warrant and because she never signed on, they stopped her money for two weeks. And she couldn't get a Crisis Loan cause she's 'No Fixed Abode'. It's like the system's fighting against us, mate. Never *helped* her while she was in there. Just give her somethin to stop her rattlin and a travel warrant and sent her back to the car park. This lady have actually been bailed to Number One, High Street Car Park - by the *magistrates!* Bailed her to a *car park,* they did!

There's a pop song called 'Invisible' and it's sung by Elton John but we sings it all the time. It goes: *'Invisible! Feels like we're invisible!'* And we *are,* mate, cause people walks past and we're totally invisible. Now, don't get me wrong: for every two people what's bad in this world, there's ten what's good, yeah? But the bad ones don't half make up for the good ones! We're not sat on the street cause we *want* to be. We'd *love* a four-bed roomed house with three kids, a car in the car park and everything going right for us. People looks at us as if afterwards we're goin to go home. They don't realise we *are* home. *This* is our home. *This* is our street. And cause we're on the streets, we gets treated as totally different. If *you* came into Housing Options with me now, we'd be treated like the next human being but if me, Rocco or Nicki walked in on our own, it would be totally different. You're writing a book aren't you, mate? Well, just for *one* day, dress up scruffy and *look* like you're on the streets and walk in there and see the reception you gets. Try it as an experiment, it would *benefit* you. You go in and you stand there and first of all you're being

135

polite 'Can I put my name down for this?' and 'Can I do that?' But then they do their best to *degrade* you. They says things in such a way that you ends up sayin 'Listen: I haven't asked you to do *effin* this or *effin* that,' and then, all of a sudden, they'll say: 'Oh, we're not havin *that* attitude. *Leave!'* But the attitude wasn't there when you walked through the door. The attitude's come back off *them*. *Do it,* mate: walk in one day like that and, honest to God, you'll see a *total* difference to what you see when you walk in by yourself.

D'you know the Job-Seekers Allowance? D'you know if I goes in for that and I don't look too tidy, they can *deduct* my money. Well, *that* is hitting *us*: the street people. Not yourselves. Not the people signin on, who've *got* houses. The only people who's goin in not lookin too tidy, is the people who's sleepin on the bloody streets. They're actually takin money away from you and makin you lower, not trying to help you out and bring you up a bit.

You're down here in the nights and at about three in the mornin you can hear gales out there and you know by six o' clock all these lights are goin to go on and the Security'll come down and sooner or later you'll have to go out in it all. And when that happens, you feel as low as you can go. A *snake* can't go no lower - and a snake *slithers.*

'God bless the Soup Runs!' is all I can say. The Cyrenians come down here about half past seven in the evenings and if you're asleep, they leaves your soup and your sandwiches on the side and if you're cold you wakes up with an extra blanket on you. They are *lovely* people, okay? *They're* the *real* people in this world. They're the people who count to me - yeah!

Every Saturday and Sunday I beg in the Kingsway. I've seen so many hidings down there, you wouldn't believe! They're all on their way to the Clubs and you say 'Help us out, boys: spare a little bit of change!' And they'll say 'Aw, fuck *you!'* and they'll walk away and all of a sudden, there'll be three or four of them come back - usually eighteen or nineteen year olds - wantin trouble and they'll grab your hats, which is not worth havin cause there's only coppers in them. And, in the end, many a time I've just had to cover up and take it.

Everybody thinks we're drinkin on the streets cause we *likes* drinkin. We drink *to go to sleep,* mate. You can never go to sleep when you're sober - not on a cold night. This lady will *not* go to sleep on her own - sober or otherwise. Some nights, I come in at ten or

136

eleven o' clock and she's sitting up on a black bag waiting for me, cause she's scared. And we get up in the mornin and we're sat there rattlin. And the worst day on the street down here, is a Sunday. On Friday and Saturday there's people about to help us out but on Sunday there's hardly anyone - except these Christians on their way to church and they'll sit down and give you *booklets!* And they say 'Read *this* tonight,' or 'Say *that*, tonight and I'll *pray* for you.' Without doubt, for anybody livin on the streets, that's the worst day. *Nobody* seems to want to help you on a Sunday. Fair do's, in the week all the workers will help us out; but Sunday? *Forget it,* mate! All those do-gooding Christians who get their best suits out to go to church! 'Read *this* book, read *that* book: *this* book, *that* book.' You can't *eat* a book! You can't *sleep* on one!

I rung my mum on the second of February to wish her Happy Birthday. I said 'I'll ring you tomorrow, mam, to see if you had a good drink or not,' cause it was her sixtieth birthday and the first day of her pension. And I rung half a dozen times on the third and there was no answer. So then I rung my dad and said 'That's funny, dad - ' but before I could say anything else, he said 'I got a bombshell for you, son. She *went* last night.' She went the night of her birthday, so she made her pension and that was *it.*

Little Ritchie come to the funeral with me: all the way to Cardiff. My father was there but me and my family are *finished*, mate. I stayed at the back. I was the black sheep there - simple as that. My mum had had bronchial asthma and she was on a walking stick but, as far as I'm concerned, all the hammerings she took, contributed a little bit to what went down, yeah?

'Number One
High Street Car Park...'

Rocco

What the psychiatrist was telling me was that I'm originally classified as a paranoid schizophrenic. Like, you could be sittin here talkin to someone and I could be walkin down by there and I'd actually run back cause I'd think you were talkin about *me*, even if you weren't. *That's* how bad it is. That's why I wear a scarf round my face, cause I'm so paranoid I keep thinkin people are *lookin* at me. I used to have medication every month but I beat up two nurses and a doctor in Cefn Coed on Christmas Eve, so I just come off it. I've got eleven brothers and one of them's doin life in Broadmoor for choppin up my nanny and grampy. He's paranoid schizophrenic as well, like, and he won't speak to nobody but me, so if any of my family want to talk to him, they got to take *me* along, too. They tried to get me to go to Pen-y-Bryn Special School when my father died but when he was alive he told me 'It doesn't *matter* if you can read or write or spell as long as you can count money and *fight*.' So I become a fighting machine and as long as I can count money - which I *can* - I get by. Give me a thousand pounds in one pence pieces and I'll tell you exactly how much is there just by *looking* at it. It's just reading, writing and spelling, I can't get. But my missus is goin up to the library to get some of them what-you-call books - them *learning* books, which she's goin to say is for a child but which is actually for me. And then she'll read them to me and I'll read them to her. I can read a *bit*, like - to myself - but I can't read to you. If I read to you I'd get confused. What really embarrassed me was when my missus's family came down and her seven year-old sister actually spelt that word '*califragil* - what-you-call - *abnosious*'. She spelt *that!* Then she picked up a dictionary and was reading it to me and then she asked *me* to read it to *her*. I had to think of an excuse and walk out.

He appears halfway through my interview with Karl: combat cap pulled low and scarf pulled high, so that only the narrow slit of his eyes is visible. He won't sit down. He wants to know if anyone's seen Nicki, his 'missus'. He's promised me an interview on several occasions but doesn't want to do it on the street or anywhere where people might see his face. The three of us - Rocco, Karl and me - go up to the High Street Car Park and sit down against a wall on the basement floor. The car park is eerily empty. The interview takes place in semi-darkness.

My name is Rocco Ricco and I'm twenty-nine tomorrow. My father was a United States Marine and my mother was a GI bride. I was originally born in Sicily but I got brought over to Alltwen when I was a baby. My father owned hotels, garages, *everything* but cause of the pressures of business and cause he'd been through the war and was shell-shocked and had seen his mates getting blown to bits, he just couldn't handle it.

His family's from the Bronx and him and me went over when I was about nine and he got drunk and we got kicked out of where we were stayin and had to sleep in Central Park. When I woke up, it was pitch-black and I had my father's jacket over me and I could hear rustlin in the bushes and next thing this big black geezer jumps out with a knife and says 'I want your money and then I want *you!*' But what he hadn't counted on was my father being an ex-Marine and Special Forces and he'd heard him coming and was right behind him and he said 'Well, are you goin to *use* that blade on my son or do I have to wrap it around your throat?' And then this geezer just run off.

We come back over and then he took me to Hong Kong. And he got locked up and I was left in this hotel, which I didn't realize was a brothel. I was nine and a half and on my own in Hong Kong and I didn't speak the language. So I phoned my mother and she told me to go to the British Embassy but by the time I got there I'd already spent over four thousand pounds, cause I knew how to use my father's credit cards. They organized two body guards to escort me - cause there were these geezers everywhere tryin to pick up young boys for prostitution - and brought me back home to my mother in London.

I came down one morning dressed ready for school and found my father naked on the floor. I thought he'd had too much to drink cause they'd both come back drunk from a party the night before but what must have happened was they'd gone upstairs to bed and he must have sneaked down on his own and took an overdose. He took Valiums, tomazipans, cocaine, speed - he took *everything.* And cause I was just a boy, it took me half an hour to drag him onto the settee, and then, before he died, he turned to me and said 'Don't worry, son, you'll never want for anything cause I'm rich and you'll have *all* the money in the world.' And then he said 'God Bless the family,' and that was it: he died in my arms. The police took my school uniform off me and my brother's and found out later, through forensic, that *I* was the last person to hold him.

They locked me and my brother in the attic on the day of his funeral but my brother kicked the window through and I climbed down the drainpipe. I was covered in blood but I got to the funeral on time. I was the twinkle in my father's eye and I tried to commit suicide over him a few times. I've actually jumped off multistorey car parks and landed on buses - that's why I've got plates in my head - and even now, I can't go and see the grave or I'll end up diggin it up.

I've got one of the biggest families in Swansea: eleven brothers and fifteen blood brothers: which can't be bad, can it? Most of my real brothers are bouncers. My oldest's a Tai Kwondo expert and is the head bouncer in Ritzies. I got put into care after my father died, went through Borstal and then straight into prison for armed robbery. I was drunk and drugged and went into this garage and said 'Gimme the money!' and the woman said 'I bet you're *beautiful* underneath that mask,' and I took it off and they caught me straight on camera. I was in the pub after and a CID bloke came in and said 'Would you like to come and watch a film?' I said 'No, I wouldn't,' and he said 'Well, it's a *good* film, and it's about *you*.' So I had fifteen years with a recommendation that I do five.

I came straight from Dartmoor down to Swansea. I come out of High Street Station with all my stuff, not knowing where I was going and the first person I met was Dan 'The Man' Piper. It was funny. I saw him and I thought: 'He looks a bit of a boy - a bit of a drinker,' like, so I walked up to him and said 'Where's the nearest Off Licence?' He took me down the road and I bought four bottles of wine and two bottles of sherry and we went and got drunk and I ended up upside down in a bush on the Mumbles Road. I stayed with Dan for a couple of months. We skippered down behind the old Water Board and we drank around the back of Tescos.

He used to be in a band called 'The Dan-the-Man Band'. Nicki and me went down the Salvation Army last Christmas to hear him sing but because he hadn't done it for so long and everybody was clapping so much, he got stage-fright and had to speak the words instead of singing them. When he died, his son gave me his phone number and said to call round any time I needed help but I won't go cause I've got my missus and I don't trust *nobody* with my missus - not even my mother. But what we're goin to do this Tuesday, out of respect for Dan, is buy two bottles of Tudor Rose - which was his favourite tipple - and twenty Marlborough and sit behind the back of Tescos and drink it.

The first time I seen Nicki was in The Big Issue office. Me and my mate Tom qualified as the best sellers in Town and we went in the office one day and Nicki was there with this guy Gary and she was starin at me all the time. The place was crowded out, so I thought I may as well show off a bit and I walked up to the guy behind the counter and said 'I want *five hundred* Issues!' *Everyone* stepped back in amazement, like, and Nicki fell in love with me.

A couple of weeks later, Tom and me was selling Big Issues by the Quadrant and she come round the corner with Gary and Gary had to go somewhere so he asked if I'd look after her for a minute, 'But you *touch* her and I'll *kill* you,' he said. It was raining at the time and when he come back, she was wearing my jacket. So he tried to fight me but what he didn't realize was that I'm a Tai-kwondo expert, too, and I almost knocked him through a window. The police turned up and everything and Tom was so drunk, he ended up getting locked up and I ended up down Debenham's Car Park with Nicki. And I've been with her now for nearly two years off and on. We've had our ups and downs but we're still together. Nicki would do anything for me - *anything*. If I had a shotgun here now and told her to put it in her mouth and pull the trigger, she'd *do* it.

Before I come down to this Car Park, I was skipping over by the County Hall with Belfast Danny but I had all my stuff pinched. I had to sleep in my boxer shorts with a black plastic bag over me but fair play to the Security Guards there, they come out and they give me a boiler suit, cause they said they didn't have nothing else. They give me a pair of shoes that was two sizes too big, coffee, tea and a great big dinner. Belfast Danny was there too, but he was drunk and started performin and they only gave him a sausage sandwich. This was Sunday afternoon, so I went and done a bit of beggin and when I come back Sunday night, I couldn't believe it: they had clothes my size: jeans, shirt, top, hat, gloves, socks and shoes that fitted me.

Since I've been down here, my mother bought me five hundred quids-worth of equipment. I had sleeping bags, a little calor gas stove, walkie-talkies, Ghurkha knives and a hat you could pull over your face like a balaclava: *everythin* you could need to sleep out in the streets and I had it all in this massive rucksack. My missus had all her stuff in another bag:

all her underwear and stuff. And because it was raining we left it all underneath the ramp. But when we come back it was gone. So I asks one of the security guards - a big, plumpish geezer with glasses - if he's seen it and he says no but later on he says he's found my missus's tobacco tin, which she kept inside a pair of knickers in the bag. Now I searched around and *I* couldn't find that tin, so how come he just *happened* to find it? The tin had all her personal gear in it: photographs of her and me, some drawings she'd done, her birth certificate - but everythin, includin her knickers, was gone. And I still believe to this day, that *he* took it all - all five hundred quids worth. But what really got me was there was a map of Vietnam in there - a proper map of Vietnam - where my father was in the war. He gave that to me for a present and it was an actual map of where he went and got his mates out. So why did he want to take my gear, like? And why did he want to take my missus's underwear?

We don't stay in one place any more cause it's too dangerous. There's been two murders in here. There was a bloke came down the ramp the other night and he had a big breeze block and he didn't see us cause we was lyin in the corner in the darkness and he come down and *smashed* a geezer over the head with it. And there was another time a bloke got kicked to death for no reason at all. Me, Sara and Rick were all down here once and a load of blokes come down steamin drunk and they were goin to beat Rick up and try things on Sara but what they didn't realize was my cousin and my two brothers were comin from *that* way, with pizzas for us and my cousin Dewi carries a gun, like, and he *will* use it and he had them up against the wall and I've never seen them blokes since.

I've got a very *dangerous* family. When I was short of money, I actually *knife-fighted* for six years. My ex-manager offered Nicki twenty five thousand pounds to get me back into it, but Nicki turned the money down and said 'I'd rather have him alive than dead,' cause it only takes one cut along the jugular and I'd be a gonner.

When Nicki first came to Swansea with her father, he was claiming for her. He was gettin his giro, spendin all the money and not givin her nothin. Makin her do the cleanin and everythin and ave tea on the table when he got home. So that's why she left. We stayed in his place over Christmas but, when he come back from Devon, he threw us out on the street and had his friends livin there instead, so we can't go back. And we can't go to my mother's cause she remarried this old bloke who's a millionaire and thinks he's my father -

which he'll *never* be - and I hit him with a sledgehammer once.

When the nurse come down, she checked my head to see if my plates were out and then she checked Nicki and said she was goin to have the baby sooner than she thought. We can't go to Housing Options cause Nicki's under age and her mother's got custody over her, so they could send her all the way back to Devon and I'm not goin to mess her about - not while she's pregnant. On her eighteenth birthday her mother is goin to send her forty thousand pounds but, until that day, we can't do nothin.

We sleeps under the ramp there. When it gets *really* cold I gives *all* the blankets to Nicki cause I've got a Para's jump-suit and with that on I can sleep in gale-force weather. So I sleeps by the side of her but I always make sure I'm on the outside and she's against the wall. Because Nicki's pregnant, what we try and do if I've got enough money is get a cheap bed and breakfast for the night. Cause it's my birthday tomorrow, my mother paid for a dear hotel for us for the last couple of days. She's got a two hundred and fifty thousand pound boat she said I could ave and she's promised that when the baby comes she's goin to buy us a flat and give us twenty thousand pounds to get us started but Nicki'll have to do all the stuff about the electric and everything cause I can't read or write or spell properly.

Some people says to me 'How come you're on the streets and you got a mobile phone?' Well, what's it got to do with them? I could be on the streets and have a *car.* I know a guy who's got a Porche and he's livin on the streets! He just runs it off Benefits he gets. It's like you're sittin down here now and, for all you know, we could be *murderers* but, in fact, there's more decent people on the streets than there is out there and, believe it or not, some people have actually given us *money* for lookin after their car, cause when we're down here nothing gets broken into and they reckon we're better security than them upstairs.

I had the DT's down here one day. I was shakin and seein things goin up the wall and the Soup Run come down and switched on the lights and I freaked out. I chased them out of the car park and, God bless them, twenty-five minutes later they come back in with torches and apologized. This old geezer was good as gold: 'Shout as much as you like,' he said, 'I'm not goin anywhere until I see you *eat* somethin.'

D'you know when the soup run's not coming around, I've seen me and Nicki getting scraps out of the skip at the back of McDonald's and eatin them. There's also a bin up by Jungle Jim's there - where all the children go. We sit around the back until the party's finished and they bring the waste food out in black bags. There's usually fag ash and stuff on it but I wipe it off and put whatever it is in a bun and eat it. That's how we gotto survive on the streets. I've been in back street bins where I've actually *seen* used condoms in a sandwich. People put them in rolls hoping street people will come along and not open them up and eat them. But I've actually taken the condom out and *ate* the roll. That's ow ungry I've been!

'Aunty Mary had a canary...'

Tom and Sylvia (1)

They live in supported accommodation on the edge of Town. It's eleven o' clock in the morning when I call. Sylvia answers the door. She has thinning copper-coloured hair and bears the faded remnants of a black eye. Somebody once described her as the Edith Piaf of Cwmbwrla. That almost exactly sums her up physically but emotionally she's much closer to Blanche Dubois. Tom is sitting in their small, neatly-decorated living room with a glass of something next to his stockinged feet. He is tall and wiry, with a weather-beaten face that may once have been quite handsome. We talk for a while as Sylvia makes coffee. She's gone a long time. When she eventually returns, she hands us the coffee and goes and sits on the other side of the room. Tom's speech is slightly slurred. Sylvia speaks in a small, mostly refined voice, nervously miming the words at times or clapping a hand over her mouth when she thinks she's said something she shouldn't have. They swap chairs frequently during the interview, Tom several times crawling across the floor to retrieve his cigarettes or his drink or just to have some breathing space...

Tom: I'm fifty-seven and I was brought up in Fforestfach. My mother worked as a cook in Waynesmore's and my father was in the Tin-plate in Gorseinon. I was a paperboy when I was young. I was deliverin the paper one Christmas to Harry Secombe's mother's house and I think it must have been her birthday, cause he was inside singin 'Happy Birthday' and I stood outside the door listenin and when I gave them the paper, he never even gave me a Christmas tip: *Git!* I used to go and see him in the old Empire, an all. 'Appy days! But we never ad much money. I had a younger brother and they couldn't afford for us both to have school meals, so I used to ave to run ome from school dinnertime, make myself somethin to eat and run back again. Then, when I left school I went to work with my mother in Waynesmore's and it was *rubbish!* Seven o'clock in the morning to twenty to six at night, five days a week. Two pound nineteen shillings for all those hours! I asked for a rise after a month and he gave me half a crown. Two shillings and sixpence extra - and that was *it*. So I walked away and went as a milk boy. But it was still up at half past six in

145

the morning and I'm not an early riser so I said enough's enough and I was out of work for a long time.I was walkin down Wind Street one day and there was the Army Recruitin Office and I went in, filled the form in and was gone in a week. Bo-boom! Oh God, I was mad! I was seventeen and a half and I volunteered. I would have gone at eighteen anyway but I just thought *'Let's go!'* I went to Bataan for training. I loved it but some of the National Service guys didn't want to be there. They knew all the scams - how to work their ticket. You had guys drinkin Brasso and other guys pissin the bed every night - deliberately, *on purpose.* But the best one I saw was this National Service guy who started walkin around the parade square one day with a dog's lead. There was nothin on the end of it and he was walkin along goin 'Come on, Cyril! Come on, ducky, ducky, ducky!' And he had breadcrumbs in his hand and he was throwin them down behind him as he went. They locked him up. Put him in Roehampton Mental Hospital and I don't know what happened to him after that but that's the *Gospel* truth! I done my drivin test there and worked in the Stores, then they posted me to Cyprus and it was great but there was still trouble between the Greeks and the Turks and - I don't know whether I should say this but - well, we was on patrol one night and I was in this jeep with this Officer and a driver and this guy came running up the road towards us and the Officer shouts 'Stop him! Stop him! He's a *thief!*' So we chased him, caught him and put him in the cooler cell. He had nowhere to go. *Nowhere* to go. The Officer said to me: 'Shoot im!' I wouldn do it. He put a gun against *my* head. *I'm* a soldier, *he's* an Officer. He says: 'It's *you* or *im!* That's true. That's the God's honour truth. And I shot im. He was a Greek. Young boy he was. Same age as me. And I shot im.

Sylvia: He did. It's lived with him to this day. He shot him. He's goin to cry now.

Tom: I'm not kiddin -

Sylvia: He shot him he did. Didn you?

Tom: He was a *plonker!* This Officer was a right *plonker!* Even the Driver said: 'Shit! You're not goin to *shoot* im, are you?'... I wasn't there to find out what happened after. They bunged me out. I had no choice. Put me on a flight to Belgium, out of the way. Oh yeah, I reported im but they wouldn't believe me. *My* word against an Officer. Commanding Officer said to me: 'Ah, yes - Davies: *Belgium!* You're off.' Two days later, I was gone. I think about it now, mind. *That* will never die. I had the choice, didn I? 'Pull the trigger *or else* -!' So I turned the gun on him and killed him personally. The Officer was a right pratt.

146

Sandhurst Boy. I don't know his name. And I wouldn't mention names. No, no, I couldn't do that. No way -

Sylvia: Cheer up. Cheer *up!* Don't be so bloody depressin.

Tom: Anyway - went to Antwerp then. Antwerp: oof! Brill! Magical! Better than Brussels. I was in the army football team. I remember the first game we played: after the match, we has our meal and gets a lift into Amsterdam - ends up in the Red Light district. Oh boy! We're passin these shops - and I'm lookin now, aren't I? - and I thought they was clothes shops - with mannequins, you know, for modelling clothes? But they was *real* women - with *numbers* on them. I said to this corporal 'What's happenin there?' and he said 'Oh, just go in there, pick what you fancy, give a number and pay at the door.' I said 'No *way!* Fuck *this* game!' but all the other boys was goin in and there's *me* standin there like a dumbo!

Sylvia: Didn't you go upstairs?

Tom: No way. Never done *that* in my life.

Sylvia: Didn't you realize it was a whore house?

Tom: In the end I did, yeah. But I was *young* then. I was a *Swansea Boy,* wasn I? I never seen nothin like *that.* Never seen girls in windows. I come home and I told my old man -

Sylvia: *I* saw them in windows up in London once, with Derek -

Tom: And he wouldn't *believe* me!

Sylvia: He took me down Soho -

Tom: This was the late *Fifties,* this was -

Sylvia: And they were all callin him out the window: 'Come here, baby!' they were goin, 'Come here!'

Tom: *Numbers* on them! Never seen *nothin* like that before. And the boys was all goin in - !

Sylvia: And I shouted 'You leave him alone!

Tom: *'Come in, Number Seven! Come in, Number Twenty-nine -!'*

Sylvia: I was shoutin and screamin out on the street 'Keep *away* from him: he's my *boyfriend,* my **fiancé**!' and he was pullin me back and they were all sat there on their window sills goin 'C'mon, baby c'mon - !' And I says 'No *way!* He's *mine!'*

Tom: Yeah, Belgium: great! Magic! Magic people. I married a Belgian girl and it was great. I used to come home to Swansea, to Ystrad Road and I'd say -

Sylvia: D'you smoke, Alan?

Tom: 'Hey! They're open twenty-four hours a day out there - *every day of the year*!' And my old man wouldn't believe me. He would *not* believe me. And it was brilliant actually, because -

Sylvia: Tom: we *don't* talk about pubs all the time -

Tom: No! I'm just tellin the gentleman what it was like in the Army.

Sylvia: We *don't* talk about pubs all the time. We don't. We talk about *life*, we talk about *living* but we don't talk about *pubs*.

Tom: I *am* talkin about *life*, love! I'm talkin about the Army. My mother and father never went abroad in their lives, till I joined the Army. The furthest they'd been was Bristol. On my life! And they come there, to Belgium - my mother, my father and my uncle - and my father and my uncle wouldn't believe they were open twenty-four hours a day. So I took them round one Sunday morning at half past ten and, oh my God, I'll never forget it! My uncle was a miner and bigger than me: six foot two and built like a brick shit ouse. I said 'We'll go in here now. And the beer is *strong* and it's ice-cold and you don't get pints you get litres. So take a tip from me and *don't* drink too fast, cause it *its* you.' Gordon Bennett! He ended up dancing on the pool table!

Sylvia: I used to go with a University Lecturer. D'you want to hear about him?

Tom: My mother and father never travelled till I was in the Army. They been to the Eifel Tower and they been to Luxembourg -

Sylvia: Miles, his name was. Nice man, he was -

Tom: And they didn't do *that* until they were in their sixties!

Sylvia: He used to take me everywhere -

Tom: Enjoying yourself?

Sylvia: I'm just telling him about my Lecturer, Miles. He was a Lecturer in the University: Philosophy -

Tom: Ave you finished?

Sylvia: Yes, I've finished. Have you *started*?

Tom: No, when I was in the Army, it was great. I met this lovely girl and I got married.I finished with the Army and she came over here to live. I ended up in the pits in Garn Goch: a miner. At the coal face. And it was *rubbish*! I likes to be out in the open. I likes to *see* life, cause I was a good footballer. I played for the Welsh League: Fforestfach. And she said 'I'm not stayin ere,' so she bogged off back to Belgium. Young boy that I am, I followed her. And I signed on again - boo-boom! - just like that. Another ten years. But it was great. I love the Army: Germany, Arnheim. Ended up in Bicester or 'Bigh-cess-tah' as they call it. Oxford! What a *dump*! It was *rubbish*! My God, it *was* -

Sylvia: That's nothing. I had to go all the way to Porth - Aberporth - and live in this big house with my father's sister *and* take the baby with me. And my aunty used to say 'Come on in, Syl. How are you doin today, Syl! And I used to say -

Tom: Is there an ashtray ere?

Sylvia: Under your nose. Under your *nose*! And I used to say 'What d'you want *now*, Cook?' - 'Cook', we used to call her - and she'd say -

Tom: Yes, Oxford was *ab-sol-ute rubbish*! You're talkin about a *big* depot now - and we had four of them. You're talkin about miles and miles -

Sylvia: D'you ever shut up?

Tom: I'm talkin about the army.

Sylvia: For *God's* sake: d'you *ever* shut up?

Tom: You had Ordnance and you had the Pioneer Corps -

Sylvia: Tell im to shut up.

Tom: And we used to book everythin in and everythin out. Then you had the Engineers, then you had -

Sylvia: *Do you ever* SHUT UP! Does the gentleman *have* to know all these things?

Tom: Okay, okay - I'm goin over there. C'mon, *you*! I've had enough of telling my life away. *Your* turn now - oh God, I'm drunk. I spilt my tea now.

Sylvia: It's not tea, it's coffee. Oh shit: he can't even hold the cup. Be *real*, Tom! He's hopeless. What did Alan Morgan say to me? Alan Morgan, his Support Worker was here and he said to me 'You could keep Sylvia talkin for four hours!' He said that, didn't he? 'You could keep Sylvia talkin for *four* hours!' That's what he said.

Sylvia: *He* knows all my history: I was born in Brynhyfryd, I'm forty-seven and I've got one brother. He was killed on the road. He was only three. And my mother had a nervous breakdown. My father was out abroad... (Is that all right, so far? I'm not borin you, am I?)... Oh, it was a tremendous childhood. Yes, tremendous. My grandfather lived with us. Datci. He was a lay preacher and Welsh - totally Welsh. He died when I was eleven. I came home from a School trip one day and they said 'Don't go upstairs,' - you know, it was like that in those days - and my grandfather had died. He used to take me up the Old Men's hut. He used to buy me gingerbread men. 'Come on, gal!' he used to say. He was totally old-fashioned. I'm sorry if *I* sound old-fashioned but I am. I'm totally old-fashioned.

Tom: Old Mother Time!

Sylvia: My other aunty - my mother's sister - lived next door and I used to go in there and she had one of those great big black things they used to cook on - a *hob*, yes that's it! - and a little frying pan and she used to cook me meals - egg and chips, always egg and chips - and I used to love going in there and sitting and reading a book with her. 'Aunty Mary,' I used to call her, always 'Aunty Mary - '

Tom: *Aunty Mary had a canary up the leg of her drawers!*

Sylvia: I'd sit down with my book and everything and 'All right, gal?' she used to say. Always 'gal'. And mammy used to cook her Sunday dinner and she used to say to me 'Take aunty Mary's Sunday dinner in,' and I used to take it in. She was an old maid, she was -

Tom: Who built Swansea Greyhound Stadium?-

Sylvia: Never got married, never -

Tom: My *father!* And his friends. All the boys from Ystrad Road. I used to carry the buckets of cement -

Sylvia: What are you talking about?

Tom: The Greyhound Stadium in Ystrad Road.

Sylvia: I never heard my grandfather preach but he was a lay preacher and he used to go round and they all loved him. He used to have a pipe -

Tom: I used to be a choir boy and every Sunday mornin the choir master - Mr. Thomas, he owned the shop in Ystrad Road - used to chase us down the road and we used to run like ell -

Sylvia: And Datci used to sit there with his pipe - always a pipe -

Tom: Oh God! He used to chase us from mornin till night. Every Sunday mornin -

Sylvia: And he used to order me around sometimes: 'Oy, *you!*' he used to say -

Tom: And if he caught you, he used to pick you up by the ear: 'C'mon *you!* Get in that vestry!' Oh, he was strict. Very strict. Know St. Peter's Church? Harry Secombe's brother? I was confirmed by him.

Sylvia: I was supposed to be baptized but I wouldn't go -

Tom: I was only fourteen and I was confirmed. A whole batch of us. Oh, *happy* days...!

Sylvia: I went to Private School: Clarke's College. Secretarial: shorthand typing, bookkeeping, office management and all that. I was only sixteen at the time and it was difficult. I used to go round with the surfers, believe it or not. Langland Bay? I used to wear a white bikini. That was the *in* place in those days. The *in* crowd. I used to wear a white bikini and I had hair down here. Long blond hair. I used to go round in all these Jags and Sports cars and I used to sit in the back and pose.

Tom: And there was *me*, fighting for my country. Gordon *Bennett!* Up to my neck in muck and bullets!

Sylvia: All my friends lived down in Derwen Fawr. Very, very wealthy people. They all had money and cars. D'you know Rachel Manning and Philip? And Penny Sokolov. She was my best friend. Her mother used to keep Thomas's Shops. Jews they are.

Tom: Jews! They are the *worst.*

Sylvia: No, they're *nice* people.

Tom: They're worse than Nazis. I can't stand em. She just asn't been around. I was in Berlin. I been there in the Army - and I been to Auschwitz!

Sylvia: Penny's a lovely girl. Her mother used to run Thomas's Shops. She was Manageress there. We used to go there a lot.

Tom: Oh God, yes, I been in Auschwitz. What a *place*!

Sylvia: I went round with all the surfers and then I met my first husband and got pregnant and had a baby and he treated me like shit. He was a drinker. He just left me in the house and I had to look after his Gran. And Gran used to go wandering, so I used to have to go and look for her. Hard work? *Tell* me about it! Then I got agoraphobia and they put me on nerve tablets: Valium, Ativan, antidepressants, sleepin tablets - you name it - I was on them all. They kept changing them all the time. Then, when I had the baby, I couldn't keep still. It's true. I knitted a forty-eight jumper in a fortnight. Knitted it. In a fortnight. The breakfast table would be laid at three o' clock in the morning. They couldn't get me down. The psychiatrist came to me and said 'We've got to do something. It's your *body*. We've got to slow it down, otherwise you'll be ill.' Kept putting me on something all the time. Then I come off them, just like that. Aven't seen a tablet for blinkin years. Had withdrawal symptoms then, didn I, babes? Oh yes, it was very hard but *he* doesn't understand.

Terrible it is! You sweat, you shake, you've got fear of everything. You think everybody's looking at you. You think the *whole world* is looking at *you*. They're not but you *think* it. I had to go to a Treatment Centre in Weston Super Mare. It cost two hundred and eighty pounds a week and I was there for nine weeks. I was in there with Charmian, Oliver Reed's ex-girlfriend, and this Cabinet Minister's daughter. And there was a Lord and a Lady. I worked in the kitchen with the Lord. It was very vigorous treatment. You had to scrub the carpets, clean the dormitories, cook the food and things like that. My friend died. She couldn't take it. She walked out one day after seein her family and they found her on the roadside. She died of pneumonia and alcohol. Charmian was very beautiful: she stood very tall and had very long, blond flowing hair but the Cabinet Minister's daughter was a right little snob. They used to talk about how they got pissed and used to get thrown in the swimming pool - things like that. And there was group therapy, mornin and night and you had to tell your life story and mine was turned down *three* times by my Councillor, cause she said it was too unbelievably *good*. And when you'd done your treatment, you got a little medal, like a kind of a half-moon thing and they presented it to you and all the group were there: Lords and Ladies - you name it - and they're all clapping and everything and you just have to go through it. I got a job on a Health Farm after that - with my second husband.

Tom: You were a *pig*, weren't you? Oh dear, I gotto laugh at *that* one. That's a *joke*, that is!

Sylvia: Give me a fag. You don't understand. I don't like talking about my life. I *mean* it.

Tom: Neither do I! But if we *say* we're gonna do it, we *do* it. It's as simple as that, as far as *I'm* concerned.

Sylvia: I got married the second time - I hope you're not going to laugh at this - *over the phone*. Yes, through one of these Dateline things. He came *fifty-two* miles to see me. From Cwmbran. And we ended up married. It only took about two or three conversations. He liked the sound of my voice and I ended up marrying him. It's *true!* He was the same age as *him*. Fifty-seven. Ten years older than me. He was a Road Safety Officer with the Police. And *he* laughs at what I'm going to tell you now, but it's *true*, even if you'll never believe it: we once took Coco the Clown in my car. Really, it's absolutely *true!* Ray picked him up and brought him back to the house because he did these Road Safety things with the Police and Schools. And he said 'D'you mind Coco coming with us?' and I said '*Who?*' and he said 'Coco the Clown! D'you mind him coming with us?' And I said 'Are you serious or what?' but there he was, fully dressed in his clown's outfit, sitting in my car, on the M4 with his feet sticking out the window. And I said 'Are you all right, Coco?' and he said 'Yeah, I'm all right, gal!' *He* laughs but it's true: Coco the clown and me and my car...

Sylvia: The marriage didn't last. He went off with a sixteen-year old.

Tom: She should ave gone off with Coco the Clown. Done me a favour.

Sylvia: I'm being serious, mun. I *ave ad Coco the Clown* in my car! *The* Coco! He's a twat, he is. He was walking round Cwmbran with these big shoes on and he was going like this and I said 'Are you serious or what?' And he says 'Come in the car with me, gal!'

Tom: She should ave gone off with him. Gordon Bennett! Saved me a bloody fortune.

Sylvia: I went into a Refuge after my husband ran off. I just walked out on him. I had *everything* in my home, right? I had velvet curtains, I had a gold lamp, I had a dining suite, wall to wall carpets, peach bedroom: *everything.* But no, he went off with a sixteen-year old and I couldn't cope with it. I lost it all and he's still with her, in that house. I came back home - to Morriston - and went in a Refuge. I can't tell you the address. It's not allowed. My husband knew where I was, though, and he used to come and see me - until I met Cyril. I met him in the Top Rank. I was about thirty-odd -

Tom: And bald...

Sylvia: ...Cyril was great. Tremendous! I had a daughter - a baby girl - off him. Rebecca.

Tom: Tell the gentleman what he done. Go on - tell him... He *abused* her.

Sylvia: He didn't.

Tom: He did.

Sylvia: He *didn't.*

Tom: He bloody *did!* **You** know it and *I* know it. What a cunt! He got five years and I want her to *say* it. Go on. Tell the gentleman what he done.

Sylvia: I was sitting in my flat one day - *expensive* flat - in Cwmorfa and my aunty phoned me and said 'There's something on the Evening Post.' And it was somethin he done to my daughter...

Tom: *Tell* the bloke! He came here for an interview. Tell im! Speak your mind. I'd tell the bloke - no problem! Do you good. Get it off your chest.

Sylvia: All right, can I skip that?

Tom: I wouldn't. I *wouldn't!* Strictly the *truth,* pal!

153

Sylvia: It's all right, if you want to know about it. Do you want to know about it? It's not too upsetting. I've got over it now. Yeah: he was ad up. I didn't know anything about it until I got the phone call. Five years he had. I phoned him but I phoned his sister up first. I said 'Rita?' and she called me everything under the sun. I said 'Rita, *who's* in prison: *me* or *him*? Grow *up*!' I said, 'For goodness sake. *Who's* in prison?' I don't know what happened. She was only two and a half - God love her - and she never got over it... What else do you want to know? Do you want to know anything else? Just tell me what you want to know. I was homeless once...

Tom: Oh God! Can I get out of here? She's telling lies, now. She's doin my head in. Even the cat's gone berserk!

Sylvia: I was *sort* of homeless. I was livin in Townhill at the time but I was havin hell up there. They were smashing my door, smashing my windows and gettin in and stealin everythin. I was livin in fear, so I rang Paxton Street and they said I could come down. I was only there for two weeks and that's where I met Dick Ead here. He came in one day for a drink and said 'I've got a flat,' and would I come back to it? I said 'What about Paxton Street? They'll check up on me.' 'Oh, fuck *em*!' he said - scuse my language - 'Fuck *em*!' he said, 'You're with *me!..*'.

Tom: I met er in the Plough and Harrow and you was black and blue, wasn you? I said 'Oo it you? A lamppost, was it?' and she said 'No. A bloke beat me up.' Her face was all brown and yellow, you know? I said 'D'you fancy a drink or something?' but she bogged off and left me! Next day, I went there again and she was there and before I could say anything, she said 'I'll have that drink now.'

Tom: When I first went to Paxton Street, they put me in the shed. On my life! I was homeless and they had a shed out the back there - it's not there now - where they kept mattresses and they stuck me in there. I was on top in a sleeping bag. Just to get me *in* the place, cause it was freezin outside and there were no rooms available. And on the Sunday, this guy signed out and I signed in. And that's how I met Dan: Dan 'The Man' Piper or Daniel Wal-ter Piper, as I always called him. Dan had been in the Merchant Navy and that's how we became friends. And when he mentioned Franky's Bar, Antwerp one day, I *knew* he'd been there, cause I was there eight years and I knew it well. It's a place where blokes - can I say this? - dress up as women and you couldn't tell the difference.

My mates took me there when I was in the Army and when I heard these two blokes say 'Two beers for two queers!' I nearly fell off my chair!

Tom: He liked his sherry, Dan. Oh God! He liked his sherry. He bought me a bottle in the Glamorgan and he said 'C'mon, Sarge,' - he always called me 'Sarge' cause I *was* a Sergeant - and we took off and we was friends. He was a cad and a bounder but you couldn't help liking him. Do you know the Water Board building? We used to drink down behind there every Tuesday morning, first thing. Two litres of cider, four cans and a bottle of sherry. Oh boy! The cider was for me, the cans were for Jimmy and the sherry was for Dan. Every Tuesday until the Duchess opened. Then we went across to the back room. *She* doesn't want to know about it.

Sylvia: It makes me ill. I don't like it. I don't like pubs.

Tom: Last time he saw me, he bought me a pint. I couldn't *believe* it! He owed me eighty quid. He said 'Here you are, Sarge. I gotto go now,' and that was the last I saw of him. Two days later he was dead. I met his mother and she got the same trouble as me: her toes. Poor circulation. They took a couple off, just like they done with me. Oh, a lovely lady! She was sittin on this bed and 'Here you are, Sarge,' he says, 'Here's my mum!' I said 'Ello, darlin.' and I sat by the side of the bed and I was talkin to her. Oh, a lovely lady. Pontardawe somewhere, I think it was. Yes - *Pontardawe!* I'm sure of it.

Sylvia: He's rabbitin again.

Tom: Oh, I *loved* him -

Sylvia: Shut up. You're rabbitin again.

Tom: He was a bounder and a cad but -

Sylvia: Shut up! You're *rabbitin* again!

Tom: He was *straight* -

Sylvia: For **Godsake**, Tom! You're **rabbitin!**

Tom: I'm not. I'm speakin the truth.

Sylvia: You *are*. Look at him: he's got a pinny on!

Tom: My Key Worker won on the horses one Saturday and we had this party in Paxton Street and Alan comes in and says 'Right: *you, you* and *you,*' - me, Jimmy and 'Frank Sinatra' Piper - 'We're going over to this pub in Wind Street.' We were almost skint and we had to get rid of her so we gave her two quid and told her to get half an ounce of tobacco and a packet of papers down the petrol station and we all bogged off to Wind Street. (Come nine o' clock she *found* us. I don't know *how,* but she *found* us.) And Dan, that night, he sang a song on the Karaoke. I'd never heard him sing before. I think it was a Dean Martin song - a very slow, laid-back number and oh my God! We all sat there goo-goo eyed. What a voice - !

Sylvia: Alan: being serious for a moment: do you want to hear about Miles now?

Tom: Miles?

Sylvia: Yeah, my Lecturer.

Tom: Who?

Sylvia: Miles!

Tom: Who the hell's *Miles?*

Sylvia: I *did* tell you about Miles. My Lecturer in Swansea University. I went out with him. Are you deaf or what? He lectured in Philosophy. I met him in the Kings Arms - before I met *you.* He was reading a newspaper and he spoke to me. 'All right?' he said. Then he bought me a drink and took me in his car: down Penclawdd -

Tom: Cockle-pickin, wannit?

Sylvia: This is my *real* life, this is, and it's true! Check it out. Why shouldn't it be? I'm not ugly am I?

Tom: I'm sayin *nothin!*

Sylvia: He said 'Can I see you again?' And I said 'Yes,' and he said 'I'll pick you up,' and, of course he's in love with me now, isn't he? And then he had to go away -

Tom: Locked him up, did they?

Sylvia: He had to go away but he brought me back a bottle of wine.

Tom: Probably stole the bastard thing!

Sylvia: And what else did he buy me? He bought me something else as well -

Tom: Gordon Bennett: even the cat's bored. Look at her: she's doin a flop -

Sylvia: It didn't last long -

Tom: Until she drank the bottle of wine!

Sylvia: And he took me down Three Cliffs - in the middle of January - and I paddled in the sea, I did. Like a twat. He was a Lecturer, Miles. A straight-faced Lecturer for Godsake and I'm paddling out up to my knees and he's standing there shouting 'Sylvia, come back! Come *back*! and I just kept on going and shouted back at him 'Oh for goodness sake, leave me a - *lone*!'

'Delta, Alpha, Romeo, Victor, Echo, Lima, Lima...'

Wayne

I started writing my life story last night and finished it this morning. It's only half a page long. Not a helluva lot happens to *me*!

I don't tell *lies* and I don't tell the *truth*. I just *exaggerate* a bit. We had a fire practice in School once and while we were havin it, a *real* fire broke out in a demountable. Some *bright spark* must have started it but when I went to tell the Headmaster, because I told so many lies when I was little, he wouldn't believe me. Until the demountable burnt down...

He's smartly-dressed in shirt and tie and a charcoal-grey suit, which has the bottom of one leg half-torn away. The backs of his hands are a mess of self-inflicted cuts. He's shaved off his moustache and beard and, for good measure, his eyebrows as well.

*One afternoon at the end of February, seven weeks after he was first admitted to the Hostel. I arrive early for the Soup Run and he greets me in the passageway with the news that his brother Terry died last night. I express my condolences but don't take him too seriously as he's told me the same story on at least two previous occasions. Both offices are in use, so there is nowhere else to go but the front seats of the Outreach minibus. As soon as he sits down, he picks up an imaginary mouthpiece from the dashboard and speaks urgently into it: 'Delta Alpha Five-Six-Five calling: Could you let me know if Lyn Darvell is wanted, please? **Dar-vell**: Delta, Alpha, Romeo, Victor, Echo, Lima, Lima - .' 'Okay. I'll get back to you: Oscar Five, out.'*

I was a bit nervous when I first came here but since I've been in the Hostel, people are beginning to respect me: outside and inside. When I go out in the mornins, nobody recognizes me any more, cause I'm washed and shaved and in a suit.

Some people still thinks 'The dirty bastards should be back inside!' but they shouldn't call us names, cause we're innocent and we're human like anyone else.

(Although, Lyn don't *smell* like a human, but that's beside the point.) Some of them still wind me up - especially in the Hostel. Lenny went out last night and told somebody I was a murderer and the bloke came back to the Hostel lookin for me: a bloke called 'Sparky'. You might know him as 'Rocco'. But normally, if anybody in here says anything, I don't go for them I just laugh it off or go and tell the staff. That's what they're there for.

When I was twenty-five, I got put in Cardiff prison for nicking a bag of sweets from Woolworth's in Neath. Four days I got - just to frighten me. Then, in 1985, a woman was murdered in a Sex Shop in Swansea and they knew it wasn't Paul and me cause we were helping the police with the barriers straight after they found the body but we got convicted and did nine and a half years in prison. We got put on Rule 43 when we were inside, which is a section for sex offenders mostly. It was supposed to be for your own protection but, some officers don't like 'nonces' as they're called, and many a time the door was opened for other cons to walk in and beat us up. Mostly they hit me where the marks wouldn't show but I was slashed a couple of times and these burn-marks on my arm were not self-inflicted: they're what they done in prison. I reported it but nothing ever came of it. I don't think the Governor liked 43's either.

I felt like suicide many a time. I didn't have visitors and none of the family came to see me until about a year after I was convicted. They noticed all the cuts and burn marks - even took photos of them - and wrote to the Home Office but they just ignored it. They separated Paul and me after a month. He went to a secure unit in Wakefield and I went to Dartmoor. It was bad luck for me because Paul was my bodyguard. He's *big* and he used to look after me. It was a godsend that my mother was spared seein it all but if she'd have been alive, I don't think she'd have let it happen. We'd have been still at home.

I didn't get to see the Rough Justice programme but I can get a copy of it if I want it. Actually, it was the Devon and Cornwall police that started the ball rollin. They had an investigation after that programme and found out about the fabricated evidence. *'Fabricated'*: that's a good word for me, especially with *my* upbringing! The one who came and saw me in prison, was David Jessell, the producer of the programme. He said in January '92 that I'd be out by July 14th or he'd put his job on the line - and by the 14th July, I *was* out. When I come out of prison I was on another programme with David Jessell and - this is serious, this is - when he went to London to do this programme with me, somebody nicked his hat and *I* got the blame for it. The day before my release, this guard said to me: 'Pack your stuff.' I said 'Why? Am I moving to another prison?' He said 'Yes, you're goin to Brixton.' I said 'What's this in aid of?' He said 'Just do as you're told and pack your stuff.' Then the Governor called me in and told me I was being released. He said 'Look, sorry about the past and what we've done to you - ' But I turned round and said 'It's no good you apologising to me *now*, because the damage has been *done.*' So I stayed overnight in Brixton and the following morning - the fifteenth of July 1992 - I had to go to the Appeal Court. I can't remember getting out to be honest with you. All the cameras and reporters were there waitin for us and I know I was carried from the Court to the ambulance, cause I collapsed - emotionally and physically. I was coming down the stairs and I fell and knocked myself out. It was in all the papers: 'MAN FREED FROM COURT KNOCKS HIMSELF OUT'. I stayed overnight in the Hilton with my brothers - Robert, Paul and Derek - and, ever since I've been out, apart from staying with my family for a couple of months, I've been on the streets.

It's been five years now. I've been back in, but not for something I didn't do. Since I've been in the hostel I've been good. I've only had one official warning - for shouting at Len the other day when he called me a murderer - and I've been chucked out once for drinking on the premises, but they let me back in again after an hour. I do lots of jobs here. I cleaned the toilet out on Sunday and they paid me time and a turd for doin it. The police came last week and tried to have me for attempted rape or something but one of the workers said 'No way. He was here nearly all day.' And he *knew*, cause that was the day we couldn't move the bins out of the Yard cause of the cars, so I had to put all the rubbish in bin bags and carry them out to the lorry.

I've settled down well. I'm not gettin no money at the moment, apart from what my brother Derek gives me out of the compensation every week, but the Hostel are sorting that out. I've got my own little radio at last and I'm hoping now to find a flat and move on to greener pastures if I can, because I know I can't stay here indefinitely. I'd like to have Lyn with me actually, cause he's a bloody good cook. He looked smart the last time I saw him. Well, he *should* do, cause I lost my suit and *he* had it on. He'd take your *teeth* if you yawned long enough! But I'm worried about him cause I haven't seen him for four days and I found out last night, he's got bronchial asthma and shouldn't be on the streets. Terry saw him legless by High Street Station yesterday. Couldn't move. So they phoned the ambulance and took him into hospital. If you see him on the Soup Run tonight, tell him to come down and see me.

Yes, I like it in the Hostel. My room's a bloody tip but around half past eight tonight I shall be having a nice shower. It's not my birthday and I don't *need* one but I'm having one, *anyway.* Remember the date: it's the twenty-third of the second, 97!

So, thank you, Alan for this interview. I was bored watching Eastenders and it's been nice to talk to somebody sensible on a Sunday afternoon. We'll continue after the Break...'

MARCH

'The Search for the Dragon's Egg...'

Nicki

I'll be stayin down here now for a couple of hours, get up enough money for breakfast and some dog food and a drink and then come back and get up enough for some Polyfiller and what we normally do is go back to the house by about two and paint a few more walls and Polyfill some more holes. And then we'll do the same thing again tomorrow and the day after, until it's all done. We've got the Electricity, the Water and the Gas coming on Monday and we've got to get all the locks changed as well. Other than that, we're *getting* there: slowly but surely.

She's exactly where Rocco said she would be: in 'The Pit', in one of the subway tunnels under the Kingsway Roundabout. She's got their recently acquired dog with her and, although it's still quite early on a bright Saturday morning, she's already begged a considerable amount of money. A dark, brown-eyed, very pretty girl, she speaks quickly and articulately and with a pronounced West Country accent.

I was born in Weymouth. My dad used to work on making and testing torpedoes down in Portland Harbour. They used to go out in little rubber dinghies but he got caught by fumes a couple of times and nearly died, so he had to give it up. He worked on his brother's trout farm after that and when I was old enough, me and him used to go off in a lorry weekends deliverin trout up to Cumbria and places. We carried something like four tons of fish and I used to control the oxygen tanks so it didn't get too low while we were drivin and kill them all. My mum and dad split up when I was about six or seven. She remarried and moved to Honiton in Devon but I didn't get on with the person she remarried so she sent me back to my dad, who was living in Axminster, about twenty minutes away. I stayed with my dad in the week and my mother at weekends and we found we got on better like that. I get on well with them both but me and my mum can't live together in close surroundings. We just argue all the time.

My dad came to live in Loughor for three years, just for a change really. He'd been doing building work in Axminster and got a job in Swansea drivin cement mixers. He got remarried just before he came here and I used to go and visit them a lot. I helped build part of Swansea prison. You know that new hexagonal extension? He laid the foundations for that and I helped him.

My mother did proof-reading for a living and still does. Every weekend she'd give me a book and let me proof-read it in the week and take it back. It was good fun. She did quite a few famous authors: Stephen King, James Herbert, James Clavell. I read one by Stephen King called 'Cujo', about a year before it came out on the shelves. And she also used to work for a video company, checking videos before they sold them in the shops. I was quite lucky I suppose: I used to read books and watch videos before anybody else had seen them.

I got on brilliantly at School. I'd have the occasional day off and then if I missed too much, I used to have private tutoring in the evenings, but it was mostly weekends and school holidays I used to see my father. I passed all my GCSE's: English, French, Physics, Chemistry, Biology. The only one I didn't pass was Mathematics cause I could never quite grasp fractions and decimals and stuff like that. I went into the Sixth Form for a while and moved around from college to college but found I'd rather go out to work, so I dropped out.

When she became pregnant, my stepmother wanted to move nearer her family, so they moved back to Devon. They split up not long after that and my father worked as a barman in Axminster for a couple of years. I used to help him behind the bar but I was only allowed to serve lemonade and waitress. I worked with a cleaning firm for a bit and then I was doin fettling: filing down the rough edges of ceramic toilet-roll holders before they got put in the kiln. I was making a hundred and twenty pounds a week doing that, for just a couple of hours a day in the evening.

I travelled around with my father a lot, living in caravans and things like that. We came back to Swansea about two years ago now. We lived in Dunvant first of all, with friends, and then moved to the Uplands. My dad started doing an electrician's course in College. He used to bring home his projects and I'd read through them and he'd test me on them, so I know quite a bit about electrics. He gets tellies and stuff like that - things people throw away - and fixes them up and sells them on. He's got a roomful of about twenty tellies and seventeen video players and makes quite a lot of money out of it.

Just over a year ago, me and my dad started having a few rows. I'd started selling The Big Issue round about that time and that's when I first met Rocco. We got so attached we decided to stay together and try and get ourselves sorted out. It was mostly the car park for that first year and the sea front: places like County Hall and that. Every now and again, when we got up enough money, we'd shoot off to a hotel down the Mumbles somewhere. It was either Issue selling or begging to begin with. We used to do really well with The Issue but I found I could make even more money begging. At first, my dad didn't approve of Rocco, mainly because of his drink problem. But then Rocco and me got together and worked on reducing his drinking and, when we last went round to see my dad a couple of days ago, he was quite impressed.

Rocco and I had a Gypsy wedding. There were only a couple of people there. One of them had to read the words and we had to jump over a stick, holding hands and then we had to swap an item that we felt was sacred to us. So we swopped our rings. And then it was a case of having one helluva drink afterwards. It was on the twenty-seventh of June, so in a year and a day from then, we've got to do it all again. But once the house is sorted out, we're planning on doing the *real* thing. And then it will be forever.

For a long time, we weren't sure what the pros and cons were about getting a house. When I first met Rocco I was only sixteen and my mum had custody of me. I thought I'd be sent back or put into care, so I didn't get up the courage to actually go to Housing Options and find out. But then, when we finally *did* go, on the very same day, they said they'd give us a two-bedroomed house. So we needn't have worried in the first place.

It's a nice place up in Mayhill. It's a half hour walk to get into town but it's only two pound by taxi, so we get a taxi up there every night and walk back in the morning. It's got two bedrooms, a living room, a bathroom, a kitchen and a couple of big closets as well as a back and a front garden. It's just a case of re-wallpapering and repainting basically and getting carpets down. We haven't got anything in the way of furniture at the moment. The City Temple helped us out with blankets and stuff and they're goin to try and get us a bed or, rather, two single beds. So we're just goin to have to join them together.

Yes, I had a miscarriage. A few weeks ago now. Rocco and I have had a long talk about it since and we decided that we *still* want to have kids but we really want to get ourselves sorted out first: finish the house and start earning some decent money.

I might go back to college part-time to do an electronics course. Cause of the work I've done with my dad, I could probably jump straight in at GCSE level and it's handy now cause if someone chucks away an old telly or wants one repaired, ninety percent of the time I can fix it. Rocco's planning on getting a job as well. I don't know what: tyre-fittin, mechanical work, painting and decorating - all sorts of things, really. The house is doing Rocco good because he's got something to concentrate on now. It's a case of not being in the same old situation and doing the same old things all the time: he's got something to *focus* on and look forward to. Once we're settled down, there's definitely no chance we're coming out on the streets again. We discussed that, too. There's no *way*. But we'll still come and see all our old friends and things like that.

I love writing. I'm writing a book at the moment. It's a story about a kid who runs away from home and goes on this adventure. He comes across a door in a mound and there are three fingers trapped in the door and when he opens it, the fingers fall off and run away. It's a bit gruesome but I *have* had a book published before, when I was about ten or eleven. It was called 'The Search for the Dragon's Egg' and it was about this little kid who went and found a dragon's egg and took it home and hatched it. My mum sent it off and I got quite a bit of money for that.

I wrote a couple of chapters in the house last night but I also write when I'm sat here in the subways - on a big A4 pad - and sometimes I do illustrations as well, cause I did quite well in Art when I was in School. Rocco's really good at doin cartoon characters, but he won't admit it. We did a cartoon book together and all my little sisters and their friends *loved* it and wanted to keep it. I'm writing another one about an archaeological dig as well cause my nan's an archaeologist and she once found five skeletons with gold coins in their mouths. They were buried down in Devon somewhere, in this burial mound. Druids or something. She's found quite a few things: like this little heart-shaped pendant I'm wearing now. It's solid silver and dates back to eighteen-fifty and she found it in a field when I was nine. It's worth quite a bit but I wouldn't sell it for sentimental reasons.

I'm always writing bits and pieces of poems and that. I've been writing about my experiences of the last eighteen months, on and off, in a kind of diary. I've changed all the names and what I'm going to do at the end is just sort of add bits and pieces here and there and make it into a book. About how life is *really* like on the streets.

'Somethin in the back of my mind all the time...'

Sara

Allo, my darlin! Sara Jayne Thomas is my name. I'm fifty-six and I was born in Gowerton. I sit here outside Iceland's most days and watch the people pass: 'Allo, Sara! they say. 'Ow are you, love!' They all know Sara and they're good to me an all. I don't beg, mind. I *ask* but I don't *beg*. 'No hat out, no hand out.' Just sit. Sometimes you get aggressive people but then I just walk away and say nothing. They say 'I'm gettin the police!' But why? I'm not doin nothin. What am I doin, innit? Just sittin, that's all. Good as gold...

Back in the Autumn, I photographed Kathy and Robert - two visitors to the Hostel soup kitchen - and later made a drawing from the photograph which was exhibited in the Cyrenians Christmas Show in the Glynn Vivian Art Gallery. I haven't seen them to speak to since.

A busy Saturday morning in Town. I sit alongside her on the pavement on her usual pitch in High Street. She's on only her second can of Tennants and is still quite cheerful and lucid. Probably the best-known dosser in Town over many years, her health has deteriorated over the winter months and the Hostel has been making determined efforts to find her a place. She speaks in a loud, friendly and often emotion-filled voice, with total disregard for who might be listening. There are frequent exchanges of greetings with a non-stop stream of passers-by...

Sara: I had a lovely childhood. Except when I got raped. My father was a collier. He was from County Cork. My mother was Welsh. An alcoholic, same as myself. That's who I follow in our family. My sisters and brother don't drink or smoke. And my dad didn't drink or smoke. He'd ave alf of Guinness but that was *it*. Anyway, after I was raped, I *run*. I just couldn't help it. Oh, I run! I was gone months. Ended up in Blackpool, in Homes up there. And daddy come up and brought me back by train. It used to stop in Gorseinon then.

That's goin back years. But e never it me in his life. E wan' a fighter but he'd shout at me and put me to bed. I was goin on twenty when he died. Of arthritis. He got it from working in water in the pit. And in them days you couldn't cure it - not like today. I lost my best friend when my father died. But no matter where he is now, I know he's *there*. I see him often. I don't know *why* that is, but I *do*. Maybe it's DT's. I still cry when I think of him. *Everybody* cries, I don't care *who* they are. He was a lovely man - God bless im - and I miss him terrible.

Passerby: *Allo, Sara, love! All right?*

Sara: *Allo, darlin!*

Passerby: *Warmer today?*

Sara: *Yeah - not bad...* Nice girl. A friend of mine... My husband died three years back. He was from Dowlais. Not that I was with him for long. After me, he was with another lady. Alma her name was. A *good* lady. Good to *him*. I was never good to him. Because I didn't love him that much, understand me? You gotto *love* a person to *know* a person. You *gotto: deeply*. Deep inside. He was a boxer: *'Dai Dowlais'*. He won one fight then took to the drink. Same as myself. I took to it when I was *fourteen*. I think we split up cause of that. I *think* so. It was all *hammer and tongs* with us.

I worked as an ancillary nurse in the *old* Hospital but I got dismissed on the spot for passin tablets through the window to somebody. I done five years imprisonment in Holloway and in them days you ad it *ard*. When I come out, I went to my grandmother. She was up in Aberdare. Lovely woman! I *loved* er and she loved me. I worked in the colliers' canteen but when my gran died the house was left to nobody, so I had to get out and come back here. And, ever since then, I've wandered. I've been from here to Scotland, Ireland - *everywhere*. Tryin to find somethin and I don't know what I'm lookin for. Understand me, *please*. Tryin to find *somethin* - but I don't know what it *is...* I was in Ireland for five years - Dublin for most of the time and then Drogheda, about ten miles outside Dublin. I got on very well with the Irish. They was good to me - put me up. You didn ave to ave none of that sleepin in car parks. But I left there and went to Stirling. *Great* friends again in Scotland! They call them *mean* but the Scotch are not mean. They'd give you *anything*.

I'm a bit too old now but I *love* to travel. I'll go anywhere. The last place I went was Cheltenham - and Bath Spa. Lovely place, Bath Spa. I stayed there for three years and Cheltenham for five. I didn't work in those places. I was with company: Rik

Macilvenny. A great friend of mine. He's in Port Talbot now. I miss im but e got to ave is little spot, aven e? Rik is from Drogheda. That's where I met him. He worked on a pick and shovel - and drillers. But he can't get a job now, cause he's gettin on a bit. He comes down once a week to see me. He wants me to go to Port Talbot but I got roots in this Town and I won't leave. I says 'No, I'm sorry. I can't. I got a family here and I worship them and that's *it*. I won't go. No way.' My daughter'd take me in this second but I'd rather kip out. No reason. I don't *know* the reason. I'd just rather kip out.

I've spent *thirty-seven* years in that car park. Yes I have and I've seen them security guards come and go. I don't like men, to be honest with you but *they're* very nice, most of them, and Vivian is a *great* person! I've ad no aggravation nor nothing in that car park, till recently. My bag was stolen three times. With my glasses - and it's hard to get glasses for readin. Three times they were stolen. Anyway, by the last time I knew who it was so the next night I stayed awake in the car park and he comes along but little did he know that a friend of mine - Cardiff Karl - was round the corner. And he chased him off. He said 'Don't you *ever* touch this woman or go near her again!' Good man what he is! Jus like my dad. My father wouldn ave let me down either. But e can't elp me now and that's what I'm so sad about all the while. Honest to God, I never forget my daddy, cause I loved him so much. And I was his two eyes and he died, just like that. Cause God said *'E gotto come with me!'* and God is good as well. I *know* he is. Cause he looks after me, he do. And I *know* he do. I pray to him each night, no matter *what.*

Just lately, I been avin trouble with my vision. Nurse come and seen me the other day - the nurse and the doctor. E said 'You got water behind the eyes.' I said 'It's more likely to be Tennant's Super.' Then he examined my chest. He said you got bad bronchitis. You gotto go into hospital. I said no. I don't want no hospitals. I don't like no hospitals. So he give me little tablets, to take, which I felt *eased* it, you know? I gotto keep takin them. Not antibiotics - I can't take *them.* Little white pills. He turned round and said to me: 'You're a *hard* woman!' I said *'Nobody's* hard in this world. It's as hard as you make it yourself. And I *do* make it hard. It's not nobody's fault that I'm in this position. It's my own. Nobody else's.

But somebody's tryin to get me a little 'ome now. And I'll tell you his name when I think of it. He's one of them in the big red van that comes around on the soup run. Good as gold, he is! He brought a form for my signature and all this and I said 'Thank you very,

very much. Thank you for your hospitality and thank you for *listening* to me, *talkin* to me.' I appreciate that very much. I *do* and I mean that. If it wasn for the soup run, I don't think I'd be livin.

And I'll tell you another thing. Please, listen to me: d'you know them that's omeless? It's a shame, cause I *know:* I gone through it for years. *Years!* To see the young ones now - *young* people out on the streets! And there's *more* of them now. Oh, it's terrible. Why don't they give them a little room or a bedsit or anything. Look at all the shops that's empty here. *Look* at them! They could be used. Course they could be! The Council could open them up and put a few beds in there - put the light back on, they could. Even if it cost you, say, half a crown to go in there. You know what I mean? You can pay somethin like *that.* If I could, I'd *do* somethin like that, I would... *Bob! Come here, boy. Ello babe!*

Bob: *Ow are you? All right?*

Sara: *Yeah. I'm fine.*

Bob: *Seen any of the lads around? Ritchie? Rocco?*

Sara: *Not Ritchie. Seen Rocco. He went with Nicki lookin for Karl. E got paid this mornin. They're all under the tunnel most probably.*

Bob: *All right! See you later - !*

Sara: *See you!* ...Anythin else you want to know, my friend? Let me explain to you about when I went to the Housing Options about a place. I didn't want a flat. I couldn't cope with it. Just a bedsit is all I'm askin. Now I know damn-well there's plenty of bedsits in the Uplands. You pay forty somethin down. My sister will do that for me. My next of kin: I *worship* the ground she walks on. A *lovely* lady! I wish you could meet her. She'd tell you and all, what I've got to go through. What I've *gone* through. But I won't *stay* with her. We're like twins. Eighteen months between us. She's coming down today. She don't drink or smoke or nothing like that and she's worked hard all her life for what she got. And she got a home. I can go there *now.* Any time I want to but I can't *rest.* I'm up and down all the time. And she wants to know why. And I tell her I don't *know* why. I'm up in the mornin at four o'clock and I'm wanderin. And *she* can't sleep. Then that worries *me* then. And I got to be goin. She'd love to take me but I *can't* settle. I *can't.* Why is that, I wonder? There's something in the back of my mind all the time. Deep down. Somethin. I don't understand it, you know? I don't... *Here comes my daughter and my son-in-law...!*

Kathy: Hello, what's appenin, mum?

Sara: I'm doin a documentary. This is my daughter Kathy and her husband Robert -

Kathy: Where were you yesterday? We were looking for you everywhere.

Sara: I was by ere.

Kathy: No you weren't.

Robert: We looked here and you weren't here.

Sara: Oh, I went in the Job Centre for a bit to warm myself by the heater. I often do that. The Manager is very good. He always says 'You can stay for ten minutes, Sara but then you'll have to go.' Which is fair enough. They're entitled to say that. I usually only stay long enough to get warmed up but yesterday he sent for the police. There was three of them turned up and turfed me out.

Kathy: This is the man who done a paintin of us.

Robert: It was in the Gallery. Our friend bought it. 'Couple,' he called it. All right, Alan? How's things?

Kathy: Go on. Carry on with the interview -

Sara: ...My dad died when I was goin on twenty and my life was shattered completely. I loved my father but my mother was a bitch. Maybe *I* am. Slamming of the door: that's all I can hear from er. She was like that. *Slam* the door, walk out on my father - for *no* reason. You know, things like that? And it plays on your mind. As you get older you get - I don't know what it is - your nerves seem to go. And when I was raped - I was tellin you about that - a man opposite to where I was brought up, done that - I had to go out to work then, in a factory... Here's Ivy and Maureen comin. They're friends of mine. *Great* friends... *Hiya, Ivy!*

Ivy: *What's the matter, girl? Ow's it goin?*

Sara: I'm avin a documentary. This is the Evenin Post. This is my friend Ivy and her daughter Maureen -

Ivy: Ow're you, love! Ave you seen the boys?

Sara: Bob's down the subway with Rocco and Nicki -

Ivy: Only, Jimmy ave ad a letter now, cause he was on the sick for so long, saying he can claim severe disability. Well, I can't fill the form in, cause I don't know how. I'll see im shortly. Maureen's coming up in court soon. Shopliftin. In Neath. They told her she's lookin at six to twelve but her previous is only two: shopliftin in 1990 and one assault on a police officer in '91. Two blokes kicking shit out of this young boy. She jumped on one and I jumped on the other -

Sara: Aw, love er - !

Ivy: And that is *all* the previous.

Robert: You get caught shopliftin in Neath and you're through. They don't like anythin like that.

Ivy: Yeah, I know. They told us that. If she's tried up there, she'll ave six to twelve but if she's tried in Swansea, she'll just ave a slap around the wrists.

Sara: What're they puttin her in the nick for? That's the Government for you! I don't agree with them, like I told you. Look at these shops - they're empty. Why don't they open one of them up? That's the Council for you! That's why people like myself got to sleep out in Car Parks.

Ivy: Right, we're goin down the subway till ten -

Sara: *See you, babes!*

Ivy: *Look after yourself now, love.*

Sara: *Maureen, you take care!*

Ivy: *Ta! Ta!*

Sara: *Ta! Ta!*... What else can I tell you? I worked in all the factories in Fforestfach before Kathy was born but then I had to give up work and Kathy was fostered out cause I got in trouble with the police - that's the only reason. Cause I *loved* er. She's my first-born. Yes. I stay with Kathy sometimes. Certainly I do! Any time I want. My daughter is more *marvellous* to me than anybody have *ever* been!

Robert: Cigarette, Al?

Sara: He's a good boy, Robert. The best my daughter 'ave ever ad. I've got two daughters and two sons. I just seen Kevin. He sat down by ere with me for about ten minutes then he had to go somewhere. I forget where. That's Kathy's stepbrother. He loves Kathy with all his heart. An I like people to be kind and nice. You don't need aggravation in this world. There's enough with wars and fights -

Robert: Here's a fiver for you. Put it in your pocket. Go on.

Sara: God bless you, love! Friday's pay day. I'm eligible for work - which I put down as a barmaid. Well, they can't dispute *that* part. What you put down, you put down. I'm a bar maid. Fair enough? I've *done* that. I've *done* it.

Robert: Excuse me. D'you want something to eat?

Sara: No, no, no. *You* ave somethin.

Kathy: I'll finish this fag first. I'll have something in a bit.

Sara: I can't eat in the day now. *Wayne!* - yeah, *that's* his name. *Wayne!* What a lovely person. Wayne comes to see me every night in that car park and he's a great person. Darling Wayne is trying his hardest now to find me somewhere. He said to me: 'Don't you worry, Sara. You'll be indoors before the month's out.'

Kathy: They been tryin to get her in for *four* years.

Sara: So I give my signature. Signed the form -

Kathy: I've tried all this before - through Housing Options. I tried *four* years ago and it's always the same old story. They promise her the earth and she's *still* out on the streets.

Sara: No. This is not the *Options*. It's nothin to do with *them*.

Robert: What Housing Options said - can I speak here? - what they said when we first went down there was Sara would be a danger to herself and other people if she had a place of her own. Cause she was an alcoholic and she would cause a fire.

Sara: I'm not a danger to *nobody*!

Kathy: That's what they *said,* mam. That's what they *told* me.

Robert: That's the excuse they give her. But I can guarantee you, that woman is no danger to herself.

Kathy: I leave her in *my* home.

Robert: No danger to herself or anybody around her when she's in a home.

Kathy: She can't get drunk, anyway. She's been an alcoholic for thirty years. She *can't* get drunk.

Robert: She gets to a limit and that's it.

Kathy: Half of them down the Hostel are alcoholics and there's never been a fire that I know of.

Sara: Well, *exactly*! I've never got a row in anybody's house and never will.

Kathy: I've left her in my house and she's *never* burnt *anything*.

Robert: Nothing at all.

Sara: No, nothing. I appreciate what people do for me.

Robert: She's *careful* with cigarettes -

Kathy: And she *can't* get drunk any more.

Robert: She gets to a level and that's *it*.

Kathy: The booze doesn't take effect. She just *can't* get -

Passerby: *Hello, Sara. Here you are, dear - I'm afraid I'm not very rich today -*

Sara: *Thank you, darling!*

Passerby: *Goodbye!*

Sara: *Goodbye. God bless!*

Kathy: See *her?* See that woman? She's *rolling* in it.

Robert: *Loaded*, she is.

Kathy: Stinkin rich. She's got *two* houses down Gower. She's always comin sniffin around. Seein what's goin on. Did you see in her bag? I see she got her *wine and cheese* -

Sara: Yeah, there she goes and *look* who this is! The Securicor Man with the wages for Iceland. Nice man. Always says ello. *Hey! Honey-Bunch -* **Gimme that box!**

'He ain't heavy...'

Bernie and the Bowls Team (2)

On the front page, above the photograph of a dozen or so worried-looking local hoteliers, was a caption: **HELL HOSTEL ANGER.** *The accompanying report claimed that the former Radnor Hotel in Langwell Road was the location for regular fights, all night revelling and frequent police visits. Guest houses nearby had been promised urgent action to shut the hostel eighteen months previously, when a murder had taken place on the premises. Now, more than a year later, the violence was still continuing, with residents claiming they'd had bottles and buckets of urine thrown at them by people living there.*

On my way to Langwell Road, I bump into Bernie, Mike and Blacky. They, and everyone else, apart from Ceri and Ray, were kicked out of the Radnor last night but returned, briefly, in the early hours when the landlord was no longer on the premises. Bernie's fairly sober but Mike has been drinking gin and is staggering along, on a long lead, behind Blacky. We go and look for Jack and Debbie and find them at an Off-Licence in Rodney Street. They've been using their giros as security there and are now collecting the balance from the owner. We go and sit in a small courtyard at the back of a church in Rodney Street. I switch on the tape-recorder and they begin telling me the full story of their abrupt expulsion from the Radnor. After about forty minutes, I realize I've pressed the PLAY button by mistake and let out a string of expletives...

Jack: **Language! Language!** There's a lady present.
Mike: We'll do it all again - in Welsh this time.
Jack: D'you siara Cymreig? Ich siara Cymreig, ser gut.
Bernie: *An labhrann to Ghaeilge?* Talk properly! It was bloody freezin down there last night, wannit?
Jack: I can't remember *tomorrow* let alone last night!
Bernie: The four of us slept rough.
Jack: Tuesday mornin the landlord knocked the door -

Bernie: And came in and caught Debbie and Tracey in Danny's old room. -

Debbie: I was on the floor and Tracey was in the bed and he comes in and says 'I want everybody *out!*'

Bernie: 'Pack your bags and *get out!*'

Mike: I was just goin down to take Blacky for a walk and he took the keys off me. I says 'Old on! Leave it *out!*' But he still took them. And there was no need for it. No need at all -

Bernie: I still had my key, but when we tried to get in again last night, he was sittin on the wall.

Debbie: That's not a hotel, it's a doss house. It's stinkin in there .

Bernie: There's no sinks. There's no water. There's no heatin. There's *nothin* in there. It's warmer out here than it is in there.

Mike: One mornin, I got up early and turned the water on for a bath. I goes back into my room to get my fresh clothes and when I comes back, the water is brown. Before I even got *in!*

Jack: The funny thing is: the hot water is *freezin* but the cold water is *luke warm!* We ave to go up his mate's house in Mount Pleasant to get a bloody bath.

Bernie: I think, myself, between the four of us, another one's goin to die on the street before long. And I know who it's goin to be. It's goin to be Ray.

Jack: Yeah, I know what he means. Bernie's got this sixth sense. It's like a dog.

Bernie: I'm psychic. Remember, I says years ago, I says 'I *know* somethin's goin to happen down here. There's goin to be a murder.' And there *was* a murder.

Debbie: Ray was hit last night but we don't know who by. We were down the County Hall at the time and when we went back to the Hotel - four o' clock in the mornin - Ray ad a black eye. So somebody ad obviously it him while we were out. But e doesn't know oo.

Jack: He can't remember. He'd paid his rent, an all.

Bernie: The landlord took his giro -

Jack: Run to the Post Office and took his money off him.

Debbie: That's the landlord for you!

Mike: He's a wanker.

Bernie: Don't say *that,* son.

Mike: Well, he *is*.

Bernie Somebody's been takin Danny's money, too.

Jack: Gerry Beynon. You met him in the Park with us. I call him 'The Weasel.'

Bernie: It's not fair, though, cause wee Danny means no harm to anybody. He's like the rest of us: just survivin.

Jack: People who care for people, *care* for people. We look after each other. Got a cigarette, Deb? I'll get a spliff together after -

Bernie: I'm not queer or anything like that, Alan, but I love *you*. I love *him*. I love *everybody*.

Mike: Oh, you've gone off *me* now, ave you?

Bernie: No, but I love *everybody*, son. I'm just tryin to state a fact -

Jack: Here comes Danny!

Bernie: Danny, son!

Jack: There's my boy! Give us a kiss, brother!

Danny: Cursin me to hell, were you?

Bernie: Oh, we don't curse *you*, Danny!

Jack: We were wonderin where you were. Did you get your money?

Danny: Hallo, Blacky! Can I squeeze in there?

Bernie: Ow you doin, bro?

Danny: Ask me that after about a quarter of vodka. It was bloody cold last night.

Bernie: I'd no blankets left, Danny, son. I put two over you, didn I, Debbie?

Danny: That's all right. But these shoes you sold me are falling apart, Bernie. *'Made for walkin!'* you said. I'm getting more wear out of my *toes!*

Jack: Ave you seen Jim about your money, cause he's waitin on it?

Danny: Oh yeah, yeah. That's where I've been. To get this... Enough to keep us goin for at least a day.

Jack: Well, give it to Bernie, cause it'll be safer, then.

Bernie: We're goin to buy a van, Danny. And *you're* drivin!

Danny: Hold on a minute. I can hardly walk, let alone **drive.**

Bernie: Put five pounds-worth of petrol in and *I'll* drive, then.

Danny: Where we goin - France?

Bernie: Doncaster.

Danny: Fag, Alan?

Jack: He don't smoke. He's a Christian. He don't swear, either.

Danny: Oh, I beg your pardon! And there was me *cursin* -

Debbie: Give us a can of Tennants, Danny, cause my can has just spilt all over the place again -

Bernie: That's it. Share and share alike. No, I'll have one after, son, but you can lend me a thousand pounds, Danny. I want to buy this van.

Danny: Hold on - I'll just check my back pocket -

Bernie: I'm skint but if these boys want to work together and get the van, then I'll drive it.

Jack: *C'mon, c'mon, let's work to-**geth**-er!*

Bernie: Well, what d'you think? You need somewhere to put your head down as well. Am I a good driver, Danny?

Danny: I don't know. I've never taken the risk.

Jack: You have. Member when we went over to Beverley's?

Danny: Oh, that's right: we hit the bank -

Jack: Yeah. Instead of brakin, Bernie put his foot on the accelerator and it was a hairpin bend and - *Whoomp!* - right up on the bank we went and over onto the roof. So we just left the car there and walked the rest.

Danny: Joe Tanner did the same but his was a write-off, wasn't it?

Jack: The Capri. Cor, what a mess! I seen it the followin day. Squashed like a fuckin orange. He was lucky to come out of it with his life. I don't know whether he'd been drinkin or not, I wasn't there, thank God. And two weeks later, he was dead anyway.

Bernie: This world's not fair. There's two sides to every story and if I had the will-power, I'd save everybody. The Government or the Council or whatever, don't care about us. All they want is money, money, money. And when somebody dies on the street, they say 'Oh, it wasn't *our* fault.' We're trash as far as they're concerned.

Mike: What amazes me is you've got night shelters in Cambridge and you got night shelters in -

Debbie: Leicester - everywhere -

Mike: But you aven't got no shelters in Swansea.

Debbie: You used to have. There used to be one by the fire station in the Strand. Every year, two weeks before Christmas. But you had to get out of there by half ten in the mornin.

Bernie: Oh, Alan! Did I ever show you a photograph of Peter Pan - ?

Mike: *I* got photos!... *Look! Look!* I'll show you my kids... Here you are: this is my youngest one... this is outside my house - that's Chantelle. She was nine then. Yeah. Awright? Look! That's er and er brother and this is my ouse and this is them in fancy dress, as Jack and Jill. And there they are again, right? And there's my mum and dad, God bless em! And this is my mum and dad's ouse, right? And I built all of this, right? And got them that Chesterfield. That's Paula and there's Stephen my son there. E was thirteen at the time. And there's me wife there. *Ex*-wife, actually. She's *black* but all my kids come out *white*. But havin said that, one of my kids could ave one, one day - awright? - and it could be *black*. And I'm not colour-prejudiced. But he don't like blacks - Blacky don't like blacks -

Bernie: Alan, sit there, brother. D'you know what this is? Have I shown you this before. That's some of Peter Pan's ashes. I been carryin them over a year now and I know I've spilt some in my wallet but I'll never lose that. Cause he *meant* somethin to me. I'm not queer but he always stayed in my room - always. And - I can't find the photograph. I don't know what I've done with it. I think it's in the bag - but that's still Peter Pan. He's not gone from me, like. He's always there and, I know it sounds crazy, but if I lost that, I'd lose my *self*.

Danny: Bernie, d'you want a fag, son?

Bernie: Yes please, brother. D'you know: you can't bring back what's lost? If I could I would. But I don't want to see what happened, happen again.

Debbie: Give us a light.

Bernie: I spoke to my brother last night - me and Debbie here - and he wants me home. But it's hard work, it is, cause you cant just walk away from the fire - if you know what I mean. I can't just leave these on their own, cause I look after them - not all the time, but I do my best.

Danny: You do your best.

Bernie: I come looking for Danny at night, cause it's cold, don't I, son?

Danny: The landlord threw us out. Me and Ray were goin up to see Bernie yesterday mornin and the landlord saw Lofty there and he says 'You - **out**!' And then he saw me and he says '*You're* not supposed to be here, either.' So I says 'Will you tell Bernie we called up to see him?' and he says 'I'm tellin Bernie *nothin!*' So that was the end of that.

Bernie: I must be honest: we drink in the Hotel but we always tidy up.

Danny: Oh, there's no mess up there.

Bernie: Debbie clears up mostly, to be honest -

Danny: She goes round brushing the carpet of any ash or debris or whatever, but we all chip in, you know? And the Landlord doesn't give two hells about us -

Bernie: Because all he wants is his *bread*.

Debbie: The Hotel's on the market: so he told us last night.

Mike: And d'you know what she said? She said 'I aint just goin to lose the Hotel. I'll probably lose my house as well - cause the Bank's repossessing.

Bernie: Cause they're on the **fraud**, man! They were **frauders**! They been fraudin us for the last three to four years. Maybe even before I came there.

Mike: They'll end up goin down.

Bernie: Well, I hope they *do*. And d'you know why? Teach them a lesson. I was taught a lesson. We've all been taught a lesson. We've all been in prison. I been in prison when my wife died. That was a crime of passion. I didn't *murder* her. She just fell. I was inside just eighteen months, brother, cause I didn't murder her.

Danny: She fell downstairs.

Mike: *My* last was three years - for fraud. But while I was doin the three years - of which I'm only doin eighteen months, aren't I? Yeah? What did I do? I killed a nonce case and I got five years concurrent, on top of that. He ended up in my cell and I bladed im. He'd been messing about with little boys and I couldn't ack it so I bladed him - bad. I killed the guy. They took me back to Crown Court and I got another five years making eight in all. I done just over four and a half in the end. I don't regret doin it because he messed about with *kids*. I don't regret that. I don't regret *nothin*.

Jack: We'll get some speed later -

Debbie: We can go by taxi -

Mike: But a nonce case done me ead in. So I killed im. Anybody can kill somebody - d'you know that? And I killed im. I was done for manslaughter. And, to me, it was a good result. Even the prison officers was glad. Same thing happened to another nonce while I was there. A couple of guys got old of him, right, stripped him and poured boilin water over him. Threw him over the rail and when he hit the wire net, his flesh went through it like chips -

Jack: Listen to this, Alan. You won't believe this. I was jus telling Danny. This guy, the other day, was sittin in the Gardens: you know, where you interviewed us? - and his pocket was on fire. On my *life*! It's a *true* story. He's sittin in the Gardens and his fuckin pocket's on fire. Oh, I'm sorry, I shouldn't swear. So we're all tellin him now: *'Look! Listen*, you're pocket's *on fire!* But it was like talkin to a bloody *brick wall.* He was startin to burn. On my life! But he just wouldn't *listen* - !

Bernie: Jack, lend me twenty quid. I haven't got a penny.

Debbie: Nor me.

Mike: Lend us a score.

Bernie: Danny, lend me a tenner, son.

Danny: Oh, *fuck off!*

Jack: Oh, come on. Give him a tenner, mun.

Mike: He just did. It bounced.

Jack: It went over there.

Bernie: Just ten pounds - for some speed. I want to inject it.

Debbie: Not with *my* pins. Get your own. I got all my own pins in here - in my Danger Box. I been doin it for fourteen years, on and off. I've gotto have it every day. I've been in rehab in Weston Super Mare -

Bernie: Jack, lend me twenty -

Debbie: I've been in Cefn Coed a couple of times and I'm waitin to go in again - and they'll section me for a month. And, hopefully, that will get me off it. They don't give methadone for that, they give Dexedrine, which is tablets but it's *pure* speed and you're only allowed eight a day. That's the most they'll give you. And I'm also on a hundred and fifty mil a day of Valium and I'm on these forty Silptics cause I can't eat properly. And then I've got this Complan stuff -

Bernie: Jack, give me twenty -

Debbie: - to try and help me out. SAND - Swansea Drugs Project - that's where I am. They're sorting out the Housing bit. I do want to come off it but it's not the speed any more, it's the needles. I got this thingy about poking needles in my arm. Needle Fever, they call it. I'm addicted to needles.

Mike: D'you know amphetamines stay in your system for two years. It stays in the back of your spine -

Debbie: I get morphine injections but my doctor does it for me. I as one of them a week. But I'm hoping to get off it all, like. Yeah, they're *brilliant* in SAND -

Mike: I been as well -

Debbie: And Jack have been. They got computers there now and they help you find a flat. So I'm hoping to get off everything, cause I've got children, you know. Three. Twins aged fourteen years and a little boy of seven. I was only fourteen when I had the twins. They're adopted. The little boy's half with my mother and half with foster parents. My mother's a Social Worker and she's avin a lot of difficulty cause he's hyperactive and goes to Approved School and everythin. I wasn't married and I don't see the father but my son still does. I was in the Homes when I had the twins and I ad to ave tutors to come there - but I still can't read. My father left when I was three and went to London and e died three years ago: of drugs and alcohol. My mother's with somebody else and they live in Ammanford. But I can't get on with my stepfather, cause he abused me when I was five years old, see. It *did* go to court but nothing came of it. They just put me in the Homes when I was five till I was eighteen. I did go to foster parents too, but I never stayed there and I don't want my son to go like I did. My mother always said I'd follow my father,' and that's what I'm doin, by the looks of it. But, hopefully, I'll get on the straight and narrow one day. Maybe this flat Bernie's just fixed up for me will help.

Bernie: I'm her bodyguard. I look after her. And she knows it. All you hear is *'Bernie! Bernie! C'mon, Bernie!'* It's cause I care for her. Don't get me wrong, brother: not in that way. But I do *care* for her. I care for *everybody.*

Debbie: That's a fact.

Danny: He does.

Mike: I woke up this mornin and I had a fuckin blanket over me but I couldn't get my fuckin legs out. My legs were stuck!

Jack: We managed to get back in the Hotel in the early hours but with a lot of difficulty.

Bernie: So they may change the lock now. It's hard to say.

Jack: Environmental Health need to go along there. This guy comes in the other day with a *startin handle* and wrecks the toilet. *Wrecks* the fuckin toilet! There's no toilet there any more.

Bernie: D'you know what I done the other night, Alan, after he'd thrown us out? I went upstairs with a hatchet and I smashed the whole place up: the stereo -

Jack: The TV -

Debbie: The Hoover -

Bernie: The sink -

Jack: Three stacks -

Bernie: And d'you know why? Because it wasn't really worth *twopence*! Cause the Landlord's so cheeky, so ignorant. Takes all the giros, takes *everything*. Steals all the stuff we buy, out of the house. He takes the lot.

Debbie: He claimed for me for six months, while I was livin on the streets.

Danny: He comes up to me this close the other day - nose to nose - and says *'Where's my rent?'* I says 'Well, look, hold on a minute - '

Bernie: I bought a guitar one time. So about eight o' clock in the mornin I was havin a little sing-song - I always sing Country and Western - nice and soft, like - and he runs up the stairs: 'Get that music **off!**' he says to me 'Next door's complainin!' So I thought about it for two minutes and then -

Debbie: He ran downstairs -

Bernie: And guess what I did with the guitar?

Debbie: Smashed it over his head.

Bernie: I was *that* bad-tempered, you see. I said 'D'you want it? You can **have** it!'

Jack: Got any tobacco?

Bernie: Let's get some speed. Jack made the joints that strong for me last night, I couldn't get up. I thought I was stuck to the chair!

Debbie: *They* smokes it but I got this thing about needles. Rob was the same.

Bernie: Who's Rob?

Debbie: The one who died the other day. In a tent on the front.

Bernie: Oh yeah! Paul stopped the van and asked if I wanted go to the funeral but I don't like funerals. I don't like them at all. Eighteen, wasn't he?

Debbie: Seventeen. No relatives, just all his friends there.

Bernie: You see, you might die but you're not dead forever, you know. Your soul leaves you. If your body's dead, your soul's still there.

Debbie: Look at the people who died in Dinas Fechan when I was there. There were seven or eight. All youngsters. All on drugs.

Danny: The people who are supposed to care, *don't* care. They just let them get on with it. It could be any of us.

Bernie: They call us the black sheep, Danny son. The *outcasts*.

Danny: We *are* the outcasts.

Bernie: But *why* do they call us outcasts? Cause we fall by the wayside. You read the Bible. I can't read but I understand the Bible. *'Who falls by the wayside, lies alone. Who's goin to pick him up? Who's goin to take him home?'*

Danny: Very few. Except us.

Bernie: Yeah. It means that you are my *brother*. There's a little song goes -

Jack: *The road is lo-ong, long enough to care -*

Bernie: *But he ain't heavy, he's my bro-ther...*That means it's a gift. Everybody's got a little gift in them. And if you haven't got that gift, you don't survive. We all die some day. Me, everybody. Nobody'll live for ever. But we're goin to a far better place. They call it *Everlastin Peace.*

Jack: *The Big Hostel in the Sky...* I think I might get there -

Bernie: But I'll tell you one thing: you'll meet all your mates and your family. And *that'll* keep you happy.

Jack: You'll meet *the Maker* as well -

Bernie: You'll meet *the Maker* first. You know what it states in the Bible: before this world's goin to end - which it will by the year 2000 - Jesus Christ will walk as a man again.

Jack: Will e?

Bernie: Oh yes - he'll walk the world a man -

Jack: In the year 2000?

Bernie: Then he'll try and tell you something. And then he'll disappear for a little while. Cause if you look at life, right: Jesus is in our head. So's God. Jesus doesn't have to come here. He's here already.

Jack: *Course* he is.

Bernie: Seven days a week.

Danny: You've taken the words out of my mouth -

Jack: This is *serious shit*, man!

Bernie: You see, God doesn't lose *us*. Nor does Jesus. *We* lose God and we lose Jesus - with our own mind. Through drugs, through drink - whatever. Whatever we take. Can you buy rum? Can you afford it?

Jack: Sometimes -

Bernie: Can you buy a rocket? Can you afford it?

Jack: No.

Bernie: God doesn't need a rocket. He's got his *own* rocket. He's goin to carry you up there in it.

Jack: In the year 2000. You're *right!* That is A B C. That is *finito,* then. At's the end of the world. *The end of the world as I know it -*

Bernie: D'you want to die? I don't. D'you say your prayers every night?

Danny: I do.

Bernie: What d'you say?

Jack: The Lord's Prayer. The Twenty Third Psalm -

Danny: *The Lord is my shepherd -*

Jack: *I shall not want. He makes me lie down in green pastures -*

Bernie: *He restoreth my soul -*

Jack: *My cup runneth over. Yea though I walk through the Valley of the Shadow of Death -*

Bernie/Jack: *I shall fear no evil -*

Jack: *For thy rod and our staff, comfort us -* Carry on -

Bernie: D'you know, brother, I could talk all night about religion. I did last night. Everybody fell asleep and I kept talkin to myself, didn I, darlin?

Debbie: I couldn andle it.

Danny: He bored us to death!

Bernie: But, d'you know what I always say is: booze is not everythin. If people could *talk* to people, they could *understand* people.

Jack: Whah?

Bernie: And if you don't talk to people, where are you? You're in the dark. So you've got to put that little torch on, right? It does no harm to listen, does it?

Debbie: Will you buy me a dog, Bernie?

Bernie: I listen. I listen to you. I listen to Danny. I listen to Debbie. I listen to Mike. He listens to Blacky -

Jack: Blacky listens to his sausages -

Danny: He's a better listener than *any* of us! Oh, he's very clever.

Jack: Eh! Any chance of a lift down to Wind Street, Alan?

Bernie: He's on foot.

Danny: D'you fancy changin shoes, then? I'm size eight. I'm not sure what size these are but they're too big and there's nothing left of them.

Bernie: I know we all talk crazy sometimes, cause we're off our trolleys half the time -

Jack: *It's the end of the world* -

Bernie: But at the end of the day, who's left? Yourself.

Danny: And your soul.

Bernie: Yourself, son, and your own thoughts. We enjoy each other's company all day. We have a good fling-up or whatever they calls it but, by the end of the day, there's only *you* left. There's nobody else.

Danny: You don't take anything with you, but your soul.

Mike: And vodka -

Danny: Oh - and a bottle of vodka.

Bernie: You can be lying beside your wife but you're still alone.

Jack: You've had enough sex, so forget it -

Debbie: *Forget it!*

Danny: Oh, I don't know about that. *I'm* always looking for a wee bit more. It's like alcohol. You get addicted to it and you always want -

Jack: *Shhh!* Somebody's comin - !

Bernie: What - ?

First Policeman: Hello, there -

Second Policeman: Ow do?

Danny: Hello, guys -

Bernie: Hello, there. We're talkin about the homeless and that, like. We're not doin no harm. He's doin a documentary.

First Policeman: With whom?

Danny: With us, Sarge. How's it goin?

First Policeman: Some people have complained -

Second Policeman: About the noise -

Danny: We're just talking -

Mike: About the homeless -

First Policeman: What is this? Just a place out of the way, is it?

Bernie: We don't drink on the streets, brothers.

First Policeman: Danny?

Danny: We're out of sight here. So we're not botherin nobody.

First Policeman: Takin all your rubbish with you then?

Jack: Not exactly *rubbish*.

First Policeman: The empty bottles and cans and that sort of thing?

Danny: Oh, yeah. We'll clean it up.

First Policeman: We don't want it to end up lookin like a rubbish tip, do we?

Bernie: We'll clear up, no problem -

First Policeman: I know you'll take the *full* bottles with you.

Danny: *What* full bottles?

Bernie: Ave a drink with us, boys!

First Policeman: Eh?

Second Policeman: Sorry?

Bernie: Ave a drink with us!

First Policeman: I'm on duty unfortunately. I'll have to wait till after hours before I can have one. Ow are you, Debbie? I aven't seen you for a while. Ow're you keepin?

Debbie: All right.

Bernie: She's not too well.

First Policeman: No?

Debbie: Waitin for a bed in Cefn Coed. Honest to God -

First Policeman: Well, as long as it's all quiet. How long are you goin to be stayin here for?

Bernie: About ten to fifteen minutes, brother. *Probably.*

Second Policeman: You're not goin to make any noise or -

Bernie: No.

Second Policeman: Keep the conversation down cause it's a residential area. *Respectable* -

First Policeman: As long as there's no mess and as long as we don't get any complaints off the Vicar.

Bernie: Oh, *the Vicar*, was it?

Danny: We're old friends -

First Policeman: He didn't complain but in case he does. If there's goin to be anythin goin on here this afternoon - *now.*

Bernie: Ten or fifteen minutes, squire, at the most. It's for the homeless people. He's took

187

pictures of us and whatever.

First Policeman: As long as you take all your stuff with you.

Bernie: Right, no problem. Take care, brothers. Thank you very much -

Jack: Goodbye -

Bernie: Thank you very much. *Ta ta, bro!*

Danny: *Ta ta, lads!* You're doin a *good* job. *See you...!* They're doin a good job - and a *dangerous* one... You got them on tape? Oh *brilliant!*

Bernie: Right, where were we?

Danny: You were on religion.

Bernie: You know, I believe there's a higher power. Cause we didn't come from nowhere. What it says in the Bible, right, is this: *'the unexpected is unknown.'* Know what that means? It means God is in the Universe. Look around you. What d'you see?

Danny: Well, you don't expect to see two *Old Bill* comin round the corner, do yer!

Jack: We shoulda asked for a lift. They aven't gone yet -

Debbie: They'll check on me now. They could be radioing through at this very minute. They *knew* me. I kept my head down but they knew me straight away. *'Allo, Debbie!'* I've got thirty-nine warrants out on me. Non-appearances. Provoking violence. Shopliftin. I can never remember the date to appear. I've got memory loss. As I said, I'm waitin to go into Cefn Coed. Waitin for a bed, to go in.

Bernie: I *love* the police I do! They're beautiful. D'you remember the policeman last night, Danny!

Danny: No I don't.

Bernie: He helped me pick you up off the pavement. You fell off the wall twice. Remember?

Jack: Ave they gone yet?

Debbie: No, they *haven't*.

Bernie: No, they're gone, pet.

Debbie: They *aven't*.

Bernie: That's not their car -

Debbie: I *know*. But they're parked up by there, mun!

Danny: Oh, they're not goin to bother us.

Debbie: They bother *me*. I got a warrant out -

Jack: No hassle.

Danny: If we were smashin bottles or fightin or shoutin -

Bernie: Where else we gonna sit? We've gotto sit *somewhere.*

Danny: I haven't met those two cops before, but I think I recognize the big one.

Bernie: How many years have we got between us? Nearly two hundred. I haven't been in jail now - oh, for years. And I'll tell you: I don't want to go back. I'm so used to fresh air -

Jack: Alan, we need a van. Ow much d'you want for the Outreach one?

Bernie: It's crazy, I know, but we all get drunk of a night and there we are, singing to ourselves *'Goodnight, my dear, goodnight, my dear...'*

Danny: And he won't let me sleep cold at night, if he can help it. He wraps me up. He's a good man.

Bernie: I look after those who look after me, brother. And d'you know why I look after you? Because you're *Irish!* And you couldn't meet a nicer person than an *Irish* person, could you, Debbie love?

Danny: Well, I don't want one of your head butts again -

Bernie: Oh, forget about that. That was just a misunderstandin -

Debbie: *Shh!* Keep your voices down, in case -

Danny: We'll set Blacky on them -

Mike: Blacky's as knackered as I am.

Bernie: If they'd wanted us, they'd have sent the bloody van down by now -

Debbie: They've gone now but that's all they got to do is check up on me -

Bernie: Ah, don't worry.

Debbie: But I *am* worryin, Bernie -

Bernie: I know -

Debbie: Well, there you are then! *Don't* tell me not to worry -

Bernie: You know, sometimes I don't *care.* I don't care what happens to me any more. I'm tryin to get back home again and I can't even do that. Can't even get home, where I belong.

Danny: I know what he means -

Jack: Let's get out of here! I'm frozen -

Debbie: That's all he wants is blow. And I wants speed -

Bernie: And *I* wants speed -

Jack: Same difference -

Bernie: Where we gonna sleep tonight, then - in the tent? We got ourselves a little two-man tent this mornin. Pitched it in a little dip behind the car park in County Hall.

Jack: Crash in the tent - or book in the Grand! And Alan's promised to get some duvets put on the Outreach van for us: half past five at St David's.

Bernie: You were tellin me this mornin, Alan son, weren't you, there's a room vacant in the Hostel? But I won't take it because I can't leave the others. And I've been inside seven or eight times, so the police would only come looking for me,

Danny: Well, I'm banned. I *can't* get in.

Jack: So, we'll see you about five-thirty outside St David's, Alan. Is that okay, that tape? *True* stories! Worth twenty quid of anybody's money!

Bernie: No, don't bother. We don't want it.

Jack: Keep it. We're all right. We're on the road a-gain -

Bernie: Well, if you're bein *refunded,* I'll sign for it no problem -

Jack: Alan's *sound.* He's a gentleman and a scholar!

Debbie: I got a pen -

Jack: All donations gratefully accepted!

Danny: What goes around, comes around -

Jack: That's right. That's *truthful.*

Danny: Can I hear a replay?

Bernie: This doesn't work, Debbie, love -

Debbie: It *do* work. Just sign there -

Bernie: Alan son, d'you want me to put just *'Bernie'* or *'Bernard John'*?

Debbie: Put *'Bernie'* down.

Danny: *'B. J. Malloy.'*

Debbie: *N.F.A.*

Jack: Well, don't put the Radnor Hotel for *Chris sake*!

190

'Geographically mobile...'

Neville

PERSONAL PROFILE: *'A good communicative person with experience of varying environments and backgrounds with fluent Spanish. I enjoy acting independently or with other individuals. A challenging position is an ideal goal for myself. A tolerant and friendly person enhanced by a wealth of experience derived from a variety of occupations both at home and abroad...'*

ADDITIONAL INFORMATION: *'I am a young 44 divorced man with a clean driving licence and enjoy leading and facilitating teams which means I can adapt readily to most social situations. My social life is very active and I am geographically mobile. More leisurely pursuits are crosswords, mah-jong and reading...'*

The times I've had in the past when I've gone into places to buy cannabis and they've all been trying to hide it because they thought I was a policeman! I mean, even in *prison* they thought I was a policeman. In Maidstone they actually got one of the guys to go through my file to see what my convictions were because they thought I was a bent copper. And they were going to do me over, because that's the way I *look*. I come across that way. I suppose it's because of my airline background. I always used to wear a uniform...

He arrives at my studio two hours early. Short, dark and good-looking with a David Niven moustache, he could well be a recent graduate of the old Rank Charm School. He always seemed like the odd man out in the Hostel environment and I often wondered what could have led to him being there. He is smartly dressed in shirt, tie, leather jacket and slacks and chronicles the events in his life articulately, with hardly a pause and in almost perfect sequence for an hour and ten minutes...

I'm forty-four and I was born in Hounslow in London. My father was in the Royal Navy for sixteen years and then in Customs and Excise up until he died. He was an alcoholic, due to the Navy rum and died when he was fifty-seven. My mother's still alive and in good health and lives in Milford Haven now. I've got a younger sister who doesn't smoke or drink and an elder brother who's Managing Director of a flight brokering company. He used to smoke but he's never taken drugs and rarely drinks. So, really, I'm the exception to the rule: I *haven't* come from an underprivileged background - my family *never* separated or anything like that - and my siblings are both very happy and successful. I wouldn't say I was 'the Black Sheep' of the family but I'm definitely *'an exception'.*

I started smoking hash when I was thirteen and quickly progressed through amphetamine to heroin and diamorphine. I first got in trouble with the police for being in a stolen car and then I got a conviction for possession of cannabis. That was quickly followed by a conviction for possession of heroin and so, at the age of fifteen, I was put under treatment with a psychiatrist at Crawley Hospital. Before I went to court, he gave me the option of either going to Borstal or being sectioned under the Mental Health Act. I chose to be sectioned and was sent to a mental hospital in Chichester for a twelve-month section, during which they would give me aversion therapy.

Rather than being traumatic, it was rather an enlightening experience because, up until then, we'd lived on a tough Council estate and I'd never really seen the countryside. The Hospital was a big Country House which used to belong to a Lord and was set in the grounds of Goodwood Race Course. The aversion therapy was experimental and optional but if you took it you'd get early release so, of course, everyone agreed. It was conducted by a psychiatrist called Dr. Daley and involved using Skolene, which is a muscle-relaxing drug derived from curari. They injected you with the Skolene and then you had eight seconds, before it acted on the brain, in which to inject yourself with the diamorphine. And then you just collapsed on the bed and, of course, you couldn't breathe because all your muscles were completely relaxed. The psychiatrist would then whisper in your ear and tell you 'You're in the toilets in Piccadily and you've overdosed and you're dying in your own vomit and *this* is what's going to happen to you one day if you carry on using diamorphine.' You could only have been under it for about thirty to forty seconds, then the anaesthetist brought you out of it. And they repeated that for five days and on the fifth day - and looking back, I think they did it *deliberately* - they didn't put the oxygen bag over your mouth properly, so you started to turn blue. Your lungs collapsed and the only muscles you could move in your whole body, oddly enough, were in your big toes and I kept banging them against the end of the bed to warn them that the oxygen wasn't reaching me. It was a most horrifying experience and I thought I was going to die.

And that sort of left me with an aversion to any injections. But, of course, a year or so later I was going abroad and had to have an injection for typhus or something and I didn't have any aversion against it whatsoever. Anyway, I stopped using heroin and got my first job and I was very successful. I've got my CV here, if you'd like a copy - . I worked for British Rail at Gatwick Airport and then, when I was old enough, for British Caledonian Airways on check-in and ticketing. After three years, I got accepted on a course for a Steward but before the course started my passport had to be sent to the American Embassy for an indefinite multiple entry Visa. But because of my drug conviction I was technically debarred from entering the States so I had to go back and tell my boss why and he was very good about it but said if I wanted to get promoted he'd *have* to send me to the States at some point or other. So, to cut a long story short, I said if he gave me a round-the-world ticket at 10% staff rate, I'd resign. He sold me the ticket and I spent two and a half years going round the world: New Zealand, Australia, New Guinea and finally Hong Kong, where I got a job as a manager in a travel agency.

Everything was fine until I went to Bangkok for a weekend. It started at the airport: some young boy came up and asked to carry my bags and asked if I wanted a nice girl or a nice boy or some ganga. He found me a cheap hotel room and when we went to get the ganga, he said 'I can get you some really good heroin from the Golden Triangle.' So I said okay and at first, because I didn't have a syringe, I smoked it but a couple of weeks later I went back and bought a syringe and started injecting - but only at weekends and only in Thailand. I was doing this for a year and then one weekend I returned to Hong Kong with a big bag of Thai grass and made the mistake of offering my flat mate a joint. He was the Company lawyer and he went absolutely berserk: 'How *dare* you bring drugs into the flat!' he said. '*I'm* living here as well and if it was found, I'd be struck off. Get rid of it straight away!' So I went and stashed it somewhere but next morning at eleven o' clock I got a phone call from my office: 'Come to the Company Board Meeting.' I went along and all the Directors were there and the Chairman said 'We understand you imported drugs into Hong Kong last night. For the sake of the Company image, we cannot tolerate this. So either we sack you - in which case you'll lose all your benefits and probably damage our good name by spreading the word around Hong Kong - or we'll give you the option of resigning, with a month's pay in advance and a ticket to anywhere in the world.' So obviously I resigned and got a ticket to London but on my way back stopped in Bangkok and had a good time. I smuggled thirty grams of pure heroin back into the UK, gave two or three grams of it away and tried to sell most of the rest because I was desperate for money by then. I didn't know any big dealer, so I arranged to sell a gram of it to a friend of mine from my old Chichester days. When I met him at Victoria Station to sell him this one gram, about seventeen Scotland Yard Drugs Squad Officers jumped out on me and I ended up getting five years for possession with intent to sell heroin.

In a strange way, prison was the best thing that could have happened to me. I was a model prisoner and because I'd been expelled from school and didn't have any qualifications, it enabled me to continue my education. I was transferred from Wormwood Scrubs to Maidstone where the Great Train Robbers and all those sort of people were. It was a Lifer's prison but it was one of the few places then - in the mid-seventies - where you could learn and study for Degrees. I enrolled for the Open University and got a distinction in the First Level of the Arts Foundation but during that time my father was diagnosed with cirrhosis of the liver and given only six months to live. It was a terrible strain for me and my mother and one day I was called into the Governor's office and told that he had died. He said I could go to the funeral but I'd have to be handcuffed to two guards. Now, apart from my immediate family, none of my relatives knew I was in prison, so I said that unless he allowed me to go without prison escort I couldn't go. He said that was impossible because I was a Category B prisoner so I burst into tears and marched out of the office. And I think that helped me with my parole eventually because within three months I was released, which is very unusual in heroin cases. And - touch wood - I haven't reoffended since.

I came out in February '78, stayed with my mother for a bit and worked at Gatwick Airport doing catering work and driving and that sort of thing, until I started at Bristol Polytechnic. I spent three years there and got a Second Class Honours Degree in Philosophy, Psychology and Sociology, with my thesis on Aversion Therapy. I worked in Public Relations in London after I graduated, moved into a house and started using heroin again but only at weekends for recreational purposes. I got a job with Thomas Cook and moved to Peterborough but I wasn't happy there and found myself going back to London to buy heroin. So, eventually I packed the job in, sold everything and moved to South America, on spec. I got a job teaching English as a foreign language in Colombia and married a Colombian friend whom I'd met when I was eighteen on a French Course at the British Embassy in London. It wasn't in the back of my mind when I went there but, inevitably, I transferred my heroin problem in London to a cocain problem in Bogota, which

194

is where I lived for nearly three years. The marriage only lasted twenty months due to my cocaine use. I don't know whether it was engineered by my wife or not - she denies it - but at eleven o' clock one morning, I had the DAS - the Colombian Secret Police - hammering on the door. The Colombians are terrified of them and if ever you have a visit from them, you know you're in *big* trouble and likely to disappear in the middle of the night. They took me to their headquarters and told me that when I'd entered the country and applied for a Green Card, I hadn't mentioned my police convictions. They had all the details from Interpol and told me they were expelling me from the country: 'There's a flight leaving at 5p.m. this afternoon - and *you're* on it!' They had a lawyer there for me but, obviously, it was one of *their* lawyers and he told me 'You can appeal but if you do, they'll keep you in custody in the Bogota prison for five or six weeks until the hearing. And you don't want to go in *there* because with your blue eyes you'd be raped straight away.' So that's how I left Colombia: I was picked up at eleven and six hours later I was on the plane to Paris.

I then went to Spain to live, because I thought I might as well make use of my Spanish. Again, I went out on spec, with a friend who had a yacht in Pollensa in Majorca. The deal was that he put me up on the boat and I helped him get it cleaned up ready for the summer but within six weeks I got a job with Intersun as an airport manager in Malaga. I worked there for a year and met a nineteen year old hotel rep from Liverpool, who I fell in love with. Her contract ended at the end of the season but mine was year-round, so I gave up the job and went back to England with her. And that was a disaster because we got a grotty flat in Stamford Hill in North London and I couldn't get a decent job and she worked for a pittance as a sales assistant in Barker's in Kensington. It was the middle of a very harsh winter and I was thirty-five and she was nineteen and we didn't have enough money to get along on, so she left me.

I started working for Whitbread as a full-time relief Assistant Manager then, which meant moving around from pub to pub and that's when my alcohol problem started. I worked there for a year and then drifted from job to job until I eventually got a job as an English teacher back out in Spain. I worked in Madrid for a year and then in Calahorra in La Rioja, where all the wine comes from. Trust *me* to get a job there of all places! I was right in the middle of it: 70p for a bottle of first-class wine. Then I met a heroin addict: a very attractive girl from one of the wealthiest families in Town. She'd been kicked out of Pamplona University for non-attendance and, of course, I started using heroin with her. So one thing led to another and I was working for myself by this time: teaching English to executives in their offices and doing quite well but, because I was getting strung-out and missing classes, all that fell through and eventually, in '91, I came back to Wales.

I worked first as a translator for a Spanish trawler company in Milford Haven and then for the NAAFI at RAF Brawdy. The NAAFI is basically a pub with a shop attached so, once again, I was back into this pub environment and drinking at all hours of the day. I started helping myself to the optics and coming on duty half-drunk and stock was going missing. Eventually, they caught up with me and did the honorable thing and said 'Look, we know you've got a problem. We can either sack you or you can resign and we'll give you a reference and a month's pay and you can get yourself sorted out.' Same as Hong Kong, basically.

And that was where I went into a rut and was unemployed - you'll see there's a gap on my CV for about two years - and lived in this farm house in Haverfordwest, paid for by the DSS. Then I went on a course in European Leisure Resource Management at Swansea Institute but because of my drinking, I didn't even take the mid-term exams. Which meant that my rent allowance, which was paid by the European Union, was stopped and I started getting into rent arrears with my landlord. I felt disgraced and at rock bottom and was borrowing money left, right and centre to spend on cider. In the end, I had to move out of the house and start sleeping down on the beach there. It was mid-summer and I couldn't wash or shave and I hadn't eaten for about two days and I was sitting on a bench by the YMCA, outside Quid's Inn when a homeless person came and sat next to me. And he was the one who told me to go to Paxton Street and that if I got there by five o' clock, they might give me a dinner. This was a Sunday. So I went down there and knocked on the door at about ten to five and John - the ex-monk - answered the door and I asked if there was any chance of a meal or a bed for the night and he said 'No, I'm sorry, we're full,' and closed the door. And as I was walking away, I heard somebody call after me and it was Julie Sheldon and John. He'd forgotten that there were ten beds free in Stembridge Avenue, so they got me back and John very kindly drove me up there. But before I went - I'll always remember it - Jimmy Dougal was on duty that day and they had a spare Sunday dinner, which was the first square meal I'd had for about two weeks.

They put me up in Stembridge for one night and I was lucky enough to get a room in Paxton Street the following day, which was better for me because it was central and I could look for a job. I stayed there for about eight weeks and it was great because I could steady myself and bottom-out with a roof over my head and three square meals a day.

From there, Caer Las got me a room in a house in Pentreguinea Road in St. Thomas. It was a nice house but I found it depressing because it was so awkward to get to.

Then everything changed. I got a job with Flyaway Travel - a good job on about £14,000 a year - selling holidays to Florida over the phone. That lasted three weeks because, with the first pay cheque I got - which was about £800 - I went on a bender and missed a day's work. And I didn't have the guts to phone in and say I had flu. So I let it go for a second day and then a third and then a fourth and a fifth. And so it went on for about ten days, until I phoned up and said 'Look, I'm sorry I haven't been in but I've been *really* ill.' So this guy told me to come into the office at 10 o' clock the following morning and when I did, they gave me my Cards.

Shortly after, I met a woman - Babs her name is - who's a well-known hash dealer in Swansea - and I moved in with her, while still keeping my flat on in Pentreguinea Road. She tolerated my drinking because her last two husbands had been drinkers, but once again I was involved with the drug culture. After eight months with her I got another good job with Jet-Tours House as a Business Manager but three days after I started, Babs's daughter was involved in a car accident and rushed to Morriston Hospital and given only twenty four hours to live. So again I started drinking and taking time off work because I was more concerned about Babs and her daughter. Until the owner called me in and said 'Look, why don't you just leave it? We'll take someone else on and when you feel that you're fit to take the job on, give us a ring back.' I left and then, within two or three months, Babs kicked me out as well, because I was drinking and rowing and becoming aggressive.

I had a stroke of luck after I moved back into Pentreguinea Road. I'd had five or six months of being really down but I went to practically the last travel company in Swansea that I hadn't been sacked from and they took me on. They're called Aircity and they're the biggest operators to Florida in the UK. They knew about me from my Flyaway days and said 'We know all about your drinking and why Mark sacked you but we're prepared to give you another chance.' That was the third of December, 1995. On the sixteenth of December, I'd just come back from a computer course at Gatwick, which they'd sent me on, and I met this beautiful woman called Rhiannon in a Club in Town. She was thirty years old and I was forty-three but we hit it off together instantly. She'd been married for nine years and had three young children but she'd left her husband because he was knocking off everything in sight. So I went to live with her and that was the best time of my life so far. I had a lovely, brand-new three-bedroomed detached house, which she rented, and an excellent job with Aircity. I was their Number One guy: Senior Telesales and I was on a fast track to becoming Manager of one of the Departments because I was the oldest and the most experienced there. But again, after about three months, I went on a bender. I came back after two weeks and explained that I was under stress. I'd been working six to seven days a week so they said 'Okay, we'll cut you down to five days a week but *don't* do it again.' But my drinking increased and I started drinking in the morning as well. I'd buy a flagon of White Lightning and if half of it was left in the morning, I'd get up at seven to have a couple of glasses before going to work. I used to do it in front of Rhiannon but then she started going up the wall, so I started doing it behind her back. Putting bottles in the cupboard behind the sink, in the washing machine - that sort of business - like you see on television. Eventually, we had a massive bust-up. And it wasn't about drink, it was about something petty. She wouldn't pick me up from work one night, so I had a drink in the office lunchtime and I went home early and we had this terrible row. She ran off and called the police. The police came round and said unless I gave them the keys to the house they were going to arrest me for assault. Rhiannon had told them I'd grabbed her by the wrists - which was true - but I hadn't hit her or anything: she just bruises easily. So I left and went to stay with the Manager of Aircity. I didn't go into work the next morning but went back to the house to look for her. My jacket with the office keys were in the house but she'd stayed the night at her mother's. I waited all day for her to come back and have a chat with her to try and sort things out but, of course, I was back and fore to the pub for a couple of pints while I waited. At about three o' clock I bought a flagon of White Lightning, drank half of it and at quarter past five Rhiannon turned up to check if any mail had arrived, saw me in the back garden and ran off. I ran after her. She called the police from a neighbour's house and they came and arrested me for common assault and criminal damage, because I'd tried to break the back door in to get my jacket. They kept me in till I sobered up, interviewed me and charged me but a few days before it went to court Rhiannon dropped the assault charge. She'd got a job in a bank by then and didn't want any adverse publicity in the papers, so I was bound over in the sum of £100 with £103 damages for the back door.

When I eventually went back to work to explain what had happened they said the younger reps were supposed to be looking up to me but discipline was breaking down on the sales floor, so they'd have to let me go. They gave me a reference and about a thousand pounds, because I hadn't had any holidays. I rented a student flat in Brynmill for five weeks, blew all the money on a two week bender, and found myself homeless by the time the students came back. But I went back to Paxton Street and luckily there was a bed available and they took me back in. They found me another flat and I've eventually ended up sharing a place in Mansel Street with another ex-Paxton Street resident. Frank is thirty and a waiter and half Spanish, so I can practise my Spanish on him and it makes him feel more at home. He doesn't smoke and he doesn't drink much, so he's not that bad an influence on me and we get on very well.

As soon as I moved into Mansel Street, I started a course with Swansea City Council doing telesales: anything from insurance, banking, double glazing to travel. It's a four week course, ending next week, and then you've got the option of going onto other courses which they run. 'Re-skilling' they call it. You get ten pound a week extra for attending the course, so it's better than sitting on your arse at home all day. I know most of the stuff they taught us but there was a lot I didn't and an old dog is never too old to learn!

I've been under the CDT - Community Drugs Team - since the 13th. March, 1996, which is when Rhianon first identified my alcohol problem. Until then, I'd refused to admit I was an alcoholic or even had an alcohol problem. Looking back on it, it was a crucial thing. They're not like the AA. They accept a tolerance level of drinking: you're allowed one or two pints, even to get pissed once a fortnight - but not paralytic. Unfortunately, I'd stopped going to them before the split with Rhiannon but, as Martin my councillor says: 'Nev, don't think that if you'd stayed with us things might have been okay with Rhiannon, because you weren't prepared to *confront* it at the time. You weren't in the right frame of mind. Now that the shit has hit the fan - to excuse the expression - you're doing it because you want to do it. We're not *making* you. The important thing now, is to *reduce* your drinking.'

I've been counselling with Martin for about six months and my drinking is under control. If I go out for a drink now, I don't wake up in the morning thinking 'God, how did I get home last night?' I haven't had a drink for about five days and it doesn't bother me. Hopefully, I'll meet another woman soon. In the past, I've been *looking* for one instead of making myself into the sort of person that would *attract* one. So that rather than *me* chase the hare, the hare chases *me*, so to speak. I'd like to achieve a degree of stability and happiness in my life and maybe have a child. Rhiannon and I tried for about four months to have one but because of my drinking I presume my sperm-count was low and she never conceived.

I'm on medication from the doctor for anxiety - I bite my nails and chain-smoke and sometimes I get so depressed I cry on my bed at night - but I've got to look forward rather than back. I still think about Rhiannon every day but not with that heartache - that kind of pain you get in your stomach. I used to ring her but she's gone ex-directory now. The last time I phoned her she said 'Look, Nev, don't phone me again. I've got two boy friends now and I'm very happy. You're bugging me by phoning. So don't phone again.' And I haven't. But I've written to her. In fact, I wrote to her on Monday and Tuesday of this week, because she's doing telebanking now, which is *exactly* what we're doing on this course. So I asked her to phone me and give me some tips about the sort of questions they ask you when you go for a job. But she *hasn't* phoned me, so I suppose she just doesn't want to know...

'Wanderin, wanderin: nowhere but anywhere...'

Kathy and Robert

Kathy: I was born in Holloway prison and brought up in Homes all my life. By the time I was thirteen, I was institutionalized. Never been on a bus or a train. Never been in a Supermarket. Never done *anything*. Basically, they locked me up from thirteen to eighteen and then I had to see a psychiatrist to see if I was sane enough to come out into the community...

Kathy is tall and big-boned with fine, gypsy-like features and hair hanging down in one long, plaited pigtail. Like Robert, she is dressed in anorak and trousers, thick thermal socks and boots. She doesn't smile much although she is friendly and talkative. She gives the impression of being a very strong-willed woman. Robert, in contrast, speaks gently and rather hesitantly, Kathy frequently having to complete his sentences for him...

Kathy: I've got two brothers and a sister but the oldest brother died. He ad a tumour on the brain but my mother won't admit that he's dead. It's got 'Father Unknown' on my birth certificate, so nobody really knows who it is. But Dai Dowlais isn't my real father. My *real* father's Billy Preece. I'm the image of him. Dai Dowlais was married to my mother, so he took me on but there's always been arguments between him and Billy about who was who. But I never lived with either of them and whenever I saw them it was always separately. Dai Dowlais was a boxer and Billy Preece was an ex-seaman. He's lovely, Billy is. When he come off the sea, he had a lump-sum and he blew a lot of it on me and my daughter. He's still about now but *then* he was travelling back and fore all round the world and even when he was home I wouldn't of known, cause I was in care anyway. I was taken from Holloway at seven months by Billy Preece and brought back to Swansea but the Social Services stepped in and put a full Care Order on me. They shuttled me around from place to place until I was thirteen, then they locked me up in what they called a 'Secure Unit'. I'd never been in trouble. It was just to see if I could adapt to the outside world, cause I'd been institutionalized so long. I had to go to a psychiatric hospital in Whitchurch in Cardiff twice a week for a year before I could come out and then it took two doctors and a Social Worker to certify me sane. But comin out after eighteen years, was frightenin. They don't tell you where to go or what to do. I didn't sign on. I didn't do anything. When I spoke to the Dole people two weeks later, the girl said 'God, you should have been here a *fortnight* ago. Where've you been?' I said 'I don't understand what you're tellin me. What have I got to do?' Social Services didn't fix me up with anything. I just had to do the streets and get on with it -

Robert: Can I say - if you'll allow me - that prior to all this: when Kathy was born in Holloway, her mother's sister and husband -

Kathy: stepped in -

Robert: and they wanted to take Kathy on and Social Services were agreeable -

Kathy: but Sara wouldn't allow it. She had the last say and she was my *mother.* She'd gotto sign the forms but she wouldn't do it. It wasn't that she didn't get on with my aunty, she just *wouldn't* do it. She signed the forms for my other brother and sister and they went away. My sister was legally adopted and went to live in Australia eventually, with her foster family, and my brother lives in Neath.

Robert: And *that*, mainly, is the reason why -

Kathy: I never had a childhood. I'm thirty two now and I got no recollection of being a child at all.

Kathy: The first place I went in was a Barnardo's. And then I spent a lot of years in and out of Barnardo's, till they realized I couldn't even recollect having a name. Sara never came and visited me and for years they told me she was dead. Then they announced one day that she was alive and would I like to meet her in Castle Gardens. My mother'd made arrangements with Social Services a week previous. Somebody from Princess House took me to meet her in Castle Gardens and left me there. And it was orrible! I didn't recognize her. I adn't seen her all my life. Could ave been *anyone.* She was drunk and, after being told for so many years that someone's dead, it was a bit of a shock, anyway. She was entitled to a visit, cause she was my natural mother but for thirteen years, she never even bothered. She'd never looked me up, never asked, never questioned. She was into barbiturates and alcohol in those days and she was violent, too. That's why they moved me so far away. When I come out at eighteen, there was nothing for the homeless, except

SASH in the old Gloucester Place and I used to go there a lot but

Robert: she used to live up by the Carrot Pond in Town Hill.

Kathy: They call it the Carrot Pond, cause it looks like a carrot. I used to live there under the tunnel.

Robert: Right alongside the railway line. The one that travels from Cwmbwrla to Haverfordwest.

Kathy: I lived there by myself for two years. No tent, just a sleeping bag. It was freezin. I used to spend a lot of time sleepin in the day and up in the night. I used to always cut my hair short and make myself look like a boy, cause if you were a girl out there, you weren't safe. I made loads of friends. I knows everybody in Swansea, from sleeping under the bridge. The old men used to bring me oxtail soup down. I had one friend who took me in and I stayed with him for a long time. He's in his sixties now. I was ill at the time and run down from not eating and sleeping properly. Just wanderin, wanderin - nowhere but *anywhere*. Know what I mean? Then, my friend Iris took me in and fed me. She got me a place in Hanover Street when I was nineteen and I lived there for a while but my rent didn't come through one week and the landlady said I ad to leave. So I left and walked the streets.

I met my husband under the tunnel by the Carrot Pond. I stayed with him in Townhill - as friends - for a good year, before we got married and had my daughter.

Robert: He virtually imprisoned you in your house though, didn't he?

Kathy: Yeah, he kept me in the house all the time.

Robert: A very jealous man. A vicious man. He locked her up. She couldn't even have a friend in the house, cause he was *that* possessive over her.

Kathy: He was an alcoholic and he thought I'd understand, what with Sara being an alcoholic and him being one as well - but no. I was only twenty -

Robert: And if you can imagine a twenty-year old who's just come out of care: Kathy was looking for somebody to look after her at that time, wasn you?

Kathy: He was very violent -

Robert: So she run away -

Kathy: Took my daughter and myself to a refuge in Newport. But he found me. It took him six months cause I was livin under a different name. But I wouldn't go back with him so, for eight months, until I met Robert, me and my daughter were on our own.

Robert: Prior to having met Kathy, I came from a good home. My father was Area Manager for Wonderloaf Bakeries. But he left there and bought his own business: a Fish Bar in Penmaes. Then he bought another one in Blaenymaes, for which he had a manager, but there was too much trouble there so he had to sell up. My father was quite wealthy and I had a really good upbringing. I was water skiing when I was nine and by the time I was twelve I was driving speedboats with wet-suits in Oxwich. So I didn't want for anything. But after I fell out with him, I turned to drugs, very heavily, and by the time I was nineteen I was a heroin addict. My father disowned me for four years - and I don't blame him. I had various bouts of drugs and detoxes up until I was about thirty two. Then I had a bad accident and I wanted to stop but there was nobody there to help me.

Kathy: Until I came on the scene. When I met Robert, he was in a homeless unit in Paxton Street.

Robert: I didn't want any sympathy. I seriously tried to commit suicide -

Kathy: He threw himself in front of a lorry -

Robert: I had a broken arm, broken leg -

Kathy: Broke one whole side of his body. He was in hospital three years and in a wheelchair in the Car Park for eighteen months. We were doin the streets at the time and I still couldn't get a place while he was in a wheelchair. They was prepared to put him in a nursin home and just leave me wander the streets.

Robert: I'd already been in a Nursing Home and I could andle that cause I was ill. But, after meeting Kathy, I felt it would have been a backwards step. If it wasn't for Kathy, I wouldn't have had any - what's the word I'm looking for, Kathy - ?

Kathy: Confidence. He wouldn't have had any confidence *at all.*

Robert: I couldn't walk the road on my own -

Kathy: He'd been married and had two sons before I met him but she couldn't cope with Robert's smack habit. And it was Robert's fault at the end of the day cause I've been to his wife's house and I've seen his wife and children.

Robert: Eventually, I had a breakdown. I went up to Cefn Coed four times but even after that, my head was down because I thought everybody knew about me. A lot of people didn't realize I'd been through three years of sheer hell and really wanted to sort my life out. They were saying 'Oh, he's a known drug-addict!' and a lot of them -

Kathy: disapproved of me being with Robert, because I've always been straight - never drunk or took drugs - and it took them a long time to come round to realizing that I'd chosen Robert as a person to live with and be with -

Robert: But now I can hold my head up. I can sit down with Sara and I can have a drink but we're not alcoholics. My father was a total, absolutely gone-to-the-limit alcoholic. Went round in a car once, with a knife, looking for my mother. He was a sergeant in the army in Africa. A very well-educated man who came from a well-to-do family. I never heard an obscene word ever came out of his mouth. But that's what alcohol can do to people. It's totally degrading. I felt really bad for *him* but before he died - ten to fourteen years before - he was absolutely straight. A gentleman. He realized in time, luckily. And he died penniless.

Kathy: I never drunk at all until two years ago. Only a glass of wine when I used to go out. It wasn't because I was worried about becoming an alcoholic. I had no intentions of becoming one. After what I've seen, know what I mean? I only mix in that circle because of my mother: see how she's getting on and who she's with, basically. I know Sara says she takes after my grandmother but my mother's memory is very *vivid*. My grandmother was never an alcoholic.

Robert: But she wasn't a very good mother to Sara, was she?

Kathy: My grandmother was very strict. I went there to live for two years when I was young. I can't remember much but I've heard all my family say my grandmother was very hard. Her ouse was left to my mother but cause my mother was getting in so much trouble with the police at the time, my oldest aunty jumped in and said 'Sara's not having this ouse! She's not *worthy* of it.'

Kathy: I was never in Paxton Street but I was in and out of the old SASH, opposite Dora's Night Club. It's closed now. So's Dora's. Oh God, you're going back a bit. They used to have a big, huge fire in there. And a chair by the fire. I was the only woman in there at the time. So that was frightening in itself. Belfast Danny was there but he was young in those days, nothing like he is now. He was just coming out on the scene, really. He wasn an alcoholic - not to what he is now. I mean he's *gotto* have a drink now. I've known him all my life. I've known all the alcoholics, the tramps, the old heads. Danny had a good job in Ireland. I've heard bits and bobs about his life but Danny don't say a lot. I seen him Saturday. Know the sandwiches I took off the Run? I took them round to him.

Robert: We helped put the tent up for Bernie -

Kathy: It's right opposite the County Hall. The new, big white building.

Robert: The Great White Elephant -

Kathy: We was down there having a drink with them and whatnot. I didn't think Danny'd make this winter, to be honest with you but e ave, thank God. Cause I've seen loads die on the streets and I've seen younger than that go. Joe Tanner was one of the last. He died in the Ableglaze building. The verdict was pneumonia but my mother *told* me he was going to die. She got a way of saying 'He haven't got long.' D'you know what I mean? She seems to know, from looking at so many. Like Sara, herself. She aven't got long. It wouldn't surprise me this time, cause I was warned this Winter, she won't make it. She's awful bad. I've never known my mother to moan as much as she ave this year. I take her ome with me and I keep her ome as long as I can. But then I can't keep her in. Once they're used to being out there, that's it.

Robert: Three days and she gotto -

Kathy: wander. Oh, it's horrendous, sometimes, having her home! I've got a normal family home, I have, with a telly and a cooker and I do my nine to five job with my children - yeah? But when Sara's there, she goes back to bein a child. It's like having *four* kids not one. After being out there so long, she can't settle. I have had her livin with me for six months - her and Rick and all of us - in Blaenymaes, the omeless flats. Waiting for a Council House we were. They'd just come back from Cheltenham and she was ill and they arrived like nothing I'd ever seen - as if they'd both been down a coal mine. They asked me if they could stay and I said yeah, as long as they behaved. I couldn't turn them away but having Rick and my mother in the same ouse is - oh! - terrible! One is okay at a time. But Rick is stone deaf, so you gotto scream and have the telly up full blast cause he can't hear a thing. No, I can't put up with Rick and my mother *together*. A week for one and a week for the other, d'you know what I mean? And then she'd get mad with Rick and say 'You're takin my daughter off me!' Like a child. Jealous, like a child.

Robert: And, if I can say: it can get very awkward for me as well because

Kathy: she gets very nasty with Robert

Robert: not because she knows I love Kathy and would never see any harm come to her but because of me being *close* to Kathy, so I gotto

Kathy: step back

Robert: a little bit and let things carry on And sometimes she gets drunk and then she gets

Kathy: violent. And I gotto take her to bed then. She's fifty-six but, like, when she goes to bed I gotto take her and undress her and put her nightie on like a two-year old

Robert: Like a baby -

Kathy: Like I take my own child of twelve to bed, tuck her in, give her a kiss, read her a book or whatever. Know what I mean? That's the way I have to treat my mother. She's sober when she comes to the house and then she aves a drink and, obviously, I can't stop her, but she can get awful violent, can't she?

Robert: And she's getting worse. She swears

Kathy: And we don't swear in front of our children

Robert: at all

Kathy: and I wouldn't expect my child to hear it. I ask her not to and she gets worse, don she? At times, I've asked her to leave cause my daughter's really scared of her.

Robert: My two children come round to see us quite a lot but they can understand

Kathy: cause they're older. But my daughter's twelve and she doesn't like no violence. She's never seen it. My mother's never bought me a Christmas or a birthday present all my life - or my daughter. I buy my daughter Christmas cards and Christmas presents and say they're off her nan. And I always have. Not having a mother of my own, I had to *learn* how to handle my own child. Sara's got four children but she's never been a mother to any of them. She goes harping on about her hard life but Billy Preece bought her her own house, at one point in her life.

Robert: In her younger days, she had it *all*. The number of men that would have taken her and given her everything she wanted! But she didn't, did she?

Kathy: I went down to Cardiff when I was sixteen and saw her working there one night. She's well-known all over the country. Everybody knows Sara. There's a lot of people in Swansea that despise her for the damage she done to her children. It's all in the library - exactly what she did. I went back once and looked it up. 1964. She'd come out of prison and had me out of Care and we went to live in Westbury Street. I was only two and a half but she left us locked up in the house for four days and four nights.

Robert: As babies

Kathy: One in a cot and three toddlers

Robert: Covered in excreta and everything.

Kathy: It's all in the papers. So there's a lot of people in Swansea don't like her.

Robert: Kathy's life has been very - how can I say? - *tormented*, because she has nobody to fall back on, no relation she can go and sit down with and have a cup of tea and a chat with and say what she gotto say. Get it off her mind. I've never been closer to any person in my whole life than this woman here but she's had no mammy at all

Kathy: Ever. She wouldn't know where to start.

Robert: Even when you see us sitting down together

Kathy: There's no love lost -

Robert: None at all. Our concern is just humanitarian.

Kathy: That's all that keeps me there. How can you love someone you never knew? You *can't*. To love your parents, they ave to bring you up. They have to look after you. They have to see to you. I do what I gotto do - cause she's getting old. Even now, I couldn't rely on Sara for a loaf of bread or a pint of milk of a daytime. I hate her for what she did. But I can't let her know that. Not at her age and the way she is. She has to die with some sort of dignity. If I gotto lie, I'll lie. Know what I mean?

Robert: Exactly. We've had long discussions about it.

Kathy: I couldn't be that heartless in the end.

Robert: There's no way you can let a woman like that die, without

Kathy: her respect

Robert: Somebody to respect her. And for *humanitarian* reasons, if that's the right word-

Kathy: Yeah, that's all I got. That's all we respect her for. You can't love someone you've never known.

Robert: Even if she gets *in* Dinas Fechan, she won't *stay* there.

Kathy: I've had a room there for her before. Four years ago. Through Housing Options. *One* day, she stayed. If they was to give her a Council place, she'd stay there. But they can't give her one unless she goes through the system, like everybody else.

Robert: The reasons they gave us was that she's a danger to herself and other people.

Kathy: But she's no danger to the public. I've gone out all day and left her. She makes me lock her in and she stays there all day. She's never burnt herself or the house, has she? She wants me to take her down Dinas Fechan after and if this room is still open, I'll take her. But she's like as if she thinks I'm goin to *stay* there. I can't *stay* there. I got a *family* to see to.

Robert: She won't settle. It's like somethin's inbred in her, after bein out there so long

Kathy: No, she won't. I know her. I told Wayne on the soup run: 'I've tried to get her bedsits up in Walter's Road and she hasn't lasted two minutes.' All she needs is somethin at night, cause she's a day person. Yeah? She keeps saying 'Take me down Dinas Fechan tonight,' I can't get it into her head, she's gotto book in in the *mornin* to get in in the *night*. 'Oh, it'll be all right, they'll let me in,' she says. And I tell her 'You have to go through the system to get what you want.' She's really hard work. And she needs things all the time. I give her clothes - good clothes - and tell her not to throw them away and she throws them away. A good set of clothes! I gets really annoyed.

Robert: Could I say this? There's a man who wants to write a book about all this. Michael Bellany. He's Kathy's mother and father and grandparents and the only person who put Kathy in touch with

Kathy: reality.

Robert: The only person she could trust and who would listen.

Kathy: He was my Case Worker. They said to him 'You've got three years to educate this child and if she doesn't come out of it by the time she's sixteen, we'll just have to certify her insane and put her in a sanatorium. I didn't *speak*, see!

Robert: She *wouldn't* speak.

Kathy: For years and years. At *all*.

Robert: Not a word.

Kathy: Just sit there, day in and day out. And he was my only Carer in this building for three years. Just me and him and three cells. He used to come in every day and do a lot of screamin and shoutin to make me scream back at him.

Robert: He had to get her to talk. Scream at her for her to scream back -

Kathy: He'd annoy me, make me lose my temper, say things about my mother I wouldn't want to hear. Anything, as long as I'd speak. But after thirteen years not saying anything and nobody listening anyway, I just didn't have *anything* to say.

Robert: They wouldn't believe that Kathy could bring up a child on her own.

Kathy: There was no one there to teach me how to be a mother. I learnt myself. I had loads of help from Michael Ballany, from when I was younger up until now. I still see him often. I phone him all the time and he comes down whenever I need him. He's like a lifeline. He's

Robert: Kathy's best friend.

Kathy: He finished as a Social Worker after me and bought a farm in Carmarthen.

Robert: He come up from Carmarthen and bought that picture you did of us,

Kathy: for his Lounge

Robert: And every time he looks at it, he says he can see something different.

Kathy: He never thought I'd make it at eighteen. And I almost didn.

Robert: It all boils back to the beginning, when Kathy was born. Sara could have signed a bit of paper when she was in prison, for Kathy to live with a relative, but she didn't. And that, of course, forced Kathy to be

Kathy: Institutionalized.

Robert: But that couldn't appen now

Kathy: No, it'll *never* appen again. The Judge of Chambers I went to to get released said 'It'll never appen again,' I've had letters of apology for it all - from the Director of Social Services.

Robert: And Michael Bellany has said categorically that what happened to Kathy, *could not* and *will not* happen again. Not in *today's* society...

'I once was lost but now am found...'

Bill and the Bible Class

A short, middle-aged man with white hair and a big white moustache, his hands twisted with arthritis. He's still talking when I slip in at the end of the Bible lesson and sit down near the door. There's no more than a dozen or so people in the Hall, including Bill and his helpers. I spot Will and Ceri straight away but don't recognize anyone else. Will is sitting on the other side of the room, heckling quietly - and not so quietly - under his breath and Ceri is sitting up front nodding in agreement with every word, whilst munching away at a packet of Rich Tea biscuits. There's a plump, red-faced man at the back with bicycle clips on, sleeping next to his bike. People are still arriving in ones and twos, in anticipation of the food that is soon to follow. It's a Saturday night like any other Saturday night, in a church hall somewhere in the centre of Town...

Bill: ... and so Jesus said *'Ought not this woman to be healed?'* She was a daughter of Abraham whom Satan had found and Satan was doing his utmost to blind the eyes of people who would not believe. Can you see that? *Why* didn't they believe? *What* had they been told? You had a people here in this synagogue who were being led by a shepherd who didn't know where he was. So what does that tell us?

Peter: It tells us that that is what is lacking today, Bill: *faith.* People just don't *believe* in it any more. They go to church as a matter of form. They sits down, they gets up and they goes home. The Bible's just like any other book to them. They haven't got the faith, see, Bill. That's why it won't work: cause E *knows* when you aven't got the faith but once E *knows* that you've got the faith - like you said yourself, Bill, E *knows* you are genuine then and everythin will be given to you in abundance.

Bill: That's right, Peter. Okay! Let's move on to Isaiah 52... Come on in, folks - !

Will: Come on in, boys! Don't wait out there in the cold!

Ceri: C'mon over by ere, Colin!

Colin: Hang on - let me finish this roll first -

Bill: This is what it says: *'Behold my servant. He shall be exalted and extolled and be very*

211

high' - put that fag out, please!

Colin: It *is* out, Bill. I just put it out. You see but you do not observe. What page are we on?

Bill: Page four-hundred and fifty-six -

Colin: What book are we in?

Bill: Old Testament: Isaiah.

Will: There's an old joke about Isaiah - !

Bill: Quickly now, folks. We want to get to the end of this little bit tonight.

Colin: I'll find it, don't worry. I go to Fellowship every Sunday in Spring Terrace. They told me last week they wanted me to be an Official. Which chapter?

Bill: Fifty-two: six eight nine.

Colin: Isaiah's a big book -

Bill: Okay, listen to what it says -

Colin: Lots of pages in it -

Bill: Quiet, now then, cause we want to get through this little passage and then we can have some soup.

Colin: Sorry we're late, Bill. The chain went on my bike down by Brynhyfryd lights. Have a look at this: I've just bought this lovely new Bible. It cost thirty-five quid but it's got all the Books in it - every one. It's got the Old Testament, the New Testament *and* the Apocrypha.

Will: The Apocalypse?

Colin: No - the Apocrypha! It's got *everything* in it.

Bill: Thank you! If you want to talk, go outside the door and wait for the Bible Study to finish. Right, where were we? *'Behold my servant! He shall be exalted and extolled'.* That's talkin about the Messiah -

Colin: He died for *me* and for *you*! Some people even go so far as to say He survived the Crucifixion -

Bill: And then it goes on to say this: *'He was despised and rejected of men and we did not esteem Him.'* So, you see, what it boils down to is that everybody in 'church' had been listening to the 'vicar'. Now let me just warn everybody in this room tonight: 'Don't listen to preachers or take what they say to be jonnick. Right? Listen to preachers and then look at the Bible. See what it has to say. If they are not preaching what the Bible says, they are *false* prophets.

Colin: The Reverend Frank Price *I* go to, in Spring Terrace, Bill. *He's* not a false prophet.

Bill: D'you hear what I'm saying? If they do not say what the scripture says, they are *false prophets*! No matter how wonderful a preacher they may be.

Colin: But he's *really* good in Spring Terrace, Bill -

Bill: No matter *how* great a Theologian they might be.

Colin: But Frank Price is *definitely* not a false prophet. He is very very good -

Peter: This woman I know listened to false prophets, Bill, and as a result she give up the chap she was engaged to be married to and called it a day cause she listened to what the man was sayin up there on the altar - the pastor or whoever it was - and after that she more or less married far below herself.

Colin: I'm a Catholic, I am, but I started going to Spring Terrace as well cause I like Frank and he gives a good service as well. It's *educational.*

Peter: She *threw* it away see, Bill, because she listened to the one man. And she lost it *all*.

Colin: *And* I go to the Salvation Army as well, cause I've got friends in the Salvation Army and I'm really enjoyin it -

Bill: Okay, quiet now! Let's go back to that other verse in Matthew: *'And when she had said these things, all his adversaries were ashamed -'*

Colin: And I used to go to St. Mary's, the Jesuit church in Bristol. I used to play the organ there -

Bill: *'and all the people rejoiced for the glorious things that were done by him.'* What does that tell you about the people?

Colin: They got a computer organ there and when I played the Voluntary, it printed it out as I was playing.

Will: Not in *manuscript* form, though?

Colin: In *manuscript* form. I played it and it did a print-out for me.

Will: Impossible! It *couldn't* have!

Colin: It **did!** As I was playing, it printed it out -

Will: I don't believe you!

Colin: On my **life!**

Bill: If you want to talk -

Colin: *I'm* not talkin, Bill. I want to concentrate on the Bible. It's not *my* fault. I'd rather listen. I'll talk to Will after.

Bill: Okay -

Colin: Later *on*, I mean.

Bill: We're comin to the end now -

Will: That's what I was tellin you at the **beginning**!

Colin: Shh! **Shhh!**

Bill: And if you look in Matthew's Gospel, you find there the fulfilment of these passages of scripture: *'The people rejoiced for all the glorious things that were done by Jesus.'* They saw this wonderful thing happening and they rejoiced. Now is that the way to be?

Will/Ceri: Yes!

Bill: I'll ask you again: is that the way to be?

Peter: Actions speak louder than words, Bill.

Colin: *'By Thy fruits shalt thou know them,'* says the Bible.

Bill: The people are looking at the priest, saying: *'This woman cannot be healed.'* And all the people *rejoiced!* Is that the way to be?

Woman: No. They should have believed before that.

Bill: That's *right!* God is calling you as well as me - as well as this priest - to believe what the scripture says, to walk according to what the word of God says. So that we are not tossed about by every idle doctrine that comes up. Listen to *men* and you'll be all over the place. You'll *lose* your salvation. You'll get all sorts of rubbish thrown at you.

Colin: Absolute **trash!**

Bill: This is what God says. *Survive this and these blessings will come upon you.* Now, folks, God is here tonight - in spirit. If you believe him. If you **listen** to him, he'll *save* you. And not in eighteen years time - and not tomorrow cause it's the Sabbath - Jesus wants you **today**. And all you gotto do is -

Colin: Can I say somethin, Bill? Can I make an announcement? For the first time in my *entire* life, I cycled all the way up Pentregethin Road without stopping. I managed to cycle **all the way** to the top. I'm just so fit, you wouldn't **believe** it! I've cut down so much on my cigarettes and my lungs have cleared up so much, I can even cycle right the way up to the top of Penlan now without stopping and *that's* ow fit it's made me!

Bill: Right, it's nearly eight o' clock: time for a break. Let us pray: Father, we want to thank you for your wonderful word which will *never* pass away. Men's ideas are just goin to be

214

burnt up as rubbish. We want to be men and women who believe *your* word. We pray for healing, deliverance and salvation and we thank you for the provision of this food, Lord, and for all the things you give us so richly to enjoy. Amen.

...A babble of voices all speaking in tongues and a scramble to the food table. Suddenly the room begins to fill up. Colin marches straight to the piano and strikes up with 'Love Divine All Loves Excelling'. Beefburgers are passed from hand to hand, soup ladled into plastic cups. Bill circulates and I sit trying to talk to Will and Ceri above the racket. Bernie and the Bowling Team arrive. Colin abruptly stops playing the piano and starts marching round the room, singing Irish rebel songs at the top of his voice. An old lady hands me a beefburger. I thank her but, not being a beef eater, surreptitiously slip it in my pocket. A moment later, somebody hands me another one. When I eventually do get to talk to Bill, it's against a background of Colin's thumping piano music and straining contralto: 'Jerusalem', 'Jesu Joy of Man's Desiring', 'Amazing Grace'...

Bill: I got saved in 1970 and it was through coming to the Lord that I started preaching. And I started coming to this church cause a guy asked if I'd help out in the Coffee Bar. Now I was as green as grass, as you can imagine. I was newly saved. I didn't know what it was all about but I said okay, little realizing that twenty-seven years later, I'd *still* be here! The guy left after a couple of months, so I was left holding the baby, as it were. So that's how I came into it. It wasn't out of any desire to help people, really, cause I didn't know what it was all about. Basically, I believed in God before but I didn't have any sense of real commitment. And coming to know the Lord actually happened *overnight*. At four o'clock in the morning in my bedroom, I asked Jesus to be my Saviour.

We're here every Saturday except for perhaps one or two odd Saturday nights and the month of August. And there's a need for a break - for everybody. There's a need of a break for these boys from us, too. Because they hear the Gospel here, as you will have noticed tonight as well as being fed and looked after and given clothing, if they need it. They all read. We have a reading round and then people are allowed to ask questions. It's not like a straight Service. People can join in - and they *like* that.

The Chapel finances the kitchen. It's mostly from people that just give. You don't have to ask them - they give. People just say 'This is for the Coffee Bar,' and they'll either give in kind or they'll give money, so we're never ever short. For the past twenty-seven years the place has been continually ticking over and I've never had to say we're short of money or we haven't got this that and the other. It's always looked after here.

I do street preaching at St. Mary's every Friday and Saturday. That's every week. It never stops. And if I'm not there, there are others who do it. But, the thing is St. Mary's is a place where you meet the boys. People who just dribble into Swansea come to hear the Gospel and they say 'Do you know anywhere where I can get food or anywhere where I can get accommodation and clothing?' So, if you like, it's a *focal* point. We can advise them on accommodation because of the network that's in place. You've got people like the Cyrenians, the Sally Army and ACTS who all do a soup run and the Council have set up this business whereby you can point people to a place where they can get help. So it's very good but it's only really happened during this past twelve months. Before that it was a bit hit-and-miss. During the cold weather these organisations provide *something,* but the rest of the time people have to fend for themselves,

Betty and Rob were marvellous in the early days. They used to run Bowen's Cafe in St. Helen's Road and they set up this place in Cambrian Place where people could get in and we used to go down there with them. And they had Dr Flood's old house in Alexandra road, which was another brilliant place. And then they had another place in Stembridge Avenue but that closed cause funds started to dry up.

I know that things are moving slowly about a Day Centre and that's really what these guys could do with. They're not so fussy about the night. It's crazy, I know, cause you'd think they'd want to get in but they don't. But a day place is somewhere where they could have a bit of a rest, like - and company. Cause they *need* that.

Any memorable moments? Oh crumbs, lots of them! But for me, the most memorable moments have been when people have got saved and brought out of the gutter into a new life. And, you know, there've been many. Like Hadyn, for example. He was a tramp and he was outside and one of the ladies fetched him in. We talked to him and after a few weeks he came to know the Lord and he changed totally. And there was another one called Vivian and he lived in a little Thames van - you know the little Thames Escort van? - behind the BBC on Clifton Hill, on a car park there. And we met him in the market one day and invited him to the Coffee Bar and for months he was coming back and fore and eventually a guy from the Bible College - a black guy from Nigeria - came and led him to the Lord. And it was *wonderful*! And as a result of that, he had some publicity in the paper and his son came from Cardiff and took him to live with him. So he was put right. And then there was a girl who had had a good position in Swansea - plenty of money and a house down Langland - but through divorce and one thing and another, her life took a nose-dive. We found her sleeping rough with the rest of the boys. Louise her name was. And we invited her to the Coffee Bar and two of the ladies visited her and led her to the Lord. And her life *totally* changed and that's wonderful to me. Now she's working with people who are autistic or have learning difficulties. There are lots of stories about people like that, and for me, it makes it all worthwhile, because it's just *wonderful* to see people coming out of the wilderness. And just looking at these boys enjoying themselves here tonight, says it *all*: *We* love *them* and *they* love *us!*

'Speaking as God...'

Steve

We sit facing each other in armchairs in the front office of the Hostel. A short, pale-faced, boyish-looking man in his late thirties, wearing a brown leather bomber jacket. He was once a pupil at a local Comprehensive School at the same time that I was teaching there but neither of us remember the other. He speaks matter-of-factly and with conviction, repeating himself over and over, for emphasis...

I was one of five children and I was born next to a police station in Clase. My mother was from a good family and my father was a rag-and-bone man, believe it or not. They weren't very happy. He used to carry on a lot. He died of thrombosis when I was thirteen and I couldn't accept his death: I had this hatred in me for *everybody* and *everything.* I loved my father. I loved him *terrible* and after he died, I didn't care about anything any more.

Two years later, my mother remarried and had a sixth child by the second marriage. My stepfather was from a very posh, well-to-do Swansea family. He was a lecturer in mathematics. He got a Master's Degree in it and he's a mathematical genius now. Before they got married, she told him she only had *three* children, so I had to go and live with my aunty and my other brother had to live with my gran. Therefore, we didn't exist as far as they were concerned.

I lived with my aunty in her caravan for a bit and then, at the age of sixteen, she threw me out and I started living on my own. A girl called Cherie, had an abortion through me round about this time and, because I was young, it affected me and I felt as though I'd committed a murder. I started going downhill after that and they took me into Cefn Coed with mild schizophrenia. It took me two years to pull myself together, then I got into Peace and Love - Flower Power - long hair, drugs and barbiturates...

When I was twenty-three, I had a shot-gun wedding to a girl called Maureen: a nice girl - and very clean. But it wasn't meant to happen, you know? I said to my brother 'It's not going to work.' He said 'It's *gotto* now: she's *pregnant.*' We lived in a Council flat in Blaenymaes and I was in Mothercare one day, with my son on my shoulders, and I bumped into Cherie again. I still had feelings towards her as a friend and I still loved her, cause she was a lovely girl and - I'll never forget it - she looked at me as much as to say: '*That* should have been *my* child.' And that started the schizophrenia up again. I started hearing voices and imagining the fridge was talking to me and that Maureen was carrying on. I got a bit better as time went on but her parents weren't supportive so we had a divorce and I kept the house on for six months and, during that time, a friend said 'Go and see Cherie.' She'd been working in Debenhams and I was going to go but she died of cancer before I had a chance. I heard later, from friends, that she'd been having chemotherapy and all her hair had fallen out. So, through taking barbiturates and various other things - like my father dying and Cherie and the abortion and the aggro of the divorce - at the age of thirty-one, I had a complete breakdown. Maureen claimed the house back and for the next two years I ended up in a string of psychiatric hospitals: in Bristol, Bridgend and finally St Tydfil's, a Rehabilitation Centre, in Merthyr. I tried to commit suicide in there. A chap left his drugs out and I took them. My heart stopped for two and a half minutes. I locked the door but they found me in time. *Luck* it was. But a Dr E.T. Reilly - a marvellous doctor - got me out of it and *how* he got me out of it I'll never know.

I was in and out of hospital in Merthyr for six or seven years and when I came back to Swansea I decided to come off all drugs. I moved in with my aunt again but she couldn't cope with me so, from there, I moved into a bed and breakfast place on the sea front. They were supposed to give me three months notice but after a week they threw me out. It was around Christmas time and it was absolutely hammering down with rain and they had no right to but, luckily, I bumped into Joe Tanner and he said there was a room going in the Hostel. I was here for about three months and it was marvellous but then, because I was still sufferin from schizophrenia, I decided the best thing to do was to go round the country on my own. I was gone fourteen months. I walked from here to Brecon, sleeping rough, then I bought some Army equipment and went from there to Hereford, London, Kent, Ireland: virtually *all* round the country.

I had a sleeping bag and a camping stove and I was able to cook for myself, which a lot of people can't do. I was averagin twenty-five to thirty miles a day. Before, I'd been on so much medication, it was unbelievable but I came off all that when I was walking. I used to stay in the woods or the forest. The only time I'd communicate with people was in the Social Security and I used to give them my National Insurance number, tell them what I was doin and say 'Please can I have my money? And I was lucky: they used to be very sympathetic and give me it straightaway. But after fourteen months, I was fed up: so many places in such a short space of time.

When I came back to Swansea, I slept rough for a while in a concrete shed up by Cockett station. I had bits of cardboard down and two blankets. No lightin, except a candle. It was below freezin and kids used to throw bricks at me thinking I was a tramp. I would pretend to trainspot but I had nowhere else to go. I cooked on the stove and I used to go to the nearest toilet to have a wash and a shave. I was there a couple of weeks. There's a guy in the flat below who used to sleep in a little park nearby but he had a gortex tent and all the right equipment. And he used to help me a lot and, if it wasn't for him, I could have froze to death. Conrad and a few of them in the Hostel got to hear about it and they got in touch with the Evening Post, who did a picture and a write-up.

After that, I was lucky. I couldn't get back into Paxton Street but I got into Stembridge. I stayed there for a while but I was getting violent schizophrenia - shouting a lot and smashing things up, so Kevin Quayle got me into Cefn Coed and when I come back out I went into a bedsitter through the Cefn Coed Project.

The Cefn Coed Project is a Care in the Community thing and it's one of the few instances where it's working. They find you accommodation and if you're ill, you have a nurse to check up on you every so often. It gives you back your dignity and it's an alternative to living in Cefn Coed or in a hostel. You can't get a flat straightaway - I had to wait two and a half years for mine - but they can help you fit back into the community. When you're in hospital and you've gotto come out, they make sure you've got somewhere to stay. You're entitled to a social worker, too. It's back-up and they won't kick you out on the street if you're havin problems. Because of the schizophrenia, I wrecked my place about eight weeks ago and they *still* kept me on cause I didn't hurt anybody.

I'm livin by the fire station at the moment. Nice place. I got Elvis Presley, Marilyn Monroe and The Beatles there now - in black and white - and Kevin gave me a photo of these dopamine cells that causes schizophrenia and I got them up on the walls as well. I done all the flat out, painted it all: bathroom, kitchen, living room and he's doin me a big oil painting as well but it's not goin to look right. It's goin to clash with Marilyn Monroe and the Beatles and the trouble is: I can't refuse it, I've *gotto* put it up on the wall.

Joe Tanner lived there for a bit and my mate, Eddie Laing. Joe was from London. A lovely man but he was going through a really bad time because of his marriage split-up and so was Eddie. Joe's wife was much younger than him and she'd thrown him out because she wanted somebody else. He took to drink then. The three of us was all in the flat one day playing cards and Joe suddenly said 'Let's all be blood brothers!' and he and Eddie slit their wrists in front of me with an open razor. There was blood pumping everywhere. They wanted me to do it, too but I ran downstairs to phone and they rushed them both into Hospital for blood transfusions. That was six years before Joe actually died - and he was *lucky* then, to be quite honest with you. Another couple of minutes and they would have both died. They put Joe in Cefn Coed for a while but he never got over the split-up. And that's basically why he took to drink and sleepin rough and ended up freezin to death in The Glass House.

I've been in hostels all over the place. I've seen hostels in Plymouth and Worcester, for instance, which are massive compared to the one in Swansea. They've got cameras, video, a pool room, Day Centres - they got *everything*. I don't understand why the Government don't give the same to Swansea as everyone else: bigger places, more facilities.

Betty and her husband Rob founded the first hostel in Swansea - off their own backs. They were very nice people. They used to run Bowen's Cafe and I used to go there regular. Betty's eighty-odd now and still going strong but I've known her since I was seventeen. I stayed in the first place they ad down by the docks. I got talking to them over a cup of tea and they could see I was homeless and looking for somewhere to stay. I'd heard they'd fixed up a house and were helping people, so I asked them and they said they didn't think I'd like it there and I oughto get myself a bedsitter. But they put me up and they used to have alcoholics there and they wasn't drinkin cider like they do today, they was drinkin *meths*. There was about twenty of them - you know, proper tramps - and they'd be screaming in the middle of the night and smearing the walls with their own excrement. But you'd have a good meal there and, fair do's to Betty and Rob, they'd make the meal and they'd have volunteers helping out as well. I only stayed there one night and it frightened me so much, I moved into a bed-sit.

I've got a very strong sex-drive. Sexual-wise, from the age of twenty-one till twenty-three, I went with *seventy-eight* different women. Besides my son, I've got three children with solicitors as well. I got a little girl by Miss Dwyer of Ledbury, Dwyer and Simpson and two boys with Miss Corbett: she's a solicitor, too. Why solicitors? I was up in court for violence and they defended me. So, I've got four kids altogether: one by my first marriage and three illegitimately. My boy's sixteen and the other three are two, four and five. I see my boy but I don't see the other three at all. I've been *deprived* of seeing them, which I think is wrong. The two mothers live in Cherry Grove but neither of them wanted to get married to me. Miss Dwyer's family owns half the Uplands and I *could* claim maintenance off her but I'm happy as I am at the moment

The children were the result of a very short relationship - just one night - and if I told you how I got them, you wouldn't believe me. Miss Dwyer gave birth in a barn down in Pwlldu. I can show you the barn as well. There's a cottage there at the end of Pwlldu lane and you can walk right down to the beach. I was in Swansea when it happened - in sixty-one Ravenhill Road. They were down there cause it was nature for them to go down there for the birth, but it could have been Carmarthen or London or *anywhere*. Her father had put a lock on the door but I stepped over the door and I went like this with my hands and my spirit left my body and I give her a child. That's the way it happens. When I says my spirit left my body, people look at me stupid. But it *did* appen. It's nature. It's part of life. I can take you down to the ouse in Pwlldu *now* if you don't believe me. Same thing appened with Miss Corbett. They both ad children: not with my penis but with my spirit. And there would have been a third woman too, but I didn't turn up.

I went to see God before the births and after. He's retired now, cause he's seventy years of age, and *I've* taken over. Dr E. T. Reilly's the retired God and I can take you to see him as well if you want, up in Merthyr. I know it's hard to explain but everythin I'm sayin is the truth the whole truth and nothing but the truth, so help *myself.* My *family* didn't tell me the truth. *Nobody* told me the truth. They didn't tell me that I was Christ and so, all my life, I didn't *know.* I only found out when my spirit left my body. And I think it's wrong: the lies they told and the way it was kept from me, cause I have been almost murdered as a result and the doctors have been gamblin with my life. They've used me and abused me all my life and I've got the scars to prove it. And then they says 'God forgives.' I know plenty of people that's got two women and if it's *nature*, you *should* be with them. And then they says 'God Save the Queen,' and they're not prepared to do nothing about it. What's all this 'God Save the Queen,' stuff and God *this* and God *that?* What's it all about? I'm entitled to respect and I should have my status as well.

I am getting better now but I got no feeling for my mother or my family whatsoever, for what they done to me. My mother's got powers, too. She's goin to die in five years time but she can make my brother go blind cause I don't get on with him and then she'll want to make me go blind as well cause she thinks I'm in the I.R.A. and all that. And I'm not. When I was twenty-two, she took a photo of me with long blonde hair and a toosh. I wanted to show it to Kevin but she wouldn't give it to me. *That's* ow orrible she is. She thought I was goin to steal it but I wasn't. That's the only photo of me when I was twenty-one and I wanted Kevin to see just how much like the original Christ I looked. When my mother found out about Miss Dwyer and Miss Corbett, she hated me. But I don't feel sorry for myself. I can cope with it. And I don't feel guilty any more. I used to ask God to forgive *me* in the past but now I've got to forgive *myself*, haven't I?

In ten years time, I can see myself in a nice little job - nice little cushy number somewhere. I wouldn't mind going back to the YMCA and then back to college to try and study cause I went on a psychology course once and never stayed long enough to get qualifications. I wouldn't mind getting into computers, either. But what I'd really like to do is write a book about my life.

Nowadays, I just go out for a little drink, stay in then and read the paper. But at the moment I sort of can't concentrate. I'm trying to read more, so I can improve myself and basically I'll read any books but nothing complicated. I'm far from being dull but I gets a bit fuddled over spelling and pronunciation of words. But if I can read better, I'll be quite happy with myself.

I suffered a bit of brain damage after my suicide attempt and it's taken me till now to straighten myself out. I still suffer from schizophrenia but people *do* get better with it and, as Kevin Quayle says, 'You've gotto live with it.' I *do* know about the mentally ill cause I've been in hospital all my life and, speaking as God, I'll say it again: Conrad and Kevin and everyone else on the staff are doin a good job. They helped me a lot in the Cyrenians' Hostels. And, fair do's, they had a lot to put up with. I head-butted the gate off its hinges once. They must have thought 'Where did *he* come from?' And when somebody keeps saying 'I'm God, I'm God,' they must think he's right round the bend. They invited Lady Diana down here once but she didn't come, so what they've gotto do now is write to her again and say 'Listen, Lady Di, we're with God now and he's tellin us the *truth* and if you don't believe us, come and meet him down at the Hostel. He wants to be your boyfriend. But only in spirit...'

'... When you first saw us, you must have thought 'Here come The Two Ronnies!' St Mary's churchyard. Summer 1997.*

Top: *Last day of the Soup Run. St David's Square, Spring 1997.*

Bottom: *'. . . Catchin the Summer somewhere else . . .'*

Top: *Tuning up ... Cyrenians' beach barbecue, General Election Day, May 1st. 1997.*

Bottom: *'Underneath the arches,' Swansea Bay, May 1st, 1997.*

Top: *'Things can only get better ...'*

Bottom: *'Music you don't normally hear' ...*

APRIL

'Left, right and centre...'

Bob

I like writin. I've written a bit of poetry and things. I was editor of the magazine of one of these Drug Rehab Centres. I wrote myself out of prison once. I wrote and rewrote this letter to a Magistrates Court and the Magistrate said 'Your letter shows such' - what's the word? - '*sensitivity* and intelligence, we'd just like to wish you the best of luck. Normally we'd send you to prison for burglary but we're goin to give you probation.'

We arranged to meet at twelve 'o clock in the subway, where he frequently drinks at that hour of the day: usually with the residents of Number One, High Street. A short, stocky man with a beard and a distinctly Rastafarian hairstyle and mode of dress. He wears round thick-lensed National Health spectacles, like John Lennon, to whom he bears a marked resemblance.

I'm forty and I was born in Trowbridge in Wiltshire. My father was a tinsmith and my mother was a nurse but most of my relatives, on both sides of the family, were farmers or gardeners. I've got a younger brother and a younger sister, who've both done really well. We lived on the edge of a little market town called Melksham and to begin with, it was a happy childhood but when I was about twelve, my mother and father started fallin apart. There was never any violence but there were always loads of arguments and, being the oldest, I used to get involved a lot. I think part of the problem with her and my father was that they both got married when they were virgins and didn't know how to give each other proper relationships. My mother became a gambler-holic - addicted to gaming machines - and just seemed to stop caring. I used to have to see to my brother and sister and go to school in really scruffy stuff and do the shopping on my way home.

I left School at fifteen and met someone who introduced me to LSD. When my mother found out, I remember *her* havin a go at *me* and *me* having a go at *her* for gamblin. We made this deal with each other: if I stopped takin drugs, she'd stop gamblin - but it never worked out. They divorced when I was about seventeen or eighteen. It was my mother that cheated on my father but he afterwards admitted that he'd never been able to satisfy her in any way. After they split, he married again, three times.

I first went on the street about a year later. My dad had left home by then and I couldn't get on with my mother, so I was livin in this little shed in a graveyard. It was a bit spooky the first couple of times, cause it was where they used to keep the coffin wagon but I got used to it. I was there for six months and survived by shopliftin and occasionally breakin back into my mother's home for food. Then my mate, who was the same age as me and squattin in Bath, got to hear what I was doin and came and got me. He was into stealin cars and by the time I was twenty-two or twenty-three, he took me on the road in a bus. And that's how I first started travellin.

We eventually went our own ways in Exeter and I ended up going to live in a squat in Bristol with some other people. They were younger than me but they showed me how to beg. And then I met this girl and settled down and got a job and all that but after two years our relationship fell apart. I got a slipped disc for one thing and couldn't carry on with the gardening job I had and, cause I'd spent so many years outside, I just couldn't seem to settle down any more.

I went back to Exeter and before long I got involved with a girl who was a speed-freak. I had competition for her so, to keep her with me, I started burglin to get speed. It quickly became a Catch 22 situation: I'd burgle to get speed but every time I done speed, I'd get the desire to go burglin. I got caught four times: I got probation, two drug rehabs and three months in a Probation Hostel. I ended up doing a three-year sentence in Dartmoor for a burglary on a Conservative Club. For the first eight months they put me in the mail bag shop but then I went on an outside job. There's a little stream there, called The Leak, which is where they first got all their water from, and we had to go for miles across the Moor cleaning all the cow dung out of it. Then we dry-stone walled it and I *enjoyed* that, cause ever since I left school, I've been an outside person. My mother and father visited me once or twice, as they have done every time I've been inside.

I'd been in trouble on and off for eight years. But when I came out of prison and started burglin again, I think they knew it was cause of the drugs this time and started giving me chances. I was in the middle of a probation and this geezer asked me to go with him to Wells, so I went on the road with him and started beggin again. It seemed a better alternative to burglary and, in fact, I saw that as part of my rehabilitation, if you see what I mean.

I've been in Swansea eight months. The reason I came here was because I'd developed a heroin habit and I knew there wasn't a lot of heroin in this Town. I'd actually o.d.'d five times and been to hospital three times in other places, so I'm really lucky to be alive. I started livin in a squat and, with the help of SAND, I went through a detox.

I've made a lot of friends in this Town: Rocco, Nicki, Slug. I met Rob in this subway. His dog started attacking mine so I told him to put him on a lead or *I'd* get involved. But after that, I got to be his friend. The last time I seen him was the day before he died. He was squattin in an old furniture warehouse up on the High Street opposite Icelands. There's piles and piles of furniture in there and loads of mattresses. I'd been sleepin there ages but he only stayed in there one night and the next day he was dead. I didn't go to the funeral. I didn't know him that well to tell you the truth. But I was *gettin* to know him. It's really sad but I've known so many people that's died on the streets, it don't affect me any more like it should, if you know what I mean? Cause with the life we lead, people drop like flies, left, right and centre.

I've slept in many sorts of places: parks, doorways, an old band stand in Exeter. Recently, it's been skipperin out in car parks but most of the time when I was travellin, it was squats. You used to be able to go to a Town, look around for a derelict building that had electric, gas and water, reconnect it all and get in there. But people started smashin places up, so that give the Tories an excuse to bring in a clause in their Criminal Justice Bill. And since that new Bill come in, you can't squat any more. The police or the owners can give you twenty four hours notice and if you haven't left by then, they're legally allowed to use force to evict you. Since that happened, there's a lot more people on the street - I mean, actually *livin* on the street.

It's sleepin on concrete that makes you cold or benches like this with gaps in them. The first thing most people do is go behind the shops for cardboard and doss down on three or four layers of that. What *I* do, is find out where the carpet shops are and get bits of carpet that have been thrown out. Not a lot of people have sussed that one out yet but it's pretty obvious really.

I *would* use a night shelter if I was allowed to take my dog in there. In Bristol, you gotto tie your dog up near the door and put a few blankets down. That's all right but in most night shelters you're not allowed to take dogs in. Most of the old alcoholics on the street - I mean, *I'm* an alcoholic but they're *classic* alcoholics - use them but most *young* people who travel have got dogs and can't. Badger's three years old. She was born in March and spent her very first Winter with me. Cause she's long and lean, she sleeps in the doss-bag with me and so she keeps *me* warm and I keep *her* warm.

The homeless do get abused by the police because they know we haven't got a leg to stand on. Half the time homeless people get locked up for trivial things. Rob's dog got taken into a pound when he got arrested for drunk and disorderly and he had to pay £15 to get him out. They took all the rings out of Rob's ears, nose and mouth and, for some reason, wouldn't give them back - which upset him a lot. That almost happened to me down here. There was four of us sittin here all with our dogs, right, and I was like halfway through my second can and there was policemen came from all directions. Arrested all four of us for drunk and disorderly. They took us up to the van but they wouldn't take the dogs and I happened to see a couple of ladies I'd begged off before who knew me and I said 'Look, there's four dogs down there and they won't take them. *Please*, will you look after them for us.' When we got to the police station, the police rang the R.S.P.C.A. and said 'There's four dogs down in the Kingsway subway that we think are bein neglected.' We knew they weren't but you've gotto be really polite and careful what you say when you get taken in. You *creep* a bit. That's probably where Rob went wrong: if he was gettin angry or abusive and didn't creep, then they would have messed him about any way they could. When I was in the cells, I told the copper I was goin 'Not Guilty' and he said 'If you do that, because you've gone NFA, they'll put you on remand for at least a week.' So, cause of the dog, I had no option but to plead guilty, even though I wasn't. They let me out and, luckily, the two ladies brought the dogs back the next day.

They should have a Night Shelter and a Day Centre in Swansea where anyone can go in and there's no questions asked. Same as they've got in Bristol. It's just a big warehouse with loads of beds in and anyone can go in and get breakfast, which is just cornflakes with powdered milk, or dinner, which is just a stew. Somewhere where people can pop in for the day and watch telly and have a chat and not have to pay rent or sign a form and things like that. Homeless people can't *keep* appointments, they can't *keep* commitments. Know what I mean? That's the way we are. That's the reason why we are like we are.

You get used to sleepin out. If you spend a couple of weeks indoors - in Winter especially - and then you go outside, you feel the cold. But after a couple of days outside, you get used to it. I can't stay indoors any more because I went so long outdoors, it's in my blood. And it's the same with travellin. I've got itchy feet right now and in the next three

228

or four weeks I'll be gone. But I'll be coming back, cause I've got a lot of friends here now. I'm always going back to the places I've been before but I'll find somewhere new this year. Bangor, I think.

It's not a bad life: beggin and drinkin and havin a laugh with my mates. Sometimes I go for long walks with my dog. It varies how much I drink but mainly it's a lot. Too much. Between four and eight cans I'd say. I don't usually get drunk until the end of the night. But, then again, I take drugs as well: the occasional bit of speed, smoke. But, at least I've done one thing since I've been here: I've stopped doin heroin.

I'd like to *write* somethin in the future but first of all I've gotto settle myself down - *and* my mind. Which might take a lot of time and effort, you know? I haven't written for a while. I started in prison. I entered this competition and I won first prize The subject was 'Religion' cause it was the church that was runnin it. I'm not particularly religious - well, I am *slightly*, yeah, but I'm not sure about my beliefs. I think everyone who's *aware* has got a belief, but you've gotto believe in what you *know.* My parents weren't religious but they made sure I went to Sunday School, so with me it's Jesus, really, I suppose. It's what you're brought up with. Buddha, White Light or whatever: it's basically all the same thing.

I've read part of On the Road and I've read The Naked Lunch and Aldous Huxley, Herman Hesse and all that. Aldous Huxley took psychedelics and Burroughs was a right junkie, wasn't he? Herman Hesse, I don't think was - although he may have experimented. But he doesn't write about it. And Aldous Huxley don't much. I don't know. But really, what I suppose my ambition is, is to write something proper. Probably about what I've been through. Or just *anythin* really.

'Bad crack. Bad crack...'

Lyndon and Douggie

Lyndon: Me and Douggie's been scratchin our heads wondering where to start. And we keep calling you Alan. Your name's *not* Alan, is it? Oh, it *is* Alan! We didn't know whether it was John or Alan. You haven't got any relations in Briton Ferry have you? Cause the vicar in St. Clement's church was a Parry. Oh, *Perry*, you are! P - **e** - double-r - y. Oh, beg your pardon!

I first met them on the Soup Run: a short, slight man with a bald head and glasses who talks very precisely and a taller, swarthier-looking man who sometimes stumbles over his sentences and speaks with an even thicker Scottish accent than Alec's. I make them a cup of tea. They sit side by side and upright - like model pupils - in my studio's cramped writing area, as though not wanting to speak before they're spoken to...

Douggie: My mother's dead, my father's dead, my brothers are dead and my wife went and took an overdose and died at thirty-two. She's buried in London. She used to work on the buses and my father and brother and me were all in the pit. My granny was a hundred and ten when she died. So my mother and another two daughters went *before* her. *Hundred and ten!* She could still knit but her eyes were goin and I can remember her doin the washin with just a what-d'you-call-it - a scrubbin board. My older brother died nine months ago but my young brother Robert died at six. My Dad called the doctor and he said 'He's just got a touch of cold.' He didne take him in. If they'd a took him in right away he'd still be here yet cause, d'you know what he had? *Pneumonia.* I came out of the mine and worked in Ravenscraig for a bit but it closed down and after that I ended up in a hostel in the Gorbals. Oh God Almighty: about sixty or seventy people all sleepin rough on the floor there and rooms no bigger than toilets! Then my mate sent me a letter from Baglan Bay to say they were lookin for men and, because there was nothing left for me in Scotland, I come down right away and I've been here now for twenty-five years.

Lyndon: I don't know where to begin, really. I was born in Neath but I've spent all my life in Swansea. I went to Gregg's College at the age of eleven and I left at seventeen. And, although I'd had a commercial training, the first job I had after leaving School was with South Wales Sand and Gravel, down the South Dock. You're goin back to '61, '62 now. As a matter of fact, it's *this* month last year that my father passed away. He was 83. And my mother passed away five years ago in 1990. My father was a tin-plate worker and a lifelong member of Briton Ferry Working men's Club. A very popular man and a *devoted* member of Neath Rugby Club. I miss them both *terribly*, cause I haven't got a big family. I got a cousin in Briton Ferry and a brother in Llanelli so I'm more-or-less on my own. Well, yes: I *am* on my own.

After leaving the Docks, I had a job with McPrice, a transport firm in Neath Abbey. But then I decided I didn't want to work in offices any more and my mother had a word with the manager of John Temple in Queen Street in Neath and he said he'd like to see me with a view to me going into shop work. So I went to see him and I had a job straight away. I used to do relief work, which brought me into Swansea and after six years with them I got a job in Dean's the bespoke tailor's in Union Street. I was with Dean's for eight years. The factory was in London and they used to send the suits down by Red Star. We had a deadline for delivery and it was nothing to see me coming down the High Street on a Saturday morning, carrying this big box of suits. After Deans I went to work in Howells in Cardiff and after Howells, I was out of work for quite a long time. Then I went for an interview with Calders in Cardiff and I had a job just like *that.* But the only problem was, the wages were very low and quite a lot of my money went on travellin back and fore to Swansea. But it was the type of job I liked. I've got a photo here of me in Calders to show you... That's me on the end in the front... Of course, Calder's closed last year and that was the end of the story as far as my employment went because I'm 51 now and it's been twenty years since I've been in the trade.

I haven't been homeless long but I've gone through quite a bit. I slept rough behind the County Hall all last summer. I've had to settle all the debts connected with selling my parents' house and the money's just *gone* really. There's round about £2,000 that I can't account for, that's just *disappeared*, either with fees for the solicitors and Estate Agents or through the Bank. I shouldn't have asked the Bank to settle everythin, because that's what I done and now I haven't got nothing.

And to make matters worse, they've cut my Benefit, too. I had to go on a Board.

Oh, it's a long story, that! But there is an appeal in and my solicitor is waiting for them to say when it will be. I had to go in for a Crisis loan last year, which has to be paid off by the end of April. What happened, Mr Parry, is that they stopped my Housing Benefit and, of course, the landlord kept me on, didn't he and, cause of the period they stopped the Benefit, I ended up owing him £400. So it's all been quite a tremendous strain.

Douggie: My father'd got money saved up, so when he died we'd all have a thousand pounds each but my brother went and stole off him. He even stole a ring - just for drink, see. Cancer he had, same as my father. Oh, all up his back! He was like a skeleton. And just a year of difference between him and me. After what he done to my father, I promised I'd never go to my brother's funeral. But I *did* go. I tried to hitchhike up but I was unlucky. I got in a lorry just down from the bottom of Wind Street there and he took me almost ninety miles on the Motorway and just before we get to the M5, he radios ahead to his mate in another lorry a couple of miles away and says 'I've got a Jock here. I'll drop him off at the next roundabout and you can pick him up and take him the rest of the way.' So he drops me off and this other guy picks me up. But I was daft. D'you know what I done? I fell asleep in the cab and when I woke up I'd landed back in *Wind Street*! I couldn't believe it. I said to him 'Oh *Christ*, mun! I was goin tae **Scotland!**

Lyndon: We've been goin to the Salvation Army regular on a Sunday mornin.

Douggie: They gie you a voucher for two pounds - for fish and chips.

Lyndon: They do the same thing in St. David's. You can have a voucher for fish and chips on certain days - I think it's Mondays and Wednesdays - if you're homeless. They don't give you money but they help you out. Father Stephens and Father Francis are marvellous people. Some of the boys from High Street are regular there but one of the things I object to is that some of them are taking *advantage*. Me and Douggie goes up to the prayer meeting in the Pantygwydr on a Thursday and the pastor there was tellin us that he knows for a fact that quite a lot are doin it. Most are genuine he said but others are takin these vouchers and *sellin* them. Some of them would do anything for drink, wouldn't they? I mean, I've helped some of them out myself. The boys I had in my house when I was livin in Llansamlet! I mean, *I* was buyin the drink. You wouldn't see *them* when they got their money at the end of the week. I mean, let's be *fair*, isn't it? They'd just take advantage.

Douggie: I like to help people, too, but there's some are so ungrateful. There's one old boy on the street called 'The Brigadier'. I don't know if you know him. He says to me the other day 'Can you help me, Jock?' I says 'Aye,' and gives him a couple of bob - about one pound twenty I think it was - and he slapped me across the mouth. I said 'What'd you do *that* for?' He said 'That's not **enough**!' D'you know what I mean? You try and help people and they say *that. It's not on!'* I used to take them in just to gie them somethin to eat, cause I know what it's like mysel. I had seven in the house all at the same time once and I took this other one in and he stole a watch and a few other things.

Lyndon: Well, tell him what happened to me about the ring then -

Douggie: Oh yes. He asked this man to stay the night -

Lyndon: And he slept in the chair and in the morning he'd gone and so had my ring. A *one thousand pound* ring! I phoned the police and they had him in for questioning but they still haven't traced it.

Douggie: And it wasn't insured either -

Lyndon:*Terrible*, that was, I can tell you. It cut me like a knife. Tell him why I moved and why I sold the house.

Douggie: A lot of the boys used to come round to Lyndon's house for a drink. I was there in the kitchen one time and three of them broke in: two boys and a woman -

Lyndon: On drugs they were. Wanted to stay the night but I'd already told them I just didn't *want* them there because, I mean, I'd been goin back and fore all night gettin them drinks and *I* was payin for them -

Douggie: And then they *started* and this and that and Lyndon got a kickin and I had to call the police. Oh, Lyndon's lucky to be here! He was cut right down here, blood all over the place. In the end, I said to him 'You cannae stay here in case they come back.' So I got him out of there and took him back to my place. He sold the house and never went back.

Lyndon: Oh aye. Bad crack. Bad crack. It *was*, you know? I didn't even *know* some of these people but I try to avoid them now, don I?

Douggie: There's several we know of who've died on the streets

Lyndon: There was two over Christmas wasn't there?

Douggie: There was some old boy down in the cellar of the old church. I think it was the rats got him.

233

Lyndon: And Dan Piper up in High Street. They had to break a door down to find him. And then there was Billy -

Douggie: Oh aye. Billy Daniels. He couldne walk, see. He'd done somethin to his knee and he was just crawlin around St James's park there. I'd to lift him up two or three times - eleven o' clock at night - to take him to my flat. And then he finally got a place down West Cross. He'd only been there two weeks and d'you know what happened? There was a fire.

Lyndon: They took him up to Morriston with burns -

Douggie: Oh, *shame*, so it was! I got a shock cause I'd seen him just the day before. We went up to the hospital but the nurse says 'If you're not related, you can't see him,' so he must have been really bad.

Lyndon: He was from Armagh in Northern Ireland. And, of course, one of his relations came over for the funeral, but it happened so quickly, you know. Nice man. *Terrible* tragedy.

Douggie: And then there was Wally Crowther: died of cancer when he was sleepin rough. Well-known old boy in Swansea. He'd had a house at one time, cause I slept in it a couple of times, but they chucked him out in the end cause he wasne lookin after the place. I used to sleep rough with him when they were pullin those old houses down behind the Evening Post. We used to get waste wood and make a fire and I woke up a couple of nights and there were rats *that* size, runnin about! Och aye, I'm tellin you: sleepin like that *gets* to you in time! I got a house in Bonymaen just after that but Wally Crowther was still there when I left. I *do* feel really sorry for down and outs but, at the same time, I've gotto tell the truth: I coulda got some of them a place - but they *don't want* a place. That's funny, isn't it? I mean, you'd think in the cold weather, they'd take a place.

Lyndon: Most of them seem to have drink problems. Like Will and Ceri. Will drinks wine all the time and once he gets to a certain stage, he starts cursin and swearin and he does it sometimes outside Debenhams. Well, I mean, there's no *need* for that. I always move away -

Douggie: He used to go in the Civic Cafe but he got banned.

Lyndon: He can't get into the Duchess and he can't get into the Railway - so I took him down to the Naval Association the other day and he had a pint of Guinness with me. Only one pint cause I was afraid he might start. But he was alright. He's very knowledgeable. That's why I like talkin to the man - *when* he's sober. And he knows a lot about yachts and aircraft as well, cause I think he was in the RAF. Sometimes he goes into the workins of aircraft and I haven't got a *clue* myself. I don't know nothin at all about it!

Douggie: Ceri's improved over the years. I was with him one day and these two men from Llanelli came along and Ceri turns round and says to them 'Oh, I'll be down Llanelli in a couple of days!' And d'you know what they says to him? 'Oh, don't come down. Your mother doesne want tae see you'. They don't want to see him. That's what's wrong with him. It's a shame, cause he *has* quieted down and I think if they *did* take him back, he wouldne be the way he is.

'Shooting off on tangents...'

Ian

Stop me if I start shooting off on tangents - I always seem to. I'm forty next Sunday but I don't feel too bad about that because I remember years and years ago thinking I'd be lucky to get to twenty-one.

A thin, bean-pole of a man with pale-blue eyes, sunk in a round face. He looks ill but he smiles frequently in recalling events and warms more and more to the task...

I was born in Yorkshire but we moved to Scunthorpe when I was six or seven and I was brought up there. I've got two sisters and a brother younger than me. Me mother's still alive up in Scunthorpe but me dad was killed in a car crash in Morocco twelve years ago. He used to work in the admin side of Construction and me mum runs a flower stall now. He left her well-looked after when he died. We was a right, tight family and we all got on brilliantly. If you can think of the opposite to a broken home, that's what I come from really. I was bordering on being spoilt - I think we all were - cause me dad had a couple of shops and we always seemed to have money when we was kids. Maybe that give me the disrespect for money that I have today: not having to fight real hard for it. So, although I haven't spoken to my sisters or my mother for a couple of years there was a lot of love in the family and I'm *definitely* the black sheep. My brother's a solid geezer and a good mate: I don't think he's ever had a parkin ticket and he *certainly* don't drink or take drugs.

I left School at fifteen, because all me friends were working and I just wanted to get out there and be the same as everyone else. They were all well into drugs at the time - dropping pills, tripping, LSD - and I just naturally followed on. A lot of them were injecting as well but I held off that for a couple of years because I had a bit of a phobia about needles. I was that scared of vaccinations, I used to run away from home rather than go to School. I'd never have believed then, that I'd be sticking needles in myself.

When I finally did start injecting at sixteen, that sent me off on a totally different direction. I mean I *liked* it. I liked the buzz. They made me feel good. What I didn't like was paying for them - I wasn't into that. So we used to break into chemists' shops and doctors' surgeries - even doctors' cars. And I had a good run of it but, eventually, I started getting caught. And once you *start* getting caught, it just snowballs after that.

I had a couple of chances before I actually did go to prison - a bit of probation, a slap on the wrists a couple of times - but then we did a major chemist's in Scunthorpe. There was a helluva lot of drugs involved and we was nicked within a couple of days. Somebody got pulled in and somebody said something and before I knew it I found myself in jail. I was seventeen. In fact, I had my eighteenth birthday inside.

Looking back, jail was no great hardship, really. It was a bit frightening for the first couple of days but the Wing I was on was for young prisoners and it was just like a big Boys' Club: like being back at school. I got remanded to Lincoln Prison and did three months there before going to court. They sentenced me to a Detention Centre and when I got there, *that* was the 'short, sharp, shock.' The case run late and we had to travel seventy miles to the Detention Centre so it was nine o'clock when we arrived and the screws weren't too pleased about having to hang about. Being on remand had been fairly relaxed. You didn't have to call the screws 'Sir' or anything, it was always 'Boss' or 'Governor' or 'Mr. So-and-so' or whatever. But it was *'Sir'* in Detention Centre and on my arrival I made the mistake of not saying 'Sir'. And I got slapped around the head and knocked off me feet. Frightened the shit out of me. But it was the only beating I got on that sentence, cause I soon learned to say 'Sir' and after that, I sailed through it. The only bad thing that happened was getting me hair cut and coming out of there with a short back and sides.

Rehabilitation? I've been in prison about six times now and I've never come across it. It's *containment.* People are going to *commit* crimes or they're not. Gaol's not a deterrent. *I'm* living proof of it. When I came out of Detention Centre in seventy-five, I spent all that summer getting *wrecked*: pop festivals and just having fun really but I was also getting into a lot of speed and most of it was coming from Amsterdam. So when Christmas came round, I thought 'Why pay over the odds? I'll go out and get me *own* for Christmas.' So I went over to Amsterdam but I made the mistake of telling too many people, cause when I got back the police and the Customs was *definitely* waiting for me. There was ructions in Scunthorpe. Only four people had known: me girlfriend, the people that lived in the flat underneath us and the guy that was financing it - and obviously *he* wasn't going to say anything, so it was down to who lived downstairs, who I thought was friends. They was given a right good hiding for it after - not by me - but by people who were disgusted with them. And rightly so.

The charge was Fraudulent Evasion of the Custom Importation Act and I think of all the charges I've heard, *that* was about the most frightening. It's like I was nineteen and I'm on a smuggling charge and the police are threatening me with five years and shit like this and, quite honestly, I *believed* them. It was a serious charge. I mean, it got me on TV and everything. Whereas before, me nickings had all been in the local paper but when it gets in the Yorkshire Post and the big Nationals, you begin to think 'Well, *this* is a bit *serious.*'

My parents were obviously supportive but they weren't very pleased about it. Me dad was a good old bloke and he was there for me all the way, really. He was a voluntary probation officer in Scunthorpe at the time, so I think his work with probation people give him a different insight into me taking drugs. He helped me in sorting out a solicitor and even got me a job just before I was due to go to Crown Court. It didn't do any good but it *looked* a bit better.

I got Borstal, which is like the next stage up the ladder to the big prisons. I went from Leeds to Strangeways to Wormwood Scrubs and finally to the Borstal so, by the time I got there, I was only nineteen and I'd done a month in three different prisons. Borstal's the same military regime as the Detention Centre, really: all bed packs and inspections. The first couple of weeks they teach you how to march. And then they march you *everybloodywhere.* Plenty of gym, hard work, road digging - things like that. They keep you busy all day: bed early, sleep and up early in the morning. Gym, work and a bit more gym...

The only good thing about being in Prison is that I've met some *really* interesting people. Just cause they're criminals doesn't mean they're shit-eads or anything. Some of them were good, solid, stand-up guys, who made gaol bearable. And a fair number of them had been fitted up one way and another and come out with little prospects of compensation. Most of them never got the publicity of the Guildford Four or the Birmingham Six or the Darvell brothers even, but it went on all the time and it's *still* going on. Although, thinking about it, I don't think *I've* ever been fitted up. I've never *had* to be. When I've been caught, I've been *caught* and I've usually put my hand up to it.

The Borstal I was in was one of the cushiest in the country and was mainly for people with drug form and while I was in there, it *did* get me off the drugs. A smoke gets you through the day or through the night or whatever and I've always managed to get a smoke in gaol but it's the wrong place to be taking heavier drugs, anyway.

I used to make a lovely brew, too. On me last sentence I used to make a gallon of hooch between five of us. Everybody contributed something: I used to make it, somebody else used to supply their cell as a drinking den, somebody else used to supply a few joints - and we all used to drink it. It was trial and error a lot with me. I used to use rice, potatoes, raisins, apples, carrots - the lot. The main thing is to cover it up, because you can smell it *Wings* away. I used to keep it wrapped up in a big bin bag and let the air out of the window now and again. But it only takes four days, so it's not that long to keep it and we used to do it in the week because the guards are busier then than at weekends. We put it down on a Monday and drank it on a Thursday. Five of us in this little Firm and we'd all get pissed. It was basically rot-gut and I can't imagine it doing you any good if you had it every day but we had a brew once a week at the very maximum and we'd all be staggering back to the Wing.

I've been in a cell where we've been aving a drink and a joint and the Governor's walked in! We was all havin a quiet little get-together, listenin to some sounds in a corner cell right out of the way and he was looking for someone in the cell across from us and wanted to know if we knew where this guy was. And it was *all there* like and obviously he couldn't miss it. It was like a little Saloon Bar. The smell of booze was more overpowering than the smell of dope. And he stuck his head in and said 'All right, lads?' And we said 'Yeah, Governor, we're just listenin to some sounds - ' - what else do you say when the Number One Governor walks in? - and he says 'All right, then, lads - I'll leave you to it.' And he shot off. But we were *freakin* then. Somebody went and stashed it with the fire rolls and we cleared everythin out of the cell and just sat there waitin for them to come steamin down to catch us at it. And we were there about fifteen minutes and nobody *came.* So me and me mate went down the Office and the Governor's sat in there with about five screws, just talkin, so we went back and sat in the cell and waited until someone saw the Governor go off the Wing. Then the screw who used to look after the landing come down and said 'The Governor sussed you there but he's told us not to do nought cause you're doin it quietly and you're out of the way.' So we shot off, got all the stuff back out and carried on...

The first thing on me mind when I finish any sentence, is to get stoned. A lot of people come out and say 'God, I need a *shag!*' but with me it was like 'I gotto get my head around some decent drugs!' If you can imagine, I had to work my *head* out first and work my way down, so a shag was just as high up the list as a new pair of trousers or trainers. I had a couple of wild months after I came out of Borstal then, after Christmas, me dad came home and said 'I've got you a job out in Africa if you want it.' and I thought 'Oh yeah! Africa! Sahara Desert! Brilliant! I'll definitely have some of *that.*' And that was it: I shot over to Algeria as a clerk in the Time and Wages Office.

Cor! It was *brilliant* out there. Best dope I've ever smoked in my life was out in Africa. It was Moroccan but it was only twenty minutes old, basically. It came straight over the border. It was so *fresh* and so *cheap.* Yeah! I mean, by Algerian standards we was getting charged extortionate prices but by our standards it was six to eight times cheaper. And the quality I was getting was *unbelievable.* And because of that and because of not wantin to lose my position, I never bothered injectin heroin and stuff. When I came back home on leave, I had a well-healthy Bank Account. Me mates had motor bikes they was sloggin to pay off on HP but *I* went out and just wrote a cheque out for one. And it was nice to have a good bit of money and know I'd worked hard for it.

The job hadn't actually finished, when I had a bit of trouble out there. It was a funny story, really. In 1977 the country was only fifteen years old and there was a military Government with a President and only one Union in the whole country. If you worked you was *in* it, if you didn't work you *wasn't* in it. And each town had what they call a Section Syndicate - which sounds a bit scary I suppose - and the Head of the Syndicate was a Union leader. And he had more power than like the Police Commissionaire or the Mayor. He was like *The* Kiddy in that Town. Well, I'd been down the desert for ten months with just a few other ex-pats, and if you wanted any form of social life you had to get on and mix with the Algerians and learn little bits of Arabic. And the first thing I learnt was all the swear words, so I'd know if anybody was *calling* me. Then when I went up the coast to a different job there was *four hundred* ex-pats and I had seven or eight Algerians working under me who were either the same age as me or older. And they resented me being there, quite rightly, because I was getting ten times more in a week than they was getting in a month. And to make matters worse, because there were so many English people there, nobody had bothered to pick up any Arabic or really integrate with the Arabs. So when I got in the Office and heard what all the Arabs were callin the English guys, I was straight *in* there, know what I mean? I says 'D'you know what this cunt's just called you?' And obviously these Arabs weren't very pleased about that and did everything they could to make my life hell. But the final straw was when I made the unfortunate mistake of crossing the Head of the Syndicate's nephew.

If I remember, I didn't even have to be in work that particular weekend, but I'd gone in this day to finish some stuff off. And I was sat behind my desk and there was only three or four of us in there but the Head of the Syndicate's nephew was in there as well and they've got elastic bands and they're firin bits of card around, you know, just playing about? Well, he turned round like and from across the desk he let one go and it got me right in the eye so, obviously, I just reached over and pulled him over the desk and I slapped him up against the wall - he was littler than me and I was a lot bigger in them days - and I grabbed somethin to whack im with and it was a can of fly- spray - but like a *huge* can of fly-spray - and in walked me Boss. Me Boss wasn't a bad guy and he says 'You better nip back to the Hotel' - cause we were stayin in a hotel at the time - and I says 'Yeah, right - I'm *gone.*' And then, obviously he found out the facts and he came back to the Hotel when he'd sussed out what had gone on and who it was I'd had by the throat and he said 'That little cunt has gone straight round to see his uncle. And they've already been on to the Project Manager - and you're *home.'* So it was well out of my hands but I'd have gone after that, anyway. I really got on with the little team I was working with and they wanted to slot me into another department but *they* wanted me off the job site. The Company didn't really want to lose me and I remember they'd just got a job started up in Bali and I thought if I played my cards right I could be out there. So they phoned up the head office back in London and d'you know where they offered me a job: *Bournemouth!* So I just packed it in altogether and went back to Scunthorpe and started getting back on drugs again.

See what I mean about shooting off at tangents, Alan? I could go off all day on tangents. But when did I first get homeless? From the age of sixteen I've always travelled about a bit. I've been all over England and I never used to class it as being homeless then. It used to be a case of 'I'm on the move.' I think what got me into the situation I'm in now - the homeless thing and that - was the last prison sentence I got. I went in in 1986 and I came out in1991 and me ead was well-messed up after that. It's a hard thing getting over a long prison sentence: sort of mixing back in with normal people and that. So I needed a prop.

And I found it in a good woman I'd known for a long time. I knew she had three kids but we sort of - well, I didn't 'sort of' at all - we fell in love and I moved in with her. And so I've gone from being in gaol to having a ready-made family and it was a relationship that was doomed from the first. Obviously, no matter what happened, she always put her children first, which was *right*, you know what I mean? She used to like a drink and a smoke but she didn't take drugs and I was already back into them by this time. I'd got a script and everything and I was dealing a little bit cause I'd been on the scene for a good twenty years by then and I knew people that had gone up the ladder and *not* got nicked and they was in good positions to put things my way. I was the middle man for a lot of people and getting good earners out of it as well. I could make a thousand pounds some days, just for putting people in contact with people who could sell kilos and things. But anyway, the relationship lasted eighteen months, two years and then she threw me out. I moved into the park at the bottom of the street - livin in a tree for a couple of days, cause the ground was wet - and all the time I was thinkin 'She'll come to her senses soon and she'll ave me back,' but she didn't. We'd had a couple of separations for an odd week or so before but she'd just finally ad it. I mean, I was really unbearable to live with, I suppose and drugs and drink don't mix, even if it's two different people usin them.

I had no motivation and I slept rough for ages, just bumming around and getting *totally* out of me face through not being with me woman any more. I lived in me mate's granny's outside toilet for three months. She didn't know I was there. But it was all right cause I could have a lay-in some days until about dinnertime. It was stupid but it was fine weather and I wasn't really bothered. This would have been about '93 and for a year I had nowhere to live. And even *then*, I never thought I was homeless really: I just had nowhere to live.

I came to Swansea via a right weird route. I was on the script up in Scunthorpe and the workers talked me into going into a rehab to try and sort myself out. Which I did and, touch wood, although I still have a smoke, I've kicked injections and heroin right out the window. I don't even drink these days. Well, anyway, I came out of there and went into a night shelter, then a hostel, then a bedsit. But, even though I wasn't really *doing* anything, I felt myself slipping. For some reason, I must *attract* criminals and people who use drugs - even to the extent of picking up vibes from them so I know what they're into and that. I'd had a couple of turn-ons in Norwich and the way things were going I'd be out thievin again if I didn't watch it. So I left there and went on the road for a bit. I guess I made myself homeless but a lot of people don't look at it as that: it's just like 'moving about'. From Norwich I went to Peterborough to Grantham to Shrewsbury and I was on my way to Ireland when I got stuck in Derby. I was jinxed for getting lifts in one direction, so I took the other way, just to get me out of the area, and I ended up in Newport. I thought I'd give it a couple of weeks there but I actually went to Cardiff the same day and stayed a year. I did a hostel there and shared a house with a couple of people and lived in the park for a while but, at the end of the year me ulcer burst and I went into hospital. All me mates in Cardiff were drinking people and it was probably the SA that was doin me ulcer in, so when I came out I needed somewhere to recuperate, cause I really didn't feel well enough to be roughin it. And I *like* South Wales. I class myself as a born-again Welshman, so I thought 'Swansea sounds all right.' A lot of people said it was a nice little place and that they'd done a bit of busking down here, so I came here on the off-chance and, luckily, I got in this very hostel the day I moved in. And, like I say, I've travelled about a bit but this is the *best* hostel I've ever been in. I got my health back together, put on loads of weight, got a flat up in Bonymaen and got a bit of direction in my life. They helped me with a grant and kitted me out with donations from here. I couldn't believe what was on offer and what I got. I've been in the flat about eight months now but I'm just about to give it up cause I've got itchy feet again.

I still want to go to Ireland and have a look around and do a bit of busking. I don't know for how long. My dad was Irish and I'd like to see the place where he was from. I've done about fifteen countries but Swansea is me home Town now and when I've finished over there, I'll definitely be back.

I'm forty next year and I haven't got two halfpennies to scratch my arse with but I've led a full, varied and interesting life. Regrets? I've had a few! I'd like to have had a good word with me dad before he died. We hadn't spoken for the year preceding his death, so it was sad that I never got the chance. It was the classic sort of thing: you don't realize how much you like someone until they're not there any more. And, obviously, I wouldn't have liked to have gone to gaol but, saying that, if I hadn't I wouldn't have met half the people that I *do* know. I'd like to say I'd never taken drugs and gone into crime and that, but it's been a *laugh*, Alan! It's been me downfall but it used to be a laugh goin out burglaring. I mean, I never used to burgle people's ouses and shit like that - it was always shops and sussing

243

ways to get into them. And it was different every time. Adrenalin is a wicked thing. It was a *buzz* - sometimes a bigger buzz than the drugs you got at the end of the day.

Everything that I've done has gone towards making me the sort of person that I am today and going through all that gaol has made me put up with *anything* now. I'm not very good at self-analysis, but I get on well with people, I think. People have got a good word for me, I *do* know that. One of me best mates in Leicester was a Lifer. We had two years together. People thought we was bent cause we was *always* together but we was pulling some good scams in there. When I got out, one of me mates was on the Works and I slipped him twenty quid out of me discharge grant and said 'Give Sean a tenner and keep a tenner for yourself.' That was on a Friday and I was back up at the prison on the Sunday taking Sean a parcel of dope - a few pills and that - cause it was Easter and you *had* to get him through the Easter. Now, after someone's left you'd always hear shit about them that people would never have said to their face - like 'Oh, that *Wilson* was a right bastard!' and things like that - but this guy had said to Sean - cause he was on my Wing: 'You know, not *one* person *called* Ian when he left. *Nobody* had a bad word for him'. And that, I think, is what I attain to in life: *not* being disliked. Him saying that, really put a smile on my face...

'Don't worry, be happy...'

Lyn

Since Wayne was admitted to the Hostel in mid-December, all attempts to get Lyn into Dinas Fechan (where his brother Terry was resident) failed, mainly through a lack of cooperation on the part of Lyn himself, who actually kept one appointment but walked off at the last minute in a huff. He continued to sleep outside the Leisure Centre on his own for a while and then moved to a deserted chapel just above High Street Station. He stayed there until early March and then took up residence near the Kingsway: in a small space alongside an oil storage tank behind the Potter's Wheel pub. It's cramped and littered with bric-a-brac: car parts, television parts, old clothes, old bedding - some of it brought there by Lyn, some of it just fly-tipped. His 'pitch' is just opposite Liberty's Night Club and twenty yards up the lane from a taxi firm which has a constant stream of traffic coming and going from morning till night. He's become the last call on the Soup Run but I look in on him whenever I happen to be passing. Often, he'll have a half-drunk flagon or bottle with him and, if he's in a good mood, I'll be offered a drink and a surreal assortment of objects, produced one after the other, as if by magic, from various parts of his person.
This particular morning, he is curled up asleep, indistinguishable from the debris surrounding him but for his gnome-like face. I approach quietly and he wakes with a start...

You're always frightenin the *fuckin life* out of me! Why the ell don't you say **'Allo Lyn!'** when you poke your head round the corner? You're like a fuckin *weasel...*!

Right, well, there's only me kippin ere and I've been here now for three weeks and it's not an improvement on the last place, cause people are taking the micky out of me all the time - I'm not goin to swear, cause you're doin a survey - but what it is: certain people take advantage. There's nothin wrong with the world - it's the people *in* it. Am I right or am I wrong? I know for a fact I'm omeless and I'm very grateful to you people coming out, giving soup runs. You don't ave to do it, cause you could be home with your own family. But people *do* disturb me. They hit me. Give me a poke. What'd appen if *you* saw somebody hitting me, Al? Would you hit them back? No, you wouldn't: you'd run a fuckin *mile*!

There's a bit of atmosphere here: you see all the crumpet goin past and what-ave-you. Before, I was in the chapel up by the Station, with all the pigeons. You got a car, aven't you: ave a box spanner! An you got kids, aven't you? Grandchildren? Nephews and nieces? Ave a teddy bear. *'Thank you,'* say. Bloke walked into the Potter's Wheel the other night, said to the Landlord 'Pint of whisky and a pint of bitter.' He put the whisky in his top pocket and drank the bitter. The barman said 'I think you've ad too much.' He said 'D'you want to make somethin of it?' And a little mouse poked his head out of his top pocket and said 'Fetch the bloody cat as well!' Get it? *'Fetch the bloody cat as well!'* What d'you call a Jewish tea-boy? *He-brew!* Why have Prince Charles got a blue one? He been dippin it in dye! Why have a cow got a long face? Well, you would if you had your tits pulled twice a day. What d'you call a woodpecker without a beak? A head-banger! How long am I goin to stay in this place - that's what you were goin to ask next, wannit? Well, about three foot two inches!

I been to Neath Fair since I saw you last but it wasn Fair! D'you know why? It's not there till next week. And I been down to Dinas Fechan to try and get in there but Terry's been performin all the time, so I couldn't. What coat catches fire? A blazer! What's Hunchback's first record? 'It Started with a *Cyst*!' What's blue and fucks old ladies? *Hypothermia!*

I had a wet dream last night. I dreamed I fell off the end of Mumbles Pier. I got up about nine o' clock this mornin. Wayne came ere and he started kickin me. So, what I've done: I reported him to the police, cause there's a warrant out for him. Now, you didn't know that, Alan, did you? No don't laugh, I'm serious. And what it is, is - here you are: ave another socket set - the warrant was issued last Thursday. Onest to God, there *is* a warrant out for him. They don't know he's in the Hostel and - you got a bit of a cold, aven't you? Ave a Lemsip. *'Thank you,'* say! Screwdriver any good to you? Handy. You never *know*, see. And you're on the phone, aren't you? Cordless telephone! Ow's that? It *is* workin - I tried it. And you're goin abroad this year, aren't you? Turkey, innit? Here's a 20,000-lira Turkish note! I'm good to you, aren't I? *'Thank you very much!'* say. 'Diolch yn fawr, ich I!'

Here's a good one for you: What d'you call a black window-cleaner? Chamois Davis! Why do Polos blush? Well, *you* would, if someone sucked your ole! Prince Charles was down here the other day - on an official visit. I couldn't believe it: he was wearing a fox-skin hat! I said 'What you wearin that for?' He said 'I told my mother I was coming to Swansea today and she said 'Wear the fox 'at!' No, there's nothin wrong with the homeless. Some of them are just people who want to do their own thing in life. Now, am I right or am I wrong? I aven't got no Poll Tax nor nothin like that, you know. It's your own choice, innit? What d'you call a Chinaman with six kids? *In Too Long!* What succeeds? A budgie with no teeth! Irishman went into a bar. **'Oh!'** he went. It was a fuckin *iron* bar! And you need a new pair of shoes, Alan. Now, you didn't know that, did you? Look at them! They're startin to go round the seams. Another five minutes now and we'll go but you'll see me all right, won't you? Last time you gave me somethin for doin a tape, didn you? And, *categorically* speakin: you're goin to play this back after, are you? Cause you won't see me tomorrow. I'm goin to poke your eyes out!

Anyway, I'm goin to finish off now with a couple of jokes. What d'you call a Jewish tea boy?' I've said that one, ave I? Oh, well: What d'you call a Welshman with a lollipop stick stuck up his arse? *A Taffy Apple!* Where's the elephant's sex organs? On his foot, cause if he stamps on you, you're fucked! What d'you get if you cross a fork-lift truck with a giraffe? *Hydraulics and high bollicks!* Well, I'll love you and leave you now, thank you very much but before I go, *you* say a few words on behalf of me. 'What d'you think of the *atmosphere* in Swansea?' Is *that* the word? *That's* what you were goin to ask me, wasn it? I think it's a load of shit! But so long as I get somethin for a drink, I don't give a fuck. Don't worry - be happy...!

'Mornin night, mornin night, mornin night...'

Randall

I was supposed to have my giro this morning but I never received it. They've stopped it and I'm waiting now till three o' clock to go back over to see what the decision is. It might be a 'yes' and it might be a 'no'. If it's a 'yes', I can pay so much off my bills and stay where I am with the Gwalia. If it's a 'no', I gotto get back over here quick as possible for someone to bleep Alan Morgan for me to confer with him over what I can do next.

A tall, thin man aged about fifty who bears more than a passing resemblance to Leonard Rossiter of 'Rising Damp' fame. There are tags on the shoulders of his navy-blue pullover, which say 'SECURITY' in white letters. He speaks quietly and with a kind of childlike naivety, sometimes confusing his words. He's called in to the Hostel to see his Support Worker about his dire financial straits and an astronomical phone bill he's just received. Both offices are in use so there's nowhere else I can talk to him but on an empty landing.

My childhood was very happy. I was born up in Brechfa in Brecon and I went to Bryn Coch School, Monmouth. That's the only place I went to and I was all right there. I used to go camping with the Girl Guides! Oh yes! We was all in one - a mixture. And then, every morning at six o' clock, I used to go fishing but not with the Girl Guides - on my own. Or with another two boys. I caught a big one once. Oh yes! It was about six foot six. A big trout - *that* big. A sewin. Caught him with my *bare hands* - yeah! I used to tickle them. Nobody taught me how - I learnt. He gets trapped under the stone and he can't turn round, see, and I've gotto tickle him and grab him by the gills and bring him out and break his neck. And that was *good* fun. I caught about one hundred and thirty six all together, like that..

My father was working underground. I went in the mines as well when I left school but it was hot underground and I didn't like it. He used to be a gravedigger, too. I never helped him with that. Oh no - I didn't like *that!* But I used to go down to the pen to hide -

to have a look at what he was doin! He died at seventy-three. I never fell out with my mother but we only had a one-bedroomed flat and she couldn't keep me, so I went from there to a hostel down in Haverfordwest. I forget the name of it but it's closed down now. I got a job in Haverfordwest cleaning buses for South Wales Transport. I moved into a house and was courting a girl for nine years but the problem was another boy called Kevin Newell took her off me and kicked me out of the house - where I was payin my rent, my food, my gas and my electric - and even chucked all my clothes and my belongings out as well. And I went to a solicitor and they couldn't do nothing about it.

I did a lot of different jobs after that: painting and decorating, gardening, mechanics and looking after kids. I was changing nappies and everything at one time. Some people don't like doin that but it doesn't bother me. When I was with the Council I used to be on the Suicide Squad: going down under the drains and unblocking them. It was dangerous work. There was gas down there and sometimes I had to fly up quick, cause the sewage came whooshing out at me. *Raw* sewage! Oh, *stinkin!* But they got cameras now to go down and see where the problem is. I was with the Council for twelve months and then I went over to Pembroke Dock on the Gardening Scheme with them but I didn't like that. I lived up with my brother for six months, then we phoned up from the Yellow Pages one day and found a hostel for me down in Swansea, in Stembridge. I was there all over Christmas and it was good. Other people were not doin what they were told - swearin and cursin and stuff like that - but I *always* did what I was told. Kevin Quayle helped *me* and I helped *him.* Some of the other boys were too lazy to work and I had to do all the house work and everything and hoover upstairs and clean the kitchen, clean the livin room, clean the laundry room, clean the passage and I didn't get paid for it. When they closed that hostel down, I went straight from there to the Gwalia place I've got now.

I'm looking after Ken's Shop at night and Jack's Chippies up there and they give me a packet of fags and discount off whatever I want but the problem is there's too much vandalism there. We get break-ins all the time and people knocking your doors and threatening you. The kids come in there at night time ringing the bell. I pick up the phone and say 'Who's there?' and they say 'Oh, I come to see Mansel Jenkins,' and I say 'He's not very well at the moment: can you call back another day?' Then the bloke up in number seventeen leaves them in and they damage the place and light fires and we get the police up but by the time they gets there, they've gone. The other day, it took them from *twenty past one* to *half past two* in the morning to arrive for a bloke upstairs with music on full-blast. We just *could not* sleep. Oh, it's a *pain* and it's too dangerous. I want to move out because of the drugs and the threats and the abuse.

Why they've stopped my giro is because I used to work for Britelite Security up in Banwen - that's why I'm wearing this. They've got eight hundred sites they patrol and I was lookin after a coalmine near Aberdare - watchin the lorries, vehicles and shower room. I was working nights till eight o' clock in the morning. Then I was on from eleven o' clock in the mornin till half past ten at night. A few hours kip and then back to work again. I was *really, really* tired. Day and night. Day and night. But what they done: they took twenty-five pound diesel off me for travel, sixty-two pound tax and insurance and the eight pound for the uniform, which I never received. It's a quiet place and we only had four incidents at the most when I was up there but it's a bit rough and there's a lot of vandals. We got stones chucked at us by the kids from Tairgwaith.

I had another guard on with me but the problem was he kept fallin asleep all the time so I went back to the office and told the other security guard in the end and he said 'Take Troy,' - one of the two German Shepherds - 'and tell him to take him for a walk around.' So I did that but it was rainin and he left the dog out in it and it was howlin like anything, so I went back to the office to say what had happened but he wouldn't listen. 'Stay over there, Randall,' he said, 'and if you see any movement, give me a buzz on the phone.' So I had a walkie-talkie and I went over and I seen somethin so I rung him up and said 'Yes, there's somethin goin on over by the main gates.' And what it was, was two blokes had come round from the back end and were tryin to break in and steal coal. So he phoned the police up straight away and they went down with a Doberman - a *nasty* old Doberman! - and the last I heard was they caught one of the fellas. I did as much as I could to help them out and we had to fill in a form - a criminal form - for to go back to the depot - the office up in Banwen. But I didn't like the way they kept me out till three o' clock in the morning and it went all the way through till the following morning and *that* really got me down. And they *still* took twenty-five pounds diesel off me and sixty-two pounds tax and insurance and eight pound uniform, which I never received. So what can I do about *that?* There was *nothing* I could do about it. A solicitor could have done *something* but I didn't want to get a solicitor involved. It would have been a court job if I did and I would have been worse off then than I was before. But it was good, in a way. I enjoyed my work but the hours I was puttin in! Two pound forty-five for a *ninety-six*-hour week: mornin night, mornin night, mornin night. I couldn't get my sleep. That's why I finished.

I don't drink *all* that much. I can go out at night and have two or three pints of shandy and come back all right but one night I went to a Singles Club in Carmarthen and I come back *steaming*. I was courting with a girl there but I haven't seen her since and now I'm getting closer with this one down in Swansea here but I don't want to mention her name. I met her at the Sunday night Disco Club in the Dolphin. She lives with her husband in Bonymaen. He hits her a lot. She's marked all across there. She wants *him* out and she wants *me* in. But I'm not going in at the moment till everything is lawful and she can keep clear of him. But she's *lovely!* I had *fun* with her on Sunday! Oh yes! I kicked one of the carpet stays off the bottom of the stairs by accident and I said to her 'There's somethin on the floor there.' and instead of picking up the carpet stay, she was trying to pick up the black mark that the carpet stay had made on the carpet! Oh, I was in *stitches!* But she'll be cursing me this morning cause I was supposed to be meeting her at half past nine but I've had to sort out my giro.

The main thing I'd like to have now is a place of my own: a two-bedroomed flat or a house or whatever it is. I want to move to a place up in Penplas - by Morriston turn-off. I've heard there's some flats going down there and if I can get Alan to find out where they are, I'll be better off. Gwalia won't allow dogs but if I went there I would like to have a dog cause I'm a dog-lover. I've seen people kicking dogs and chucking them on the Motorway in a black bag. I found six on the M4 last April and I stopped with a mate of mine in a lorry and we picked them up and put them in the cab and took them to the RSPCA in Port Talbot. They was alive but they was tied up and I said 'Look what I just found!' They said they'd contact me again and I'm hoping they'll get back to me and that I will have a job with them in the near future.

Alan's helped me a lot. I asked my other Key Worker to lend me money to buy food but he wouldn't do it so I finished with him. If I don't succeed in getting my giro this afternoon I've gotto get Kevin Quayle or whatsername - the lady downstairs: *Julie!* - to bleep him out and tell him that Randall has been over and he did *not* succeed. He got *nothing*. So then I'll want further allegations made as to *why* I got nothing.

There's a lot of things I'd like to do but there's no jobs going anywhere at the moment. There *was* a job in this new Kennels down in Penllergaer - taking dogs for a walk and cleaning them out - but it's voluntary. So I'm hoping I will get my money this afternoon, cause if I don't, I won't have no food in the house and if I don't pay my bills I'll be homeless again.

What it is mainly is: I don't have enough to pay my phone bill. They don't give you enough on the dole. So I've been cut off. Oh yeah! I've been using it a lot. I've been phoning my girlfriend and my brother. Ave you seen the bills? Ooh, I tell you what: if you want a shock, ave a look at *them! I've* got a stack *that* big of them and *Alan's* got one *even bigger!* Some are for BT and others are for outside phone calls. But the funny thing is: I was *not* in the phone book and I was on *incoming* calls only. But it's only my girlfriend contacted me. Nobody else. Oh yes - and I *have* been phoning around to see if I can get a dog from somewhere.

'Good as gold...'

The Collective

'...Squatters have moved into an empty shop in Swansea's High Street and declared it a free cafe and commune. Up to half a dozen people moved into the former Downs Furniture Centre opposite Iceland a week ago but have only just put up noticeboards revealing their plans. They have painted murals and signs on the shop declaring it Waste of Space and No-Cash Cafe. A poster in the window reads: 'Coming soon: no cash cafe, meeting space, information stall, recycling, rehearsing space and workshops. As caretakers of this wasted space, take notice that we are nice people. We intend to turn this space into a useful and creative place for the use of the people of Swansea and the multiverse...' The Landlord of the nearby Cardiff Arms pub said 'We thought they were going to have a rave on Saturday but there were no problems. So far they have been as good as gold...' The property has been empty for more than a year and is being sold by Dawsons's. No one was available for comment from the Estate Agent...'
South Wales Evening Post, March 27th. 1997.

Ingrid: All of us were completely blown away by the positive feed-back we had from all areas. In our first week in particular, we had a constant stream of people just shoving their heads round the door and saying 'I think what you're doin is *brilliant!'* And because of that, it came as quite a blow to find the papers had been served on us. We've been up and running for two weeks and they've given us just *seven* days to prepare for court. Now, if we'd been open longer we'd have already researched things like Agenda 21 but we're just *so* busy: not only trying to keep the cafe in running order but trying to clear up the rest of the building as well. The case is tomorrow morning. *Everyone* is doing their best to support us - Councillors and social workers alike - but, to be honest, the Council is in a bit of a predicament since they're facing an election and have to be careful with their words

The eve of the County Court hearing. Reporters from the Evening Post and The Big Issue have turned up as well as several representatives from Caer Las. The cafe is in full swing

253

and customers are being regaled with an impromptu song-cycle from a drunken Terry Darvell who has wedged himself and his crutches next to the counter. There's a whole pack of dogs yelping and cavorting in the midst of it all as Ingrid gets up to show the reporters around the building and Damien and Ben take their places on the settee. Damien is thirty-four and from Carmarthen and Ben twenty-two and from the South West of England.

Damien: I've been here approximately fourteen days and since then we've been managing to feed, on average, thirty people a day for nothing as well as provide tea and coffee. We've got a registered child-minder on the premises, basic creche facilities and people trained in First Aid and Fire Regulations.

Ben: The support has been phenomenal. Businesses and the public alike have been contributing in so many different ways. From the old dear who comes in from her shopping and gives 20p, to the plumber who reconnects our water free of charge. All sorts of people. We've had a couple of band practices and community dances.

Damien: And the cafe's been thriving. I went down to the market the other day and we got three trolley-loads of food from people chasing me round saying 'Are you from the Squat? C'mon over here! We've got food to give you!' Half of which, we had to give to the Cyrenians. So we're looking to support other groups in whatever ways we can, just as they are supporting us.

Ben: I've been staying at Holt's Field for the last two years and there are similar sorts of issues there. People have lived there all their lives, in an area of outstanding beauty, and now the landowner wants to uproot them and build luxury flats. Holt's Field is an example of a really quite unique community facing problems that a lot of homeless people face: the fact that the law and the system place property before people.

Damien: Our petition for the Court tomorrow totals six hundred and seventy two signatures, including sixty seven from Holt's Field. Inevitably, we *will* be evicted, just due to law but if the Local Authority would grant us access to one of their many derelict buildings - which are becoming more and more derelict as time goes on - we are prepared to do a similar thing to what we've done here. They've admitted they've got five hundred empty buildings, so we'll pick one. Or let them offer us one and we'll probably take it.

Ben: The amount of energy that's been put into this place in two weeks just goes to show what can be done when people get together for a common purpose! We tend to forget it but there's people living on the streets who *do* have a lot to offer. We've had alcoholics come through that door, people like John there, who came in late one night and was given a bed and the next day was asking what he could do to help. He said if he's got something to do, it takes his mind off the booze.' And what we're doing is bound to have a positive effect on levels of crime, too. People don't have to steal any more, cause there's food and work available.

The actual eviction order is very impersonal. Whoever thinks up the wording to these summonses hasn't much imagination. They just slap it on the door. They're not interested in communicating with people on a personal level. That's the law and there's no room for negotiation and dialogue.

For the past week, since we've known about the Summons, we've been asking people who've supported us if they'd like to attend court tomorrow to show their feelings. And I think a lot of them will turn up. Besides that, we've got no fewer than half a dozen affidavits and we've still got them coming in. About twelve have been promised in all: from a wide range of organizations including Shelter, the Cyrenians, Swansea Drugs Project, Acts, people working on homeless issues, a group working on disability issues and youth employment; there's one from a music shop, from two churches and from a couple of respectable individuals who've got a lot of influence in Swansea. So, given the weight of that, I'm quite optimistic about the outcome. I mean, the Law is the Law and at the end of the day we *will* get evicted from here but I think we have a lot of room for negotiation.

We'll continue what we're doing for as long as we can. We believe in self-help and DIY and we want to give people a chance to renovate the place themselves. Local Agenda 21, which was something they agreed to at the Rio Earth Summit in 1992, stated that the community *has* to be involved if development is to be successful. It needs to be on all levels and this is a good example of what can be achieved when people at street level are involved in taking responsibility for their lives and not leaving it to bureaucrats and politicians.

I'm studying Social Anthropology in Swansea University but the exorbitant rents we're asked and the grants students get, aren't sufficient to live on and it's forcing a lot of people into very dire economic situations. I go to college from here every day. I've got my finals coming up soon, so I'm going to try and balance working here and helping out with what's going on. There's a lot of different sections of society - homeless people, travellers, Ethnic minorities - are being marginalized and impoverished by the policies of this present government and the System as a whole.

I think I speak for the majority of people here when I say that the policies of the Conservative and the Labour Governments are very, very similar. Jack Straw has talked about beggars and squeegee merchants and how they should be criminalized. Jack Straw, Michael Howard: I don't see much difference between the two. I don't believe in trusting the running of a country to a Government which is out to serve their own interests and the interests of a minority before others. I think people are increasingly beginning to realize this and taking action for themselves, as we're doing here. The Government's power comes from what we give them. And by doing things like this, it undermines it. People need to start taking control of their own lives.

I was down Holt's Field the day the bailiffs came. There we see it again: a similar disrespect for people and people's homes. They came that first time and there were three hundred angry people there to meet them from the surrounding community, to say 'Look, leave these people alone.' So they went away and had to have a bit of a rethink about their strategy. The second time they came, despite assurances from the Sheriff that they'd come after nine o' clock for the sake of the children - so they'd be in School and wouldn't have to go through the trauma of it - they came at half past seven in the morning and started knocking people's homes about and throwing people out. They went to my friend Karen's home - and Karen's is a single parent family with two young kids - and what I saw there was just a blatant disregard for people's lives, basically. For all that they've built to achieve. And that is just because *that* is the law. I knew for a fact that a lot of those bailiffs didn't know the issues. They'd been told it was just another job and *that*, at the end of the day, is what keeps it all going: it's a job. Just a job. That is the justification for so many things. And that's all it'll mean for the bailiffs who'll ultimately evict us from here - *a job.* Nothing else comes into consideration.

'Show me the way to go home...'

Bernie and The Beach Boys

After being kicked out of the Radnor back in March, they pitched a small two-man tent in a grassy dip near the car park at County Hall and alternated between sleeping there and back in the Radnor, once the landlord was off the premises. We included the tent on our Soup Run. There were three of them - Bernie, Jack and Mike - crammed into it, plus Blacky. I managed to find them a similar tent and, for a week or so, they were able to spread out but eventually both tents were stolen. They returned to Victoria Park and started sleeping there - together with Debbie and new arrivals Leanne, Rocco and Lenny. Since Nicki had left him to return to her mother's house in Devon, Rocco had temporarily abandoned their Council House in Townhill and teamed up with Leanne, his former wife. She's a Big Issue seller in her early thirties, who occasionally uses the Soup Run and Lenny is a former resident of the Cyrenians' Hostel, who was admitted urgently during a cold spell in February but recently excluded due to his wildly drunken behaviour. They all seemed happy with each other's company but, in anticipation of the bowls season, the police moved everyone on, warning them not to return. I got them another tent · this time a bell-tent - from the Emergency CRISIS fund and they took to the foreshore, somewhere in the dunes between Brynmill and Blackpill. They were spotted one day, sleeping on the sand in Busby Berkeley-style formation: in a circle, toes facing inward, the tent draped over them like a blanket.

At the beginning of April, they'd made up their minds to move on, maybe for a week, maybe for the whole of the Summer.

The Slip, one Sunday in mid-April. They are all there, spread out on the sand at the foot of the bridge: Jack, Bernie, Mike, Rocco, Leanne, Debbie, Lenny, Ray - almost the full team. The sun is shining and the tide is halfway in or halfway out. Across the busy Mumbles Road, a huge roar rises from St Helens rugby ground, where Llanelli are playing Cardiff in a SWALEC Cup semi-final. They all look suntanned and disgustingly healthy, in sharp contrast to the day after their expulsion from the Radnor. Mike looks like something out of the Pirates of Penzance: a brightly-coloured bandana round his head, Bermuda shorts and salmon-pink legs and Rocco has at last discarded the scarf which permanently hid the lower half of his face. Bernie is sleeping some yards off, sandwiched between Debbie and Leanne...

Jack: The nights are definitely getting warmer now. And fair play to Ray: he puts us up now and again. He's still stayin in the Radnor and if the weather's too rough we try and sneak in there. But we're out of there by six or seven in the mornin cause of the Landlord.

Rocco: Last night we had about eight or nine crammed into one room. Blacky bit me on the nose in the middle of the night cause I was goin to give Mike a kiss!

Jack: But the update, basically, is that we've had two tents stolen since you interviewed us last and the dome one got ripped.

Mike: You told us it was easy to put up but it took us *hours!*

Jack: It's funny lookin back but it wasn't funny at the time: It was bloody freezin. We use it as a ground sheet now, cause Lenny dragged it through the bushes one day and it ended up getting ripped.

Jack: We woke up this morning and found a pair of knickers hanging from a bush.

Rocco: A pair of black and white knickers. We were all sleepin in the same bush down in the dunes there and nobody knows where they come from.

Mike: Len may have put them there. He's a milkman, he is, you know. We wake up some mornins and there's a couple of bottles of milk beside the bush. He must get up early to get it. I call him Ernie.

Jack: We've still got the tent but, as Mike says, it's been torn. But we're plannin on pullin out anyway. It *was* going to be Doncaster but it's changed to Hereford now: strawberry-pickin. The girls are plannin to go up by bus tomorrow, so we'll follow them up on Saturday. We're still trying to buy a little car we've got our eye on.

Mike: A Sierra Estate. You'll get about six of us in there: four in the back, two in the front

Rocco: and one in the boot.

Jack: We'll kip in that but, usually, when you get a job strawberry-pickin, they put you up in a barn. It's a bit rough but it's warm.

Mike: I've done strawberry-picking before. It's a good laugh. Trouble is, you eat that many, you're sick at the end of the day. The season lasts about two months, but we'll only stay a couple of weeks. See ow it goes. I have to come back to get me giros.

Rocco: In the winter then, we're goin apple-pickin

Mike: And down to Kent for some hop-pickin. Just travel around

Jack: We're decidin on the car next weekend - we'll all chip in. It's just a matter of waiting till Friday or Saturday. But money doesn't go anywhere, does it? Especially when you're on the street. If it wasn't for the bloody Soup Run we'd starve half the time. It's our main meal. Unless we're sensible enough to get up to the City Temple - the Christian place, you know? You get a hot dinner up there, once a week on a Thursday.

Mike: And Bill's coffee bar's still goin. We were there last night.

Rocco: They had cream slices.

Mike: What we do, we all get around the piano for a sing-song. Not necessarily hymns. It's all-sorts. We leave there about quarter to ten. The last one we do is 'Show Me the Way to Go Home.'

Jack: They're glad to see us going. But they're good people.

Mike: We make them laugh. I took over the sermon there one night, didn I? Bill was gob-smacked! I went on for ages - and I was *steamin* as well!

Len: I'm definitely tryin to go strawberry-pickin as well. I could have had a job with the gypsies on the tarmacking this summer but -

Mike: I've done that! What they do is, they'll give you like twenty pound on the first day and then every other day they'll offer you a fiver.

Rocco: I done tarmacking with them, too - about four hours work - and what they done to me was they gave me two pound fifty and told me to go and get a couple of bags of chips. And I fell for it and by the time I came back they were gone. And this was up in Gloucester, so I had to make my own way back from Gloucester down to here.

Len: *Cowboys,* they are.

Mike: They take all the gear with them and mix it up there and then and *you* do the work. And they promise they'll give you the money but half the time they don't. My mate Shane went tarmacking with them and they only gave him a fiver a day cause they'd given him a caravan to stay in, so he ended up burning it down. They're not real gypsies. They call them Didicoys. My mate Terry Foreman was a tarmacker. He was a gypsy boxer: a bare-fist boxer. He did actually go professional. He had twenty-two fights, yeah? Twenty-one knockouts and the twenty-second one jumped out the ring. Money used to go on it. But he used to do the tarmacking as well and he's doin this driveway for these people this day and he says 'For an extra sixty pound,' he says, 'I can put all these white chippins in it for you.' and they says 'Yeah, we'll go for it!' And he just went up the road and got about a quid's worth of Polo mints - right? - got a hammer, smashed them all up and just strewn them down and rolled them in. Couldn't get away quick enough, in case it rained. That's true! That's what he did: quid's worth of Polo mints and just smashed them up, chucked them down and rolled over them. *That's* Terry Foreman for yer! Mind you, when I ad me carpet warehouse I used to do all the caravans out for them, yeah? They wouldn't ave cheap stuff but you ad to ave the money off them first, otherwise they'd do a runner on yer. They used to ave thirty to forty bagged rolls off me a week. I was makin a *fortune* off them! And they used to go round door to door selling these six-by-twelve rolls as twelve-by-twelves. Good business people, give them their due. And some of their caravans - whoof! - you wanna see them. You ave a cup of tea in a gypsy caravan and it's the best tea you can get. It's *all* tea-leaves, d'you know what I mean? And it's all fancy china and everythin. Oh, it's lovely! I only ever got ripped off once by a gypsy. I done a carpet for them and the people wasn't in but the daughter was and she says 'Come back later.' When I went back later to get the money, the bloody caravan had gone. They'd pissed off. That was the only time I got ripped off by them. But I didn't mind, cause I'd nicked the carpet anyway...

Mike: To be honest with you. I never thought *I'd* be on the street.
Rocco: Well, look at *me.* I got a two bedroom house in Heol Gors, right? and I haven't been there for a month. And the only reason is cause Nicki's left me now. There's too many memories for me in that bedroom. I admit it: I ends up cryin every time I goes in the room. So I aven't been up there. I think my ampsters must ave keeled over by now. There's two ampsters and a goldfish. One of them's an albino and that's rare. Cost a fortune, but I got it off the back of a lorry. They're small and white with pink eyes. An albino hamster. But my next door neighbour's got the front door key - a little old lady - and she might be goin in feedin them. I haven't been up cause, like I say, Nicki's gone back to her mother's in Devon - that's what her father said - and if I wants her back, I knows the telephone number and I knows the address, so I can go over and get her. I've already done that once. I've actually thumbed lifts and gone on lorries all the way to Devon just to get her back. But I'm sick and tired of doin that. I'd rather stay with the family here and

have a laugh. Know what I mean?

Len: The hamster was sittin on his head one day.

Jack: Yeah, serious.

Rocco: Yeah. Nicki called her Sparky Junior, after me. That's my nickname, Sparky. Cause I sparked a fourteen stone bloke up once. I hit im so ard he just flew over the sand dunes.

Rocco: When I come to Swansea, Len was the second person I met and, fair play to him, he put me and my missus up for about a month. And every mornin he used to go out and come back with twelve pints of milk cause he said we needed nutrition.

Len: I was doin good then. I had my own flat. So I gave them my room and if they were havin sex or whatever, I went somewhere else.

Rocco: But we had a dog and the dog was runnin around and Lenny was getting gyp off the bloke down below, so the landlord said if me and my ex didn't leave, then Lenny's goin to get kicked out. So we left and then Lenny went and handed his keys in and *he* left but he also left both our mobile phones in his room and all my clothes.

Len: We *did* lose a lot of stuff. I lost my clothes and I lost my room but I didn't mind. I said 'Look, Rocco, leave it there,' I said. 'No point in argument,' and I gave the flat up. I'd been there about seven and a half years.

Rocco: So, he gotto go beggin now.

Mike: When the check clears, it'll be Friday and we'll probably go down Saturday mornin. The girls are goin to go tomorrow. I've got the address and we'll go down there, see how things go, probably stay a couple of weeks and come back in the motor.

Jack: What would be ideal is the red Transit with the Soup Run. That would be the answer. Just rip all the seats out and get a double mattress or two in the back. We'd all cwtch up. Brilliant! Cause we're all there in the Radnor at the moment. Just imagine it: eight or nine of us in one little room.

Mike: Last night we ad arms and feet goin everywhere. I was layin on the floor and I had *his* feet between my legs and Ray's up my backside. I ad *him* layin on me half the time

Rocco: and then I rolled on top of him and

Mike: then Blacky jumped on his bollocks

Rocco: He was jumpin on everybody.

Mike: He bloody *knackered* me!

Jack: I'm sure he's been on that wacky baccy or somethin.

Mike: Wouldn't surprise me!

Rocco: And then I went to sleep thinking about my ex-wife and when I woke up I was cuddling Bernie. Touching him up, like. I thought 'Where's her you-know-whats gone!' Cause she's got a lovely big pair and then I started touching his leg up and I thought 'What's this lump doin between her legs - and it was *Bernie,* it was!

MAY- OCTOBER

'Like something out of Clockwork Orange...'

Evelyn

A slim, attractive woman in her early forties. I've already met her on a creative writing course I ran at the Drugs Project Centre. Her Key Worker there said she was terribly nervous about the interview and when we talk in the Bar of the Brunswick she laughs a lot to hide her nervousness. She warns me in advance that, due to her amphetamine addiction, she might wander off the beaten track but I give her free-rein...

My father's from Greenhill and my mother's from Liverpool. Coming to Swansea to live was a helluva wrench for my mother. A lot of people didn't speak to her cause of her accent and thought she was a bit of a snob but she wasn't really. We all lived in the same house in Winch Wen and it was like Upstairs Downstairs: my grandparents upstairs and my mum and dad downstairs. Most of my childhood was spent with my grandmother, which was beautiful cause we went to Clyne a lot and we had a chalet down in Three Cliffs. I didn't go to School until I was six and I started to play the piano - well, when I say *play* I mean my father paid two-and-six a time up in Cwm Chapel for lessons for me from when I was five till I was fifteen. But I found out later my father wanted to learn to read music but he couldn't afford it in his day so he sent *me* and I taught *him*. He used to play with Terry Williams of Dire Straits's father and the Billy Hole Jazz Band. They did gigs in the Patti and when I was a kid I used to drag the amplifier around for them. My father's seventy-nine now and still playing and writing his own music. I remember going to Billy Hole's in Hanover Street and Billy would be sitting there like a mad professor playing the piano with all these kittens beside him and a swarm of kids running round wild. They were great people and he died quite young but we went camping with him a lot and that's why I say we had a lovely childhood.

I didn't know it at the time but my mum had a nervous breakdown. She had thirteen operations all together and spent a lot of time in and out of convalescent homes. As a child I was lonely and couldn't understand why she hardly ever went out. I wasn't allowed to have school dinners and she used to come and fetch me and carry me everywhere and I'd sit at the table and wouldn't eat. Often, I'd come home from school and there'd be an ambulance outside the front door and it might sound terrible but I used to say to myself 'Oh *great!* I'm sleepin up with *Nana* now!'

We don't often talk about the cause of my mother's breakdown. Before I was born they told her down in the old Swansea Hospital that she couldn't have children. They tried for nine years but when her youngest sister up in Liverpool, who was an unmarried mother died, the family all got together and said she could have Winnie, who was twelve at the time. So they adopted her and as soon as the adoption papers came through my mother found she was pregnant with me. I was a year old up in Winch Wen when Winnie fell down the steps and died. My mum was ill after having me and all I know is that Winnie died in the old Swansea Hospital and dad said they were throwing the clothes off her as she went down to the Theatre and they took out eight pints of blood and put eight pints back in but they did it too fast and when she came back out she was wrapped in foil. And my dad said what they done to my mother as a result it's a wonder she didn't end up in some sort of asylum.

And then we moved into two Council flats and he worked for the Steel Company of Wales and as soon as he'd finished his shifts he'd go straight to Glamtax or Fussells - the taxis in Swansea - or anywhere to save enough money to buy a house. Eventually, we moved to St. Thomas and within a year my mother passed her driving test and got a job in Spontex and within three months of getting the job she became Supervisor. And as soon as she started going back to work she went from eighteen stone to size twelve and started going dancing. It was like a different person!

My grandfather died when I was seventeen and three days before my eighteenth birthday my grandmother died. I remember my father taking her up to a kind of hospital in Brecon and I thought she was coming home but within a week she was dead. I walked into this hospital and she was in a kind of crib or a cot and she looked at me and said 'I want to go to the toilet.' So I automatically pulled the cage thing down and then this Matron shouted at me 'She's **not** to get out of bed!' It upset me a lot. The last words my grandmother said to me was *'Look after the baby for me,'* and I realized the baby was her son - my *father* - cause that was her only child. And I *knew* then that she'd *gone.* And when she died it was like I lost my mother so, on the spur, I did something totally out of character: I signed up in the WRAF. For six years. All my friends in school couldn't believe it. It was so *unlike* me but at the time I felt I just *had* to get away. My Gran died on the thirty-first of January and I went in on the third of February.

I did my training in a place near Grantham in Lincolnshire. I was seven stone when I went in and *nine and a half* stone when I came out! My parents came up for the pass-out and I was in the front row when we did the eyes-right and I was *looking* straight at them but they didn't recognize me!

After Grantham, I was posted to RAF Uxbridge in Middlesex as a telephone operator in Communications, the place where Winston Churchill apparently won the War. We had American GI's next to us and I was in Nine Signals Unit and we did Communications for Heathrow Airport. Sounds as if I had a marvellous job but it was shift work and there'd be like one girl and nine men on a shift and I was always complaining that there should be *two* women. I got insulted one day by a sergeant who asked me to sit down on his lap so we could talk about 'the first thing that comes up'. I was so innocent I ran back to my dorm and they put me on a charge. I could have been kicked out cause that's desertion but he had me on jankers cause I'd also drank a bottle of vodka. I kept pretty shtum about what he'd said and they didn't *charge* him but they *transferred* him and I never saw him after that. And the third time they locked me up was also for drinking vodka and it came up at the Court Marshal that I'd been singing 'House of the Rising Sun' outside the Naafi and when the MP told me to move on, I said **'Balls** to you!' and this was all read out in court: '**Balls** to you! I'm stayin *here*!' so the six of them carried me and I woke up in the cell. *Great* fun! I had to report to the Warrant Officer and he gave me two weeks on the Parade Square. The day I finished I said '**Yes! Yes!** It's *over!* And he turned round and said 'It's one o' clock: you're not supposed to be stepping on the training square - you're *charged* again! And *his* jankers was cleaning the toilet with a *toothbrush!*

After four years I got married to a service man, left the WRAF and went to live with him in Malta. Although we split up out there it was the best three years of my life. He had six months left to do when I left him out there but I wrote to Mintoff first to ask if I could carry on living there on my own and I had a lovely letter back - actually *from* Mintoff - saying 'Thank you for loving our island and wanting to stay but as you can appreciate there isn't enough work for Maltese girls never mind the British,' which was *understandable*, you know?

It was hard to pick up the pieces when I came back. I didn't have to sign on for the first three months cause he was still sending me money but after that he sent me a letter saying when are you going to get a job? So I got a job with United Biscuits on Fforestfach Trading Estate. That was the time when you didn't need to go to a Job Centre. You'd finish a job on a Friday and be in another one on a Monday.

I have to explain something before I go on. It sounds from what I've told you that I was all sweet and innocent when I was young but I was not. I was smokin dope and drinkin at sixteen. I used to go in the old Scrumpy Bar in the Tenby where all the old men used to drink. I was still in School uniform and doin my O levels and scrumpy was something like eight pence for half a pint. There used to be sawdust on the floor in there and all these old men off the sea. That's where I first met all the old crowd - all the old Hippies: Peter Curry and Dan 'The-Man' Piper and Micky Baker and Joe the Boxer and Mav. Mav's still alive but a lot of them are dead now. They used to call me 'Ev The Rev' in those days and some of them still do and I don't like it. And I always remember the old landlord went on holiday and left Dan The-Man in charge and he spiked a barrel of scrumpy with acid and all the old men were swaying back and fore to the bar and saying **'Elluva** kick on the scrumpy tonight, Dan!' I drunk some too, and it took me three and a half hours to walk from there to the Number 10. Don't ask me where I went. I'll never forget it the pavement was like an escalator and Charlie Chaplin was coming towards me and when I got home my intestines came out on the floor and I *ate* them. My father used to drag me out of there sometimes but I used to love sitting with the older men. And I forget who it was - it's many years ago now - but someone said you're sittin in the *famous seat* and it was the *actual* bench where Leon Atkin used to drink with Dylan Thomas. I knew Leon Atkin's son Gary. He's dead now but he used to go in there as well. Always in and out of prison and always for something trivial. Leon Atkin's church was opposite Joe's Ice Cream Parlour and my father told me he was the first man to open a crypt up for all the old tramps and meths drinkers. He was very well respected and he always had a big congregation and none of them complained at least not to his face when he opened it up. The powers-that-be and the City Council might not have liked it but it was *his* church and he could do what he wanted and what's a church for if it's not to help the unfortunate? He must have been a lovely man. I don't know what the relationship was between Gary and him but I *do* know he gave him a row once for playing the organ in the crypt. Gary'd gone right off the top in Cefn Coed through taking too much LSD and he'd gone down the crypt late one night - and Dan would tell you this if he was alive, cause he was *there* - and there was an old organ down there that hadn't been played for years and I don't know whether he thought he'd give them some *live* entertainment or what but he started playin and Dan said it was like something out of a Hammer Horror film. I can just imagine it - all the old tramps woke up and started freakin cause they thought it was a ghost and Gary was sat there white and gaunt like Boris Karloff and then his father rushed in shouting hell fire and brimstone cause he'd upset the old men and Gary only meant it as a practical joke but I don't think they spoke for a long time after that. But although they didn't get on his father never turned him away he always took him in and whenever I saw Gary he'd always say I'm back with my dad now. And then of course Gary died. I don't know of what and his father wasn't long after and when he died it was horrible to see that lovely church all boarded up. There was mesh on the windows and they took all the lovely glass out and it was like that for years and then the next time I saw it it was like two cinemas in one and on the big board where it used to have **The Reverend Leon Atkin** and the name of the Church it had **Studio One** and **Studio Two** and what had happened was the Castle cinema had closed and they took all the X films from there and put them in the church. In the *Church!* He must have been turning in his grave. They didn't even knock the old Church down and put a new building up. I thought it was wrong. The man was dead and he couldn't stand up for himself and to my mind it was like going from Good to Evil. I know that sounds a bit over the top but d'you know what I mean? They couldn't have done anything *worse* if they pulled it down altogether.

I had bedsits all the way up Constitution Hill when I left home and then I got married and had a son but it didn't work out and I moved into a Refuge. It's a bit awkward to explain how I first became homeless because I've never been *exactly* homeless. I had a flat and it was in Eversley Road in Sketty. But I couldn't cope so I made myself homeless if you know what I mean. I was just so glad to get up to Sketty. It was like a stepping stone. The landlord's office was on the bottom floor and then there was two flats and I was on top. And at first it wasn't to do with the landlord it was to do with the neighbours below. You know, constant pressure all the time. It was totally weird. They opened *my* mail because it was *their* home and I couldn't have friends there. *They* could hear my feet and *I* could hear them talkin. I felt I was being watched all the time. I mean, I'd pull the carpet back and

I could *see* them! Through the floorboards! That's how bad a state the house was in. We had two years of living hell. They told the landlord *everything* and he *believed them.* They told him my son was havin rave music on all night and it was totally untrue. They were retired from Shropshire. I found out he was a watchmaker and he'd been a bachelor up to the age of forty-nine and got married and she was from a wealthy family and she lost everything through him going bankrupt. And from living on a big farm up in Shropshire they had to put up with a tiny little flat in Sketty, which is *sad* because I imagine he was a very good watchmaker and an artist with old clocks and things but as he told me when I was talkin to him once, when batteries came in he was *finished.*

In the beginning my son and me started stayin in other people's houses and I used to go back there at twelve o' clock at night - not to have a bath or anything - just to pick up fresh clothes but I'd only have to *see* the place and I'd go to pieces and get these panic attacks so I told the landlord I was leavin and I went and told my Key Worker in SAND and she said no don't do that you'll lose everything but I thought no I can't go on. It was a time when you're *that* low it's hard to explain. It's a horrible feeling, *unnerving,* like being an outcast. Although I *had* that place I *didn't* have it. Although there was friends who said we'll put you up I had to explain to them all the time that I wasn't *really* homeless. Over and over I was explaining this so in the end the stress had built up so much I thought enough is enough and I went on the streets. I put my son in my mum's cause if he was on the street with me they'd have taken him into care. I must have started in April cause I remember I was freezin and d'you know Jock's Pet Shop by the Albert Hall? I slept outside there for two nights. Now anybody who was *truly* homeless would *not* sleep outside Jock's Pet Shop and after that I went on the beach. My son was a scout so I'd taken his sleeping bag and his rubber underlay but that got nicked.

There's good and bad on the beach. People like Belfast Danny are fine and the older, *gentlemen* tramps who *chose* to be homeless who light a fire and ave a few drinks. I felt safer with them but the older men get mugged by the younger men and I couldn't handle that. They bashed one chap and I could have stepped in but there was *five* of them and they had dogs and weapons as well and this old man had done *nothing* and in the end he was *throwing* his money at them and I was just standin there crying. It was like something out of Clockwork Orange I don't know if you've seen it where he batters the tramp in the underground? Well that was what I was watching and I've never forgotten it.

And *all* for three pound in ten pence pieces. People *do* steal on the streets but you don't expect them to beat up their own kind for money and certainly not anyone over sixty.

I was walking miles and miles and miles wearing myself out when I came off the beach. I lost a stone in weight. I went into SAND one day cause I had an appointment with Dr. Robinson and she said 'Ev, I've got seven beds in D Ward in Cefn Coed. I can't *force* you but wouldn't it be nice to have three square meals a day and a bed and no worries? I turned it down at first, cause of the stigma but three months later I went back and signed myself in the same day.

I know quite a few people who got flats with the Cefn Coed Project. I've known Steve 'Nipper' Norris since I was sixteen. He's lovely. You know he's always smartly dressed, always has been going back years and you should see his room - it's *spotless!* Everything clean and in its place and people take the mick out of that but that's his *pride.* There's five people living in that house and to me it's like a Kibbutz. They all look after each other and they're great. They've got Key Workers but they tend to leave them alone. They've got their privacy. I stayed downstairs there with a dear woman called Phyllis and she thinks that people are doin somethin to the light bulbs all the time. She's very well read. I think she's an ex-teacher and some days she says don't put the TV on today because Mr Big is watching us but she's the best cook I've ever seen and she knows all about vitamins and garnishes and she's so *healthy.* There's a couple of schizophrenics there and on the top floor there's this witch who comes out of her room and cackles *heh! heh! heh!* and then runs back in again. But I tell you: what a house! They *all* support each other. I went there five weeks ago and Steve had this big beam on his face. I said 'What's up with you?' and he said 'I've bought a washing machine and I don't have to use the downstairs spinner any more,' so *good* for him! And now he's just bought a car I don't know what make it is but it's *red* and when I saw him, him and his mate were sanding down the front bumper and he said 'Come back at one and we'll take you for a run down Gower,' I said 'Thank you very much but I think I'll *leave* it today.' But they're all right both of them except that Steve thinks he's God. And that's when I have to tell him off. I was with him and a friend of mine one day and that's when he came out and said he had two children by Miss Dwyer. I said 'I didn't know *that!*' He said 'No, Ev, I mean like the *Virgin Mary.*' I said 'Pull the other one, Steve!' and this person I was with said 'Don't upset Evelyn now, Steve!' and he said 'How long have you known me now, Ev - twenty-eight years isn't it?' I said 'Is it as much as *that?*' He said 'How d'you feel now, Ev after all that time, sitting here talking to God?' And that's when I got up and hit im! Not in the face but on the shoulder and d'you know what he said to me he said: 'That's *it*! I'm not coming here again. I will *never ever* come near your flat again and don't phone me cause I'm *not* in.' When he said 'I'm God and I'm protecting you,' I thought he was joking but when I went to see if he was all right, cause I felt terrible that I'd smacked him, I knew he wouldn't answer the door so I rang downstairs and said 'Is Steve all right?' and next thing Steve heard my voice and came running downstairs '**Morning**, Evelyn!' as though nothing had happened. But I was worded up by the schizophrenic upstairs that when he goes like that the best thing is to *ignore* him.

'The background, the foreground, the light, the shadows...'

Frank

I can only talk about my *own* experience, can't I? But you don't want a *'poor me'* attitude, do you? *'I* was on the streets and *I* was in the gutter,' sort of thing. You want something that people can look at and say 'Well, I can see he's used his experience and he's turned it all to the good...'

A hot day in Balaclava Street at the end of May. He comes to the door as he did on my last visit: stripped to the waist, barefoot and bronzed. Until about a month ago, he shared this house with Nick and two other people - now Nick's gone and nobody seems sure exactly where. We sit either side of some steps in a small courtyard at the back of the house, the sun streaming down on us and birds singing. He looks much fitter than the January day when I recorded him and Alec in the Hostel. His body is muscular and tattooed and when he talks, his voice runs a whole gamut of emotions from wild laughter to smouldering anger. There are two pieces of broken concrete paving resting on the wall either side of us, which bear the faded remnants of some designs in oil pastel which Nick did.

I never knew my father. I was more-or-less brought up with my relations and the least that was said about him, the better. When I *did* enquire about him, it was kind of a taboo subject, so I dismissed it cause either they really *didn't* know, or if they *did* know, they didn't want to tell me. And it was left at that. So I was the cuckoo in the nest. My mother was still around and she was a nice, kind woman. I can see her now - funny how you can talk about someone and you can *see* them - I can see her as she *was*. Course, you're talkin about the end of the war now and I can still see the remains of wartime all around. I remember someone showing me a gas-mask and saying 'This thing can save your *life.*' And I thought 'Jesus! What kind of a planet am I on, that I've gotto wear a *gas-mask?*' But it was instilled in me that this gas-mask could save my life and they showed me how to put it on and - you know how things go through your mind - I thought 'Have I gotto go through life with *that* thing on?' I don't know what it was like for you but it was frightening as a child to be told that this little thing in a box could save your life: *always* have it at hand. But now you look at the ozone layer and the pollution and the different diseases and people going around with asthma pumps and everything else that's goin on in the world: and it's a far cry from the gas mask, isn't it?

I had a good job as an electrical linesman when I left school but I developed a bit of a drink problem and the job eventually fell through. I got caught up in life on the road then and I couldn't get out of it. I was going from town to town like a zombie, without feeling, without consideration. It was as if I'd switched off and gone to sleep and was waiting for someone to wake me up an say 'Hey! The music's playing: it's *your* turn to be on the stage!' It became a way of life to me. There wasn't a family in society for me and I always identified more with the outsiders - the ones that didn't fit in. Material things didn't interest me. I couldn't understand people wantin a car. I felt I'd be far healthier walkin. The stream's gotto be flowin and changin and not stagnatin. I was waitin my *turn*, so I had to lose and go with all the losers and become like them: become like the forces of darkness in order to *understand* the forces of darkness. You had the visible, the half-visible and the invisible and I had to see the *invisible* to see the *visible*. I had to look *inwardly* to see *outwardly*. D'you you see what I mean?

In school I always wanted to be an artist. Art was my top subject. It fascinated me. I loved painting the West Country waterfalls with the water coming down and the trees at the side. This *tranquility!* I always like painting *nature.* And I've seen nature change from when I was a boy to what it is today. I can remember when you could sit out in a place like this and the swallows would dart back and fore. Not any more. I've seen the *world* change. I've seen things come and go. People who stood up and had a voice, no longer have a voice. They had their time, they had their place. Like the flowers, they came up - and they're gone. But they come up again in a new form. The beginning is the end and the end is merely the beginning. Nothing is ever lost. Nothing's ever gone. It remains somewhere else. Like the dinosaurs: they *still* exist. Not here, but somewhere else. Are you with me? They're big and powerful and no-one stands in their way. And we've had a lot of dinosaurs in this country, haven't we? And a lot of Hitlers. That Telephone Jock: *he* was a Hitler. Oh, yes! Within that little realm of Hanbury, he was a dictator: 'Do *this!* Do *that!*' But all he *really* was, was a *little* cog in a *big* watch.

Bishop Briggs just outside of Glasgow was the last of the old 'Spikes' to close down - just recently. It was right near the prison, so there wasn't much difference between the prison and the Reception Centre. It was a regime where no-one spoke to each other. There was this beautiful scenery all around but what did they make you do all day? Break rocks - for road infill. What sort of activity was *that* for someone? I thought in this day and age and with the Scottish temperament, this couldn't happen but the mentality there was *bad*. Even when it was good times, you could feel the *gloom*. People were dyin within themselves. People were *dead* within themselves. People who'd tried to make it and just couldn't make it. It was like 'All You Who Enter Here, Abandon Hope.' When you see people on the streets, it's different to seein them in an institution. Put them in an institution and you see them for what they *really* are, with all their guilts and complexes and fears. You see that they scratch, they itch, they feel pain, they're enclosed and faced with themselves. Once they're out on the streets, they're so preoccupied, they don't get *time* to look at themselves. They laugh and joke and pretend everything's *great*. But I think most of them *knew* they was doomed. They'd be people who were on a search, looking for something but not sure what, didn't like themselves and didn't particularly like other people. They were sort of lost within society. They didn't seem to have the *love* or the *hope* and they wouldn't communicate. Everything was evasive: like as if they didn't want to get involved. Nobody wanted to admit the truth: they just accepted things as they were. So, because they become evasive, *you* became lost, cause there was nothing for you to relate to within *them*. They switched off. They didn't question. They didn't want to *know*. They were like slaves. Always looking for this *something* that was going to change their lives. There was nothing on a spiritual level: everything boiled down to work, money and drink. The majority of people I knew on the road, ended up committing suicide. That was a common thing. If they weren't killed, a lot of them had just had enough and couldn't take any more.

Up and down, up and down the motorways: I was going nowhere and it was an *experience*. I went around these places to see what they were like. Sometimes you were lucky and you got in. It wasn't easy but I was only *waiting*, wasn't I - biding my time? Okay, a lot of those memories are pretty-well blocked off now and you try to forget that it ever happened but sometimes it comes home to you. In the end, you had to take on a new person and leave that old person behind.

I can look back and say I met some great people and it's the *people* I remember the most, not the *experience*. The ones I drank with and admired. That's the only memories I have: the concrete, the cold, the hunger and the *people*. You don't remember much else. Cause it's people that are *life*. The rest is just background, innit?

Some of these institutions with all their egotistical fuckin officials with their own pre-conceived ideas, who thought they were *better* than you! It's almost like an apartheid system in this country, isn't it? Class distinction. I remember prisons when they'd look for *anybody* to put in, just to make up the numbers. But look at it today: they don't *need* to now, do they?

I was in most prisons: Swansea, Cardiff, the Verne, Portland, Pentonville, Dorset, Dartmoor. It was mostly for petty nonsense but you could go to prison for virtually *anything* in them days. I've seen guys doin five years for shoplifting because they were habitual shoplifters. But what is shoplifting today? It's just a way of life, isn't it? It's just a slap on the wrist. So we've come from a different mentality. Proportions and attitudes have changed. The world has moved on. We realize now that the people who actually run a country are the biggest crooks of the lot - and *International* crooks at that! Who takes you to war? Your Petroleum companies. Tate and Lyle, the sugar people. These are the ones who are makin millions a day and can *afford* to take you to war. It's all a game and we're all playin our little parts. Once you get into politics, you automatically become a millionaire, anyway, don't you? That's what it's all about. And when their time's up, they write a book and make a fortune. They *all* do it. And we're caught up in it. We go along with it until *our* day comes and then we say 'Right! We seen *their* little game, now we'll have *our* game.' Cause everythin has its time, don't it?

I came from Scotland to Swansea. Straight down from Glasgow. I had people chasing me up there for various reasons and cars coming at me, etcetera. I just woke up one morning and something said to me: *'Swansea! That's* where you've gotto go!'. It was almost as if I was programmed, as if God had said 'Okay, *I'll* take over from here. *You'll* give up on yourself. I know where you've *been* and *I* know where you're *goin.* You're *mine!* And it all *happened.* Know what I mean?

Everything just clicked when I came here. *This* connected with *this* and *that* connected with *that* and, lo and behold, I started to awaken. I started to get introduced to people and then I started to get introduced to *myself.* And everything started to spin and I couldn't spin out of it. D'you know what I'm sayin? I *tried* to get out of Swansea, cause I've always been a mover, but something was always stopping me. I'd go for a bus and just as I got there, the bus was either full or leavin. I'd go for a train and it would be just pullin out. Something was always telling me 'You *can't* get out.' Something was drawing me back like a magnet all the time, until I just surrendered and said 'Right. If it's *here* I've got to face myself, *here* it will be.' I would say I was here for a good many years before I realized I *was* here. And it's flown by. But Swansea's been the best move I ever made. I wouldn't say I'm here for good but I believe I'm here for a purpose and when my purpose is achieved, I'll move on to the next place.

I don't *plan,* cause I don't *know.* There was a lot of truths in myself that I didn't *want* to face and that I *had* to face. There was a lot of battlin goin on within me: myself and myself, my left and my right hand, the dark and the light. And the battle *still* goes on: there's actually white cells and red cells at war in our bodies all the time fighting *this* infection and *that.* But I've come good in Swansea and I'm grateful for it.

Nick's gone to Australia. Australia or America. I had a vision - a dream. I saw him boarding a plane at Heathrow. Him and me used to confide and he told me a lot of things in confidence: that his father was in Special Services, for instance. He regretted telling me that because he said it was better not to talk about those things. I used to go on to him about that scar on his nose and then one day he showed me his legs. And, oh, it was a wonder he could even *walk!* It was as if somebody had got a sword and just hacked at his legs. He said '*This* was painful - not the nose. *That* was nothing.' And I could see it had been nasty, but it had healed. I got the impression that it had healed on its own, that he'd either been in some country in a jungle or some situation and something had got his legs and he'd had to survive. He wouldn't go into detail. I tried to get him to, on different things, but all he would say was '*This* was painful.' I think a lot of his life was painful, too. He talked a lot about his wife and his little boy and about Capitalists and aristocrats and people like that. He thought we should go back to helping each other and sharing and realizing that it's *us* that makes a world and not *money*. And I noticed that when he was drunk and talked in his sleep, he never once spoke in an English accent: it was always German or Russian. He had a lot of respect for me - used to cook me meals and share everything - but I never quite knew *who* he was and I don't think he quite knew who he was himself. I think he was looking for something and wasn't quite sure what it was. I think Nick was just sort of destroying himself, cause the drugs and the alcohol had got a hold on him. In my opinion, I think there was a death-wish in him. Sad to say.

He worked for the Psychic Research people, you know, but he wouldn't go into detail about that, either. He said that *he* wasn't particularly looking for *them* and *they* weren't particularly looking for *him:* they just sort of *picked up* and it came together. That's about as much as I could get out of him. You had to make your own mind up: put the jigsaw together yourself, like you did with his drawings. His life was very much like his drawings: it was 'see in it what you want.' But it was always a woman was at the centre and the rest was just background. And even when he was drunk and sleepin on the settee and talkin in all this foreign language, it was always the woman who would come into it: 'Oh, *Baby Baby*, I *love* you, *Baby!'* His life was centred around this woman. The rest was just words, jumbled up.

Don't get me wrong: we had our battles, me and him, but we had a lot of respect for each other. People tell me he was intelligent. Well, I think he *was*. But for *what?* It's not an intelligent man who pumps shit in his veins, is it? I think he was on course for self-destruct. I don't know why. Perhaps I never will.

Nick had been to a lot of Far Eastern countries where people had absolutely nothing, so even if *he* had nothing, he felt as if he was really well off compared to them. Not having any money didn't worry him much and he was as honest as the day. He went into the toilet one day and found a money-roll with a couple of hundred quid on it, which he guessed must have belonged to Ruth upstairs, so he gave it straight back.

He was kicked out of the Hostel cause they said his behaviour was disruptive and he *was* disruptive but he didn't *mean* to be. Cause *he* was on self-destruct, everything around him was goin to self-destruct as well.

But, anyway, I definitely seen him getting on a flight. I seen him at Heathrow. On his own - nobody with him. Somebody was obviously getting him out of the country. I think his own people, cause, as you know, an SAS man is looked after for life. So, if Nick *is* the

277

son of an SAS man, there's probably a place in Australia where they look after their own.

I've spent years and years on the street but I'm still *here.* There's no-one I can say 'I remember *you* from the Sixties,' to, cause they're all gone. Their lifestyle killed them eventually - or did they have a death-wish, too? I don't know.

I go back a long time. I couldn't read in those days and I *still* can't and I can remember bread and water in prison. But I can look back on my life and I've got good memories of growing up. All my times - even the hard times - were happy, compared to what some people have had to put up with. A lot of people live with hate, don't they but if you do that, you have a very sad life. I went through a phase of hating certain people in my family but I learnt it was better to live with love, otherwise you destroy yourself. My life's been a clutter but I *needed* that clutter. If I hadn't known *that,* I wouldn't know *this.* And if I hadn't gone *there,* I wouldn't be *here.* Because it's all connected. Everything's related to everything else: like the parts in a painting. As a little boy, there's always a room in the house that you're frightened to go into but that room is actually inside your head. These are the fears that you have as a little boy. You imagine you're being watched or there's somebody under the bed. All these fears of the Unknown but there's no such thing as the Unknown. All the Unknown is, is that which we don't know about *ourself.*

I've tried to give you a picture which you, as an artist, can see and appreciate: bits of this, bits of that - the background, the foreground, the light, the shadows. See what I mean? Like a painting. But it's all related: all those years on the road and in prison, right down to the gas mask I had to wear as a child. For me, *that* was terrifyin. That was makin me into a monster. D'you understand? D'you see the connection? It took away my innocence, because eventually I *became* that monster...

'The Landlord, the Butler,
the Cook and the Maid...'

Gavin

Am I the furthest you've actually travelled to interview as a landlord? We are the last village, on the way to Pontardawe, which is actually just *within* the City boundaries. Some people find that a problem: 'Oh, *six* miles into Town!' they say, whereas others - who've come from perhaps Liverpool or Brum, where you're talkin about *twenty* miles to get from one end of Town to the other - find it no problem at all. Bus-wise, it's excellent until six o' clock, then you'd have to walk up from the Mond, which is about a mile down the road. It's more rural in the other direction. There's a small hamlet with a row of cottages, one pub and then a long road that stretches for about three-quarters of a mile and takes you into the village of Craig Cefn Parc. Locals get used to it but it *is* a bit strange for anyone used to living in a City centre. One thing that might put people off living around here is that the only pub which *was* licensed for Karaoke has just had its licence revoked. And not *just* the music licence: the *whole* licence. Some miserable sods have been complaining about the noise, so it's going to be boarded up. The only music around here now will be the Working Men's Club, which has its singing and its concerts on a Saturday. There are several other pubs around but whether they'll go for Karaoke now or not, is hard to say. I'm told that the one pub in the village, which used to have a band *every* weekend and some days in the week, is now down to *six* bands a year!

A rainy evening in early June. I've been dropped on the main road and have to make my way there on foot. It's a lot further than I expected but I'm still there in good time. Number 27 is in the middle of an anonymous-looking row of postwar semis. There's no-one about. The bell isn't working and when I knock, a dog barks from somewhere within. The whole place looks dark and deserted. I walk down the street and back again, wait five minutes and then start to write him a note. Just then, a short, raincoated man with dark hair and glasses and a shopping bag turns in at the garden gate. We introduce ourselves. His appearance doesn't tally at all with the precise, rather old-fashioned voice I heard over the telephone. He reminds me of Rodney Bewes the actor and speaks with a distinct West Wales accent. We go inside. His living room is chaotic and cluttered and home to two cats and a dog. I squeeze into a small space on a settee and he sits in an adjacent arm chair. He doesn't seem to think he'll have anything useful to say but is prepared to be as helpful as he can.

My grandmother and me bought this house jointly from the Council and when she died I thought I may as well make use of the rooms. I'm forty years old now and I've been a landlord, on and off, for the past twenty years. Before I was married, I got my tenants through my work: colleagues who, because of transfers from other parts of the country, were coming down and staying here for some months until they found their own permanent places. And then, after I was married, we seen the Cyrenians' advert and I applied to them and went on their panel of landlords and have been with them ever since. I've had between forty and fifty lodgers all together. Most of them are short term: just sort of travelling and wanting to get a fixed address so they can be in receipt of Benefits and then they usually move on when they're successful in getting work or a place nearer the centre of Swansea. I take two maximum or a couple at a push. That is: two singles or a couple together and one single by themselves.

It was bed *and* breakfast when I was married but it's just *bed* now and we all do our own cooking. We also chip in four pounds a month each for the hire of a washing machine. They don't have to be in at a certain time. They've got their own keys and they just make sure they bolt the door when they come in and lock it when they go out. There's one here now who's a keen night fisherman, so he's either going out at two o' clock in the morning or coming in at four o' clock in the morning, sort of thing, but I never hear a sound.

There's such a great *need* for accommodation round here that if I'd had the money when the former Convent went up for sale, I could have bought that and had every room filled three or four times over - and *that* is a twenty-four bedroomed building. In the wintertime - once October, November comes - on average, I could have three or four calls a week from the Cyrenians, enquiring about rooms. I'm the only one on this road doing it. There are a few people letting out flats but I would say, at a rough guess, there might be only twenty or so flats, on and off, in the whole of the area. There *is* one man owns a street of converted flats but he's so full with his books that perhaps you're lucky if you get *one* flat a year becoming available, if he's unfortunate enough to have had a tenant dying or moving out.

The only sort of problems I've seen from the Cyrenian referrals is that they've got this sort of bee-in-their-bonnet attitude, when they arrive here, about having not only a landlord but a butler, a cook and a maid as well. They want *everything* rolled into one and expect to be waited on hand and foot while *they* are quite happy to sit around all day without washing a cup or a plate. There's no sense of *gratitude* coming from them whatsoever. No feeling that without the room, the possibility was that they could be sleeping on a park bench or under a tarpaulin on the beach. It's just as though *they're* all doing *me* a favour and *I* should count myself lucky I was having *them* rather than the other way around.

I've had all-sorts here and there's quite a few that come readily to mind. For instance, there was one couple who were on mild drugs. Teenagers they were. That wouldn't have been a problem in itself but they couldn't control themselves when they were on the drugs and we had fits of giggling and stupid things being done that could have been potentially dangerous if they had been by themselves: simply because they were stoned out of their mind and didn't realize what they were doin. The cooker, for example, nearly went on fire because the chip-pan was left unattended while they were upstairs smoking some blow. Mark Sullivan, the boy's name was. He was of mixed-race descent and used to burst out laughing like a hyena at the slightest thing. You could come in and say that some maniac had just opened up with a machine gun on the street killing ten people and he'd be sitting there *grinning* - at something as serious as *that!* And then another one came here with a leg injury and, I don't know what he was expecting but I think he thought he was moving into an annexe of some Nursing Home or other.

There were others then whose names I can't recall because their visits were so fleeting. There was a Jack-something-or-other who *claimed* to be a miner and he *did* get a hobble at a pit at the valley here but when a friend of mine - who was widowed from a man who worked *all* his life in mining - asked him some basic things, he was *completely* in the dark. On only his second day here, I found him up the garden smoking blow with my neighbour's fifteen year old son. He used to come back here inebriated and there was many a time where, if I hadn't of been here, my wife - as she was at the time - would have been molested or possibly even *raped*. In the end, we had to evict him because of *that*. And then a few months later he came back, still wanting accommodation and no sooner had he walked in through the door, than he tried it on *again!*

And another one, who I believe is back with the Cyrenians - or may even be dead as far as I'm aware - whose surname was Smith-Vickers but who insisted on being called just Vick, was on very heavy drugs. And, apparently, what had affected him was coming home one day and finding his father hanging from the bannister. When he was rational he was quite a pleasant chap to talk to but there were times when he'd go overboard and do completely crazy things.

Then there was a guy calling himself Terry Allbright and claiming to be married to a Norwegian and his real name was something else but he took the wife's name. He came from a hostel in London run by an order of nuns and I even had a nun on the phone here once. He'd gone up to London for a few days and had seen them and she was basically ringing to ask how he'd settled in down here. And, again, it was all *Walter Mitty* with him. He *claimed* to have been a Regular and I had a TA man lodging here at the time and one weekend he went on a Nuclear Biological Warfare training exercise and he had on his rubber suit - or Noddy Suit as they call it - and this Terry Allbright, who *claimed* to be a Regular, didn't know what it was. And the only difference in the design of them over the past forty years is they've gone from *black* rubber to *camouflage* rubber!

In fact, I've had quite a few claiming false pasts, so whether they are *hiding* something by changing names, I just don't know. There was another one here who was on TV a few times and he was a *known* criminal who used about four different aliases. And I had to have the police up on several occasions and they used to ask him 'Well, what name d'you want us to charge you under, *now*?'

There was one who stayed a few nights and sixty-odd pounds went missing from my wife's purse. He *was* caught and he admitted it. Then he was let out on bail and went straight over to his father's place and they haven't been able to serve the warrants on him, so he's been written off and, consequently, I'm down sixty-odd pounds! Another left owing forty pound on a phone bill and then another one left and I found out a few weeks later when I went to look for it, that he'd stolen a leather blouson jacket valued at about a hundred pounds.

There was an Irish bloke - Kieran something - and he used to come out with such weird and wonderful things that I began to wonder whether it actually *was* his real name, in the end. He claimed to be an ex-soldier, in the REME, but wouldn't even join the local branch of his Regiment's Association because he was convinced the IRA had infiltrated all manner of organizations and he'd be making himself a target. And, rather than walking, he was goin around *dartin* from place to place so that no marksman could get a bead on him. You know: all sorts of nonsense like that. I mean, you've got a shirt on there with a tartan design, for instance. Well, *he'd* take that as a sign that you were here, not as a reporter writing a book, but as an MI6 Agent and the tartan shirt was the trademark of MI6, just like the long mac was the Gestapo trademark. He may well have been schizophrenic without having had the treatment, for all I know. A friend of mine, who entered the Ministry and done his training in Ireland told me he was in a cafe in Kilkenny where he was studying and he suddenly dived under the table when this Kevin went past. He just *didn't* want to speak to him because of all the *rubbish* he used to be coming out with. After Kilkenny, he came back across the water and the last known sighting of him was in either the Birmingham or the Coventry area.

Then we had another one here who had only been an Army *cadet* and yet, to hear him talk, you'd think he'd been a *Mercenary* with several years overseas campaign service: something like Colonel Mike Hoare. He tried to claim this, that and the other but, in reality, he was on the twenties side of thirty and if every campaign he'd been in for the length of time he claimed, was added together, he'd be older than Noah! He took an air rifle to the conservatory eventually and wrecked a few sheets and pillow-cases and I had to get the police out. They came with riot shields and dogs and everything.

The neighbours are usually pretty good. A few of them *have* phoned the police themselves because of various disturbances but, other than that, there's been no animosity because they take the attitude that not being able to control some of my lodgers is much the same as not being able to control the wife, were I still married.

There was one old guy - I forget his name now - with grey, unkempt hair and disfigured teeth and very *vocal* in himself - who was so lax about his personal hygiene that he only lasted *two* days. He seemed to be relyin on livin just on *tea.* He would *not* make *any* sort of solid food for himself. He was a bachelor or a divorced man from down Carmarthen way. He had been livin with his brother and they'd fallen out because of this personal hygiene problem. The other one that was here at the time was only stayin for a few months while his house was being renovated. He was sleeping on a mattress in this room but he was threatening to pitch a tent in the garden, rather than stay in the same house with this man. After just *two* days!

Most of my lodgers have had this attitude of expecting to sit here not lifting a finger all day. But I had one here, for example - a young girl - who was the exact opposite. She had been working as a wine waitress or a receptionist in a hotel in East Grinstead and the contract just ended so she came back down this area to live because she had relatives down here and just happened to call into the Cyrenians in passing and they put her on to me. Her attitude was more like: 'I'm grateful to be here. Now *I* am *your* servant and not your source of income.' I came home many a time and found her washing the curtains and doing the polishing and things like this - especially when my wife went into hospital. She moved out after about eighteen months and, the last I heard, she married her boyfriend and is now living in the Manselton area.

As I say, it's been mostly male tenants but I have had the odd woman, both in numbers and in attitude. There was one who apparently just alighted from the Paddington to Swansea train one day and I had the Probation Service phoning me at eleven o' clock on a Thursday evening, enquiring if I could put her up. And on the Friday morning my wife phoned me at work to say she'd asked her to leave because the first thing this woman had asked her in the morning was 'Where's the nearest drug joint, so I can go and get an ounce of heroin?' So we phoned the Probation Officer and he came up and put her back on the train and I assume she's the Met's problem again, now.

And then I had another one who was heavily tattooed. She stayed a few nights, went out for a packet of cigarettes at three o' clock in the morning and we're *still* waiting for her to come back. And one of my lodgers is still waiting for the return of his jeans. She asked if she could borrow a pair while she was washing hers and after she'd gone, we noticed that both the wet jeans *and* the jeans he lent her had been taken from the line. No sign of her since. And she would be *very* distinctive if ever she *is* seen around Swansea, because she's always in the habit of wearing a very brightly-coloured beret and a ring in her nose and - unless she's since had it removed - a butterfly tattoo on the side of her face.

This is the problem with the Cyrenians. If they've had somebody who's on probation or out of prison after a few years - for say theft, or something like that -all they can tell me is 'He is *known* to the police.' They can't say '*This* one's done time for *this*,' or '*This* one's done time for *that*.' So, I told them straight, after this Jack Howells bloke left: 'It's pointless you sending anyone like that again because what could have happened if I wasn't here and he'd been an ex-rapist?' But they took umbrage then and again it was back to the old attitude of '*You* should be grateful that *you're* having *them*,' and not vice-versa.

But what I think I will be specifying in future - because of the attitude problems I've encountered - will be *'females only'*. I find them more helpful because, once they get over the initial shock of having a male landlord living on the premises, they seem to be able to settle in quite well and there's no problem. Mind you, there *has* been some quite malicious gossip in the neighbourhood about some of my tenants and my relationship with them. I shouldn't say this, but when a young couple moved in here a few months ago, I was shocked to hear that certain people in the village were spreading it around that *he* was *bending* for me and *she* was *opening her legs* for me. Shagging and bumming! That's *all* they thought was going on here! And I know that for a *fact!*

It'll be a paperback, will it? And the contributors: will they be named or will they be anonymous? By all means put down 'Clydach' - the only ones that would know it was *here* are those that have *lived* here - but I'd rather be anonymous if it's all the same. I can just hear that Mark Sullivan saying 'Look what that *bastard's* said about me!' and next thing you know, I could have a brick through the window - or a *Molotov*!

'Takin off again...'

Tom and Sylvia (2)

Sylvia: He nearly *kills* me sometimes. He thumps me to death - well, you can see the bruises, yourself, can't you? - but we're still together after two years. The last thing the doctor said to me last week was 'Any more violence?' I said 'No, he's all right at the moment. He's been *good!*' What a *liar!*

One thirty on a sunny afternoon in June. Sylvia hasn't changed at all in five months but Tom looks paler and thinner and is walking with a limp. The room is still light and airy and they've acquired a new cat and a new carpet.

Tom: *She's* had problems and *I've* had problems. She got problems with her family and she was afraid to go out and all that and then, in the end, *her* problems got to *me* and we split up. We've been back together for about ten weeks now and things are slowly gettin sorted but I was really fed up after she went. I'd been sittin here for about two and a half weeks, I think it was, and I kept thinkin to myself 'I'm on my *own.*' And I'd lost my cat as well, so I had *nobody* to talk to!'

Sylvia: And I was quite happy staying with my friends. They were kind to me. We'd go into Town every day and sit talkin and havin a laugh and a joke. I was lucky: I had company. I *enjoyed* myself! But he didn't have *nobody* down here. And he's not one for goin out, are you?

Tom: I didn't fancy goin down Paxton street cause of my leg. It was swollen out here. I used to walk across there and never think anything about it, but I could never get across like that. Not that I know anybody down there now, except Alec, and he's always over the Duchess. I was pretty miserable. I had to do all the shopping myself - everythin. Couldn't stick it in the end, so I got in a taxi, went over there, knocked the door and -

Sylvia: I *refused* to come back. He was up to *here* with drink, hadn't washed, hadn't shaved and he looked like a tramp, didn you? He said 'What am I gonna *do?*' *Boo-hoo!* 'What am I gonna *do?*' I said 'I'm not comin back - no way! He said 'But there's a taxi waitin for us outside. It's *waitin!* I said 'Nope! No *way!* **Go!**' And he went.

Tom: Yeah, I went. Got back in the taxi, left it another week.

Sylvia: Come back again then and *begged* me to come back. I'm not one to give in easy but I'd mellowed a bit by then. It was Bank Holiday Monday. He came in and we talked and my friend said he could stay with me while we worked it out, so he stayed for a week.

Tom: More than a week, wannit? End of March we got back together and I stayed up there after Easter, didn I?

Sylvia: That's right, you did. Cause there were Easter eggs there for the babies.

Tom: I think she was surprised to see me the second time. She didn't think I'd go back again. But in the end, she admitted she was missing me as much as I was missin her. Well, *so* she *said!*

Sylvia: But I wouldn't give in for a *week.*

Tom: They're a married couple we were stayin with. Nice people. Haven't been married long.

Sylvia: But it's not the same when you're stayin with someone else, is it? I'm used to runnin a home: cleanin it and things like that but you can't relax in someone else's home no matter how welcome they make you feel. You don't feel comfortable. You feel awkward goin in cupboards, even if it's your own things in them. They'll say to you 'Oh, don't worry, *I'll* do this and *I'll* do that,' but you don't feel the *same.* You don't feel *right.* I didn't anyway.

Tom: It was like a holiday for me, though. I enjoyed it, I did. Everythin was done for us: it was *great!*

Sylvia: But he was really sobbing when he came to the door that first time. I said 'No. *Definitely* not! I am *definitely not* coming back!' 'What am I gonna *do?'* he said, 'What am I gonna *do?'* I said 'Do what you *want* to do! I'm *not* coming back and that's *it!'*

Tom: But she *did* come back and it's goin all right at the moment. My foot's not hurtin so much now. Went to the doctor's three times. He put a surgical bandage on it. Wanted me to go into hospital, but I wouldn't go.

Sylvia: The ambulance came once -

Tom: But I wouldn't go. I had my tablets and I said I'd do it here. He said 'Alright, but if it doesn't work, you'll *have* to go.' As long as the old legs are gettin better, I'll be alright. Cause I likes to walk, me. In the army we was out *all* the time. *She* won't believe it, but in Belgium I was always in a track suit. Trainin in the mornin, trainin in the night. And then we'd play on a Thursday and a Saturday and sometimes even on a Sunday as well. Cricket, football: I'd volunteer for *any* sport, just to get away - out in the open. I *can't* be stuck in. I goes potty - *really* potty. I've been really bad these past six weeks but I think I'm over the worst of it now. Takin off again, diggin in, gettin fit stage by stage. It'll take a bit of time I suppose but we'll get there.

'The Dam Busters...'

Wayne and Lyn (2)

Lyn: I believe in God cause he died for us, didn he? He give up his life. Wayne don't believe but he was a Catholic once, wasn you?

Wayne: I was baptized. The vicar put my head in a bucket of water and said 'D'you believe?' I said 'Yes, I *believe*.' He said '*What* d'you believe?' I said 'I believe you're tryin to fuckin *drown* me!'

The grounds of St Mary's churchyard on a bright sunny day in mid-July. People strewn across the grass, sunbathing and eating sandwiches; Bill preaching through a loud-hailer down the lychgate end; a five-piece brass band - which Wayne was earlier conducting - oompah-ing in Castle Gardens, and a traffic-jam of taxis beeping outside Littlewoods.

Wayne: Christ, those taxi-drivers are horny today!

Lyn: An they're stoppin all the buses this afternoon.

Wayne: Why's that?

Lyn: To let the people off!

Wayne: Ow many people d'you think are buried in here, Lyn?

Lyn: I dunno.

Wayne: Ow many d'you think's buried in here that are dead?

Lyn: All of them.

Wayne: Thas right. It's a dead loss, innit?

Lyn: I got booked yesterday. Here's my charge sheet for you to have a look at. What happened was, I was in Singleton Hospital visiting Terry cause he got beaten up and I'd had a few drinks and I went over the top. Over the *limit*, as they say. I collapsed on the floor and this policeman charged me and now I gotto go to court. No violence caused nor nothing like that. It was just a *petty* thing. Is that the word?

Wayne: He went in at one o' clock in the day and came out at one o' clock at night.

Lyn: And I didn't ave no food or nothin. So I said to the Sergeant 'Ave you got any food?'

289

and he said 'No, but if you find any, let me know.'

Wayne: And when he come out the Sergeant said to him 'Have you got a roof over your head?' and he said 'What d'you think I am - a *car*?

Lyn: I've been to court a couple of times before: mostly for drunk and disorderly. But the last time was for pinching onions from Neath market. The judge said 'Any more of it and that's *shallot!'*

Wayne: And I got done for drinkin battery acid the other day. They put me in a cold cell and charged me in the morning.

Lyn: He ought to drink my favourite drink: vodka and carrot juice. The vodka gets me drunk and the carrot juice sees me home!

Wayne: Well, that's better than my brother Terry. He drank a bottle of varnish last week. Elluva death but he ad a beautiful finish!

Lyn: Anyway: ow do a policewoman part her hair?

Wayne: And where do they live?

Lyn: *Nine nine nine Lesby Avenue!*

Wayne: And why do a prison officer always have a chain?

Lyn: Cause no shit-ouse is complete without one!

Wayne: Bloke come past Swansea prison on a camel and a police car pulled him up. He said 'What you got a camel for? 'Don't know,' he said. 'Where d'you keep it?' 'Search me,' he said. 'What d'you feed it on?' 'Haven't a clue,' he said. 'Is it a girl or a boy?' 'Oh, it's *definitely* a girl,' he said. Sergeant says 'All the questions I've asked, you've said "I don't know." Ow d'you know it's a girl?' 'Cause when I came past the prison, some con shouted "Look at that cunt on the camel!"'

Lyn: D'you reckon it's like the Muppet Show: me and him? Ow about gettin us into the Grand Theatre one night and me and him will give a show. What d'you think of that? Do a pantomime or somethin, cause why should we go round actin the goat like this, when we could be earnin thousands? Have I got a good point or not?

Lyn: You know as you go down by the Cardiff Arms? There's an old warehouse on your left: that's where I am. Behind the green door.

Wayne: *'There's an old piano an they play it hot behind the **green door!**'*

Lyn: Oh God: ark at Shakin Stevens! Behind the *sliding* door. Where the squatters used to be. I wouldn't say it's one of the best places I've had but as I've said before: there's worse people off than ourselves. There's only me there and an old mattress and a couple of pigeons. And an edgeog and an owl.

Wayne: What d'you get when you cross an edgeog and an owl?

Lyn: A prick that stays awake all night! Why can't owls have sex in the rain?

Wayne: Cause it's too wet to woo!

Lyn: It doesn't matter where you sleep as long as your health comes first. I could have gone into Dinas Fechan long ago but with me, see: I'm too dull. I stay there a day and if it's not too good I leave -

Wayne: You're a *wanderer.*

Lyn: I'm a wanderer but if Wayne had *his* way, he'd be in bed all his life, wouldn you?

Wayne: I like it in the Cyrenians. I've got food every day, a bed, TV -

Lyn: And at least you're not *out*, and you can ave a wash whenever you want. You got all the *facilities*. What more can you ask for, innit?

Wayne: They've promised me a flat and if I get one, I'm goin to get Lyn in with me cause he can cook and I can't.

Lyn: My brother Derek said he'd try and get me a flat. He's got his *feelers* out but he's in Spain at the moment.

Wayne: I know where *I'd* go if I had the money?

Lyn: Where?.

Wayne: Rumania.

Lyn: Rumania?

Wayne: No: *remain ere!* I wouldn leave *you.*

Lyn: Have you been abroad?

Wayne: Yes, I've been a *broad bean* - and I been a *runner!*

Lyn: So what are you goin to do now when you get your money on Tuesday?

Wayne: Take you to Port Talbot to ave a bath.

Lyn: No, don't take the piss. *The Bath's* the name of a pub we go to.

Wayne: I thought we could either go there or up The Ring of Feathers.

Lyn: Where's The Ring of Feathers?

Wayne: Round a duck's arse!

Lyn: And don't forget: you owe me a fiver for a bar of soap.

Wayne: That's *life*, boy!

Lyn: Money's like water, though, innit? It's in one hand and out the other. I can't get *nothin* from the Social. It's a waste of bloody time.

Wayne: Go over and ask for a Crisis Loan. I'll come with you and whatever you get I want half. So, say you get twelve pence, I want *six* pence of it.

Lyn: What I find is: the more you do for people, the less you're thought of. Like last night: what did I do?

Wayne: He come over the Hostel and put all the seats back in the Outreach van -

Lyn: And cleaned it -

Wayne: Took him an hour. And then when we went some bugger took them back out again!

Lyn: Ow're we doin so far? Any particular *topics* you want us to cover?

Wayne: Or Mars Bars?

Lyn: When you first saw us, back in January, you must ave thought 'Oh fuck! Here come The Two Ronnies!'

Wayne: My favourite comedian's Max Boyce.

Lyn: And mine's Les Dawson - and Jimmy Cricket.

Wayne: I met Max Boyce in real life, once, in Neath.

Lyn: What's e like?

Wayne: Well, he's got curly hair, two eyes and a nose and a mouth - and he's a bit of a card.

Lyn: I was in Neath last Friday. A tramp came up to me and said 'I haven't had a bite for days,' so I bit him!'

Wayne: I went with him. I said to this old woman 'Your stockings are wrinkled.' and she smacked me in the mouth. I said 'What did you do that for?' She said 'I'm not wearin any!'

Lyn: What's got ninety balls and makes old women sweat? *A game of Bingo!*

Wayne: Where would you keep a rubber trumpet? *In a rubber band!*

Lyn: What d'you call an Irishman hanging from the ceiling? *'Sean-delier!'*

Wayne: What did the policeman say to the stomach? *'You're under a vest!'*

Lyn: What do donkeys have for dinner in Brighton? Half an hour, same as the rest of us.

Wayne: I can make you swear. Spell 'bone'.

Lyn: B - o - e - n.

Wayne: Take the 'f' out of it.

Lyn: There's no 'f' in 'bone'.

Wayne: Little boy in School. Teacher said 'Give me a word beginning with 'b'. *'Bastard.'* 'Get in the corner!' she said. Ten minutes later she comes back: 'Give me a word beginning with 'd'. *'Dwarf.'* 'That's better,' she said. 'Excellent! Ten out of ten - you said that without swearing. By the way: what *is* a dwarf?' 'A short little cunt *that* big!' he said.

Lyn: So, d'you think we done alright, like? Good session there? Good *atmosphere*? Is that the right word? So what's the position now, then? We give up our time to do this and I reckon I've done more than Wayne, haven't I?

Wayne: And it's like I said, Al: it's a good thing you're doin this book, cause no other fucker'd do it!

Lyn: You was a teacher before, wasn you?

Wayne: And before that, he was a bouncer for Mothercare!

Lyn: What you goin to call it?

Wayne: How about *'The Life and Times of the Down and Outs'*? or *'On These Streets'*?

Lyn: *'**Within** these Streets'*? or *'People...**Unfortunately**'*!

Wayne: *'Unfortunate People **Within** these Streets'*?

Lyn: *'People in Need'*?... *'Survival'*?... *'Persevering'*?... Somethin shorter?

Wayne: *'Boxer Shorts'*?

Lyn: *'Public Problem'*?

Wayne: *'Public Enemy Number One'*?

Lyn: *'The Dam Busters'*?

Wayne: Or you could change it into a joke book.

Lyn: The Terrible Twins!

Wayne: The Community Service is going alright. I missed a few weeks for medical reasons but I'm goin again now. It's landscape work mostly: doin gardens and everythin. From half past nine till half past four every Wednesday but, If I had to have a proper job, I'd like to do glazin again. *Smashin* job, that was.

Lyn: And I wouldn't mind doin farmin. Anythin to occupy my mind.

Wayne: But nobody knows the future.

Lyn: You could be here today and gone tomorrow. Gotto live day by day, innit?

Wayne: One day at a time.

Lyn: Sweet Jesus.

'A good night were ad by all...'

Sid

I've ended up the way I am through things that have gone off over the past four or five years. I can't blame anybody else: it's just summat that's happened - through *circumstances*, if you understand me meaning. I mean, I can go through my whole history but it depends on what you want to know and how much is goin to be put in book. Perhaps the best way is for *you* to ask *me* questions, cause I don't want you to go one way and me go another, type of thing. As long as you're aware that some things might be quite *upsettin* for me, to a point...

The photo on the office desk showed a middle-aged, bald-headed little man with spotty skin and a disproportionately large waistline. He was sitting down on a chair in the middle of what looked like a pub or a club. All around the room were laughing and giggling groups of drinkers with 'red-eye', mostly young and middle-aged women dressed for a night out. Various items of clothing were strewn on the floor. The man was down to his string-vest and underpants and the beautiful and practically naked young girl straddling his legs was smearing cream on his face, while he fumbled with the catch on her bra. He didn't seem to be embarrassed or aroused. Behind the thick-lensed glasses, his sad watery-blue eyes stared up into hers, expressionless...

There's something anachronistic about his appearance - as though he's just stepped out of a Heath Robinson cartoon. We sit in the corner of the empty Lounge a couple of minutes after opening time. This is the venue of his choice, as he doesn't want our conversation overheard in the Hostel. Only with great reluctance has he let me buy him a drink. There's No Smoking in this part of the Lounge, so his pipe and matches and tobacco-pouch lie impotent before him as he speaks: loudly, haltingly and with a thick Yorkshire accent.

I *was* on Disability but when I went to Park Ouse, they knocked me off it. 'Fair enough,' they says, 'you've got arthritis - we're not questionin that - but it's not as bad as all that.' Apparently, you've gotto ave fifteen points and over to qualify and I only ad six - summat lak that. And yet, when me doctor saw me, he says 'You *can't* work. You've got *osteoarthritis.*' I says 'Is *that* what you call it? I thought I just had *arthritis.*' I've already *been* X-rayed for me chest but now I want him to get the rest of me X-rayed to *prove* that I actually *have* got what he says I've got. I mean, they're only two big Quacks down at Park Ouse anyway. I didn't know they *could* knock you off just like that but what can you *do*? I'm not a *fighter*, so I'm probably just goin to ave to live on forty-odd quid a fortnight instead of an undred-and-odd.

I can't complain about me upbringin. I always got on wi me mother and father but for the first five or six years of my life, I were never out of hospital. Your childhood is the most important part of your life but I lost most of mine and I've never actually caught up. It's all in me medical records - the lot. They couldn't suss out what were wrong wi me: 'We just don't know,' they said. But it must have been *somethin* cause I were in and out wi me lungs for a long time and, I mean, I *still* suffer from bronchial trouble to this day.

I've got a sister but she's passed on and I've got a brother up in Alltwen but he don't want much to do wi me. Me mother worked part-time in a bettin shop and me father was a manager for Cemtex, until he got made redundant. Him and me were more like good friends than father and son. He used to say 'Fancy goin for a walk?' and we'd go straight to Club and have a couple of pints. If ever I needed advice, he'd gie it to me. If ever I needed the proverbial 'ticking-off', he'd gie it to me. And that was *that*: 'Is it *my* round next?' he'd say and that's the sort of relationship you *need* with your father.

I had a stack of jobs when I left school: steelworks, forging - even worked for a couple of bakers - then I ended up on Railway. When I first started I did checking - you know: checking things on and off wagons - then I went on to shuntin and then I went as a Guard in Scunthorpe. Then my father died and, cause my mother was left on her own, I got a compassionate side-step back to Sheffield. I filled in some forms and they pushed it through for me. Within a month I were back in Sheffield and me mother said 'I'm glad you've come back because I'd ave probably ended up goin round bend.' Losing me father was the first bereavement I ad and that *definitely* upset me. And then I had to go through losin me sister and then through watching me mother die - and *knowing* she was goin to die - and not being able to tell er what was appening. And, of course, avin to hold a job down at the same time. The time before last that I visited, she said 'I've got somethin to tell you.' I said 'I already know. I've known for six months.' And she didn't like it that I'd known. That were about five year ago. It were somethin to do wi lung. And, of course, afterwards I just went to pieces and that's what's caused the problem wi me now - that and drinking. I were goin through a real bad patch, up *ere* in me ead. Me boss says 'We know you've got problems and we'll try to accommodate you but you must try and get your act together.' But I couldn't and in the end he says 'I'm afraid we'll ave to let you go.' I just couldn't get me act together and even now, after all this time, I *still* can't. How can I put it? I'm all right *normally.* I'm like everybody else: I'm out for company more than owt else. A couple of beers and that's *it.* But I'm now, in a sense, *lonely.* I've nobody to turn to. Me brother's not all that interested and things mount up and, you know what happens then: you just ave *one* too many.

I've never been married and I've got no kids that I'm goin to admit to, if you understand me meaning. Mind you, I've had to leave *that many* towns in my time! I'm fairly experienced I suppose and I'm gullible for a laugh as long as it's in fun - as you'll ave seen from that photo in the office! I mean, that night it *were* good fun. It were comin up to me forty-sixth birthday and I suddenly thought 'It's me birthday soon, and I'm a bit pissed-off' like, so I had a word wi me old Landlady in the Red Chrysanthemum in Pontardawe and I gave her some money and told er to arrange a birthday party. She says 'Oh, *no* problems!' And then, about a fortnight before, somebody says 'We've got a little surprise for you afterwards, so keep yourself sober' and then her daughter spills the beans and says they've got this female stripper lined up for me. I'm not goin to go into the full story of what was supposed to ave appened afterwards - but it *never* appened. It never *materialized.* And I think you know what I mean by 'afterwards'. Let's put it this way: if she'd ave done exactly what she were supposed to ave done, it would ave been rather *naughty.* I'll go so far, but in private's *one* thing and in public's *another,* cause this stripper were one of these who'd have done a - how can I put it? - a *blow-job* type of thing on me, if you get me meaning. When she turned up, there must ave been 280 to 290 people there, summat like that, and there were still a lot that didn't come cause of prior commitments. They couldn't get them all in the same room. I says to the Landlady 'I wouldn't advise her to take me trousers down cause I've *no* pants on!' She says 'We were goin to ave your pants off, in any case! 'I said '*Forget* it. I'm *off!*' But I didn't get very far: 'C'mon and take your punishment!' they said - and that photo was the result. Everyone else was up to ere and I ad to stay sober as a judge, more's the pity! Afterwards, I were walkin round sayin 'Alright, oo's nicked me shoe? Oo's nicked me sock? Must ave taken me all night to find me shirt! A bloke comes up to me and says 'Eh! You ad some *gumption* with that stripper, didn't yer? Cause *I* wouldn't ave done it!' Oh, it were in good fun and a *good night* were ad by all! I mean, I left at half past twelve and they were still suppin at three o' clock in't mornin. And that were from *eight o' clock* at night. Landlady ad to give me fifty quid back cause they took *that* much over the bar. I ended up payin for the stripper but I didn't bother askin how much it cost to get her. Actually, I ought to ave charged at the door: it would ave cut me bill down a bit. I says to the Landlady a few days later 'Any complaints about party?' 'No,' she says, 'we all enjoyed it. We all had a good laugh at your expense!' I says '*Good!* That suits me down to the ground!' I might do it all again on my fiftieth birthday - as long as they don't get me another strip-o-gram. That's 2001, so I better start saving *now*.

I had to sell me ouse back in Sheffield when I left Railway. I didn't even get my holiday money. I got nowt. The only thing I walked away with were a week's wages. And that were *it*. GTFN. On yer bike! Then I moved down ere cause my legs started to play up and I thought, well Ponty were *just* the right place cause everythin's flat and I don't ave to go walkin up and down hills all the time. My brother'd been down here fifteen years through his job but, of course, when I come down he weren't bothered about me. I get on with me sister-in-law okay but me brother's a bit of a - I don't quite know ow to put this - a bit of an **asshole.** And that's puttin it politely! I can't even *talk* to im. He's only one I've got left and whenever I go to him he just turns around and walks away: 'I'm not interested: I've got me *own* problems.' He wants owt to do wi me and, I mean, who else could he turn to bar me? I'm *family*.

I lived in a bedsit for a bit but one of the blokes there were a right mischief-maker. They all knew e were a bit of a nutcase but he done nowt but cause trouble. *I* was supposed to have done *this* and *I* was supposed to have done *that*: and I weren't even anywhere *near* the place! But *I* ended up gettin kicked out. The little bit of money I ad for the house were almost all gone by now so I slept rough for nearly two weeks: on a park bench by the Leisure Centre. I used to put newspaper down and an overcoat over me and that were *it*. I let things get on top of me. Then I saw the Homeless Officer in Neath and they rang up the Hostel for me.

I'm not prepared to say anythin about the Hostel. I have ad words with somebody in there about certain things but I'm glad to say he's *off* it now, if you understand me meanin. But there's two others who are still on it. I said 'Avin a drink's *one* thing, avin a smoke's *another* but I definitely don't hold with *that!* You know? I told them to wait till I get out and then they can do what they like. And I'm not goin to say any more than that.

This is first time I've ever been in hostel and I'll be glad to get out actually and into me own place. All bein well, by next week I'm hopin to be in Neath in a bedsit. I had a telephone call the other day and I've just had another one this mornin: to confirm it. They're goin to pick me up and take me over there next Tuesday I think, just to have a look. It's a place just outside Neath: *British Ferry* or summat. I've heard of it before but I can't quite pinpoint it. But I *do* know the name and, fortunately, I *do* know one or two people livin nearby.

If there were some sort of job I could do, I'd do it - just to keep me out of mischief, cause I feel *useless* at present. Before I came down here, I went for a washin up job in Clydach - just washin pots. I told them I were forty-odd and he says 'Any illnesses?' I says 'I've got a bit of *osteo*.' He says 'No chance. You'll not work here. We don't want anybody who's goin to be off for two or three weeks at a go or makin excuses for bein sick and if you'll take my advice: don't even *consider* workin. You'll find you're virtually *unemployable*.' I mean, that were only *his* advice. In fact, him and somebody else who said exactly the same: 'You're unemployable because of arthritis.' I can only go on what people tell me. Whether they're right or whether they're wrong, I don't know. I might be able to get a little part-time job in Neath. I'd be all right then. But I won't be keepin in touch with my brother in Ponty any more. As far as I'm concerned, he can go and take a long walk off a short pier. And his wife can go wi him!

I keep avin a recurrin complaint with me breathin, you know, cause I suffer from bronchitis and it keeps goin into me left lung. Doctor just keeps tellin me 'Stop smokin! Stop smokin!' I said 'I've ad it for years, so *smoke* is not goin to make any difference. Last Friday, I had a bit of a turn in Hostel. I were avin pains in me chest and I thought 'Oh, it's blinkin wind or summat,' so I ad a couple of rums to try and get rid of it but it didn't work. Then I must have just passed out. Hit me head on the dining room door and woke up in the ambulance. Me ead still urts a bit but I'm as right as rain now. I says to them in hospital 'Look: I've got pains in me chest - just ere,' and then they asked if I'd taken anythin and I had to admit to it: 'Yes,' I says, 'I had a couple of rums to try and get rid of it but - *'Oh!'* they says 'You've been *drinkin!'* I says 'Look, I've *admitted* I've ad a couple of rums - I can't *dispute* the fact - ' Then they just fobbed me off. They *said* they wanted me to stay overnight but the way the doctor were performin, I said 'You might as well discharge me,' so they gave me a form to sign and I left. I thought 'I'm not goin to get any satisfaction ere,' and, I mean, all they ad to do were give me an X-ray and they'd ave seen it all.

Twenty-one years I were on railway. If I could get me brain box workin, I could sit down one day and start reminiscing and you could write a book about it, depending on what type of stories you want to know. I'm not sayin a *thick* book but a *small* book and you could make a *fortune* out of it. All funny stories - what d'you call them - *antidotes!* You'd be surprised. You'd enjoy it. You see, I'm no good at puttin things down in writin. I can sit here and talk to *you* about it and then you can probably put it down cause I'm no good at owt like that meself. I mean, why should I put in *five* pages, what I could say in *two* words. When I were on Railway they were always askin you to put in reports: can we have your report about *this* incident or *that* incident? And they always used to get just three words off of me: **'Eff off!'** or **'Balls!'** That's what I always put down. And they used to play *bloody* ell wi me! I says 'You ought to know me by now. I'm **no good** at writin, so them's the only three words you're ever goin to get out of me. They says 'Fair enough,' and then I used to tell them what they wanted to know and they used to write it down for me but if ever they sent me a letter, they knew there were only three words they were ever goin to get and you've got all three on tape: **'Eff off!'** and **'Balls!'**

I'm just goin to have a pound on bandit now and then I'm goin. I don't know whether you can use any of that stuff cause most of it's probably a load of *crap!* No, I don't want payin. It'd upset me. You bought me a drink and that's good enough. Just put me name in book somewhere.

'Don't look back in anger...'

Paul (2)

Paul: I met her over in Balaclava Street and she seen my eyes and I seen hers and that was *it*. Love at first sight! She was on this Family Housin Support Scheme. I'd gone over there to see someone else and when I walked in she was on her way to bed but I said 'Go and have a bath and come down and watch TV.' I could ave fucked er that night, like, but I'm a fuckin *gentleman* I am. I said 'No. If you want full-blown sex, you'll ave to wait till the time is right and then we'll go the full fuckin og.'

I've had my *time* and I've had my *women* but now it's time to pack it in, cause I've found the *right one* at last. I wanted to marry her after three weeks but she said no, it wasn't long enough. We've had our ups and downs but we've sorted out our differences now. She's very easy-goin and considerate, on times. I didn't want someone who was all airs and graces and always on about her family background. I couldn andle that. She's from Treherbert. You know, up in the Rhondda Valley, where they made Jurassic Park. Fuckin dead up there, it is. The best thing about it is the fuckin beer is cheap. All the rest is *shite.* They gotto find out what their fuckin shoe sizes are, for their wellies - and they all wear fuckin *wool* on their backs!

The Rat and Carrot, Oystermouth Road, early afternoon, August 1st. A grey, overcast day. The Bar is already quite busy but there are still a lot more people to come. It doesn't take me long to spot Paul. He's standing in a corner at the end of the Bar, nervously sipping at a half and trying to look inconspicuous. With his tall good looks, flowery waistcoat, white shirt and tie and pink carnation, he looks like a Mississippi Steam Boat card-sharp.

Paul: It's goin well so far but I feel a right *cunt* in what I'm wearin. Not used to it, see. I'm *cool* and I'm a real tough cookie, like, but once I see the limousine, the old false teeth are gonna start rattlin. It's *my* day and it's *Gabrielle's* day and it's *really* exciting but at the same time, I'm not goin to go through this *ever* again. It's a big ordeal and it's not just *three weeks* away or *a day* away it's only - what? - *fifty* minutes away now. I never thought I'd ever get married. I know Gabrielle's not Patsie Kensitt but I seen Patsie's and Liam's fuckin weddin and it was fuckin *shite!*

Yeah, John Patterson in the Hostel payed for everythin and, if it wasn't for him, this wouldn't have been possible. We paid for the rings and what she's wearin and what I'm wearin but he's done a lot and he's kept my head together at times and stopped me goin off the rails.

I had a sort of a Stag Night. But at the end of the day, you know, it's just me and er. It's like Batman and Robin, innit? And *I'm* fuckin Batman, aren't I? I'm the guy *from dusk till dawn!*

I spoke to her earlier on. She'll be there and she'll be all dolled-up, like. I haven't seen the dress, so I'm lookin forward to that. She's had her make-up done in David Evans. Wish *I* had some fuckin eye-liner on. I'd be like fuckin Roger Daltrey then, wouldn I? Like Quadrophenia.

Her family are alright but it's not as though I'd carry a picture of the mother-in-law in my wallet, like. I was up Gabrielle's house yesterday but it was fuckin ectic, you know. Her father and me had words about this and that and in the end I said *'D'you want to eat fuckin pavement?'* In other words: 'D'you want to get beaten up?' So, you know, I'm just a wild, tough cookie, like. I told him 'Whatever we do in the future is up to *us.* I'm *myself.* I'm my *own* person. No one can change me. I've done my bit for Society and no-one else can fuckin say to me 'Nah, nah, nah!' and all that.

The Twins from 'Twin Town' will be coming - Rhys whats-is-name and his brother and Kevin Allen and Paul Durden and Raymond Fuseli. He's related to the Fuselis: they're like the Krays up in Birmingham. They own all the Night Clubs and that. You know: *Big Time,* like!

'Swansea's a pretty, shitty city,' as you once said, Al, but we're goin to live over in Mount Pleasant. We're over there now: The Promenade.

Gabrielle isn't working at the moment and neither am I but we're both goin to get work. I'm stable now. I done my time with 'Twin Town' and that and I want to follow that up. Start off small and build myself up. A lot of people wouldn't have taken the chance but I *did* and I'm grateful. There's a lot of pressure when you're doin it but the way I look at it is, that either you've got it or you haven't.

I met a lot of famous people and I reckon I can do even better than I did. I'm just waitin for the next film now. Some parts of 'Twin Town' they took off me and I know that cause I seen it on the editin before anybody else seen it and I did a better fuckin job than what the Sex Pistols did with fuckin E.M.I. When they released it, they'd cut a lot of things out and I was a bit disappointed by that. There should have been more of me in it. I've still got the T shirt that I wore, though. But next time around, I'll have a really good part, I hope.

I've got to go over to the Registrar's now to meet the Evenin fuckin Post photographer. Comin...?

...This is the part I hate: goin over to this fuckin joint... Feel a right fuckin twat, *I* do!... Last time I was over the County Hall was seein the fuckin Social Worker and all that... There's Gabrielle's father over there with the fuckin walkin sticks. If he starts shoutin and all this now, I'll say 'Fuck off!' Like fuckin Oasis, isn't it?... You gotto be cool if you want to be a pop-star like me and always remember 'Don't look back in anger!'... I'm one good, tough cookie... I got loads of friends. I don't know why. I should start my own fan club... There's Kevin Harwood and Conrad and Julie and John... and there's Paul Durden! Over there in the big red Pontiac, talkin to the photographer...Eh, **Paul!**

Photographer: This looks like the bridegroom now - !

Paul Durden: Ow about takin one of me in the motor, then? Biggest fuckin engine in Wales!

Paul: Hey, **man!** Glad you could make it -

Paul Durden: So, what's goin on then, Paul? What time's kick-off?

Paul: Five minutes.

Paul Durden: Nervous?

Paul: Naw! But I feel a right fuckin pratt in this outfit!

Paul Durden: Marriage is a wonderful institution, Paul. D'you know what the best thing about a blow-job is?

Paul: What?

Paul Durden: Three minutes of fuckin *peace and quiet!*

'Take it as it comes...'

Baglan Benny

Late Autumn. He rests his crutches at his side and makes himself comfortable in the office armchair. A sturdily-built young man, dressed all in black, he has recently started coming to the midday soup kitchens in the Hostel. Before the accident, just over a year ago, he was surly and resentful. Now he is over-grateful and all smiles...

Benny Lewis is my name and I'm thirty now. I was born in Sandfields estate, just across the water. I went to Sandfields Comp but I didn't stay on to do exams. I emigrated with my parents to Western Australia when I was fifteen and got a job as a kitchen hand on a holiday island out there: washing pots and pans. And through that and working well, I got an apprenticeship. I did four years - three at college and one on the job - and got a Trade Certificate from South Fremantle Technical College. I was out there for fifteen years, working around in hotels, restaurants, holiday camps, sporting venues and a few other places. The standard of living wasn't much better than it is here but it was quite good. It was hard work but I enjoyed it.

I was twenty-nine when I got back here. There was no decision to come back. I follow my feelings a lot. If I *feel* I need to move somewhere, I do, you know? I've ridden motorbikes a lot and lived a rugged sort of life which isn't suitable for everyone. I got a short-term job cooking, up London way. Came back this way, got a flat in Taibach. The last job I had was in catering, but I had my car and all my money stolen and everything started goin downhill for me. I ended up in Swansea jail: *three months* for stealing a bottle of Lucozade. Three months was a long time for just a bottle of Lucozade. I couldn't believe it *then* and I *still* can't. And I had to do the *full* three. It's chronic in there with all them criminals! This was about eighteen months ago and after coming out, I've been on the streets ever since. I just didn't bother going back Sandfields way. I found it much easier to live outside. I drifted into homelessness but I'm happy living out there at the moment. I'm content with it.

I go round scrounging. There's nothing else to do. Over there - around Aberavon, Taibach and the actual beach area - people just keep *passin* the homeless but it's a lot easier over here. I wouldn't work again. I hate work. Me and work don't get on any more...

This happened less than a year ago. It was in the paper. I was mindless on the day. I'd taken a bit of powder - amphetamine - but it wasn't the drugs that were the problem. It was walking day and night on the streets. I was on the railway track - just crossing over - and I didn't realize the train was coming and *BANG* it just caught me on the right hand side and flung my leg underneath. Tore my right leg off and sent me flying down the bank. The paramedics found me. I don't know if the train stopped or if the driver even knew he'd hit me. I know nothing about what happened although I was conscious the whole time. I knew I'd lost it as soon as it had hit me. It was the Swansea-Paddington train - the Llansamlet track, the long one. I was in hospital three months. In Morriston. It was torture in there, too. It was touch and go for a long time.

This one's artificial but I'm walking now, no problem. I don't want to bother with relatives. It's not that I'm a loner. They've got a hard enough life on their own and they haven't got much but I do like to go and see them when I can. As I say, I always follow my feelings. I'm not bothered about life. There's no plan. Take it as it comes. I just want to ride bikes. You know: *freedom*, like..!

Epilogue

'Waiting for Eric...'

Sylvia (3)

I've heard from her Key Worker that she's been drinking a lot and that if I want to speak to her again, I'd better do it quickly, as she's going away. When I call at the flat, she's locked herself out and has to wait for her Key Worker to come with the key. It's nearly nine months since I last visited and six weeks since Tom's funeral...

Sylvia: ...Come on in, babes. I'm right in the middle of packin, so we can talk in the bedroom. It's alright - I'm not goin to *eat* you! I'm goin away for a few days. The old gent - Eric - is takin me to his home. Well, what've I gotto do here on my own, isn't it? So I may as well. He lives down Worcester way somewhere and he's comin for me at three o' clock, so I haven't got much time. He's got somebody that'll drive us. But just look at the state on this room! It's a mess. Total and utter chaos and mess. I haven't even made the bed. What day is it today - Wednesday? Thursday? I'll be back by Saturday. I told my Key Worker that Eric wanted to move in here and he said, 'Well, I don't think the Housing Society will be too happy about *that*.' I said 'Oh, don't be so stupid! There's nothing wrong in an old gentleman stayin with me. He's not goin to *sleep* with me or anything. He's upstairs with Denzil at the moment but it's cold and dark and gloomy up there and he needs a little flat. 'Don't worry about *me*,' I told my Key Worker. 'I'm quite stable and I'm a grown woman. *Trust* me!

There you are, look, I've even rolled the carpet up cause I thought I'd be movin. But I've seen this room in a worse state than this. I'll tidy when I come back. I've only been away once since Tom died, so I've *gotto* have a break, aven't I? Did you come to the funeral? I didn't notice to be honest. That day I was in a daze. I was terrible. I'd blanked out. But, that's right: you *were* there, sweetheart. I'm sorry - I forgot. I was absolutely blanko at the time. Cause I found him, didn't I? I was the only one with him. I don't know to this day how he died cause he was sittin right next to me, right? And I'm a chatterbox I am, aren't I? Never shut my mouth. And he was talking to me one minute and I was still talking and I must have been talking to myself for ages until, in the end, I poked him and said 'Wake up, Dozy, will you! Wake *up*!' And there was no response. And his head was back and his eyes were closed. And that's all. And I felt his hands and they were icy cold. And they were like *that* - you know - *stiff*? And I couldn't even move. I've never seen a dead body before. I slept then and then I called the police. Well, they got to do whatever they got to do cause, for all they knew, I could have *done* something to him. I could have poisoned him or harmed him or *anything*. I had to notify the police, doctor, and ambulance. And they all had to come. And then they took him away then, in a black bag. The policeman took me in the kitchen. He said 'Come with me, my love and ave a cuppa tea,' I didn know what was appenin. I was walkin around like this, goin round and round in circles. Didn't know what the friggin hell I was doin. He said 'Now calm down and have a cup of tea with me.' I had hysterics then, didn I? 'What am I gonna *do*! What am I gonna *do*!' But I've calmed down a lot now. The doctor gave me anti-depressants. It was a helluva feeling, mind. I'd never seen a dead body before. That was the first one. And he was sittin right next to me, like we normally did. And to turn to talk to somebody and find that that person's dead - . He hadn't been feeling ill that day. He never said a word. He never said 'I've got an aching leg' or anything. Now normally he'd say 'Oh, my leg or my foot is playin up,' but he didn't. He never said a word. He just *went* like that.

We were gettin on so well, too. *He* didn't do this. I gave *myself* this black eye. I walked into the friggin door, didn I! Cause I'm still in shock. I'm still walkin round in a daze. Some days I go up the shop and if you ask me where I am, I go 'Er...er...er - oh! *Manselton!* But I've got to *think* about it. It's goin to take me a while. The doctor's put me on valium *and* sleeping tablets cause I'm awake all night and all day. This woman came up to me in Quicksave and said 'My husband has been dead thirty years and I *still* aven't got over it.' I thought 'God, you're a *great* help, like!' But what I'm tryin to do now is busy myself. I'm helping with Eric - my gentleman friend - just like I did with my mum and dad - and that's all I can do, isn't it? Tidy up the house as best I can, make sure that's clean. My Key Worker said something about me taking over the tenancy. I hope so, cause all my property's here, right? Tom and me moved everythin up from the Marina and I couldn't move everythin out again. Not on my own, I couldn't. We've got everythin settled now. I know where everythin is, all my nooks and crannies. The same as in your home, isn't it, babes? I know which drawer is which: one for tea-towels, one for linen, you know? Everybody knows where their own property is. And I'd have to do it all again and I don't fancy that. Plus I know the area - I know all the neighbours. They all say hello to me or talk to me. I mean if I went anywhere else I'd be a total stranger, wouldn I? I'd be worse off than I was now. Cause without Tom, I'm lonely. At least somebody says hello to me. And that's a great help, isn't it?

Eric's upstairs at the moment. I don't think you've been up there, ave you? Denzil lives up there - and he *smells*. He's *onkin*. He doesn't even open the windows - but Eric's *lovely*. He's gettin on a bit but I told him 'Don't worry, I can *see* to you, cause I nursed my mother *and* my father, so I know all about that. And there's no problem gettin nurses. E can afford it can't e? E's loaded. At least, I *think* he's loaded. He proposed to me the other day and I accepted. So, anyway, I went to this bloody wedding last week and they were all there, in this huge mansion of a place - all his family and friends - and the gardens were - oh - *miles* long: flowers and everything, lawns and, you know: these snooty, fat bastards - scuse my French - everywhere. And I walked out, cause they were *sayin* things to me: you know, nit-pickin all day about *'Where d'you live?'* and *'How d'you manage?'* and this and that and *'Oh, you live in a **flat**?'* And I couldn't take it any more. It was as if they were puttin me down all the time. So I said 'Thank you very much for the meal, thank you very much for the reception.' I said 'I'll see you, my darlin,' and I walked out. And about two days later he moved in upstairs. No, not Denzil - *Eric!* Eric's the one who proposed to me. And, apparently, he's loaded? Did you know that? Where did I *meet* him? God knows! I can't remember. Don't ask me cause I don't know. But I take pity on everybody, don't I, babes? I'm always runnin round here, there and everywhere, helpin others. The only one that's gettin on my nerves at the moment is whatsisname upstairs: *Denzil!* He's filthy. And I didn't know, right, until a couple of weeks ago that he'd been in prison twice. I was on the phone to somebody and it came out that he'd been in prison twice. For killing. Well, assault, actually. And that's why they put him here. And whenever I go up there he's always feeling me, touching me. *'Can I see your thingumabobs?'* You know: *crude* remarks, if you understand me. Which other men wouldn't make. I mean, you wouldn't stand there and say to me 'Oh, can I feel your *privates*?' would you? But *he* does. And he's got it *out*, in full view, as we're talkin. He just drops his trousers and leaves them at half-mast. 'What d'you think of *this*? Ooh, look at *this* - a German helmet! Isn't it a *big* one?' Well, you don't *do* that, do you? You **don't!** And I go up there and I take a cup of tea up, have a chat, cause

I'm lonely, aren't I, without Tom? And I sit there and he's always like that. But you don't do it, you know, you *don't.* I said 'Don't do *that*! Have a *conversation.* Have a cup of *tea.* Do *anything.* But don't do *that*!' I said 'We're not married and we're not related' - you know - 'we're not *anything*!' We're just neighbours and that's *it*! That's where it stops. I'm not - how can I put it? - I would, never *ever* go with him. He's dirty, he's stinkin, he doesn't shave, he doesn't change his socks! How can he *think* I'd ever entertain gettin into bed with him? Be realistic! It's a dream that he wants to fulfill but, not with *me* he won't. I say to him, 'Right: go out and find a girl if you want it that bad,' and he says 'Oh, I've gotto ave it. I've *gotto* ave it.' 'Well, I don't want it!' I said. 'I don't *want* it!' And you know *me,* I'm a little madame, aren't I? I'm only small but I've got a big mouth. 'I don't flippin **want** it!' I said. I used to joke with Tom when he used to say 'Oh, I've got the horn. I've got the *horn*!' I used to say 'Well, don't look at *me*! **Do** somethin with it!' Other men will take that with a pinch of salt, won't they? But Denzil always takes it the wrong way. He thinks I'm serious and, after all, I'm only a neighbour, aren't I? And even if I *was* going with him - or married to him - you don't do that, do you? You know, it's annoying. I mean - come *off* it - I've been married twice - leave alone Tom - so what does he think I am: a naive person? It's obvious I know about - you know what. I'm a woman of the world, aren't I?. But he won't take no. I lost my key again this mornin. Couldn't get in my flat and I was stuck, wasn I? And whenever I'm stuck he seems to *know.* So then I have to go up there and wait till somebody comes with a key. And he can be quite aggressive. It's like as if he thinks 'Well, you can't get *in,* so you'll have to stay *here.*' He came up to me with his fist clenched this mornin and you could see the anger and he said 'Don't talk to me like that or I'll smack you on the other side of your face!' I was frightened to be honest. I was terrified. Oh, but upstairs in his place is terrible. He doesn't open the curtains, so it's pitch-black up there and you walk in and you don't know where you're treading - especially me, cause I've got bad eyes. And you're stumblin around and you can't *see* and you're thinking: 'Oh God, let there be **light**!'

But we've got a tidy little home here, haven't we? I know: I still keep sayin 'we' even though Tom's gone. We kept it tidy and we'd do it half shares, even though he couldn't get around much towards the end. You've gotto do that in a partnership, aven't you? You've gotto... You haven't got a light ave you, Doll?... thanks... And now, I suppose you want to know what's happened since the funeral? Not a lot: I met Eric, I nearly got married and I'm goin away. To Eric's mansion in Worcester. Is that somethin worth knowing? No, I told you before: I don't know *how* I met him. It just happened to be, didn't it? My Key Worker asked me that and I said 'Mind your business!' It wasn't through *Denzil* though! Can you imagine me marrying a *tramp*! Be *real,* will you! I had a good upbringing, I did. I went to Private School. I wouldn't marry a *tramp*! No way. Eric's a good age. D'you want to meet him? You can. He's up there now, in Denzil's place. He can't talk very much though. He's *trying* to talk but it's difficult for him. *I* can understand him, though. You get used to it. With some people you *do* - you get used to it, don't you? I go up every day to see to him. But those bloody nurses! They left him, right, in that cold bathroom - in a ***light bulb*** of all places! I was furious. It's terrible to see the circumstances he's livin in. Oh, it's terrible. I was disgusted. I'm trying to talk to him and help him and all Denzil does is sit in the living room on his fat arse watching telly. Come up and see and tell me if I'm wrong. In a *light bulb*! I said 'What're they *doin* to you, babes? Why don't they get the light bulb out or buy a *new* light bulb, get you a lamp and sit you in a comfortable chair - a wheelchair?' It's very hard, if you can imagine, talkin to somebody like that. In the end, your neck starts to go. So sometimes I just give up. I go 'Alright, alright, sweetheart, I'll get you anything, anything at all but what d'you *want*?' And then Denzil starts shouting 'What are you *doin!* Get out of my bathroom, get *out*!' I said 'I'm talkin!' 'Talkin to *who*, you stupid cow! You're a *loony*!' But Eric's a genuine person and he *is* alive. They wouldn't put him in the bath if he was dead, for goodness sake, now *would* they? I mean it's common sense, like... I think his name is Eric. Eric *something.* His family are snobs but he's lovely, he is. He calls himself God. And he's takin me to Worcester at three o' clock. You'll find it very very difficult to get through to him but if you're slow and take your time, it's alright. Denzil hasn't got the patience. He just shouts and screams. Well, you can't do that with a sick person, can you? You've gotto have time and patience. You've got to *listen* to him. I'll take you up and you can talk to him. But *I* can't talk to him for too long cause, like I say, I'm so short and I'm like this and my neck starts to go, so I've gotto go and sit down, to get my breath... Let me just find my bleedin shoes and we'll go up and see him... Oh, don't tell me I've lost them again... I can never find them when I need them. What's that my Key Worker says: 'Put your head on! You're goin bloody *daft*, you are!' Oh God, am I goin mental or what! I'll find them now... let's ave a look...sorry to keep you waitin... I don't want to empty all these bags again. I'm goin senile I am. Literally *senile*: where's this and where's that and half an hour after, I'll *find* it. I think all women are like that sometimes, though, aren't they? I'm not the *only* one... Ah, *here* they are...!

...*Denzil! Is it alright if I bring someone up?... the gentleman who's writing the book... **The gentleman who's writing the** -* Oh, God, he's so *stupid! - Is it alright if he comes up? He's writing a book - you know: about people who've been homeless!...We're not goin to* **do** *anything. He's not here to* **steal***. He just wants to talk to Eric, that's all...*

...Yes, he says it's alright. Come on up, Babes. Up here...in the bathroom... Come in and close the door... that's it, sweetheart, close the door so *he* can't hear. What could you *steal* anyway - the bath? The toilet basin?...There... There's Eric. D'you see him? In the light bulb? And they thought we were a couple of flippin lunatics... *...What're you doin, Eric? Did you have a nice bath? ...What?...who?...mmm? I don't know what you're sayin, darlin...take your time...this gentleman is writing a book and he wants to know about us. Alright? Help him now, then, there's a good boy. Go on - for me. Alright... I know... I know...What are you trying to say? What? What's that?... Puff some steam out for me! Show a bit of red. Go on: red and blue, please. Go on, for* me*! Oh go on, darlin!...Come on, sweetheart... ...*Sorry it's takin so long but you've gotto have patience to talk to him... *...What?...who? mmm?... ...*Love him! He's trying so hard.... all these little whispers... *...What? Did you have a nice bath? Eh? Yes... Show the gentleman how you can go through the ceiling. Go on: show him. Put yourself through the ceiling...* watch him now - there he goes! Look!... How he does that, I don't know. It's a miracle... ...He claims he's God. He took me up to his mansion last week... *That's it!...* He's gone through again and he'll come back without makin a crack in it. Is that a trick or what? I don't know.... *What time are we goin?...Pardon?... 3 o' clock? Okay, I'm ready when you are... ...Hmm hmm... don't you laugh at* me, *you bugger!..* Can you understand him? They're all laughin cause I talk to a light bulb. But as I said, I can't talk to him for long cause my neck goes. In my estimation, it should be a bigger light bulb and on the table. And it should be in the livin room. Not stuck in a cold bathroom like this. D'you understand it? I'm furious. Absolutely furious. I'm tampin. They stuck him in the bath and it was stinkin. Denzil hasn't bathed since he's been here and that was *before* us. And we've been here over a year now, aven't we? *Well* over a year, me and Tom. So I sponged the bath out - stupid, friggin bath - cause he couldn't do it himself, poor guy... I just don't like the situation, you know? So I'll look after him. I done it with my father and I done it with my mam. I fought and fought and I got everything for them. New clothing, new socks, new towels. I said 'You can't live in *this.'* And I was washing every day. But they were getting threadbare, you know, with them wearing them all the time. I told the Social 'I've *gotto* have them. They've gotto use them every day.' So I said 'Help me out. I need the money.' And they did, fair play, I had a giro. I said 'Thank you, very much.' And then dad's underwear started to go, so I had new underwear for him and new underwear for my mum. He's 87 and she was elderly too and stuck in a wheelchair. She couldn't do anything for herself but I got the money. They've never denied me the money. I had a giro for £401 the other week. Admittedly it was back payment for Tom as well. So I've always had money out of Social. Some people go down and rap the counter and say 'Give me the money! I'm desperate - *desperate.*' And they only want it to go to the boozer. But they can't get it. And when I get giros, through the door, for four hundred-and-odd, they want to know why: 'How d'you do it?' they say 'How d'you *do* it?' and I tell them 'Well, I don't go down screaming and shouting. I just go in as I am and explain the situation and they always listen to reason, you know?' *...I know, sweetheart, it's weird, isn't it? Eh?... They're all lookin at you, weird... we've got to get you down out of that light bulb... would you like that? Would you... to come down here? In my flat? Would you? If I put you in my lamp? It's not nice up there is it? All on your own, stuck in there every day, twenty four hours a day. It's depressing, innit? It depresses me, let alone you... So, would you like to? Yes. Alright. When we come back, is it? Will you call somebody out to do it? Cause they'll have to take the light bulb out... And then I'll wash you and clean you. I'll clean the bath for you. I done that for my father and my mum. But I can't do it when you're up there, cause I can't get you down. If you're on floor level, I can do it. If you only got a wheelchair, I can wheel you in and out, whisk you back and fore... don't smile at me, you bugger...hmm hmm... you happy now? That's alright, don't thank me... no, don't worry, I'll do it, babes, alright?... But, it's ridiculous, I can't reach you up there. I can't. Hasn't anyone suggested this to you before? Getting a Home help or something. No? Well, where's your family? Oh yes, we're seein those this afternoon, aren't we? So I'll want to know why. They've got the money, haven't they? They've got your money. They're rolling in it. Yes. So, I'll see about it. Not shoutin and screamin or anythin but if you've got the money, you're allowed to get a home help - even if it's in my place. Why shouldn't we be entitled to a home help?... Mum had a home help... Are you listenin? ...Sorry, babes, I can't look at you all the time. My neck is bad...* and she used to come down to Mum every mornin, but they *do* cost a bomb, right? So dad stopped her on a Sunday. But all through the week, I used to get my mother up, wash her, dress her and put her in a chair. The home help used to come in and have nothing to do just sit and have a cup of tea and a fag, no shoppin or nothing cause I'd done the shoppin and everythin and then I'd do the dinner and then in the afternoon I'd sit down and I'd be exhausted. I'd be panting, like this - yes! It was so tiring. And it wasn't just mum, it was having to cope with dad and cook dinner for my daughter and son. Oh God it was exhausting. I met my daughter the other day. Rebecca. She came to the flat. I didn't know who she was. And, if you can understand, they're all sayin I must have been imagining. But I never believed in ghosts. Do you? Well, this isn't a story, it's *true*... She came to my window, and I had the washing in the machine, right? And I had a pile of dishes there cause I'd run out of water and I could see somebody flashing by me... it was just a shadow... and I went out and looked and... there was nobody there. I said 'Hello, who is it?' Nobody spoke back. And then somebody said 'Hello, mum. Mum. Mum! *Mum!* And I said 'Rebecca?'... and she stopped: 'Yes, It's *me*, mum. It's *me*.' But she couldn't stay, she had to go outside, for some reason, and talk to me from there. A ghostly figure. I know it sounds weird. They're all tellin me I'm a loony but it's *true*. She was there and she was talkin to me through the window as I was doin the dishes. She was sayin about her father and everything. She took an overdose but she's forgiven him now. I said 'What happened to you, sweetheart? Why did you *do* it?' but she wouldn't say why. 'I don't know, mam,' she said. 'I don't *know*, mammy.' It was on the front of the Evening Post. He had five years and his girlfriend had three and a half. I don't know the details or what happened. I haven't got a clue. I said 'Why have you come to mummy now?' And she said 'I want to *live* with you, Mummy. I want you to come up and live with me...' I've had quite a few experiences like that since Tom has died. I had all my family here one night, in the living room. *Ghosts!* But they were alive. They were all comin in and out. And there were people that I didn't know were dead. So don't tell me I was imagining *that.* One's name was Valerie and she came with her mother who passed away 12 months ago - but she was still *alive.* She walked in and she said 'Hiya, Syl!' And they were all very bubbly and chirpy, you know? I said to Valerie 'What's happened to you?' Because normally she was very depressed and morbid and an office worker, you know. *'Hiya, Syl!'* she said. And then Phyllis came in, my other cousin, and I spoke to her. And then my mum came in - *walkin.* And she'd been in a wheelchair with a stroke. And I said 'Who's that?' I said. And they said 'It's your mother, Syl.' And I said 'Oh mum, I'm *sorry*! I didn't recognize you.' I was talkin to all the ghosts. I know it sounds weird but I was *talkin* to them. They come, every so often. They might come tonight, I don't know. And they talk to you and they're sat around. And I was goin through all my family. They all arrived. One after the other. And the following morning - was it the Saturday mornin? - I had Elvis Presley and Buddy Holly turn up. They were singin outside my window downstairs. Elvis was singing all the old numbers: Love Me Tender and Jailhouse Rock and he was prancin up and down the path and I was goin 'Shut up!' cause Denzil was tryin to sleep. **'Shut up! You're keepin the neighbours up!' '...Went to a party in the County Jail!...'** I was goin spare. I was goin scitzo, wasn I? And Buddy Holly was goin **'Peggy Sue! Pretty pretty pretty pretty Peggy Sue.'** It's *true*. It *did* happen to me. So if you want to call in one evening, they *do* pop in from time to time but not until about half past nine. That's when they come. And they're absolutely fabulous. They're fabulous. They say 'Who d'you want to meet?' And you just say who you want. As long as it's a dead person, like. They're all in heaven and there's a God up there. Well, who d'you think my old man is? *Who* d'you think Eric is? Yes, that's right, sweetheart: he's God. I died and I went to heaven - it's a weird story isn't it? - last week. That's when I was goin to get married to him. Tom was up there but I didn't bother with *him*. He's livin it up with all those women! He's got one after the other. He's not waiting for me. He told me not to bother with him any more. I said 'I don't *intend* to!' No, don't laugh, it's perfectly true. But: good luck to him! God tried to put me in heaven too. I went up the morning before the weddin, right? And he dressed me all up in this regalia and the coffin was there and everythin and I said 'No. No way. I'm too alive and bubbly to be dead.' I said 'I'm not ready for it yet.' I was just about to say 'When God tells me' but he *is* God, isn't he?. So I came back. I couldn't go through with it. I'm sorry, I just couldn't. I mean, I'm *me*, aren't I? When I'm lyin on the floor and you can't get an ounce of breath out of me, then I'll know I'm dead, isn't it? I'm 48, I'll go on till I'm 80. God willin. Look at *him* laughin...Why did he chose a light bulb, I wonder?... *Don't worry, we'll get you down from there, my sweetheart... alright?... 3 o' clock we're goin?... I'm all ready... but who's gettin you down? I can't reach...who's gettin you down, eh?...* Angels look just like us, you know: smart and tidy and the complete opposite of Denzil. The only thing is, I was gaspin the other night and they were all in the front room puffin away and when I went over and asked for a cigarette, it evaporated...

When you go up there, it's fantastic, it's just like home. It's a lovely place. But I couldn't stick it for long, so I come home. I didn't like the idea of bein married again. I suppose after death it's lovely but to be there when you're still alive and all your property's down here, didn't appeal to me at all... *I'm sorry, Eric. I just couldn't go through with it, my love... He got his own office up there, haven't you?...* And when he's there, he's sittin in a chair, behind the desk. But where's all his family? That's what I want know. I'm goin to have a *word* with them.

Eric's only come *since* Tom died. Of course *that*! I was devoted to Tom, as you know. We had our ups and downs: the hammerings and the tongs. Like all couples do. He nearly killed me once or twice, so I left him. Went and stayed with friends. But I soon went back, cause I was grievin for my own home, wasn I? You can't do things in someone else's home. When you're in your own home you're free to roam around, do whatever you want. I mean, that's what I was tellin my Key Worker when he was talkin about me movin. I couldn't uproot myself now. I'm not a youngster, I'm not 17 or 18 any more. No, I couldn't move again. Not at my age. It's a big upheaval.

What are my happiest memories of Tom?...Or the funniest? I'm tryin to think now... I think when he fell over... in the Marina with all the carrier bags, and they split open, all the tins and everything went flyin and all the holiday makers were walkin past and I said 'You silly moo!' And he said 'Fuck off, *you*!' Well, you know his language was foul. Every other word was effin and beein, wasn't it? I took it with a pinch of salt in the end. I thought 'Well, if you can't beat them, join them, isn't it?' But that was one incident. Oh God, there's so many to be honest... let me think... ...I know this sounds weird again but when I was in here on my weddin day talkin to Eric, a voice piped up out of nowhere: 'Don't you ever come to me again!' I said 'Who's that?'... *'Tom!'*... 'Oh,' I said - on my *life*! - 'I don't want you anyway.' 'Well,' he said, 'I've got other things on my mind now.' I said 'Yeah: other women!' Cause when you go there they change your whole future. For a start, I wouldn't have had this black eye if I'd stayed there. My hair would have been blonde, which it used to be. And it would have been short, curly or whatever my style would be and my eyes would have been beautiful. And they make you younger. If you go in about 54, they make you look about 48. You look younger when you come out. Eric will tell you ...*are you listenin, Eric?... If I come in there when I'm 60, ow old will they make me look?... 64! I'll give you, you bugger!*...

Yes, Tom was very athletic when he was younger. He was a sergeant and he had strong views about - how can I say? - being clean and neat. You had to be disciplined. If I'd left that cup in the sink, he'd wake up out of his grave if he seen it and if I said I'd left it on the draining board, he'd get up in the morning early to clear it up. And it'd be neatly put away. It was his training. It was all the army discipline. Whereas me, I gets out bed and I say 'Oh where *am* I, like?' Am I *here*? Am I on this earth? We were together for three and a half years and it was quite a time, I can tell you. I'm always bubbly - just to please others more or less - but I *miss* him. In the night mostly. I cry all the time. I miss him being *there*, cause when I come home, I walk in and there's like a hush-hush atmosphere. But when I used to come back before, he was always sittin there. Always. I'm sorry, babes: I don't know where I *am* at the moment, whether I'm comin or goin. But all I want to do now is marry a rich millionaire. And that's Eric...*we're goin on a cruise, aren't we, darling?...* Aren't *we?...* we were talking about that last night, seriously. He's thinkin of takin me on a cruise... *A world one?...*he's nodding. He was so excited earlier... *weren't you?...* So excited. He'd never thought about a cruise. Cause on board you've got everybody at hand to help you while you relax. ...*And you can watch me in the swimming pool and everywhere, can't you?* ...oh, he's lovely... but you can't understand him, I know. It's very difficult. But he shouldn't be up there. Not like that. He's a human being. And I believe that every human being has a right. Don't they? So I'm goin to have a word with his family. Why is he stuck in a light bulb up there? Imagine talkin to a light bulb like this. I mean, I know he's human. I understand what he's sayin. But to be stuck up there: it's ridiculous, isn't it?... *What is it, babes? Is it three o' clock yet?*

What time is it? We'll ave to go or Denzil will be *startin* again. And I've gotto finish my packin. I don't know where I am at the moment. I'm really down in the dumps today. I'm not in the mood for anybody. I've told Denzil off, I've told *everybody* off today. It's just one of those days. And yet, I'm still perky, you know? My sense of humour's all that keeps me goin. Being alive and being bubbly for everybody else, even if you feel deadly inside.

I'm tryin to rebuild my life, on my own, without a man. It's hard but I'm tryin to do it and it'll take me a while. But I tell you what. I can gamble on one thing: I'll meet another man! I always *have* done. And if it's not Eric, it'll be *somebody*. I don't know who or where or when but it's never *long*. After every relationship I've had, I've always found a man. Within about three months, usually. I get my hair done, buy a new outfit and I look a new woman. At the moment I can't be bothered. It's too *soon* yet. But you *watch* me: I'll be off down the disco, jivin, before you know it!... Look at *him* laughin up there... He doesn't *believe* me. He thinks I'm havin you on... *but I'm not, darling, I'm* not....*You just* **watch** *me...!*

AFTERWORD

WILL

At the time of writing, Will is living rough in the Marina area of Swansea, within sight of his beloved yachts.

PAUL

When 'Twin Town' was eventually released Paul's part had unfortunately been cut, although he was still to be seen - if only fleetingly - in one of the crowd scenes. Gabrielle and Paul now have a baby son.

DARREN

Shortly after this interview, the Hostel admitted a young female resident. Within two weeks, Darren had proposed to her. They both moved into a flat on the outskirts of Town.

VINCE

Vince also moved into a flat, several weeks later.

WILLIAM AND TERESA

Shortly after moving into their house, William and Teresa split up. William still lives in Swansea.

BELFAST DANNY

Danny's condition deteriorated rapidly over the spring and summer. He continued to drink heavily and was having periodic fits. In May, he was taken into Cefn Coed for a detox and was transferred from there to Morriston Hospital where several abscesses were drained from his lungs. Less than a week later he was back in hospital with pneumonia, but signed himself out within a few days and against doctor's orders. He recovered from the pneumonia and continues to sleep rough.

NIGEL

Nigel moved to a caravan site in Scotland shortly after this interview.

ALEC

In early July there was a police raid on the Duchess and Alec was arrested along with six other people and detained in a cell overnight. Most of the charges were drug-related but Alec was charged with being drunk and disorderly and fined. The Hostel found several odd jobs for him to do in order for him to raise the money. He has now left the Hostel and is living in rented accommodation in the Port Tennant area of Town.

WAYNE AND LYN

In early August, after several warnings about his unpredictable and often temperamental behaviour, Wayne was given notice to quit the Hostel. He slept in a skip at the back of the Co-op for one night and was then admitted to the Dinas Fechan Hostel. After serving short sentences in Swansea prison, both Lyn and Wayne are still sleeping rough.

JOHN

Is still a Support Worker and active fund-raiser for the Cyrenians Cymru.

NICK

Whereabouts unknown.

RICHARD

Whereabouts unknown.

FRANK

Still lives in the St. Thomas area of Swansea.

LITTLE RITCHIE

In the middle of March, Ritchie had to quit the Hostel due to his disruptive behaviour. He returned to sleeping in the High Street Car Park but when that became a lock-up one, reverted to sleeping in shop doorways. A year later, after being rushed into hospital with internal bleeding, he died.

CERI

At the beginning of May, Ceri stopped taking his medication and his condition deteriorated drastically. He became more and more difficult and abusive on the soup runs and was eventually arrested for disturbing the peace. He was banned from the Hostel and from sitting in the Outreach van, although efforts were still being made by the nurse from Caer Las and the Hostel, in conjunction with Cefn Coed and the police, to get him sectioned. He was now alone in the Radnor and a serious risk to himself. Around the third week in May, following an incident in Tescos, where he stripped off his shirt and threatened to take on all-comers, he was finally taken in to Cefn Coed. There, his condition rapidly began to improve and in early August he was once again back in the Radnor.

BERNIE AND THE BOWLS TEAM

Went their separate ways over the summer months but reappeared, one by one, in the Autumn.

TERRY

In August, Terry moved to a flat nearer his sisters and parents in the Townhill area of

Swansea. He had to give up the flat, due to his drinking, and is once again resident in the Hostel.

CARDIFF KARL

A few weeks after this interview, Karl was admitted to Dinas Fechan. He left there to go into detox in Cefn Coed but didn't complete the treatment. He returned to the streets and, in mid-march was arrested by Cardiff police for various warrants which were outstanding on him. In early May he was back with Sara and Little Ritchie and the others but, since the Government had introduced their Zero Tolerance policy, they had moved from the main road into a side street. A few days later he assaulted Wayne Darvell - who required hospital treatment - and just over a month after that, he received a six month's sentence for GBH.

ROCCO

Rocco finally returned to his house only to discover the hamster and the gold fish dead. He slept rough in Swansea for a while then moved into his new girlfriend's house in the Mumbles.

TOM AND SYLVIA

Tom and Sylvia split up and got back together several times since the last interview I had with both of them. In April of the following year, Tom died peacefully in his sleep.

NICKI

Nicki is still living with her mother in Devon where, according to Rocco, she gave birth to his child.

SARA

Sara was admitted to Dinas Fechan in late March but left of her own volition after six weeks. She slept rough for a while and then moved into the 'Waste of Space' as a permanent 'guest'. Her health began to cause concern at this time and attempts were made to get her admitted to hospital but she refused to go. When the 'Waste of Space was forced to close down, Sara once again returned to the streets. She eventually found a place in Dinas Fechan.

NEVILLE

Still lives in the Tenby area of Town.

KATHY AND ROBERT

In July Kathy and Robert split up. By Christmas, they were back together again.

BILL AND THE BIBLE CLASS

Took a well-earned rest in August. Bill has since retired, due to ill health.

STEVE

Steve is still living in accommodation supplied by the Cefn Coed Project.

BOB

Whereabouts unknown.

LYNDON AND DOUGGIE

Still live in separate flats in the Mount Pleasant area..

IAN

Whereabouts unknown.

RANDALL

Randall continued to accumulate massive bills. His support worker arranged for a Social Work assessment which established that he had learning difficulties but did not merit any special treatment or care.

THE COLLECTIVE

Its members dispersed and plans to establish another squat in the Wind Street area, never came to fruition.

EVELYN

Still lives in the Tenby area of Town.

GAVIN

Still runs a guest house, though is now taking only female residents.

SID

Sid moved to a flat in Baglan.

BAGLAN BENNY

Became a resident in the Hostel for several months but is now back on the streets.

DEDICATION

This book is dedicated to the memory of Betty Williams and also to the following former residents of the Paxton Street hostel who died, directly or indirectly, as a result of their time on the streets:

Jack
Sid
Peter
Stan
Rob
Alan
Jane
Paul
Terry
Dave
Danny
and Tudor

ACKNOWLEDGMENTS

I am indebted to all those who helped in the writing of this book, particularly to my sixty co-authors and the residents and staff, past and present, of the Cyrenians Cymru Hostel for the homeless in Paxton Street, Swansea. Thanks are due to Carwyn Rogers and the West Wales Arts Association for financial support in the early stages; to Gareth Perry for his time and patience in formatting the text; to Paul Harwood for formatting the cover design; to Sally Roberts Jones of Alun Books and especially to Conrad Watkins for his constant encouragement and advice at all stages of the project.

With a few exceptions, all names have been changed by request. All royalties due to myself as author of this book, will go to further the work of the Cyrenians Cymru Hostel in Paxton Street, Swansea.

A.P.